THE CAMBRIDGE COMPANION TO STAND-UP COMEDY

Stand-up comedy is one of the simplest theatre forms in existence. The comedian stands on a (usually) bare stage, talking straight to the audience in the hope of getting laughs. Yet it has never been more popular, with national scenes developing across every continent except Antarctica. In this insightful and accessibly written volume, diverse chapters explore the subject from many angles, ranging from national scenes, live venues, and recordings to politics, race, sexuality, and the question of offensiveness. Chapters also consider the performance dynamics of stand-up in detail, examining audience, persona, and trauma. Interspersed throughout the chapters are a series of originally commissioned interviews with comedians from nine different countries, including Maria Bamford, Jo Brand, Aditi Mittal, and Rod Quantock, providing rare insights into their craft.

OLIVER DOUBLE is Reader in Comic and Popular Performance at the University of Kent, where he established the British Stand-Up Comedy Archive. His books include *Stand-Up! On Being a Comedian* (1997), *Getting the Joke* (2005, 2014), and *Alternative Comedy* (2020). A former professional comedian ('Surprisingly Funny' – *Guardian*), he currently compères Funny Rabbit Comedy Club.

CAMBRIDGE COMPANIONS TO THEATRE AND PERFORMANCE

The Cambridge Companions to Theatre and Performance collection publishes specially commissioned volumes of new essays designed for students at universities and drama schools, and their teachers. Each volume focuses on a key topic, practitioner or form and offers a balanced and wide-ranging overview of its subject. Content includes historical and political contexts, case studies, critical and theoretical approaches, afterlives and guidance on further reading.

Published Titles

The Cambridge Companion to African American Theatre (2nd edition)
Edited by HARVEY YOUNG
The Cambridge Companion to International Theatre Festivals
Edited by RIC KNOWLES
The Cambridge Companion to Theatre and Science
Edited by KIRSTEN E. SHEPHERD-BARR
The Cambridge Companion to the Circus
Edited by JIM DAVIS and GILLIAN ARRIGHI
The Cambridge Companion to American Theatre since 1945
Edited by JULIA LISTENGARTEN and STEPHEN DI BENEDETTO
The Cambridge Companion to British Theatre of the First World War
Edited by HELEN E. M. BROOKS
The Cambridge Companion to British Theatre since 1945
Edited by JEN HARVIE and DAN REBELLATO
The Cambridge Companion to Modernist Theatre
Edited by BRAD KENT and DAVID KORNHABER
The Cambridge Companion to Stand-Up Comedy
Edited by OLIVER DOUBLE

Forthcoming Titles

The Cambridge Companion to British Playwriting since 1945
Edited by VICKY ANGELAKI and DAN REBELLATO

Related Cambridge Companions

The Cambridge Companion to the Actress
Edited by MAGGIE B. GALE and JOHN STOKES
The Cambridge Companion to British Theatre, 1730–1830
Edited by JANE MOODY and DANIEL O'QUINN
The Cambridge Companion to English Melodrama
Edited by CAROLYN WILLIAMS

The Cambridge Companion to English Restoration Theatre
Edited by DEBORAH PAYNE FISK

The Cambridge Companion to Greek and Roman Theatre
Edited by MARIANNE MCDONALD and MICHAEL WALTON

The Cambridge Companion to Greek Comedy
Edited by MARTIN REVERMANN

The Cambridge Companion to Greek Tragedy
Edited by P. E. EASTERLING

The Cambridge Companion to Medieval English Theatre, second edition
Edited by RICHARD BEADLE and ALAN J. FLETCHER

The Cambridge Companion to Performance Studies
Edited by TRACY C. DAVIS

The Cambridge Companion to Theatre History
Edited by DAVID WILES and CHRISTINE DYMKOWSKI

The Cambridge Companion to Victorian and Edwardian Theatre
Edited by KERRY POWELL

THE CAMBRIDGE COMPANION TO STAND-UP COMEDY

EDITED BY
OLIVER DOUBLE
University of Kent

CAMBRIDGE
UNIVERSITY PRESS

Shaftesbury Road, Cambridge CB2 8EA, United Kingdom

One Liberty Plaza, 20th Floor, New York, NY 10006, USA

477 Williamstown Road, Port Melbourne, VIC 3207, Australia

314–321, 3rd Floor, Plot 3, Splendor Forum, Jasola District Centre, New Delhi – 110025, India

103 Penang Road, #05–06/07, Visioncrest Commercial, Singapore 238467

Cambridge University Press is part of Cambridge University Press & Assessment, a department of the University of Cambridge.

We share the University's mission to contribute to society through the pursuit of education, learning and research at the highest international levels of excellence.

www.cambridge.org
Information on this title: www.cambridge.org/9781009009737
DOI: 10.1017/9781009000635

© Cambridge University Press & Assessment 2025

This publication is in copyright. Subject to statutory exception and to the provisions of relevant collective licensing agreements, no reproduction of any part may take place without the written permission of Cambridge University Press & Assessment.

When citing this work, please include a reference to the DOI 10.1017/9781009000635

First published 2025

Cover image: Hannah Gadsby performs at the Edinburgh Festival Fringe on August 16, 2013 in Edinburgh, Scotland. Photo: Scott Campbell / Contributor / Getty Images Entertainment / Getty Images.

A catalogue record for this publication is available from the British Library

A Cataloging-in-Publication data record for this book is available from the Library of Congress

ISBN 978-1-316-51857-1 Hardback
ISBN 978-1-009-00973-7 Paperback

Cambridge University Press & Assessment has no responsibility for the persistence or accuracy of URLs for external or third-party internet websites referred to in this publication and does not guarantee that any content on such websites is, or will remain, accurate or appropriate.

For EU product safety concerns, contact us at Calle de José Abascal, 56, 1°, 28003 Madrid, Spain, or email eugpsr@cambridge.org

Contents

List of Figures   *page* ix
List of Contributors   x

Introduction   1
Oliver Double

Comedians' Insights: What Do You Do to Prepare to Go Onstage?   13

PART I   TIME AND PLACE

1. Stand-Up in the United Kingdom   23
   Oliver Double and Neil Washbourne

2. Comics, Minstrels, Satirists, and Hacks: A History of Stand-Up Comedy in the USA   43
   Beck Krefting

Comedians' Insights: The Audience You Attract   61

3. Where Stand-Up Happens   67
   Morten Nielsen

4. Recorded Stand-Up from Radio to Netflix   83
   Brett Mills

Comedians' Insights: A Particular Performance Technique You Use in Your Act   97

PART II   INTERPRETATION AND MEANING

5. Stand-Up Comedy and Gender   107
   Ellie Tomsett and Rosie White

6	Stand-Up Comedy and Sexuality *Joanne Gilbert*	124
7	Laugh No Limit: Black Stand-Up Comedy *J Finley*	140
8	Jewish American Stand-Up Comedy *Debra Aarons and Marc Mierowsky*	158
9	Stand-Up Comedy, Disability, and Social Justice *Sharon Lockyer*	175
10	Stand-Up Comedy and Offence *Simon Weaver*	189
11	Stand-Up and Politics *Sophie Quirk*	206

Comedians' Insights: Your Writing Process — 222

PART III PERFORMANCE DYNAMICS

12	Audience *Ian Brodie*	233

Comedians' Insights: Who Are You Onstage? — 249

13	Persona *Oliver Double*	255
14	Stand-Up Comedy and Trauma: Hannah Gadsby's *Nanette* *Mary Luckhurst*	273

Comedians' Insights: Why Do You Do Stand-Up? — 290

Select Bibliography — 297
Index — 304

Figures

1.1	Mo Gilligan performing on the Alternative Stage at the Leeds Festival at Bramhall Park on 24 August 2018 in Leeds, England	*page 36*
3.1	A guest walks into the Comedy Cellar in Greenwich Village as arts venues reopen on 2 April 2021 in New York City	75
5.1	Jo Brand. *The Peoples Assembly Presents: Stand Up against Austerity*. Live at the Hammersmith Apollo, London, 2014	118
7.1	Eric Andre performs onstage during the Beach Goth Festival at The Observatory on 22 October 2016 in Santa Ana, California	151
8.1	Lenny Bruce at the Jazz Workshop, 1961	167
9.1	Rosie Jones performs live on stage at the Henham Park during the Latitude Festival in Southwold, Suffolk	178
11.1	Jessica Fostekew, Deborah Frances-White, and Katie Melua attend a live podcast recording of *The Guilty Feminist* by Deborah Frances-White during the London Podcast Festival at King's Place, London, 26 September 2020	207
13.1	Russell Kane performs in his production *Smokescreens and Castles* at the Pleasance as part of the Edinburgh Festival Fringe	265
14.1	Hannah Gadsby performs *Nanette* during the Assembly Gala Launch for the Edinburgh Festival Fringe at Assembly Hall, Edinburgh, 2 August 2017	274

Contributors

DEBRA AARONS is a linguist working at the University of New South Wales in Sydney, Australia. She is the author of *Jokes and the Linguistic Mind* (2012). Together with Marc Mierowsky, she has written a series of articles on Jewish comedy, focusing specifically on licence, obscenity, and the development of the comic persona.

IAN BRODIE is Professor of Folklore at Cape Breton University and author of *A Vulgar Art: A New Approach to Stand-Up Comedy* (2014). He researches the intersection of folk culture and mass media, ranging from local radio song contests to the supernatural in children's television. Ian currently serves as the President of both the Folklore Studies Association of Canada and the International Society for Contemporary Legend Research.

OLIVER DOUBLE is Reader in Drama and Theatre at the University of Kent. Before becoming an academic he worked as a stand-up comedian on the national comedy circuit ('Delightful' – *The Guardian*) and set up the Last Laugh, Sheffield's longest-running comedy club. He continues to perform occasionally, for example in his one-man shows *Saint Pancreas* (2006) and *Break a Leg* (2015), and as the compère of the Funny Rabbit Comedy Club. He has written a number of books, chapters, and articles on stand-up comedy and popular performance, notably *Getting the Joke: The Inner Workings of Stand-Up Comedy* (2005, 2014), *Britain Had Talent: A History of Variety Theatre* (2012), and *Alternative Comedy: 1979 and the Reinvention of British Stand-Up* (2020). He helped to establish the British Stand-Up Comedy Archive, and he presents a podcast about it, *A History of Comedy in Several Objects*.

J FINLEY is Assistant Professor of Africana Studies at Pomona College in Claremont, California. She is an interdisciplinary scholar who studies Black women's history, performance, and cultural expression. In addition to teaching courses on the history and theoretical aspects of humour and comedy, she also teaches her students the practice of stand-up comedy based on her own experience as an amateur performer and the knowledge she's gleaned from working with professional comedians and comedy educators.

JOANNE GILBERT is the Alma College Charles A. Dana Professor Emerita of Communication, author of *Performing Marginality: Humor, Gender, and Cultural Critique* (2004) and contributing editor to *Studies in American Humor*. Her work also appears in *Text and Performance Quarterly*, *A Cultural History of Comedy in the Modern Age*, and many other publications. Her numerous honours include the Lilla A. Heston Award for Outstanding Scholarship in Interpretation and Performance Studies from the National Communication Association.

BECK KREFTING is Professor of American Studies and Director of the Center for Leadership, Teaching, and Learning at Skidmore College. She is co-founder, co-President and co-Executive Director of the Critical Humor Studies Association and has published widely in feminist comedy studies, focusing primarily on the stand-up comedy industry, history, and its performers. Her book *All Joking Aside: American Humor and Its Discontents* (2014) examines the history of stand-up comedy aimed at social justice.

SHARON LOCKYER is Honorary Reader in Sociology and Communications at Brunel University of London. She is the Founding Director of the Centre for Comedy Studies Research. Her research interests include critical comedy studies, identity politics and comic media representations, and the sociology of popular culture. She is widely published in these areas in books, journal articles, and blogs. She is the Founding Co-editor of the Palgrave Studies in Comedy book series and has served as President of the International Society for Humor Studies (ISHS).

MARY LUCKHURST is Honorary Professor of Theatre and Screen Arts and was Head of the School of Arts at the University of Bristol from 2019–2023. She was a Research Fellow at the University of Cambridge in 2024. She is the co-founder of the Department of Theatre, Film, TV and Interactive Media at the University of York. From 2014–2019 she was a Research Professor in Theatre at the University of Melbourne. She has authored thirteen books and many articles in the areas of dramaturgy, theatre history, theatre and social justice, women in theatre, and the processes of acting and directing. She is currently working on a book on celebrity actresses.

MARC MIEROWSKY is an Australian Research Council DECRA Fellow and Lecturer in English at the University of Melbourne. He is an associate editor of *The Cambridge Edition of the Correspondence of Daniel Defoe* (2022) and co-editor with Nicholas Seager of Defoe's *The Fortunate Mistress [Roxana]* (2024) for Oxford World's Classics. With Debra Aarons, he has written a series of articles and chapters on Jewish comedy, focusing specifically on licence, obscenity, and the development of the comic persona.

BRETT MILLS is Honorary Professor of Media and Culture at the University of East Anglia. His books include *Animals on Television: The Cultural Making of the Non-human* (2017), *Creativity in the British Television Comedy Industry* (with Erica Horton; 2017), *The Sitcom* (2012), two editions of *Reading Media Theory: Thinkers, Approaches, Contexts* (with David M. Barlow; 2007/2012), and *Television Sitcom* (2005). He was the Principal Investigator on the Arts and Humanities Research Council-funded research project 'Make Me Laugh: Creativity in the British Television Comedy Industry' (2012–15).

MORTEN NIELSEN is a social anthropologist working on socially sustainable urban development – and stand-up comedy. Since November 2018 he has been based at the National Museum of Denmark, where he is now a research professor and Head of the Research Center for Social Urban Modelling. He has carried out ethnographic research in southern Africa (Mozambique), Latin America (Brazil), the US (New York City), the UK (Scotland), and Denmark.

SOPHIE QUIRK is Senior Lecturer in Drama and Theatre at the University of Kent. Her research explores the politics and craft of stand-up comedy. She is the author of *Why Stand-Up Matters: How Comedians Manipulate and Influence* (2015) and *The Politics of British Stand-Up Comedy: The New Alternative* (2018).

ELLIE TOMSETT is Senior Lecturer in Media at Birmingham City University and co-founder of the Mixed Bill Comedy and Gender Research Network. She is the author of *Stand-Up Comedy and Contemporary Feminisms: Sexism, Stereotypes and Structural Inequalities* (2023) and has written on feminist comedy, self-deprecatory humour, and media representations of women's paid labour.

NEIL WASHBOURNE is Senior Lecturer in Media Studies, School of Humanities and Social Sciences, Leeds Beckett University. His work increasingly focuses on the thick description and theoretically rich analysis of comedy/humour. He teaches the module Comedy Media and Diversity. His research projects include the development of an adequate superiority theory of comedy/humour through close case studies of contentious comic performances, past and present. He formerly published on representative and alternative politics and media and political and other forms of celebrity, and his work on comedy is informed by conceptions of comedians as representative figures and comedy performances as mediating symbolic cultures.

SIMON WEAVER is Senior Lecturer in Media and Communications in the Department of Social and Political Sciences, and a member of the Centre for Comedy Studies Research, at Brunel University of London. Simon's research focuses on the connections between rhetoric, humour, and joking. This has included the rhetorical nature of racial and racist humour and, more recently, the relationship between comedy, irony, and populism.

ROSIE WHITE was Senior Lecturer in Contemporary Literature, Theory and Popular Culture at Northumbria University, UK, retiring in 2024. Towards the end of her career, she published widely on popular media and gender, with a focus on women and television comedy. Her last monograph was Television Comedy and Femininity: Queering Gender (IB Tauris, 2018)

Introduction
Oliver Double

Form

On his 1959 album *The Future Lies Ahead*, Mort Sahl describes the performance he is giving as 'a primitive form of theatre'.[1] Although stand-up comedy is rarely thought of as theatre, Sahl's description rings true. Stand-up comedy is one of the simplest and most popular forms of theatre in existence. Famously, Peter Brook wrote that 'all that is needed for an act of theatre to be engaged' is for somebody to walk across an empty space while someone else is watching.[2] Superficially, there is little more to stand-up than that: a single performer walks onto the stage, talks to the audience, and walks off again.

Of course, behind that apparent simplicity there is a lot going on which might be unacknowledged or taken for granted. Tony Allen, a pioneer of the British alternative comedy scene, wrote that the stand-up comedian 'walks onstage relatively naked. He speaks directly to the audience in the first person. There is no contract, only a nebulous agreement that the performance is spontaneous and authentic. Even though the set-piece jokes, skits and monologues may be learned word for word, the audience will overlook any deceit so long as they get to laugh and feel included.'[3]

This is useful in helping to pin down the core elements that define stand-up as a theatre form. First, it centres on the identity of the performer themself. The comedian typically performs 'in the first person', without adopting any obvious character. There is a sense of self-revelation – hence being 'relatively naked' – and this creates a feeling of authenticity.

Second, the comedian 'speaks directly to the audience'. There is no fourth wall separating stage from auditorium, and the audience plays a crucial role, validating the performance with their tangible reactions – laughter, applause, heckling, and so on. At the end of a show recorded in the late 1950s, Shelley Berman thanks his audience directly for their part in the show, acknowledging, 'But I can't be funny without you. Alone,

I'm *not funny*. In my bathroom, for example, where I'm as *alone as I can be* – I'm not *funny*. I may *look* a little strange but I'm not funny. [laughter]'[4] What Berman is acknowledging here is that without an audience, the performance would be incomplete. The size and nature of the audience might differ dramatically. The first audience Maria Bamford performs to in her 2017 Netflix special *Old Baby* consists of just her husband and their dog.[5] At the other end of the scale, according to Guinness World Records, the biggest stand-up audience ever happened on 12 July 2008, when 67,733 people assembled at Berlin's Olympiastadion to watch the German comedian Mario Barth. In both cases though, the aim remains the same – to get the audience to laugh.

Third, even though the material might be more or less fixed, it has to at least appear to be 'spontaneous'. Unlike a play, it is comparatively rare for stand-up material to be written down word for word, and there is always the possibility of improvisation. As Lenny Bruce told Studs Terkel in 1959, 'I don't actually sit down and write out a routine. I'll ad-lib it on the floor, but line by line, and eventually it'll snowball into a bit. I'll never actually do the same routine twice.'[6]

History

It is not easy to say exactly when, where, and how stand-up came into existence. The earliest known usage of the term 'stand-up comedian' occurs in an article about a musical comedian called Finlay Dunn in the *Yorkshire Evening Post* in 1917,[7] referring to the form his act had taken years earlier than that. The term didn't come into common usage until the second half of the twentieth century, by which time the theatre form itself was well established.

Some accounts trace its origins to the USA in the nineteenth century in blackface minstrel shows, vaudeville theatre, and public appearances by the author Mark Twain. By about 1900, arguably the most popular type of vaudeville act was the 'monologist', which was defined by Joe Laurie Jr as '[a] man or woman who does an act depending entirely on talk; using no foils, stooges, musical instruments, songs or dancing'.[8] Other accounts place stand-up's origins in the music halls of the UK, with comic song evolving into comic patter in the late nineteenth century and becoming 'front cloth comedy' in twentieth-century variety theatres.

In both American and British traditions, there were distinct stages to stand-up's development. Following its early development in theatrical forms which presented a series of unconnected acts, it then moved out of theatres and into less formalised venues. In America, after vaudeville's demise, stand-up found new homes in a varied array of venues, including the Chitlin' Circuit, the Borscht Belt hotels in the Catskills, the showrooms of Las Vegas, and nightclubs across the country. In Britain, once the variety theatres disappeared, working men's clubs became the main location of stand-up comedy. This change of location led to a simplification of the form, with smartly dressed comedians telling standard gags from a shared stock of material.

Following this second phase, both America and Britain saw a radical reinvention of stand-up in the mid-to-late twentieth century, establishing an informal, individual style, more firmly rooted in the performer's personal biography. In the USA, this transformation was instigated in the 1950s and 1960s by performers such as Mort Sahl, Lenny Bruce, Dick Gregory, Phyllis Diller, and Joan Rivers, labelled at the time as 'sick comedians'. These comics were part of the inspiration for the UK's alternative cabaret movement of the 1980s, which effected a similar transformation, establishing a new circuit of venues in which performers such as Alexei Sayle, Tony Allen, Pauline Melville, Rik Mayall, and French and Saunders challenged the existing stylistic and political conventions of UK stand-up.

A strikingly similar – if less acknowledged – origin story can be found in Australia. Australian vaudeville theatres produced 'patterologists', solo comedians who performed 'material that was strong on satire, highly parochial and often written the day it was performed',[9] and solo patter-based comedians went on to thrive in variety shows after World War I. Australia's equivalent of the British working men's clubs were the licenced clubs of New South Wales and Queensland. In the second half of the twentieth century, these were home to a breed of stand-ups described by Rod Quantock as 'joke "borrowing" suit and tie types'.[10]

Quantock was a key figure in the evolution of Australian stand-up, taking an approach to performance that would prefigure and inspire the radical reinvention of the form. He emerged from the Melbourne cabaret scene of the 1970s, where he developed his solo comedy routines as part of the Razzle Dazzle Revue. Fellow Razzle Dazzle performer Mary Kenneally claims that Quantock 'kind of invented' the modern style of Australian stand-up: 'There wasn't anybody but Rod ... there wasn't that direct talk.'[11] Quantock's loosely structured performances saw him talking directly to the audience and rooting his act in his own perspective on the world: 'There was nobody here who wrote comedy in any contemporary way at the time ... I just got up and talked ... I'd get up and tell a

15-minute, 20-minute story about an event in my life ... so that's what I was doing, autobiographical stuff.'[12]

By the 1980s, the opening of venues such as the Comedy Café's Banana Lounge and the Last Laugh's Le Joke were more conducive to small-scale performance and thus encouraged a wave of solo stand-ups to follow in Quantock's wake. Something similar was happening in Sydney, with the opening of the Comedy Store. The way the Australian stand-up scene developed in the 1980s closely mirrored the UK's alternative cabaret scene happening at the same time, but this parallel evolutionary process was happening more through coincidence than crosspollination. When John Pinder brought British alternative cabaret group the Bouncing Czecks over to play at the Last Laugh in 1984, lead singer Richard Piper was amazed to discover a thriving comedy scene in Melbourne: 'It was quite stunning to discover all this was happening 12,000 miles from Britain and that it had been going on for over ten years without any of us knowing about it.'[13]

When the Melbourne International Comedy Festival was launched in 1987, it not only established links with comedy scenes in other countries but also made Australian comedy much more visible around the world. Today, Australia has a stand-up scene that spreads right across the country. Andrew McClelland, who started performing stand-up around the beginning of this century, explains: 'There's scenes in every city and in some towns as well ... In every capital city there are scenes. And then in smaller cities like Wagga Wagga or Castlemaine ... there is a lot of stand-up in Australia.'[14]

Global Spread

Notably, the parallel evolution of stand-up comedy in the USA, the UK, and Australia has happened in predominantly English-speaking countries. These are probably the countries where stand-up has existed the longest – each with a tradition of well over a century – so it would be tempting to see it as essentially an anglophone theatre form.

However, if this was once true it is certainly no longer so. The last twenty to thirty years has seen stand-up spread across the globe surprisingly quickly, with national scenes cropping up across Europe, Africa, the Middle East, South and East Asia, and Central and South America. The only continent to lack a vibrant stand-up scene is Antarctica. In the last few years, the British and American comedy industries have started to pick up on stand-up's global spread. UK comedy promoter Mick Perrin brought over comedians from Italy, France, Germany, and Russia to play the 2014

Edinburgh Fringe, as well as promoting comedy shows across Europe and in South Africa. BBC comedy producer Ed Morrish devised a show called *Welcome to Wherever You Are* for Radio 4 (2016–2019), in which Andrew Maxwell compèred comedians from around the world performing from their own countries to a live audience in the UK via a video link. In 2019, Netflix released a series called *Comedians of the World* featuring half-hour sets from stand-ups who are French, French-Canadian, English-Canadian, Saudi Arabian, Palestinian, Jordanian, Mexican, Brazilian, Dutch, German, Indian, South African, Australian, New Zealander, American, and British.

The fact that Netflix have picked up on the globalisation of stand-up is telling, because video streaming is one of the factors that helped it spread to countries around the world in the first place. Ed Morrish points out the significance of the fact that video streaming allows content to be viewed internationally: 'It's the ability of people to watch stand-up all over the place that has really fuelled a sort of simultaneous spread of comedy all across the world. It's not all these countries developing their own cultures of stand-up. It's, "Oh, we can all get on YouTube and watch clips, and we can all get Netflix."'[15] He recalls Brazilian comedian Nil Agra telling him he was inspired by seeing Chris Rock and Dave Chappelle on Netflix. Similarly, Gursimran Khamba has acknowledged that Canadian comedian Russell Peters' popularity on YouTube helped to inspire the Indian stand-up scene. The Indonesian Muslim comedian Sakdiyah Ma'ruf – who fearlessly jokes about issues such as Islamic extremism – lists Sarah Silverman, Margaret Cho, and Ellen DeGeneres among her influences, naming Louis CK as her favourite stand-up.

However, streaming footage of stand-up is not enough in itself to engender comedy industries in countries new to the form. Janet A McLeod – who runs Melbourne's Local Laughs, the 'longest running stand-up room with one solitary operator in Australia' – points out that a 'scene doesn't just come out of nowhere. You've got to have people supporting it, you've got to have that framework.'[16]

The particular way that frameworks are established to support comedy scenes differs from country to country. Scandinavia has several long-established stand-up scenes, and according to Norwegian stand-up Anders Olsen, the key moment in Norway's scene was when Jånni Kristiansen opened the first stand-up club there, Reis Deg Komikerklubb, in 1994.[17] Romanian comedian Radu Isac pinpoints the exact moment that Romania's scene sprang into existence: 'It started in a tea bar in 2003 as a workshop for actors. Three people who were on in the first night are still professional comedians today.'[18] Indian comedian Anuvab Pal recognises the importance of Don Ward opening a branch of the Comedy Store in Mumbai in 2010: 'I think the big moment was when the Comedy Store of London opened the Comedy Store in Mumbai. It sort of institutionalised a very fragmented kind of, essentially, theatre that existed … the idea of writing your own narrative kind of formalised when the Comedy Store showed up in India.'[19]

In some cases, a single organisation has managed to introduce stand-up to a new country. Louis Zezeran is an Australian who moved to Estonia via Sweden and Finland. Having performed stand-up in both of those Nordic countries, he decided to start running shows in Estonia. He recalls: 'Because there was nothing here, I understood we essentially needed to construct an industry end-to-end … So we became very independent. Almost until very recently, we did everything on our own.'[20] His Comedy Estonia organisation finds new talent by running open mic nights, staging professional stand-up shows, and mounting tours by the biggest comedians, as well as managing its artists.

It is important to acknowledge that when stand-up scenes spring up, they are sometimes preceded by an earlier performance tradition with similar qualities. For example, Liisi Laineste has shown how the recent stand-up scene in Estonia was preceded by a similar comic tradition that had been introduced in the 1960s during Soviet rule: *estrada*.[21] Similarly, despite stating that Romanian stand-up dates back to 2003, Radu Isac points out that '[o]bviously we had comedy before. A lot of it was monologues that would be indistinguishable from stand up today … I'm pretty sure we've had "stand up" in Romania way before we had recording equipment and way before Romania was a country.'[22]

In fact, these earlier performance traditions are often easily distinguishable from stand-up today. Olga Mesropova argues that Russia's stand-up tradition stretches back to the 1930s, but acknowledges that it is different from its 'Western counterpart', displaying a 'literary orientation' in that 'comics read their monologues directly from a script and rarely resort to improvisation'.[23] Dutch comedian Rayen Panday explains: 'The theatre form that was here before stand up, but looks most like it, is called Cabaret. It started around the 1890s as far as I know. It is more storytelling, more theatre with acting and/or music and less interactive.'[24] Belgium has a similar tradition, and the difference between cabaret and stand-up struck Nigel Williams, who has a successful stand-up career there – performing in Dutch – but originally comes from Bristol:

> The thing is, you had a culture here of the French-style *cabaret*. It'd be a guy or a woman coming onstage – and it used to get on my nerves 'cos they talk for about ten minutes without a laugh. And then they usually have, halfway through, a little bit on the piano where they sing a song and everybody has to cry. And then they tell a little bit more story and you can laugh now and again.

It was the late 1990s when Williams first saw stand-up in Belgium, in a form he recognised from the UK: 'I was just in a bar and I thought, "Hey, these guys are doing stand-up comedy".'[25]

Language

Despite these earlier traditions, the modern stand-up scenes springing up in countries around the world betray their origins in anglophone countries in the words they use to name the form. In France it is *le stand-up*, in Italy *la stand-up comedy*, in German *die Stand-up-Comedy*, in Finland *stand up-komiikka*, in Sweden *ståuppkomik*, in Russia стендап-комедия (*stendap-komediya*), and in Hindi स्टैंड-अप कॉमेडी (*staind-ap komedee*). Louis Zezeran recalls that when he kick-started stand-up into existence in Estonia, one of the things he needed to do was 'to name the art form' because, 'There's no word in Estonian … So we decided on, in Estonian, *stand-up koomik*. Which is, *koomik* is Estonian for comic. But we kept the *stand-up*, because I looked around at different countries … and every country had some derivation of stand-up … and it was like, "We want to be cool internationals".' In fact, the Estonian Language Inspectorate chose a different word, *püstijalakomöödia*. However, according to Zezeran, *stand-up komöödia* has become 'more colloquially accepted'.[26]

Stand-up's anglophone origins can also be seen in the fact that some non-anglophone countries initially use English as the language to perform in. English-language stand-up is still popular across Scandinavia, for example. At first, stand-up was performed in English in Comedy Estonia's shows. Louis Zezeran explains why:

> So when we started in Estonia, only ten years ago, the people accepted English before Estonian. There was sort of some cultural disbelief that stand-up and this sort of humour could work in their own language. And well, OK, we started the first shows in English … it took a couple of years and then the Estonians started to step up and we realised … it works fine in Estonian. There's actually no grammatical reason why it couldn't. And then that kind of took over … One of the big moments for us was a guy called Sander Õigus came along, and he's now probably the most popular comedian in the country … and he was very committed to Estonian-language stand-up.[27]

However, in countries where a range of languages is commonly spoken, switching between more than one of them can be a useful performance tool. For example, there are eleven official languages in South Africa, but English is widely spoken and is the preferred language for business and government. South African comedian Tats Nkonzo switches between languages in his act. He explains that 'when you speak in someone's language, you've already won their hearts over. It's one of the tricks that we use here. Even if you don't speak the language, you greet the person in their language – and already their hearts are a little bit more open to you.'[28] Ed Morrish remembers Nkonzo giving a slightly different reason for language-switching: '[T]hey speak English. But then you do the punchlines in your native language. Which undercuts it in sort of status, but also makes it a bit exclusionary – to the English[-speaking] people. Like, the bosses can't understand us.'[29]

A similar pattern exists in the Indian Hinglish stand-up scene, in which performers use a mixture of Hindi and English. On one level, this reflects how the performers speak in their offstage lives, as Aman Deep acknowledges: 'That's how we talk you know, with friends.'[30] Similarly, after starting performing in English, Amit Tandon now uses Hinglish because, 'It's how I usually speak. Comedy works best when you are yourself on stage.'[31] Thus, Hinglish helps to create the feeling of intimacy and authenticity which stand-up requires.

On another level, switching from English to Hindi is a useful performance technique, signalling a shift from formality to informality. Anuvab Pal has a joke which precisely plays on the different connotations of English and Hindi in terms of class and status. In it, he describes 'a certain kind of Indian person' who thinks English is superior because of 'postcolonial nostalgia for Britain' and has 'an assumption that people in Britain speak English in a certain Victorian sort of way'. He shows this character going to London and being thrown by encountering the way English is actually spoken in the UK:

> [T]he character I have is sort of somewhere right outside the Victoria and Albert Museum asking for directions. And he's confused because various accents are coming into play. So I try and do different sort of British accents. And he can't understand what the directions are and then finally sort of his colonial thing is just wiped off his face. And then he thinks to himself, *'Yeh kya bol raha hai?'* So the punchline is in Hindi. And the line is, 'What the hell is he saying?' ... and then he has to confront the fact that he can't understand these accents ... but that 'What the hell is this guy saying?' can only work in Hindi ... and then that gets a big laugh because I'm

referring to a certain kind of elite Indian person, who's sort of unmasked, if you will, for an Indian audience, who really enjoy that. Because, you know, nobody likes posh, arrogant people.[32]

Pal argues that Hindi's informal connotations mean that the Hindi-speaking stand-up scene is India's biggest:

> [I]n India the biggest comedians will perform in Hindi. It's just most relatable, it's what everybody'll understand ... The big stadium comedians and the auditorium comedians are all Hindi comedians. They're the really large comedians in India, because they are, you know, mass market ... imagine if Michael McIntyre's main asset was that the *language* was different. And *that* is what made him relatable, right?[33]

On the other hand, in another linguistic context it is English that allows comedians to let their hair down and share intimate experiences. Vietnamese comedian Phuc performs in English because, 'In Vietnam, swearing and [talking] about sex is very taboo, and the language is designed in such a way that if you talk about it, it's very awkward. When you swear it's different. When you talk about sex, it's very weird.'[34]

'What's Happening Here?'

Because stand-up is such a simple theatre form – and because it has such a long tradition in Britain, North America, and Australia – it can be easy for audiences based in these countries to mistakenly assume it is a universal type of performance. However, when it arrives in a country with no previous tradition of it, it can seem strange and unfamiliar. When Louis Zezeran was looking for a venue to run his first shows in Estonia, the bar owners he spoke to were often confused when he tried to explain stand-up to them: 'In Tallinn, they were like, "What is this? What, do you want to step on a coffee table or something? This is weird".'[35]

Audiences can find the form of stand-up similarly confusing, and sometimes need it to be explained to them. Anuvab Pal states, 'I remember when the Comedy Store started [in Mumbai], people would often shout, you know, "What is going on?" Like, "Is something going to begin after this?" They just couldn't comprehend that *that* was the thing. And others were laughing. So there was a lot of, "What's happening here?".'[36] Janet A McLeod remembers producer Toby Sullivan telling her about seeing a stand-up showcase in Kuala Lumpur: 'And he said it was so interesting because basically the host came out and ... described what stand-up was – "And they'll be telling you these stories from their own life, and they're not characters, and blah-blah-blah." And then the show began.'[37]

Stand-up's informality, directness, and emphasis on comedians presenting themselves in the first person – sharing what are more or less their actual experiences and opinions – can be hard for audiences unfamiliar with the form to understand. As Anuvab Pal explains, it was this that confused some among the first audiences at the Mumbai Comedy Store:

> Everything in India, just to be a little careful, is usually melodramatic and heightened and kind of like the films. It sort of works its way around reality. But here, to have a person say, 'This is my age and I'm divorced and I'm this and I'm that' … That kind of honesty never existed, that artform did not exist. So the Comedy Store allowed people to discover their own voice, and kind of allowed us to ask, 'What do we think about things?', which was very uncommon in a culture like ours … Not because there is a certain institutionalised repression of it, but because it just didn't exist.[38]

What stand-up's global spread reveals, then, is the particularity – even peculiarity – of a form that imitates everyday conversation, with comedians sharing the intimate details of their lives with a roomful of strangers, and audiences replying with their laughter.

This Book

Starting this book with an account of stand-up comedy's global spread might seem a quirky choice given that – in the UK at least – it has received little media attention. Instead, popular discourse has been dominated by other aspects of stand-up – for example, the impact of 'culture wars' and the #MeToo movement, the growth of arena comedy, the rise of the so-called dead dad show, the enormous success of Hannah Gadsby's *Nanette*, the devastating effects of coronavirus on the comedy industry, and the sudden emergence of online performances on platforms such as Zoom. All of these are covered here, and it is important to recognise that they have happened in the wider context of stand-up becoming a truly global theatre form.

The book is divided into three parts. Part I situates stand-up in time and place. There are chapters on stand-up's history in the UK and the USA, while others examine the venues in which live stand-up takes place and how it has adapted to the recorded form, from radio to Netflix. Part II focuses on interpretation and meaning, looking at how stand-up reflects different aspects of identity as well as the ethics and politics of the form. Chapters on identity discuss the importance of performers who are female, LBGT+, Black, Jewish, or disabled. Others tackle debates around offensiveness in stand-up and the politics of the form in terms of both content and organisation. Part III examines the performance dynamics of stand-up, with chapters on the role of audiences, how a comic persona is constructed from elements of the performer's offstage self, and how stand-up can deal with personal trauma.

The contributing authors are a diverse group, based in six different countries and representing a range of disciplines, including theatre, media, communications, folklore, English literature, social and cultural anthropology, sociology, linguistics, American studies, and Africana studies. Three of them have worked professionally as stand-up comedians, and others have been involved in professional comedy in other ways, for example as professional reviewers or by running workshops.

Scattered between the different parts of the book, there are a series of short statements by stand-up comedians from nine different countries, articulating thoughts about their own work and the craft of stand-up more generally. These offer a different perspective on stand-up, giving a performer's-eye view which emphasises creative processes more than critical interpretation. The comedians who generously shared their thoughts reflect on how they write or devise their material, how they prepare to go onstage, the performance techniques they use, the audiences they attract, the stage personas they adopt, and their motivation for becoming stand-ups in the first place.

Notes

1. Mort Sahl, *The Future Lies Ahead* [LP] (USA: Verve Records, 1959).
2. Peter Brook, *The Empty Space* (Harmondsworth: Pelican Books, 1972), p. 11.
3. Tony Allen, *Attitude: Wanna Make Something of It?* (Glastonbury: Gothic Image, 2002), p. 28.
4. Shelley Berman, *The Edge of Shelley Berman* [LP] (USA: Verve Records, 1960).
5. Maria Bamford, *Old Baby* (USA: Netflix, 2017).
6. Kitty Bruce (ed.), *The Unpublished Lenny Bruce* (Philadelphia: Running Press, 1984).
7. 'Stage Gossip', *Yorkshire Evening Post*, 10 November 1917, p. 3. For more on this, see Oliver Double, 'The Origin of the Term "Stand-Up Comedy" – Update', *Comedy Studies*, Vol. 9, No. 2, 2018: pp. 135–137.
8. Joe Laurie Jr, 'Monologists', *Variety*, 29 December 1931, p. 22.
9. Richard Harris, *Punch Lines: Twenty Years of Australian Comedy* (Sydney: ABC Books, 1994), p. 3.
10. Rod Quantock, email, 20 February 2022.
11. Mary Kenneally, interview with Oliver Double, by Zoom, 14 February 2022. Kenneally is an important comic performer in her own right, particularly known for her comedy character Debbie, which she performed in the 1980s TV show *Australia You're Standing in It*. She is also married to Quantock.

12. Rod Quantock interview.
13. Harris, *Punch Lines*, p. 106.
14. Andrew McClelland interview, by Zoom, 31 January 2022.
15. Ed Morrish interview, by Zoom, 7 April 2022.
16. Janet A. McLeod interview, by Zoom, 2 February 2022.
17. Anders Olsen email, 23 January 2022.
18. Radu Isac email, 16 June 2022.
19. Anuvab Pal interview, Camden, 7 April 2022.
20. Louis Zezeran interview, by Zoom, 27 January 2022.
21. Liisi Laineste, 'Stand-Up in Estonia: From Soviet *estrada* to Comedy Estonia', in L. Laineste, D. Brzozowska, and W. Chłopicki (eds), *Creativity and Tradition in Cultural Communication, Volume 1, Jokes and Their Relations* (Tartu: ELM Scholarly Press, 2012), pp. 73–90.
22. Radu Isac email.
23. Olga Mesropova, 'Stand-Up Comedy', in Tatiana Smorodinskaya, Karen Evans-Romaine, and Helena Goscilo (eds), *Encyclopedia of Contemporary Russian Culture* (London: Routledge, 2014) p. 293.
24. Rayen Panday email, 3 March 2022.
25. Nigel Williams interview, by Zoom, 28 January 2022.
26. Louis Zezeran interview, by Zoom, 27 January 2022.
27. Louis Zezeran interview.
28. *Welcome to Wherever You Are*, BBC Radio 4, 7 December 2017.
29. Ed Morrish interview.
30. Zubin Miller, 'Stand-Up Comedy and Young India: The Expression and Construction of Identity', *Changing English*, Vol. 27, No. 4, 2020: p. 452.
31. Manali Shah, 'Why an Increasing Number of Stand-Up Comedians Are Choosing to Talk in Hindi', *Hindustan Times*, 23 March 2017.
32. Anuvab Pal interview, by Zoom, 10 May 2022.
33. Anuvab Pal interview, Camden.
34. Jwyanza Hobson, 'How Vietnamese Stand-Up Comics Juggle Culture, Identity and Language on Stage', *Saigoneer*, 14 January 2018.
35. Louis Zezeran interview.
36. Anuvab Pal interview, Camden.
37. Janet A. McLeod interview.
38. Anuvab Pal interview, Camden.

COMEDIANS' INSIGHTS

What Do You Do to Prepare to Go Onstage?

Edward Aczel (UK)

Think about what's the worst that could happen.

Stephen Bailey (UK)

A spin class.

Maria Bamford (USA)

Imagine a room-sized version of my mother (she is deceased), sitting on the crowd.

Daman Bamrah (UK)

I memorise my jokes and the order in which I want to tell them. I've noticed after doing this for a few years now that most nerves I experience on stage come from lack of preparation. If I'm onstage desperately trying to remember what my jokes are and the order in which I want to say them, it knocks my confidence which can affect my delivery and consequently the audience's perception of me. So I always learn what I want to say. Even if it's new material that turns out to be rubbish … that rubbish needs to be memorised!

Angela Barnes (UK)

I'd like to say that I do breathing exercises and go over my set. But the truth is I usually look at the audience and go through all the reasons that I think this particular audience will hate me. It fits in with my worldview – if I expect the worst, I'm never disappointed! I now acknowledge that that is part of my process. I have to imagine worst-case scenarios. Then when I realise I can survive them, I am OK.

Jo Brand (UK)

Very little. Have a coffee and on and off over the years (on at the moment) smoke fags.

Jo Caulfield (UK)

Focus. Get in a bad mood. Allow myself complete artistic freedom. Check my shoelaces are tied. (A bad mood + jokes = a joyous celebration of Anger!)

Tanyalee Davis (Canada/USA/UK)

I watch the comedians before me to get a sense of the audience and to listen if I could potentially CALL BACK to a previous comedians set. Audiences love that.

Tiernan Douieb (UK)

I often make sure I know the first thing I'm going to say, and the very last thing. I'll have run through my set in my head a few times earlier in the day and so as long as I remember what the first and last gag will be, I know the rest will fall into place. I used to run it all through in my head right before the show but now I prefer to just be relaxed, having a chat with the other acts or stage manager, or whoever is around before walking on.

Alex Farrow (UK)

I read through my notes from a previous gig. Listen to my set. Just before – look out at the room. Walk around the gig if possible/practical.

Mary Gallagher (USA)

I watch every comic before me, tap into what's happening onstage, survey the room and see what is unusual or interesting and if in a new location,

I write the first few minutes of my act with jokes just for them to personalise it.

Justin Herman (USA)

I always write out the set list I want to do, identify the riskiest joke in the list for that crowd and write alternative jokes for the set if it bombs, to remind myself to always stay loose and be prepared to respond to the moment.

Bec Hill (Australia/UK)

I'll usually run through my bullet-point list on my fingers a few times. If it's a big gig and I'm nervous, I'll say the Lord's Prayer under my breath (sometimes repeatedly). It's very meditative and calming.

Harry Hill (UK)

Pace up and down, write stuff on my hand.

Matt Hoss (UK)

I always feel like I will forget my jokes, so I practise saying the first joke, so that the rest of the set can flow really nicely.

Tom Houghton (UK)

Empty my pockets and bowels. Then hop about a little to get myself in a playful mood.

Charmian Hughes (UK)

Decide running order – then run the content of my set as if it is a real memory of things that actually happened through my mind.

Robin Ince (UK)

Sometimes I will be taking to people at the side of stage until the moment I go on. I do think, 'Whatever happens, make sure you are giving fucking everything' (I think of Rik Mayall) and often I am onstage as the audience come in and I chat to people or pootle about.

Radu Isac (Romania/UK)

I don't really sit down and write. I book gigs and prepare a set in my head. I've written more than half of my jokes in the hour before going on stage. The stress helps me concentrate. When things get serious, I listen to the recording of past gigs and edit bits.

Milton Jones (UK)

I pace up and down a lot. I practise new bits. And I pray that the audience experience joy.

Jackie Kashian (USA)

I do laps and look at my set list a lot.

Brian Kiley (USA)

I make a list of all the jokes I'm going to do that night and then take a picture of my setlist on my phone to look at when I'm at the club. I put my new jokes in bold and rehearse them in the car. I also will listen to previous sets on my way to the gig. Then, just before I go on, for good luck, I peek at a picture of my kids.

Athena Kugblenu (UK)

Drink water or coffee depending on my state.

Beth Lapides (USA)

Check in on the material, chit-chat to get loosened up, hair and make-up to get centred, coffee and ricola lozenge, chi chant with the band, pee obviously, and finally just surrender to be of service.

Stewart Lee (UK)

Nothing.

Pope Lonergan (UK)

If I suspect the audience is going to be difficult, or not fully invested, I go out and mingle with them (shake hands; introduce myself). I think it's more difficult for the audience to reject you completely (which, thankfully, happens very rarely) if they've gotten to know you – albeit briefly – offstage.

Elf Lyons (UK)

My dad said, 'Treat yourself like an athlete', and that is what I do. I do a full warm up, squats, planks, stretches. Before I get announced onto stage it always looks like I am prepared to run the 100 metres. I have to get myself frightened and pumped up, otherwise – what is the point?

Jimmy McGhie (UK)

Very little in fact which is lazy and often results in struggling off the top. A good stretch and even some vocal warms can help so much, but you just feel like such a wally doing them in a green room!

Andrew McClelland (Australia)

Pace about nervously with my script held, totemically in my hand. Even if it's towards the end of a season and I know the show inside out, I'll still glance at my script before I go on. It becomes a comfort script.

Aditi Mittal (India)

Smile, with my whole body – even if my mind is not feeling it that day, my body tricks it into thinking it is.

Alfie Moore (UK)

No ritual other than to glance at set notes before walking out.

Martin Mor (Northern Ireland/UK)

Change into stage clothes, this always gets me into 'work' mode. Breathing exercise to raise endorphins.

Al Murray (UK), who Performs as the Pub Landlord (UK)

My pre-stage preparation is for as little as possible to happen. We'll even be watching *The One Show* or something normal and boring just before I go on. So that going onstage is where the thing begins, rather than like a sort of psyching-up process. Because I've never felt that's helpful. And I certainly don't get into character, or any of that actor-y stuff. You know, I just go on and get on with it.

Sander Õigus (Estonia)

Ideally tell jokes and have fun with other comedians so that I can go on stage happy, laughing and in a good mindset. Also, that helps avoid getting nervous and overthinking things. Nice, happy and loose is the way to go.

Anuvab Pal (India)

I drink an espresso and write down my whole set at some point during the day before the gig. And every gig, I try to add a little bit.

Rayen Panday (Netherlands)

Subconsciously I notice that my head starts to puzzle the set together the day before the gig and I love to shower right before the gig, put on comfortable shoes and a polo.

Lucy Porter (UK)

I used to have rituals and real superstitions actually. I used to have to eat a banana before a gig, wear a certain outfit, do my make-up in exactly the right order. I got into a thing in Edinburgh at the Festival where I had to give money to someone. Because I'd done that once, and I was like, 'Oh yeah, do a good deed and that'll get you in the right mood'. I was chasing round the streets of Edinburgh trying to find homeless people for half an hour before my show. Anyway, so all of this I decided to kill because I could see the way it was heading which was into really compulsive behaviour territory. So now, if at all possible, I try and be chatting to someone. If there's no one around then I'll be playing my *Countdown* app on my phone. And I try to create as little friction between on and offstage as possible, so that I'm carrying a conversation that I was just having in the dressing room onto the stage with me as I go.

Rod Quantock (Australia)

I wish I could say I prepare. I might brush my hair. I always gather the audience in the foyer, lead them in, greet them at the door individually, and do that in reverse order at the end. The show always starts before the show starts.

Mark Simmonds (UK)

I don't perform well if I'm nervous beforehand. The more relaxed I am the better I am. So, before walking onstage I continuously tell myself, 'I don't give a shit, I don't give a shit, I don't give a shit'.

Mark Thomas (UK)

I arrive two hours before the show and have a ritual of tasks. Say hello to the tech team. Sound check, sing a song down the mic, shout and click my tongue and make noises. Find out where the edge of the stage is. I know it is obvious but it is good to go and hang your feet over the edge of the stage. Look at the space you are working in. Try and get to the furthest seat at the back. I often just sit and have a think in the furthest seat. If the show is a theatre show I run though the tech changes, making sure I have got the muscle memory for cues, running any interactive audio and film. Do a speed run of the show. Especially if I have not done it for a day or two. Make sure I have water onstage. Then talk to duty manager about merch, latecomers, trigger stuff like flashing lights. Iron my stage stuff, trousers and shirt. Always do this. The audience have made the effort so should you. I have a pair of shoes I wear for stage only, I call them the show wheels. Run through bits or think of new ideas. Wash and shave. Audience make the effort … Inhaler if I am chesty. Water, coffee. Brush teeth. Run any bits that are tongue twisty. Think. Maybe look at news. Wee. Water. Go. In interval, iron shirt for second half. Notes on first half. Wash and clean underwear. I know, I know, but I like to start the second half clean and fresh.

Nigel Williams (UK/Belgium)

I try to get on stage with an 'open mind' so the spontaneous doesn't get 'shut out'. I try to think of laughter, comedy, pace around, and drink water. And talk as little as possible to anyone hanging around backstage – concentrate.

Bilal Zafar (UK)

I'll jot some bullet points on the back of left hand and try to make sure I know what I'm going to say. It helps me focus and is probably the result of always losing my place in my first few gigs I ever did. I also make sure my Casio is set to stopwatch. I know comedians that can do 20 minutes without even glancing at a watch but my material is all stories of varying length and I might end up improvising some nonsense and accidently running 10 minutes over if I'm not careful.

PART I

Time and Place

CHAPTER 1

Stand-Up in the United Kingdom

Oliver Double and Neil Washbourne

In the final episode of his TV series *Stewart Lee's Comedy Vehicle,* Lee tells his audience at the Mildmay Club in Stoke Newington that he is disappointed with their reaction to a particular joke: 'D'you know what? I've been running this in live for about six months and there is normally applause there. [laughter]' This small complaint grows comically vast, as he starts to snipe about how the audience fails to understand how hard it is to be a comedian: 'We lose, it's very stressful, we lose a lot of people to the – [a few laughs] We you know, like Hancock and er – Lenny Bruce, all these guys, 'cos it's, it's, y-you, you-' This builds to an outrageous accusation: 'I mean, audiences like you, you know, you – [a few laughs] you as good as murdered Robin Williams. [outraged laughter, seven seconds]' As his complaints get ever more outrageous, Lee takes the audience to task for their incompetence:

> A car, right, a car is a lethal weapon, right? You wouldn't, you wouldn't get behind the wheel of a car if you couldn't drive, would you? No, and likewise – a comedy audience, right? [laughter] Chipping away at people's self-esteem. That is a lethal weapon right, and you should not be in a comedy audience – [laughter] if you can't follow the development of an idea through.

After telling them he walks onstage every night 'through a forest of ghosts' of dead comedians – and pretending he can see these ghosts right now – he shouts more accusations out into the crowd. He tells them the blood of these comedians is 'on you', and included among the dead are 'the old music hall guys!'[1]

In this routine, Lee turns a common assumption about stand-up on its head, implying that the audience – and not the comedian – are to blame for the failure of a gag. A review of a live show performed a few months before this routine was filmed notes his skill in 'deconstructing the art form he's performing while performing it',[2] and this ability to deconstruct and reinvent stand-up is often seen as central to Lee's work.

Yet the routine is also absolutely rooted in the defining features of stand-up comedy. Tony Allen's definition of the form, as quoted in the Introduction, conspicuously applies here. Lee is performing 'in the first person'. The routine is about *him*, about his complaints and frustrations as a comedian, and it is his persona – the hangdog arrogance of the disappointed idealist, undercut by barely hidden playfulness – that makes it funny. He 'speaks directly to the audience', berating them as a group and singling out individuals for particular scorn. Finally, there is a strong sense that 'the performance is spontaneous'.[3] Even though at the time of filming, Lee had been performing this routine for months, and its basic structure was set, he was still able to respond to things happening right in front of him on this particular night.

What is particularly interesting about this routine is that it shows such a strong awareness of the history of stand-up in the UK. It references the roots of the form in nineteenth-century music hall. One of the comedians mentioned, Tony Hancock, started his career in the variety theatres of the mid twentieth century. The Americans mentioned, Lenny Bruce and Robin Williams, influenced the beginnings of the UK alternative comedy movement of the 1980s. Even the venue in which it was filmed is significant. The Mildmay Club is a working men's club, part of the club circuit which became the main location for stand-up in the 1960s and 1970s.

The routine also relates to history in another way. By focusing on the job of the comedian and the working conditions that comedians experience – for example, suffering audiences that 'can't follow the development of an idea through' – Lee offers a clue about one of the main drivers shaping the way stand-up has evolved in the UK.

Music Hall

Music hall developed in the north of England during the 1840s and later spread to London and throughout the UK.[4] For two generations the audiences were working-class and lower-middle-class patrons of all ages. At first each music hall was a one-off, but northern entrepreneurial performers developed small chains of such venues, benefiting from economies of scale in employing performers and spreading the risks of any specific venue making losses. Large-scale, nationally oriented chains of music halls did not emerge until the 1890s. During that time the large investment needed required broadening the audience to include the middle classes. Differentiated ticket prices ensured both a degree of respectability for the middle classes and practices of class segregation in the hall.

In the heyday of music hall there were no stand-up comedians. Comic performances consisted of songs sung in character. Dagmar Kift suggests that the characters portrayed in music hall songs came in three types. First, there were characters representing the 'man-in-the-street and his everyday attitudes and habits at home, at work and at leisure'. Second, there were regional, national, and racial stereotypes, including Irishmen, Scots, Northerners, Cockneys, and Black people – the last of these portrayed by white performers in blackface. Finally, there were characters based on gender reversal, with male performers cross-dressing as women and vice versa.[5]

The way in which the songs were performed was crucial to music hall's identity, and it was this performance style which paved the way for stand-up in the UK. A disapproving press report on a music hall show, published in 1856, described the nature of the performances: 'They are sung, or rather roared, with a vehemence that is stunning, and accompanied with spoken passages of the most outrageous character.'[6] The spoken passages are particularly significant, and not just because of their 'outrageous character' – an indication that sexual innuendo was a popular theme. According to Peter Bailey, in the 'patter' – the spoken sections – the singers 'insistently broke through the fictions of their impersonations with an ad lib gagging commentary'.[7] In other words, they were performing spontaneously, in the first person, and speaking directly to the audience.

By the turn of the twentieth century, patter was becoming increasingly important, largely due to the success of one of music hall's biggest stars, Dan Leno. In a biography published shortly after Leno's death, J. Hickory Wood notes that: 'One calls his performances on the halls "songs" for want of a pithy word that is better; but they were not really songs at all. They were diverting monologues in a style of which he was as undoubtedly the originator as he was its finest exponent.' He goes on to praise Leno's 'amusing wealth of monologue or "patter"' and describes the actual song verses that surrounded his talk as 'a somewhat unnecessary interlude'.[8] Similarly, in 1904, Max Beerbohm suggested that Leno differed from the 'classic tradition' of music hall because he 'shifted the centre of gravity from song to "patter"'.[9]

The recordings Leno made fail to capture the excitement of his act, because he died in 1904, long before it was possible to make live theatre recordings and thus capture the comedian playing to an audience. However, they give a reasonable idea of his style. For example, the recording of his song 'The Grass Widower' starts with four sung lines, followed by over a minute of patter, before finishing with a few more lines of singing.[10] The song is about a man seeing his wife off at the station for a few days away by herself. Here is a section of the patter, which we have broken down into a series of gags reminiscent of the type comedians would use in variety in the decades to follow:

> So I said, 'Well what has the doctor ordered?' She said, 'The doctor says I must go away for a week.' Oo! All alone for a week! I couldn't help laughing! She turned round and said, 'You brute! You massive brute!'
> She said, '"I don't believe you care! I believe you wish I was dead"!' Isn't it funny how wives guess your thoughts?
> I said, 'No darling!' I said, 'You must hurry up and get the train in the morning.' So I put the clock on four hours, she had to get up before we went to bed.

The first two gags play on the comic stereotype of the monstrous wife, which was common in both music hall and variety. This explains Leno's glee at the prospect of being without her for a week in the first joke, and the punchline hinges on describing him as a 'massive brute', given he was actually a short, thin man. The stereotype is also behind him wishing death on her in the second gag. The third joke comically reinvents how time works – and anticipates one of the jokes in Monty Python's classic 'Four Yorkshiremen' sketch.

Leno's dominant use of patter has led John Fisher to identify him as 'the archetype of the modern stand-up comedian'.[11] Other accounts identify different origins for stand-up, such as the spoken comic elements of the blackface minstrel show, whose development was contemporary with that of music hall and which has been recognised as contributing to the rise and performance of stand-up in the USA.[12] However, what makes Leno so convincing as a key figure in the development of UK stand-up is that he was part of a continuous tradition of comic performers, stretching back to the mid nineteenth century and forward to the comedians who would populate the stages of variety theatres in the mid twentieth century. Although there were blackface acts in Victorian music hall, few survived through the variety era, and those that did were not solo comedians. G. H. Elliott, for example, sang straight rather than comic songs, and Nosmo King mainly worked as a double act with his son.

Variety Theatre

With the rise of national music hall chains, the way the entertainment was organised was radically altered. By the late nineteenth century, music halls had come to resemble conventional theatres, and changes to licensing laws meant removing alcohol from the auditorium. Around the same time, the policy of running one long show lasting the whole evening was replaced by the 'twice nightly' system, with a shorter, tighter show playing twice a night. What had been known as music hall now came to be more normally referred to as variety theatre.

The front cloth comic – one who performs in front of the painted backdrop that hangs nearest to the front of the stage – was central to variety. The 'stand-up' (though that phrase was not commonly used then) performed by such comedians was crucial to the smooth running of variety shows. It allowed for elaborate acts with large stage set-ups (magicians, dance troupes, animal acts, big bands, speciality acts, and so on) to be organised out of sight of the audience during the front cloth comic's act; therefore, for the show to 'run without gaps'.[13] It was this controlled and controllable organisation of variety that allowed for two complete shows per evening, making variety economically more sustainable than the music hall. This also made front cloth comedy central to variety as both a cultural and a commercial proposition.

The change from music hall to variety also led to changes in audience behaviour. Music hall's drinking audiences tended to be rowdier, with chatter from the bars and the people wandering through the gallery at the back threatening to drown out the unamplified acts on the stage.[14] In variety, the audience members were not drinking during the show and were seated in the orderly rows of a conventional theatre auditorium. As a result, they were quieter and more attentive. Whereas music hall singers had to 'roar' out their songs – as described in the 1856 account – variety performers could adopt a quieter approach, particularly when theatres began to introduce microphones and public address systems in the 1930s.

It is likely that these new working conditions encouraged comedians to use more patter, allowing them to adopt a quieter, more conversational style. An advertisement for Standard Sound Reproducing Equipment in a 1937 issue of *The Era* shows a comedian speaking into a microphone, suggesting that his ability to convey his jokes to the audience was mainly attributable to the use of the company's products.[15] The skill with which comedians wielded the spoken word to stimulate laughter from audiences ensured their importance to popular culture of the time. Famous variety comedians often also enjoyed success in radio (BBC and European stations broadcasting into the UK from Europe), gramophone recordings, and the British film industry.[16]

The subject matter joked about by the front cloth comics of variety echoed that of their music hall predecessors, with jokes about marital strife and a delight in innuendo. For example, a routine by Suzette Tarri recorded at the Argyle Theatre in Birkenhead in 1939 includes the following: 'Only this morning, I said to my 'usband, "Where were you last night?" He said, "It's a lie!" [laughter] Oo! Oo, what a washout! He goes to bed every night in his tin 'elmet. [brief laughter] Says he needs to be ready for any emergency. [laughter, nine seconds]'[17] This short section includes two types of innuendo, comically suggesting both sex – the implication of her husband's infidelity – and toilets, with the suggestion that her husband might use his helmet instead of a chamber pot if an emergency required it.

Max Miller – arguably variety's most celebrated front cloth comic – put innuendo at the very heart of his act. In a review published in 1940, George Orwell praised the 'startling obscenities' in Miller's act, noting that they were 'only possible because they are expressed in *doubles entendres* which imply a common background in the audience'.[18] Miller dressed in garish suits, was an enormously skilled and charismatic performer, and played a sexually confidant bar-room philosopher, giving the audience the choice of books from which he should choose his jokes – the jokes from the 'blue' book often dripping with innuendo – though completed *as* vulgar (sexually explicit) gags *only* in the minds of the engaged audiences.[19]

This was just one example of how he turned the delivery of innuendo into a game played with the audience. Miller's act was recorded live at various points of his career, and this kind of game features in many of these recordings. At the Finsbury Park Empire in 1942, he takes the audience to task for picking up the obscene possibilities the word 'do', which he uses while introducing a song: 'I'll do "Josephine". Do "Josephine". [laughter] What's wrong with that, go on, make something of that, go on, make- [laughter] Nice lot of people, eh, Finsbury Park! [laughter]'[20] Fifteen years later, at the Met, Edgware Road in 1957, he is still using the same trick of blaming the audience for understanding what he was clearly implying: 'Oh you – you wicked lot. [laughter] You're the kind of people who get me a bad name. [laughter]'[21]

Miller's use of innuendo plays on core qualities of stand-up, relying on his garish persona, and his direct interaction with the audience, commenting on their reactions with apparent spontaneity. The way Miller blames the audience clearly anticipates how Stewart Lee would berate the people watching him in 2016. Like Lee, Miller would also directly comment on his working conditions. For example, at the Holborn Empire in 1938, he tells the audience that its manager, Bertie Adams, hears all his songs and gags 'because he tells me what to cut out, you see? [laughter] He does, he tells me, I don't take any notice, but he tells me. [laughter]'[22] He then says Adams is on the side of the stage right now, keeping a close eye on him. While it is unlikely that Adams was really watching him from the wings, Miller's suggestion was not entirely fanciful. Variety theatres were subject to de facto censorship from local Watch Committees, and the standard contract issued by the Moss Empires chain forbade performers from 'giving expression to any vulgarity or words having a double meaning'.[23]

Working Men's Clubs

During the 1950s, the circuit of variety theatres that once dominated the British entertainment industry went into sharp decline, its demise significantly hastened by the arrival of independent television in 1955. By the beginning of the 1960s, there were only a few of the theatres left, and the form of stand-up needed somewhere else to grow and develop. Britain's club circuit filled that gap.

Since the mid nineteenth century, working men's clubs had sprung up in working-class communities all over the UK. A central organisation – the Working Men's Club and Institute Union (CIU) – was founded in 1862 to represent the interests of working men's clubs. There was a rapid rise in the number of CIU-affiliated clubs in the mid twentieth century, reaching a peak of 4,033 in 1974.[24] Entertainment had played an important part in such clubs since the late nineteenth century, and its importance increased significantly after the decline of variety. Alongside the working men's clubs, there were also privately owned nightclubs and theatre clubs. Manchester had a number of these, most notably the Embassy Club, established by the comedian Bernard Manning in 1959. Perhaps the most famous of the privately owned venues in the club circuit was Batley Variety Club. Between its opening in 1967 and closing in 1978, this legendary club attracted a series of famous stars – including Shirley Bassey, Eartha Kitt, and Louis Armstrong – to appear in the small West Yorkshire town in which it was located.[25]

The style of stand-up that proliferated on the club circuit was conservative in style and content. Material took the form of standard jokes, as shared in workplaces, neighbourhoods, schools, and society as a whole. A 1975 performance by George Roper gives a good idea of the style: 'One Irish fella went into a shop, he said, "I want some nails. I do. Yis. I do." The lady said, "How long do you want them?" He said, "I wanna keep them." [laughter] Fella went to a transport caff, he said, "I want seven cups of tea in a flask. Two without sugar." [laughter]'[26]

These gags were based on standard patterns, structures, and stereotypes and often began with the same opening lines. A 1971 documentary about comedians in working men's clubs took its title from one of the commonest opening lines: *There Was This Fella ...*[27] As this suggests, jokes tended to be about a generalised third person – 'this fella' – rather than being personalised to the comedian. Moreover, gags were seen as common property. When Bobby Knutt started developing his stand-up act in the early 1970s, he began by taking material from another performer and then added some gags his uncle had told him until 'I'd probably replaced about half of the material with other stuff'.[28] Ken Goodwin recalled appearing on club comedy showcase *The Comedians* around the same time: 'I had my list of jokes. So every time I heard one of mine told [by another comedian], I had to cross it off. I was adding and subtracting all the time.'[29]

The northern Irish comedian Frank Carson's catchphrase, 'It's the way I tell 'em!', articulates the role of jokes nicely. The interchangeability of gags meant that it was the manner in which they were performed that differentiated one comedian from the next. This was noted by the London-born comic Mike Reid, who asserted that 'I'd nick anyone's material. But to be fair to myself, I have to say that once I've given it the Mike Reid treatment, they wouldn't recognise it themselves.'[30] This claim notes both the overwhelming focus on jokes and also the profound importance of performance skills and styles in a setting where jokes and formulae for jokes are well worn. This is particularly true given that 1970s club comedians tended to adopt similar stage wear – velvet jacket, frilly shirt, bow tie – described by Bobby Knutt as 'the standard uniform of the day for all the comics'.[31]

Club comedy was as conservative politically as stylistically, reinforcing old-fashioned attitudes by drawing on common stereotypes. Jokes were populated with nagging wives, mean Scots, thick Irishmen, and so on. Racism was rife, with South Asian immigrants a particular target. As Bernard Manning acknowledged: 'Everybody's giving the Pakistanis an hammering.'[32] The violence of this image captures the implicit violence in such material. This gag, told by Marti Caine in 1975, was in circulation throughout the 1970s and 1980s: 'Ey, you don't see many Pakistanis these days, do you? Chinese have discovered that they taste like chicken and – [laughter and applause, six seconds]'.[33] This manages to cram in two racist insults in the space of two lines, both reinforcing stereotypes of Chinese people serving types of meat Westerners would see as inappropriate and imagining Pakistanis being literally butchered.

Again, this style of stand-up developed in response to working conditions. Bernard Manning recognised that 'audiences in clubs are very, very, very critical',[34] and Bobby Knutt argued that they could be actively antagonistic: 'They didn't give a shit about the "Turns", as we were all called.

We'd worked with many a good comic ... and seen lots of 'em die on their arses for no other reason than that the punters just weren't listening.'[35] In a book published in 1971, David Nathan summed up the problem: 'In many of the clubs the performer is treated with little respect and sometimes with contempt. The club is there for other purposes and could exist without him ... Bingo, bar sales, hot pies, lottery tickets and gaming tables take precedence in many places.'[36]

Standard jokes based on common stereotypes made sense in a context where audiences could be indifferent, talkative, or even hostile. Such material is well suited for short attention spans, because if one gag is missed, another will be along shortly. This was comedy for audiences that, as Stewart Lee might put it, couldn't 'follow the development of an idea through'. As for the politics of the material, this reflected attitudes that were built into the structures of working men's clubs. Women were not allowed to become full members, and in 1977 Sheila Capstick began a campaign for equal membership for women – it was not until 2007 that the CIU would agree to this change.[37] Some working men's clubs even operated a formal colour bar, refusing to allow entry to people who were not white. In the 1970s, the CIU went to court to defend the rights of the East Ham South Conservative Club and the Preston Dockers' Club to continue to operate a colour bar.[38] If such policies reflected the attitudes of the audience, it is easy to see why jokes about wives or Pakistanis proliferated, particularly as they may have helped comedians to deflect hostility away from themselves.

Alternative Comedy

Meanwhile, a different stand-up scene was developing across the UK, in the folk clubs that were growing up from the 1960s. Notable comedians emerged from this scene, each with a strong regional identity: Billy Connolly (Scotland); Mike Harding (north of England); Max Boyce (Wales); and Jasper Carrott (Birmingham). In each case their stand-up careers recapitulated the rise of stand-up comedy out of music hall – starting with the singing of often comic songs, to specialising in comic songs, to becoming primarily a spoken word performer. Each of them continued to perform comic songs as part of their act well into the 1980s, though typically songs became a minor feature of their acts, there to provide variety within their mainly spoken performances. Folk comedy was dominated by white, male performers, but the best of them avoided the sexism and racism of working men's club comedy and preferred personal anecdotes and observations to standard jokes. The style of delivery was gentler and more conversational, so that the personality of the individual performer became the centre of the act.

It was not until the end of the 1970s that the conservatism of working men's club comedy was fundamentally challenged. On 19 May 1979, the Comedy Store opened in Soho. It was intended as little more than a showcase for new acts, modelled on a venue of the same name in Los Angeles, but it acted as a magnet for a group of performers who had been struck by the artistic and political potential of stand-up. A working-class Marxist art school graduate, Alexei Sayle, was the first compère, and he was soon joined by anarchist squatter and Speakers' Corner veteran Tony Allen, followed by Andy de la Tour, Jim Barclay, Maggie Steed, and Keith Allen, as well as double acts the Outer Limits (Peter Richardson and Nigel Planer) and 20th Century Coyote (Rik Mayall and Ade Edmondson).

A few weeks after the Comedy Store opened, some of these performers formed themselves into a loose collective called Alternative Cabaret, staging shows around London and beyond and taking up a ten-month residency at the Elgin pub in Ladbroke Grove. This sowed the seeds of a live comedy circuit made up of small clubs, often based in pubs, which continues to this day. In October 1980, another set of performers who had met at the Comedy Store opened a club called the Comic Strip, which garnered national press attention, leading to a tour, a live LP, and a long-running series of television films.

These initiatives spawned an entire scene which became known as 'alternative cabaret', the name of the loose collective losing its uppercase initials to become a generic term. Although it was also known – and tends to be remembered – as alternative comedy, the word cabaret was more commonly used. This reflected the fact that the emerging circuit played host not just to stand-ups but also performance poets, singers, street performers, and speciality acts. It is not surprising that this rich mixture of styles and genres would encourage the new alternative comedians to take an inventive, innovative approach to stand-up, refusing to conform to the dominant, established norms.

Punk was a major influence on alternative comedy, and a number of the performers took on its aggressive approach. Rik Mayall and Ade Edmondson's Dangerous Brothers routine, for example, was a loud, violent slapstick deconstruction of a standard joke.[39] Alexei Sayle verbally assaulted the audience while compering at the Comic Strip, calling them 'fuckfaces' and telling them: 'This is a People's Collective, you do what I fuckin' tell you, all right?? [laughter]' He would even jab at them for approving of him, following a political gag by mockingly imagining their reaction to it: '*Yeah, political satire, yeah! This is what we've come from Islington for, eh??* [laughter]'[40] A journalist described Keith Allen's approach to the audience at the Comedy Store as 'on the brink of violence, brooking no criticism from the audience, outstaring them with a look from his roll-around popout eyes', and noted that he assaulted a heckler 'with his own beer'.[41]

This kind of aggression was as much a response to the audience at the Comedy Store as it was an expression of punk attitude. The shows started late and attracted audiences which could be apathetic, hostile, and often drunk. For the first few months, the venue adopted a gong show structure that empowered rowdy audiences by encouraging them to shout 'gong' to get rid of acts they were not enjoying. Sometimes they would simply talk among themselves rather than listening to the act on the stage. Yet instead of falling back on formulaic jokes as comedians had done in working men's clubs, some performers responded to audience hostility with aggression of their own.

The comedians also took action to change their working conditions. Alexei Sayle believed that 'sexism and racism were rife in the entertainment business and needed to be challenged', and thus used his position as Comedy Store compère to 'impose my own view and gong off a comic I thought was stepping over the line'.[42] Tony Allen took similar action, inviting left-wing actor friends to come along to the Comedy Store so they could outnumber the more traditional acts, and rigorously promoting a non-sexist, non-racist approach. Gradually, this changed the nature of the Comedy Store as a venue. Moreover, both Alternative Cabaret and the Comic Strip were set up to create performance spaces that were less hostile than the Comedy Store.

The Elgin, for example, attracted an alternative crowd made up of activists, anarchists, and squatters, who were sympathetic to experiments with form. Sayle has recalled performing a routine there based on an audience quiz in which he would threaten people who got the answers wrong with an air pistol. This went 'really well' at the Elgin, but when he tried it later that week at the Comedy Store it just confused the audience and provoked them to shout, 'Gong!' He realised that the reason it worked at the Elgin was that the regulars there 'tolerated my experimenting with material'.[43]

As the circuit grew, the audiences that were attracted to the alternative cabaret clubs springing up around London tended to be more like that at the Elgin than the Comedy Store – young, open-minded, and left wing. Generally, comedians and audiences had similar political sympathies. Yet rather than simply confirm the audience's beliefs, comedians would mock them – albeit from an insider's perspective. Pauline Melville, for example, usually performed as Edie, a character who constantly made *faux pas* while trying to show off her left-wing credentials:

> It's so radical here, I could faint. I mean, isn't it, isn't it, I mean there's nothing bourgeois at all! Nothing bourgeois in sight. I wouldn't be here if there was! No, I wouldn't've come if there was anything bourgeois. I've just come from the thrush workshop for women in room 14. [laughter] No you see – I don't see why you laugh, it's about time radical ornithologists got together. [laughter][44]

As well as shifting stand-up to the left, alternative comedy was a vital step in the stylistic evolution of stand-up in the UK. The autobiographical, conversational style that dominates today had begun to develop in America from the 1950s when comics such as Mort Sahl and Lenny Bruce reinvented the form, and many of the early alternative comedians were aware of – and influenced by – not just Bruce but also more recent stand-ups such as Richard Pryor, Steve Martin and Robin Williams. Indeed, Williams would sometimes turn up at the Comedy Store to perform a set.

Alternative comedy allowed the UK to catch up and create its own tradition of stand-up, with self-authored original material based on personal perspective. Tony Allen's material, for example, reflected his worldview as an anarchist squatting rights activist, with a strong interest in sexual politics. One routine saw him imagine a postcoital conversation between a man and a woman:

'You didn't – you didn't *finish*, did you?'
'Doesn't matter. [laughter]'
'It matters to *me*. [laughter]'
'Look, look I said, it doesn't matter.'
'Look, it matters to *me!* Look, when I sleep with a woman –'
'Look, will you get your ego out of my c***? [laughter and some applause]'[45]

The characters Allen conjures up here allow him to send up the subtle ways that men assert their dominance. The man is overbearing and insistent on his sexual potency, symbolised by his ability to give his partner an orgasm ('It matters to *me*'). The woman tries to avoid upsetting her partner ('Doesn't matter') and only puts him down – thus providing the punchline – when really pushed to it. Allen paints a vivid comic picture of male touchiness around sexual performance and refuses to let himself off the hook. Following the imaginary conversation, he confesses to seeing some graffiti written in mascara on the mirror of his flat: 'Postpone. Post-coital.

Postmortems.' The sexual frankness and explicit language in this routine goes far beyond the innuendo of the variety comedian, and the way its comedy is rooted in close observation of lived experience is fundamentally different from the standard jokes told in working men's clubs.

Black British Stand-Up

Although there were a few Black comedians in the working men's clubs of the 1970s (such as Charlie Williams, Jos White, and Sammy Thomas) and the alternative comedy circuit of the 1980s (such as Felix Dexter, Sheila Hyde, Buddy Hell, and Kevin Seisay) – as well as the individual success of Lenny Henry around the same time – it was not until the 1990s that an autonomous Black circuit began to emerge. The Black Comedy Club started at the Albany Empire in 1989 with the aim of fostering new talent and attracting new audiences.[46] A few years later, in 1993, John Simmit started his Upfront Comedy Club at the Crucible Theatre in Sheffield, and has run shows under this name at theatres and arts centres around the UK continuing right up to the present. Simmit explains, 'We, unbeknownst to us, were creating a circuit which was friendly to Black audiences. So we came on talking to our peers, so we didn't have to make the compromises some of our pioneering predecessors had to.'[47]

The Black circuit has produced its own stars – including Angie Le Mar, Curtis Walker, Gina Yashere, Slim, and Richard Blackwood – who can pull big audiences while often remaining largely unknown in the mainstream. This is because, despite occasional exceptions such as *The Real McCoy* and *The Richard Blackwood Show*, television commissioners have either failed to notice the popularity of the Black circuit or failed to recognise the talent it has nurtured. Some Black comedians – notably Gina Yashere – only achieved major recognition once they moved to the USA.

Recently, Black British comedy has begun to attract more recognition, particularly through the stellar success and conscious intervention of Mo Gilligan (Figure 1.1). Gilligan was working in retail when he first began to perform at the Sunday Show at the Slug and Lettuce in Soho, going on to become its regular host, and later running his own Cracking Up Comedy nights. However, he felt that though he got some of his stand-up education from the US *Def Comedy Jam*, there was no route in the UK for him to play such venues as the Comedy Store, let alone '[b]reaking through to the mainstream'.[48] His breakthrough came when his social media videos started going viral, particularly his Cockney 'geezer' character with his 'coupla cans' catchphrase. In 2017–2018, his online success allowed him to

Figure 1.1 Mo Gilligan performing on the Alternative Stage at the Leeds Festival at Bramhall Park on 24 August 2018 in Leeds, England
Photo: Carla Speight / Contributor / Getty Images Entertainment / Getty Images.

play big venues on *The Coupla Cans Tour*, which encompassed a West End run and dates in Australia, eventually selling 50,000 tickets. He has gone on to star in a number of popular television shows.

Gilligan has used his success to draw long-overdue attention to the Black British comedy scene. He has headlined two live shows at the O2 Arena, entitled *Mo Gilligan + Friends: The Black British Takeover*, featuring comedians such as Slim, Babatúndé Aléshé, Thanyia Moore, Richard Blackwood, Eddie Kadi, Angie Le Mar, and Kyrah Gray. He also presented a Channel 4 documentary, *Mo Gilligan: Black British and Funny*, focusing on the history of the scene, talking to its stars, and examining the problems Black British stand-ups have experienced trying to break into the mainstream. In the programme John Simmit – one of the key pioneers of the Black British comedy circuit – argues that it 'came on the heels of the alternative comedy circuit' because 'it's people talking about their real experiences, not stereotypes'.[49]

This highlights the importance of the Black British comedy circuit in opening up the autobiographical, conversational style of stand-up to new voices, articulating different types of lived experience. A moment from Mo Gilligan's second Netflix special, *There's Mo to Life*, provides an excellent example. In a routine about his experiences working in retail, he talks about having to 'code switch' and illustrates the point by asking a Black person called Anton in the front row what he does for a living. Hearing that Anton is a carpenter, Gilligan replies: 'Carpenter! Wow! Great job, man! You must be code switching all the time! [laughter]' To illustrate, he imagines Anton talking to his friends in a strong multicultural London English accent: 'You're chillin' with the guys – "Yeah fam, that's I was saying, cuz. Man might go out this Sa'urday, you know?"' Then he mimes picking up the phone and shows Anton adopting a completely different voice, posh and full of forced brightness: 'Hallo? [laughter] Hi! Ha! Yes! Yes, yes! OK. Can I make a rocking horse? OK. [laughter] Yes! Yes, OK! OK, you need it for Friday, this Friday? Yeah! OK. All right, I'll see you Friday. OK. Bye bye! Bye bye! Yeah.' He mimes putting the phone down, and shows Anton snapping back to multicultural London English: '"Man ain't makin' no fuckin' rocking horse, cuz!" [laughter and applause]' This moment encapsulates what John Simmit says about the Black British comedy scene as a whole. By building it out of a conversation with an audience member, Gilligan is 'talking to [his] peers' and emphasising that he is 'talking about their real experiences'.

UK Stand-Up Today

In the 1980s, alternative comedy grew from an anarchic, loosely organised scene into a professionalised commercial circuit, with the most successful comedians being able to tour big venues. Perhaps the most powerful symbol of this change was the UK's first arena comedy show, *Newman and Baddiel Live and In Pieces*, staged at Wembley Arena on 10 December 1993, with Robert Newman and David Baddiel performing solo stand-up sets and a series of sketches as a double act.

Since then, the live comedy scene has continued to grow, with a night out at a comedy club or a tour show by a well-known comedian becoming an established part of British popular culture. By 2010, it had become normal for the most commercially successful comedians – including Lee Evans, Peter Kay, Eddie Izzard, Russell Howard, and Michael McIntyre – to appear in multi-date arena tours. For example, in 2012, McIntyre's *Showtime* tour saw the comic gross £21 million for performing seventy-three arena shows to a total audience of over 600,000 people.[50]

The working conditions that comedians experience when playing arenas have encouraged them to develop a distinctive style of stand-up. Large projection screens are used as a backdrop, showing a live feed of the comedian in close-up, to make the performance accessible to the people seated furthest away. Arena comics take a very physical approach to stand-up, running up and down around the enormous stages, and using their entire bodies to act out exaggerated, cartoonish impersonations. This physical style demands headset or clip microphones rather than handheld ones that would restrict the comedian's movements. The sheer number of people in the audience encourages material with the broadest possible appeal, avoiding difficult or controversial subjects in favour of universalised observations.[51]

While some comedians tour arenas, other have reacted against the commercialisation of stand-up by establishing smaller, quirkier venues appealing to more niche audiences. In 2007, *The Guardian* published an article recognising the emergence of a new scene, describing it as a 'refreshing antidote to slick, male-dominated mainstream comedy' and labelling it 'DIY comedy'.[52] More recently, the comedians associated with the scene have revived the term 'alternative comedy'.

Josie Long is one of the pioneers of this new wave of alternative comedy, her early stand-up style being based around large presentation pads filled with her own delightfully amateurish art. In her 2006 show *Kindness & Exuberance*, she lists 'the smallest things that make me happy', starting with 'when bus drivers stop in the street to have conversations with each other'. As she delivers the line, she smiles proudly and reveals a colourful cartoon of two red double-decker buses, with the passengers represented by faces cut out from magazines – getting a big, warm laugh from the audience. After acting out her imagined conversation between the drivers, she confides: 'Artistically, this is the genuine best I can do. [laughter] And I've also thought about who's on the bus. Like, who's on this bus?' She points to one of the magazine faces and declares, excitedly, 'It's *The X Files*' Gillian Anderson! [laughter] Don't leave me on my own, I *will* make a collage. [laughter]'[53]

She explains that when she started to establish herself, she struggled to make her playful approach come across to audiences in London's comedy clubs: 'I was temping every day, I was gigging every night, and just dying on my arse every night. I was, like ... "Well, I don't want to do anything else, so I guess this is my life forever" ... And then when I started doing my own shows, it got a lot easier.'[54] Running her own clubs and touring her own solo shows meant that she attracted new audiences with similar interests to her own. Like the 1980s alternative comedians before her she was helping to create a new scene, running her own shows in order to attract new and different audiences. By changing her working conditions in this way, she opened up the space for her to experiment with the form of stand-up and develop her own distinctive comic voice.

Best Living Comedian

Stewart Lee's flair for analysing and commenting on the art of stand-up even while performing it has won him widespread critical acclaim – in 2018, *The Times* put him number one in a list of the '30 best living comedians'.[55] The routine quoted in the introduction to this chapter is a typical example, with the relationship between Lee and his audience becoming its very subject. As much as it is a routine that shows awareness of the history of British stand-up, it also reflects the influences of that history. Lee began his career at the end of the 1980s, becoming part of what was still known as alternative comedy. The influences of the pioneers of that scene are very visible in this routine, from berating the audience as Alexei Sayle did, to deconstructing the process of joking in the manner of the Dangerous Brothers.

In turn, Lee became an influence on the new wave of alternative comedy that has grown up in the early years of this century. Josie Long says she was 'utterly obsessed' by *Fist of Fun*, the TV show written by and starring Lee and Richard Herring in 1993 and 1995,[56] and later, in 2005, Lee chose Long as his tour support. In 2013–2014, he also supported the new scene by curating a TV show for Comedy Central – *The Alternative Comedy Experience* – which showcased alternative comedians such as Long, Simon Munnery, Bridget Christie, and Tony Law.

Yet although Lee's style reflects the ethos of alternative comedy, it also shares features that go right back to the roots of UK stand-up. As well as sharing stand-up's defining features of being performed in the first person, directly to the audience, with the feel of spontaneity, music hall performers were known to draw attention to and comment on their own performance techniques. For example, Little Tich – an unusually short comedian who became one of music hall's most celebrated stars, particularly for his 'Big Boot Dance' – was praised for the 'sophisticated presentment' of his material, as he 'took the audience slyly into his confidence, tipping them the wink, or remarking as he kicked his cap around, "Comic business with hat!"'[57] There is clearly quite a distance from this kind of knowing comment to hurling mock-furious accusations at the audience while claiming to surrounded by a forest of ghost comedians. Thus, Lee's routine shows both a connection with stand-up's music hall origins and how far the form has evolved since then.

Notes

1. *Stewart Lee's Comedy Vehicle* [TV] (BBC2, 7 April 2016).
2. Helen Dalby, 'Stewart Lee Review: Stand-Up Masterclass at Newcastle City Hall', *ChronicleLive*, 5 June 2015.
3. Tony Allen, *Attitude: Wanna Make Something of It?* (Glastonbury: Gothic Image, 2002), p. 28.
4. Dagmar Kift, *The Victorian Music Hall: Culture, Class and Conflict* (Cambridge: Cambridge University Press, 1996).
5. Kift, *The Victorian Music Hall*, p. 45.
6. Quoted in Peter Bailey, 'Conspiracies of Meaning: Music-Hall and the Knowingness of Popular Culture', *Past & Present*, No. 144, 1994: p. 148.
7. Bailey, 'Conspiracies of Meaning', p. 144.
8. J. Hickory Wood, *Dan Leno* (London: Methuen, 1905), pp. 115–116.
9. Max Beerbohm, *The Bodley Head Max Beerbohm* (London: Bodley Head, 1970), p. 375.
10. Dan Leno, *Recorded 1901–1903* [CD] (UK: Windyridge, 2001).
11. John Fisher, *Funny Way to Be a Hero* (London: Frederick Muller, 1973), p. 14.
12. Lawrence E. Mintz, 'Standup Comedy at Social and Cultural Mediation', *American Quarterly*, Vol. 37, 1985: p. 72.
13. Oliver Double, *Britain Had Talent: A History of Variety Theatre* (Basingstoke: Palgrave Macmillan, 2012) p. 24.
14. Double, *Britain Had Talent*, p. 133.
15. Double, *Britain Had Talent*, p. 126.
16. Neil Washbourne, 'Social and National Difference in the High-Speed, Popular Surrealism of Tommy Handley and Ronald Frankau's Double Acts, 1929–1936', in Helen Davies and Sarah Ilot (eds), *Comedy and the Politics of Representation: Mocking the Week* (London: Palgrave Macmillan, 2018), pp. 117–136.
17. Various artists, *They Played the Empire* [LP] (UK: Decca, 1982).
18. Sonia Orwell and Ian Argus (eds), *The Collected Essays, Journalism and Letters of George Orwell, Volume 2, My Country Right or Left 1940–1943* (Harmondsworth: Penguin, 1970), p. 191n.
19. Double, *Britain Had Talent*, pp. 101–103 and John Fisher, *Funny Way to Be a Hero*, 2nd ed. (London: Preface Publishing, 2013), pp. 102–123.
20. Max Miller, *Max Miller* [CD] (UK: EMI Comedy, 2000).
21. Max Miller, *There'll Never Be Another* [CD] (UK: Castle Communications, 1998).
22. Miller, *Max Miller*.
23. Valantyne Napier, *Act as Known: Australian Speciality Acts on the World Vaudeville/Variety Circuits from 1900 to 1960* (Brunswick, Victoria: Globe Press, 1986), p. 149.
24. Ruth Cherrington, *Not Just Beer and Bingo! A Social History of Working Men's Clubs* (Bloomington, IN: Authorhouse, 2012), p. 32.
25. Maureen Prest, *King of Clubs* (Pontefract: Route Publishing), 2017.
26. *The Wheeltappers and Shunters Social Club* [TV] (ITV, 15 February 1975).

27. *There Was This Fella …* [TV] (ITV, 7 December 1971).
28. Bobby Knutt, *Eyup Knutty: The Life and Loves of a Stand Up Comic* (Sheffield: ALD Print, 2009), p. 118.
29. In Ken Irwin, *Laugh with the Comedians* (London: Wolfe Publishing, 1972), p. 31.
30. Mike Reid, *T'rific: The Autobiography* (London: Partridge/Transworld, 1999), p. 138.
31. Knutt, *Eyup Knutty*, p. 205.
32. *There Was This Fella …*.
33. *The Wheeltappers and Shunters Social Club* [TV] (ITV, 29 March 1975).
34. *There Was This Fella …*.
35. Knutt, *Eyup Knutty*, p. 118.
36. David Nathan, *The Laughtermakers* (London: Peter Owen, 1971), p. 222.
37. Pete Brown, *Clubland: How the Working Men's Club Shaped Britain* (Manchester: HarperNorth, 2023), pp. 245–247.
38. Brown, *Clubland*, p. 260.
39. See Oliver Double, *Alternative Comedy: 1979 and the Reinvention of British Stand-Up* (London: Methuen Drama, 2020), pp. 102–106.
40. *The Comic Strip* [LP] (UK: Springtime Records, 1982).
41. Richard North, 'Have you heard the one about … ?', *Observer Magazine*, 23 March 1980, p. 28.
42. Alexei Sayle, *Thatcher Stole My Trousers* (London: Bloomsbury Circus, 2015), p. 175.
43. Sayle, *Thatcher Stole My Trousers*, p. 189.
44. *Alternative Cabaret* [LP] (UK: Original Records, 1981).
45. Unpublished recording of Alternative Cabaret, ADC Theatre Cambridge, 29 May 1981 (British Stand-Up Comedy Archive, University of Kent).
46. John Connor, 'Black Comedy Club', *The Guardian*, 11 October 1989, p. 45.
47. *A History of Comedy in Several Objects* [podcast], episode 33, 30 October 2018.
48. Mo Gilligan, *That Moment When* (London: Ebury Spotlight, 2021), p. 149.
49. *Mo Gilligan: Black British and Funny* (Channel 4, 15 October 2020).
50. Sharon Lockyer, 'Performance, Expectation, Interaction, and Intimacy: On the Opportunities and Limitations of Arena Stand-Up Comedy for Comedians and Audiences', *The Journal of Popular Culture*, Vol. 48, No. 3, 2015: p. 588.
51. Lockyer, 'Performance, Expectation, Interaction, and Intimacy', pp. 590–93.
52. Tim Jonze, 'Laugh? I nearly DIY'd', *The Guardian* (*The Guide* section), 4 August 2007, p. 4.
53. Bonus feature on Josie Long, *Trying Is Good* [DVD] (UK: Real Talent, 2008).
54. Josie Long interview, the Quarterhouse, Folkestone, 1 July 2023.
55. Dominic Maxwell, 'Go On, Make Me Laugh: The 30 Best Living Comedians', *The Times* (*Saturday Review* section), 21 July 2018, pp. 4–5.
56. Josie Long interview.
57. Archibald Haddon, '"Little Tich." Memories and Anecdotes. The Evolution of the Boots', *The Observer*, 12 February 1928, p. 23.

Further Reading

Allen, Tony, *Attitude: Wanna Make Something of It?* (Glastonbury: Gothic Image, 2002).

Bailey, Peter, 'Conspiracies of Meaning: Music-Hall and the Knowingness of Popular Culture', *Past & Present*, No. 144, 1994: pp. 138–170.

Brown, Pete, *Clubland: How the Working Men's Club Shaped Britain* (Manchester: HarperNorth, 2023).

Cherrington, Ruth, *Not Just Beer and Bingo! A Social History of Working Men's Clubs* (Bloomington, IN: Authorhouse, 2012).

Double, Oliver, *Alternative Comedy: 1979 and the Reinvention of British Stand-Up* (London: Methuen Drama, 2020).

Double, Oliver, *Britain Had Talent: A History of Variety Theatre* (Basingstoke: Palgrave Macmillan, 2012).

Gilligan, Mo, *That Moment When* (London: Ebury Spotlight, 2021).

Kift, Dagmar, *The Victorian Music Hall: Culture, Class and Conflict* (Cambridge: Cambridge University Press, 1996).

Lockyer, Sharon, 'Performance, Expectation, Interaction, and Intimacy: On the Opportunities and Limitations of Arena Stand-Up Comedy for Comedians and Audiences', *The Journal of Popular Culture*, Vol. 48, No. 3, 2015: pp. 586–603.

Sayle, Alexei, *Thatcher Stole My Trousers* (London: Bloomsbury Circus, 2015).

Washbourne, Neil, 'Social and National Difference in the High-Speed, Popular Surrealism of Tommy Handley and Ronald Frankau's Double Acts, 1929–1936', in Helen Davies and Sarah Ilott (eds), *Comedy and the Politics of Representation: Mocking the Week* (London: Palgrave Macmillan, 2018), pp. 117–136.

CHAPTER 2

Comics, Minstrels, Satirists, and Hacks
A History of Stand-Up Comedy in the USA

Beck Krefting

The history of stand-up comedy in the USA starts with boats, slavery, and commerce as much as it starts with whistles, amusing stories, and wooden shingles scuffed with the imprint of dancing feet. Boat passengers rolling in from Long Island would have seen Bob Rowley, an enslaved man, dancing in Manhattan's Catherine Market – today's China Town – close to the boat slips on the Lower East Side. Known in the market as Bobolink Bob, his dancing pleased patrons and his signature whistle was picked up by performers across comedic cultural forms. These performers were known as *minstrels*. Their comedic performances were appropriated by white performers and repackaged as *blackface minstrelsy* – that is, white people darkening their skin to 'act' Black. In the early 1800s, men performing in blackface were called *Ethiopian Delineators*, ensuring that audiences knew Blackness was the explicit target of humour. This term shifted to *blackface minstrels* as more travelling performance troupes emerged. Blackface minstrelsy grew in popularity and was the dominant form of comedic entertainment by the mid-1800s. The institutionalisation of blackface minstrelsy created the backbone – the familiar performance tropes (call and response, monologues, sketches) and archetypal stock characters – of vaudeville and twentieth-century comedy forms such as radio comedy, television comedies, and stand-up comedy.[1] Comedic tropes are durable. Similarities in musical and performance tropes across regions in the USA can be traced back to African cultural traditions which were modified according to the political, physical, and cultural constraints imposed on those traditions. Historian W. T. Lhamon argues that 'Blackface was the first Atlantic mass culture' and to extend this logic further, stand-up comedy can be traced back to West African performance traditions.[2] Bobolink Bob is but a footnote in the history of comedy but the comedic conventions introduced by him and other minstrels – using comedic songs, stories, and dance to entertain an audience – withstood the test of time and can still be seen today.

Blackface Minstrelsy

Colonial settlers brought European performance traditions with them, but minstrelsy was the first original American performance tradition. Early influences were enslaved minstrels on plantations who would gather for corn-shucking dances, song, and worship and Black (and sometimes poor white) minstrels performing in northern urban markets. Playfulness, comic exaggeration, satire, and laughter were all part of these early performance traditions. The slave trade in 1619 in North America supported immense economic growth, and by the late eighteenth century the slave economy and the manufacturing of a caste system was deeply entrenched in the new republic called the United States of America. If you were among the thronging crowds gathered to watch Black men dance on shingles for money, eels, and public amusement at Catherine Market, you would have been watching freepersons *and* those who were enslaved. These early minstrels were entrepreneurs selling produce, poultry, or shellfish using performances to draw attention to their wares and any merchant who paid them to do the same.[3] These performances are part of the history of Black cultural production in ways that early blackface minstrelsy disallowed since Black people were prohibited from performing on stage until much later in the nineteenth century. This is not to say that early performances weren't fraught, uncomplicated, or uncontested. Lahmon describes these early market performances as creating patronage for a particular performance style that elicited audience appreciation for a variety of reasons, not all of them positive. Scant sources exist to paint the picture of audience reception but that this tradition carried on into blackface minstrelsy and vaudeville indicates audiences enjoyed consuming this kind of racialised comedic performance – as a means of connecting with folk culture, as a performance mode that reaffirmed racist assumptions about Others, and/or as a reflection of the current political and cultural climate in a rapidly industrialising nation with changing demographics.[4]

The Black minstrel tradition existed long before white men appropriated it. Elsie Williams documents enslaved performance traditions on plantations which she calls 'survivalist humor', a term that calls attention to humour as a coping mechanism for the millions of Africans wrested from their homelands. Black minstrels on plantations sang, danced, told stories, and played instruments. A painting dating back to 1790 in Williamsburg, Virginia's Ludwell Paradine House features enslaved Black musicians and dancers entertaining a group of fellow African Americans. As Williams describes it, 'the painting, while depicting slaves at work on the plantation – at the same time – portrays a private folk behavior and locates the true genesis of blackface minstrelsy in a genuine folk figure and situation'.⁵ Some performances included making a mockery of white European notions of civility embedded in comportment, social expectations, and ceremonial rites. In other words, white men watched enslaved people mimic white bourgeois pretensions, then re-presented this co-opted performance as 'authentically' Black, thus rerouting the mockery away from white people and onto African Americans. In New York City, the multiethnic neighbourhoods surrounding Catherine Market, such as Chatham Square, Five Points, and the Bowery, indicate that the earliest white men in New York City performing as Ethiopian Delineators in blackface were not simply enacting Northern white fantasies of African Americans. Interracial marriage and social mingling notwithstanding, white Northern men used exaggeration and ridicule to reinforce racist attitudes, social inequalities, and white cultural power, much to the delight of audiences. The public lionised the performances of white men travelling across the country as Ethiopian Delineators, such as T. D. Rice, George Washington Dixon, and Micah Hawkins, 'purport[ing] to do authentic black songs, dances, and jokes'.⁶

Performances in the early 1800s by Ethiopian Delineators were more improvisational and included dancing, comic monologues, singing, and clowning, but by the 1840s the minstrel show standardised into three parts. The first part consisted of a group of four or five white men in blackface (using greasepaint or burned cork). The two on each end of the semicircle were called the End Men, named Tambo and Bones, the names drawn from the instruments they played: the tambourine and bone castanets. The performer not in blackface was the interlocutor who acted as a straight man – the foil to Tambo and Bones. The jokes invariably made Blackness their target and were interspersed with songs and sometimes dancing. The second part, called the *olio*, produced some of the most long-standing comedic performance tropes and most resembles modern stand-up comedy. Comic monologues called stump speeches often featured a pretentious Black dandy character (called a Zip Coon) whose soliloquy was filled with mispronunciations and malapropisms demonstrating that Black people were unable to speak 'proper' English. This archetype of Black professional failure reinforced racist beliefs about the intellectual ineptitude of Africans. White men in blackface delivered cross-dressed 'wench' performances stoking Americans' delight in seeing Black emasculation (through watching men dressed as women), while such performances simultaneously perpetuated the image of Black women as highly sexualised objects. (Such lascivious performances worked to exonerate the men who raped Black women and the white women who did nothing to intervene.) The third part of the minstrel show, the *afterpiece*, was a one-act sketch ending in a dance called the prize walk or 'cakewalk', a pre-Civil War dance tradition that began on plantations. Enslaved people would pair off and dance elaborately in a circle. That they were mocking the highbrow dances of white people was lost on the white people in attendance. The best dancers were rewarded with a cake. In the context of minstrelsy, this dance was reinstated making for double mimicry – white people making fun of Black people who were originally making fun of white people.

Before the Civil War, minstrelsy performances generally endorsed plantation life and slavery, while after the Civil War, they expressed nostalgia for a bygone era. The long-standing success of minstrelsy can be linked to its ability to adapt over time, its use of sexual innuendo – bawdy, at times homoerotic – and its focus on folk culture.[7] African American culture has fascinated whites since the invention of race intended to justify enslavement. Eric Lott wrote that '[t]he very form of blackface acts – an investiture in black bodies – seems a manifestation of the particular desire to try on the accents of "blackness" and demonstrates the permeability of the color line'.[8] Blackface performance challenged race as a stable category while simultaneously strengthening a racial caste system by lampooning the race(s) placed at the bottom. In ways that were racialised, gendered, and classed, blackface performances created a 'formula for funny' that reinvented itself alongside the emergence of each new comedic cultural form.[9] Blackface minstrelsy found a comfortable home in vaudeville and expanded the mockery to include immigrants hoping America's promises of freedom and democracy would extend to them.

Vaudeville

The term vaudeville derives from the French phrase *chanson du Vau de Vire*, which translates as 'a song of the valley of Vire', a valley in Calvados, Normandy,[10] reputed to have inspired merriment and revelry with its musical traditions, which were mainly bawdy songs.[11] The word was changed to 'voix de ville', meaning street voices, and later became simply 'vaudeville'. This entertainment form began in the 1880s and was running at full tilt by the 1900s. Minstrelsy was reborn in vaudeville, which routinely featured *olios* and elaborate sketches set on plantations, songs with sexual innuendo, stump speeches, and 'coon songs' (a genre of music founded in stereotypes about Black people). Impresarios such as Tony

Pastor, B. F. Keith, and H. R. Jacobs standardised vaudeville throughout the 1880s, making it a commercial and widespread activity for the entire family, irrespective of class. Edward Albee, general manager for B. F. Keith, publicly stated, 'we are doing our share by making vaudeville more acceptable to the fastidious and the religious', with the results of expanded patronage and increased revenue.[12] Acts varied across theatres and among travelling troupes but vaudeville shows included a smattering of the following: juggling, acrobatics, regurgitation (usually with sharp or flaming objects), singing, dancing, musical acts, sketch comedy, minstrel acts, comedic monologues, trick cyclists, hypnosis and mind-reading, animal acts, and feats of strength. To maximise profits, shows ran back-to-back often beginning mid-day and ending late at night. Accessibility, an affordable admission price, and invoking a working-class sensibility made vaudeville the most popular entertainment until it could no longer compete with moving pictures in the 1920s.

Vaudeville was successful because it provided space for comedic response to crises in American culture – dramatically changing demographics, economic dislocation due to industrialisation, massive rural to urban migrations, and the subversion of traditional rural values.[13] Blackface minstrelsy or any mockery of racial and ethnic Others – from China, Italy, Germany, Ireland, Hungary, and Poland and, of course, African Americans, Native Americans, and Jewish people – became *the* comedic staple of vaudeville. While African Americans could now perform on stage, they were required to perform in blackface, meaning they too would darken their faces and use make-up to exaggerate facial features.[14] To perform in blackface as a Black American meant performing racist stock characters or controlling images established in the minstrelsy tradition. Elsie Williams identifies this period as one of accommodationist humour, that is African Americans and other performers of colour made complicit in their own mockery. In segregated areas of the country, racist depictions often stood in as truth-reinforcing white supremacist attitudes and beliefs.

Vaudeville offered a home to the earliest comedic monologists such as Charles Case, a mixed-race vaudevillian passing as white in the 1880s and 1890s,[15] and Beatrice Herford, a white woman who started entertaining audiences in 1885. Charles, who preferred to be called Charley, was born in upstate Erie County, New York on 27 August 1858.[16] He found a way to be Black with public approval – by performing comedy in blackface for more than twenty-five years. Blackface also 'hid' his identity, making it more difficult for the audience to identify his race. Importantly, Case did *not* use stereotypes with his blackface act. Instead, he told elaborate stories about his parents and fictitious siblings and made 'off-beat observations about human nature'.[17] He and monologists influenced by him, such as Frank Fay who regularly sold out the Palace Theater in New York City with his comedy shows in the 1920s, set the stage for the next generation of comedic monologists who would use vaudeville stages as training ground before parlaying those talents onto radio and the silver screen.[18] These early stand-up comedians who went on to become comic legends of the twentieth century, such as Bob Hope, Jack Benny, and Milton Berle, modelled how to migrate across media before the advent of stand-up as a recognisably distinct cultural form.

Charley Case was ten years old and only dreaming of the stage when Beatrice Herford was born in 1868 into a large family living in England. Herford distinguishes herself somewhat from Case in that she performed in the format of a one-person show, which gave her more stage time (sixty-ninety minutes). At the time, theatrical and musical performances could last up to three hours and Herford had no interest in performing for such a length of time. In an interview, she explained this rationale: 'It is a favourite theory of mine that as a rule our programmes of concerts and entertainment are far too long ... And I have a suspicion that all of us appreciate most what is not prolonged.'[19] Herford's performances proved the viability of a single *comedic* performer enchanting an audience for an extended period of time and dislodged the notion that performances need to last several hours to get your money's worth. She debuted in London and then delighted American audiences with her novel performances featuring a range of 'mirth-provoking' characters – a woman out on a shopping excursion, a store clerk, a woman at an agency seeking to hire domestic help, a book agent, a woman packing for a trip, or a long-term boarder.[20] She became known for her distinctive style of using clipped dialogue to transition between characters, vividly bringing to life entire tableaus.[21] Her brother, Oliver Herford, published Herford's early monologues, leaving records of one of the earliest character acts. Future comedians such as Stan Freberg, Bob Newhart, Richard Pryor, Lily Tomlin, Whoopi Goldberg, Judy Gold, Mike Birbiglia, Maria Bamford, John Mulaney, and many more would mimic her zany character work.[22]

The Chitlin' Circuit and the Borscht Belt

Having already secured the whole family as revenue streams for vaudeville, entrepreneurs stood to lose profit if they were unable to secure the patronage of African Americans subject to Jim Crow laws mandating segregation. The term Jim Crow derives from the legend that a white man named T. D. Rice donned blackface to impersonate an impoverished Black man named Jim Crow. The real origin of the term, routinely obscured by this oft-recited folklore, derives from 'a widespread African-American folk dance impersonating – delineating – crows, based in agricultural ritual'.[23] Growing up poor in multiracial enclaves in New York City in the early 1800s, T. D. Rice would have seen the minstrels in Catherine Market and more generally witnessed the cultural gesturing of performance from African Americans in his neighbourhood. W. T. Lahmon conducts a book-length exploration debunking this folklore cycle, writing: 'The apocryphal tales indicate instead, how distant our stories are from the way people produce culture and how starved they are for legitimating detail.'[24] Importantly, the Jim Crow minstrel character became the namesake for the set of local/state statutes systematically restricting movement, housing, and education and legitimising violence against Blacks. This speaks to the power of performance, specifically comedy, to introduce, reinforce, and sustain bigoted attitudes and beliefs that shape our laws, policies, who is seen as fit to govern, and the social and political institutions structuring society. In some cities segregated facilities meant deposing Black patrons to the balcony or back of theatre, but this sometimes caused problems because Black and white customers weren't laughing at the same things. Mostly, this meant exclusion of African Americans or separate entertainment venues across the country. In the late 1800s, Black entertainers formed their own travelling performance companies. Sissieretta Jones managed the wildly successful Black Patti Troubadours, a musical revue company performing in the vaudeville tradition. The company thrived for two decades but when Jones retired in 1915, they disbanded.[25] Seeing the marketability of Black performance troupes, in 1907 a group of theatre owners banded together to develop the Theatre Owners Booking Association (TOBA), which became known as the Chitlin' Circuit (named after a dish made with pig intestines and connected to the creativity African Americans demonstrated when given the offal of animals to eat while enslaved). TOBA produced Black-only vaudeville shows in venues scattered throughout the eastern seaboard, Midwest, and South.

Performers on the Chitlin' Circuit would grace the same stages on which the Black Patti Troubadours performed but some venues, such as the Apollo Theatre and the Cotton Club in New York City, originally only allowed white patrons, barring people of colour attending as audience members until the mid-1930s.²⁶ Some of the most famous venues on the Chitlin' Circuit included: the Pekin Theatre in Chicago, the Beacon Theatre and Lafayette Theatre in New York City, the Royal Peacock Theatre and Fox Theatre in Atlanta, and the Strand Theatre in Boston. Black performers suffered gruelling schedules, were paid lower wages than white performers, and dealt with inhospitable people and conditions on the road. It wasn't long before performers began resentfully referring to TOBA as: Tough on Black Asses. Henry Louis Gates Jr. wrote that 'Crisscrossing black America, the circuit established an empire of comedy and pathos, the sublime and the ridiculous: a moveable feast that enabled blacks to patronize black entertainers.'²⁷ This circuit was home to some of the most formidable comic talent during the twentieth century. Dewey 'Pigmeat' Markham was born in 1904 and his career spanned the life of many comedy forms of which he took advantage. Formerly a tap dancer, Markham commanded the Apollo as house comedian, performing in blackface long after vaudeville theatres dimmed their lights. He is best known for his routine as a judge whose mockery of courtroom etiquette was reminiscent of the stump speeches delivered a century earlier during the *olio* portion of a blackface minstrelsy show.²⁸ Cultural historians cite his foot-tapping 1968 recording 'Here Come the Judge' as an early precursor of rap and hip-hop. Jackie 'Moms' Mabley, who was born Loretta Mary Aiken in 1894, started performing on the Chitlin' Circuit a year after TOBA launched and was the first female *and* lesbian comic to perform at the Apollo Theatre. She performed her brand of blue humour on stages from the 1920s to the 1970s, taking on a grandmotherly persona who spoke openly of desires for young men and wore a housedress or mismatched baggy clothing, while peering out from under a worn hat. Moms Mabley 'adopted appearance and speech that subverted the constructions of the sassy mammy',²⁹ and disarmed audiences who would otherwise have recoiled if she performed as herself – an intelligent, Black, gender queer, lesbian usually wearing 'men's' clothing. In 1923, she was performing at the best theatres in New York and by the 1950s she garnered the top billing wherever she went, earning $10,000 a week. Like Mabley, many comedians on the circuit became crossover successes, migrating to perform in front of white audiences, including Redd Foxx, Nipsey Russell, LaWanda Page, Dick Gregory, Flip Wilson, Bill Cosby, Richard Pryor, Paul Mooney, and Whoopi Goldberg.

Stand-up comedy flourished in some respects in other cultural forms. Burlesque, wild west shows, circuses, and music hall performances featured emcees using jokes to entertain patrons between feature acts. Early humourists toured the country for speaking engagements – think: Dan

Rice, Mark Twain, and Will Rogers.[30] Film, radio, and television ushered in numerous cultural forms invoking the tropes and traditions that would later become associated with stand-up comedy, as when television variety shows featured a solo comedy act or when a radio programme such as *Amos and Andy* capitalised on racist comedic archetypes first disseminated by Ethiopian Delineators in the early 1800s. The Chitlin' Circuit survived the death of vaudeville in the 1920s and remains active today, coinciding with de jure and now de facto segregated entertainment spaces. The integration of performance spaces did little to dispel beliefs of Black inferiority, making it imperative to have Black-only spaces wherein comedians could joke about Black people and cultural traditions – warts and all – without fear of instilling or strengthening stereotypes circulating in popular culture. Indeed, the contemporary Chitlin' Circuit theatre saw a surge in the 1990s corresponding to the spike in cultural production by Black artists alongside a rise in Black middle-class consumers who could patronise the circuit.[31] Similarly, religious and social persecution made it necessary for Jews to create leisure and recreational spaces where they could safely congregate. This network of venues scattered throughout the southern Catskill Mountains which offered safe harbour to Jewish comedy acts became known as the Borscht Belt, referencing the beet soup common in Jewish cuisine.

Anti-Jewish sentiments began rising as Adolf Hitler rose to power in Germany and Franklin Roosevelt rolled out New Deal policies. The stock market crash in 1929 and ensuing depression catapulted millions into poverty and the optics of Jewish financial success made Jewish people useful political scapegoats for the economically depressed.[32] Jewish people suffered anti-Semitism in a variety of forms: through anti-immigration laws, hiring practices, quotas in higher education, and stores barring entry. Jews also faced assimilation and pressures to adopt cultural traditions, dress, and foodways, and as a reward they were incrementally granted access to white privilege throughout the twentieth century. Jewish comedy drew from acculturation pressures but rarely focused on the indignities and suffering of those belonging to the Jewish diaspora. At times, Jewish comedy *did* reference a history of persecution, but like Blacks, Jews were compelled to perform in stereotypes. By the 1930s and 1940s – and as Jews needed refuge more than ever from rising anti-Semitism – an informal network of Jews in the entertainment industry crystallised into the Borscht Belt, a region in New York's Ulster and Sullivan counties that hosted millions of Jews vacationing in kuchalayns (boarding houses with shared kitchen facilities), cottages, bungalow communities, hotels, and resorts.[33] Comedians regaled vacationers on hundreds of stages every night during summer months. Individual performers called tummlers (Yiddish for someone who generates excitement) would command the audience using all manner of songs, jokes, games, and antics to sustain attention.[34] The demand for comedic entertainers created the need for an extended one-person performance that Beatrice Herford modelled decades before and would become the standard for stand-up comedy specials by the late twentieth century. The Borscht Belt flourished until the 1960s but waned in the 1970s. Many comedians would hone their craft on stages in the Borscht Belt,[35] helping them to migrate onto Broadway, radio, television, and film. Some of them, such as Phyllis Diller and Joan Rivers, devoted stage time in their early careers to the small venues emerging exclusively for stand-up comedy and larger stages in the Borscht Belt. They would both go on to become comedy icons of the twentieth century, and in a sea of male comedians, they offered a model to young female comic hopefuls.

Early Stand-Up Comedy

By the mid-twentieth century, stand-up comedy was attractive enough for an audience to gather though these shows weren't in the palatial theatres in which vaudevillians performed. 'Pigmeat' Markham and 'Moms' Mabley were still performing comedy in theatres on the Chitlin' Circuit whereas mainly white comedians were booking shows in still-segregated pizza parlours, coffee shops, and nightclubs such as Hugh Hefner's Playboy Clubs. Small, dingy folk music venues also doubled as the earliest comedy clubs and over the next twenty years became all-comedy establishments in metropolitan areas such as the hungry i in San Francisco or the Bitter End in New York City. The emerging comic sensibility accommodated anecdotal humour, such as the stories that Charley Case and Frank Fay used to tell on vaudeville stages. Comedians such as Jean Carroll, Danny Thomas, and Sam Levenson reintroduced this style which remains a fixture in stand-up today.[36] Unlike the apolitical humour that avoided polarising audiences in the Borscht Belt and on radio and television programming, comedians such as Mort Sahl, Dick Gregory, and Lenny Bruce used political and social critique to address tensions fuelled by segregationist opposition to the Black Civil Rights Movement and the hunt for communists under the watchful eye of Senator Joseph McCarthy, not to mention the looming threat of nuclear Armageddon. The whispers of civil unrest in the 1950s turned into howls in the 1960s as Chicano/as, queer people, women, African Americans, and farmers all took to the streets for civil rights. US soldiers withdrew from Korea and relocated to Vietnam to engage in a war against communism. Opposition to the war, social inequalities, and human rights abuses coincided with increased cynicism towards the government and authority, all of which found its way into stand-up comedy. Indeed, the public clamoured for the anti-establishment humour of comedians such as Richard Pryor, George Carlin, Lily Tomlin, Robin Tyler, and Paul Mooney who started performing in the 1960s and became voices of political protest in the equally tumultuous 1970s.

The 1970s provided fertile ground for experimentation, producing a small army of comic hopefuls willing to perform wherever they could. The LPs brought laughter into the homes of the masses and had the distinction of not being subject to the same censors muzzling comics on network television and radio programming. Los Angeles-based Laff Records single-handedly produced more comedy LPs in the 1970s than any other company.[37] Significantly, all their comedians were African American. This inexpensive and accessible media primed the pump for the subsequent comedy boom, together with the opening of comedy clubs such as the Improvisation and the Comedy Store on the West Coast and Catch a Rising Star, the Comic Strip, and Pip's in New York City.[38] Comedy club owners routinely exploited comedians by paying them little or nothing at all, promising, instead, room to hone their craft and eventual exposure to talent agents and television bookers. Comedians grew tired of performing with little or no financial reward, and in 1979 Tom Dreesen organised Comedians for Compensation to picket the Comedy Store in Los Angeles, which was a club run by Mitzi Shore. The strike was successful, not because Shore paid the compensation she agreed to (she didn't) but because it standardised a national compensation model for comedians. The outcome of the strike brought economic reassurance – to comedians who sought fair payment and to club owners who sought profitability in this venture – and led to the 1980s comedy boom. Over 300 comedy clubs sprang up in the years following the strike and hundreds of mainly coastal comics began touring, performing in national chains across the country.

Other factors in the 1970s, beyond establishing a national compensation model, led to the first comedy boom. Comedy became a more profitable investment, there were increased opportunities to perform on television, and comedians demonstrated that they could draw enough fans to fill arenas and movie theatres across the country. Phil Berger published *The Last Laugh* in 1975, a book devoted to exploring the craft of comedy which quickly became the bible for stand-up comedians. At the same time, venues devoted exclusively to stand-up comedy became profitable. As Kliph

Nesteroff explains: 'The Comedy Store and the Improv demonstrated the business model. *The Last Laugh* demonstrated the artistic model.'[39] The syndicated television show *Make Me Laugh* provided career-enhancing exposure for comedians, and in 1975 Home Box Office (HBO) aired an inaugural stand-up comedy special featuring Robert Klein, who was nominated for a Grammy for best comedy album that year. This successful experiment garnering nearly 600,000 new subscribers signalled what was to come: the explosion of comedy on network and cable television.[40] The next HBO special featured Freddie Prinze Sr emceeing a comedy revue or a series of sets by several comics. This became the template adopted by television for ensuing decades. In 1976, San Francisco hosted an international stand-up comedy competition that would become an annual affair, showing that comedy was attracting global attention.[41] A year later, Steve Martin, whose madcap comedy performances earned him film roles and repeated invitations to host *Saturday Night Live*, secured enough popularity to fill arenas with far more seats than a large theatre could accommodate. Never, at least for a comedian, had such a business enterprise proven lucrative.[42] Around the same time, Robin Tyler would use her notoriety as stand-up comic and social activist on the frontlines of the gay liberation movement to launch a series of annual women's music/comedy festivals on the West Coast and in Georgia that would last into the late 1980s. Movie offers transitioned from a trickle to a steady stream for Richard Pryor when theatres across the USA screened his special *Richard Pryor: Live in Concert* in 1979. These commercial successes demonstrated that comedians had other ways of getting their content to the masses and producers outside of live performance and network television.

The 1980s signalled the institutionalisation of stand-up comedy – there was a critical mass of comedians, myriad ways of reaching the consumer, and standardised performances. African American comics had for a long time performed to audiences on an entertainment circuit separate from white comedy venues – by racist social design at first, but later as pursuit of profit in the 1980s supported by an upwardly mobile Black middle class. Because television ushered in greater visibility for many comics in the 1980s, more female and Black comics were able to cross over into the mainstream. Known for his crass and homophobic material, Eddie Murphy was the comedy superstar of the 1980s and droves of comic hopefuls sought to model a career on his seemingly overnight rise to stardom. Many comedians set their sights on securing a sitcom, a televisual vehicle that made comedians famous, such as Roseanne Arnold, Jerry Seinfeld, Brett Butler, Tim Allen, Martin Lawrence, Ellen DeGeneres, Ray Romano, Sinbad, and George Lopez. Beyond sitcoms, the 1980s brought a cornucopia of employment opportunities and comedians migrated into any cultural form where comedy flourished. This included film, comedy writing, radio, sketch shows, and late night television. Comedians had to earn their chops on stage, but no longer was that the final destination.

Alternative Stand-Up Comedy

The 1980s comedy boom saturated the market and by the early 1990s there was a discernible lull in consumption. This allowed for greater experimentation because comics were less invested in making comedy that sold; instead, they were doing it for each other and the love of the craft. Pursuit of the non-traditional and unconventional gave rise to the alternative comedy scene which emerged on the West Coast in the 1990s. This comedy sought to investigate the boundaries of comedy – the gems mined from stream-of-consciousness prattle, anecdotal humour or storytelling, or comedic commentary on traditionally avoided topics such as death and trauma. It sought to shirk performance conventions and circumvent the comedy club circuit, opting instead for the kinds of venues in which comedians performed in the 1950s, such as comic book stores, coffee shops, pizza parlours, and music venues. This was especially appealing to minoritised comedians unwilling or unable to penetrate the nearly all-male club circuit and those who found comedy clubs unsafe spaces rife with misogyny, racism, and homophobia.

Alternative comics cultivated an approach to comedy that grew quickly, becoming mainstream by the 2010s. Most of those involved early on were white comics who had the means to create comedy without much compensation. Motivated by the desire for public venues where they could experiment, Kathy Griffin created a weekly comedy revue called Hot Cup of Talk, Laura Milligan did the same at a venue called Tantrum, and in 1994 Beth Lapides opened the wildly popular UnCabaret, all in Los Angeles.[43] You could find comedians such as Janeane Garofalo, Patton Oswalt, Dana Gould, Sarah Silverman, Andy Dick, Andy Kindler, David Cross, Tig Notaro, Jack Black, Maria Bamford, Bob Odenkirk, Julia Sweeney, and Jeff Garlin at these venues and others such as Largo and Luna Park in West Hollywood. The first wave of alternative comedy paved the way for another (much more racially diverse) generation of alternative comedians working in the early twenty-first century such as Marina Franklin, Hannibal Buress, Donald Glover, Eric André, Baratunde Thurston, Victor Varnado, and Baron Vaughn. Our concept of the 'alternative' is relative to who we are. White male alternative comedy rejected the formulaic humour that had become the staple diet of consumers. Women's alternative comedy rejected gender conventions and social pressures to behave, even perform comedy, in particular ways. For example, Kristin Schaal and Maria Bamford routinely skewer gendered expectations by using seemingly foolish characters to critique female inequality. Black alternative comedy offered up Black 'nerd' humour, which was only technically 'alternative' because it deviated from racialised expectations about Blackness – from diction to language to mannerisms.[44] It allowed Black comedians a chance to perform on their own terms and without the pressure to perform in ways that conformed to racist notions of the Other. Pioneering Black alternative comedians paved the way for a new generation of Black alternative comedians including: Ron Funches, Phoebe Robinson, Amanda Seales, Jessica Williams, Michelle Buteau, Naomi Ekperigin, Calise Hawkins, Dulcé Sloan, and Rae Sanni.

Twenty-First Century Stand-Up Comedy

In many respects, the 1980s boom ended up diversifying the pool of comics and the 1990s bust provided new means of getting comedy to niche audiences. As the century turned, technology such as CDs and DVDs continued to work on behalf of the success and growth of alternative comedy, Black comedy, and queer comedy by placing more content on the market for consumers. Longer specials recorded to either CD or DVD could be sold to an ever-growing fan base. Because of the surge in televised opportunities for comedians in the 1980s, Black comics established a national audience for their humour in the latter twentieth century and in the twenty-first century revived the travelling revue format used in the past. Comedy tours featuring multiple performers reaffirmed the profitability of the large-scale arena events that Steve Martin and Richard Pryor modelled two decades prior. Producers invested in *Kings of Comedy* (2000), a filmed version of a national tour featuring comics Bernie Mac, Cedric the Entertainer, Steve Harvey, and D. L. Hughley. This model venture was exceedingly profitable and set off a scramble to secure profits. *Queens of Comedy* (2001) came next, then the *Blue Collar Comedy Tour* (2003) and *Comedians of Comedy Tour* (2005). These comic showcases travelled the country just like early Ethiopian Delineators and vaudevillians, using the same revue format that Freddie Prinze Sr made popular in the 1970s. Showcases assured a broader fan base – if you like this comic, you will like this one too – and calcified allegiances based on gender, race, and profession, although the designation 'blue collar' also offers rhetorical beard for comedy fans to congregate around whiteness and masculinity.

In the aftermath of the attack on the Twin Towers on 9/11, humour was aimed at the perceived villain and there was a sharp rise in anti-Muslim and anti-Arab humour. Arab American, Middle Eastern, and Muslim comics organised a calculated response rebutting the character assassinations aimed at entire nations and millions of practising Muslims. Shortly after the attacks, in 2003 Dean Obeidallah and Maysoon Zayid co-founded and co-produced the New York Arab American Comedy Festival, which is still held annually. From 2005 to 2011, Maz Jobrani, Ahmed Ahmed, Aron Kader, and Dean Obeidallah performed in the *Axis of Evil Comedy Tour*, a turn of phrase used by then President George Bush Jr to describe the countries he believed responsible for terrorism in the West. The popularity of this tour and other commercial enterprises around Arab American comedy signalled the collective desire to consume comedy that contextualised conflicts – domestic and global.[45]

There was a proliferation in comedy production and consumption during the 2010s. Technologies continued to offer new ways of accessing stand-up comedy. As a result, consumers could sift through comedy content on streaming services and online to find their preferred comedians. This decade's stand-up comedy was characterised by an explosion of new media, the relaxing of censorship, and experimentation. Maria Bamford performed her comedy in non-traditional venues such as a bowling alley, a bookstore, and in her parent's living room. Chelsea Peretti put live animals in seats at her comedy special and Drew Michaels incorporated no audience at all. Another outcome for stand-up comics was that international comedians could take advantage of the growing revenue stream. In 2018, Tasmanian native Hannah Gadsby became an overnight sensation in the USA when Netflix released her special *Nanette*. While Canadian and US borders have long been porous for comedy production, there was a spike in specials from international comics outside of North America. From the UK, Suzy Izzard has long been a comedy commodity and US audiences have also been charmed by Ricky Gervais, Gina Yashere, Stewart Lee, Amer Rahman, Trevor Noah, Daniel Sloss, Katherine Ryan, Rosie and Nicola Dempsey – known as Flo & Joan – John Oliver, Bridget Christie, London Hughes, and many more.

The global pandemic of 2020 meant that comedians had to be innovative to sustain their careers as clubs shut down and people quarantined at home. It would be inaccurate to call this period a bust: this would belie the copious comedic cultural production that continued to take place. More accurately, stand-up comedy saw seismic shifts in production, distribution, and consumption, most of which eliminated third-party vendors. Comedians weaponised media platforms in the service of comedy, pumping out content in micro-doses over TikTok and Instagram, ramping up podcast output, and telling quarantine jokes over Zoom to hundreds of viewers. Jenny Ylang used a social simulation game called Animal Crossing to reach her fans, writing jokes for her cat-character who performed shows on a fantasy island. Outdoor shows emerged – in parks, on rooftops, at drive-in theatres – once states began lifting shelter-at-home ordinances during the summer of 2020. Comedians shared their quarantine experiences, weighed in on the upcoming election that would end with Donald Trump losing the popular and electoral votes to stay in the presidential office, and took a stance for/against Black Lives Matter protests erupting across the country. The pandemic reminded us of how nimble and adaptable comedians can be and the resurgence of live comedy in the aftermath of the pandemic revealed the value we confer to stand-up comedy as rhetorical weapon and entertainment commodity.

Any attempt to make legible a history of stand-up comedy will fall short of capturing all the kinds of comedy performance and the vast number of performers using comedy to comment on the world around them. It was born of so many other comedic cultural forms – minstrelsy and vaudeville chief among them – and continues to be a generative force shaping who we are as individuals, as communities, and as a nation. While comedic forms will come and go, history demonstrates that we will always find ways of incorporating comedic stories, songs, and dance into our entertainment landscapes, which is just a contemporary iteration of a performance tradition connecting us to our minstrel ancestors performing in Catherine Market.

Notes

1. Jeannette Dates and Mia Moody Ramirez, *From Blackface to Black Twitter: Reflections on Black Humor, Race, Politics, and Gender* (New York: Peter Lang, 2018).
2. W. T. Lhamon Jr, *Raising Cain: Blackface Performance from Jim Crow to Hip Hop* (Cambridge, MA: Harvard University Press, 1998), p. 58.
3. Lhamon, *Raising Cain*, p. 12.
4. Lhamon, *Raising Cain*, p. 3.
5. Elsie Williams, *The Humor of Jackie Moms Mabley: An African American Comedic Tradition* (New York: Garland, 1995), p. 16.
6. Williams, *The Humor of Jackie Moms Mabley*, p. 15.

7. Alexander Saxton, 'Blackface Minstrelsy and Jacksonian Ideology', in Lucy Maddox (ed.), *Locating American Studies: The Evolution of a Discipline* (Baltimore: Johns Hopkins University Press, 1999), p. 115.
8. Eric Lott, *Love and Theft: Blackface Minstrelsy and the American Working Class* (New York: Oxford University Press, 1993), p. 6.
9. Alison Kibler, *Censoring Racial Ridicule: Irish, Jewish, and African American Struggles over Race and Representation, 1890–1930* (Chapel Hill: University of North Carolina Press, 2015).
10. 'Oxford Reference: Vaudeville', www.oxfordreference.com/view/10.1093/oi/authority.20110803115310374.
11. Eddie Tafoya, *The Legacy of the Wisecrack: Stand-Up Comedy as the Great American Literary Form* (Boca Raton, FL: Brown Walker Press, 2009), p. 110.
12. '"Beautiful Surroundings Are Uplifting to All People," Says Edward F. Albee', *Brooklyn Daily Eagle*, 15 March 1925, p. 93.
13. Lawrence J. Epstein, *The Haunted Smile: The Story of Jewish Comedians in America* (New York: PublicAffairs, 2001).
14. John Strausbaugh, *Black Like You: Blackface, Whiteface, Insult and Imitation in American Popular Culture* (New York: Penguin Group, 2007).
15. Both parents self-designated as white on census records so the presumption is that one or both was also passing.
16. Tim Brooks, *Lost Sounds: Blacks and the Birth of the Recording Industry, 1890–1919* (Champaign: University of Illinois Press, 2005), p. 173.
17. Brooks, *Lost Sounds*, p. 172.
18. Wayne Federman, *The History of Stand-Up: From Mark Twain to Dave Chappelle* (Beverly Hills, CA: Independent Artists Media, 2021), pp. 20–21.
19. Archibald Cromwell, 'A New Entertainer of Society: A Talk with Miss Beatrice Herford', *The Windsor Magazine*, 1897, p. 454.
20. Cromwell, 'A New Entertainer of Society', p. 455.
21. John B. Herford papers, MT historical society.
22. John B. Herford papers.
23. Lhamon, *Raising Cain*, p. 181.
24. Lhamon, *Raising Cain*, p. 153.
25. Maureen D. Lee, *Sissieretta Jones: The Greatest Singer of Her Race, 1868–1933* (Columbia: University of South Carolina Press, 2013).
26. Dates and Ramirez, *From Blackface to Black Twitter*, pp. 57–58.
27. Henry Louis Gates, 'The Chitlin Circuit', in Harry J. Elam, Jr and David Krasner (eds), *African American Performance and Theater History: A Critical Reader* (New York: Oxford University Press, 2001).
28. Tafoya, *The Legacy of the Wisecrack*, p. 121.
29. Bambi Haggins, 'Moms Mabley and Wanda Sykes: "I'ma be me"', in Linda Mizejewski and Victoria Sturtevant (eds), *Hysterical: Women in American Comedy* (Austin: University of Texas Press, 2017), p. 213.
30. Judith Yaross Lee, *Twain's Brand: Humor in Contemporary American Culture* (Jackson: University Press of Mississippi, 2012).
31. Rashida Shaw McMahon, *The Black Circuit: Race, Performance, and Spectatorship in Black Popular Theatre* (Abingdon: Routledge, 2020).

32. Epstein, *The Haunted Smile*, p. 106.
33. Tafoya, *The Legacy of the Wisecrack*, p. 123.
34. Epstein, *The Haunted Smile*.
35. Those included (but are certainly not limited to): Jerry Lewis, Danny Kaye, Belle Barth, Jackie Mason, Red Buttons, Judy Holliday, Don Adams, Shecky Greene, Sid Caesar, Rusty Warren, Milton Berle, Jerry Stiller, Buddy Hackett, Jack Benny, Myron Cohen, Henny Youngman, Jack Carter, Mel Brooks, Totie Fields, Rodney Dangerfield, and Dick Shawn.
36. Gerald Nachman, *Seriously Funny: The Rebel Comedians of the 50s and 60s* (New York: Pantheon Books, 2003).
37. Kliph Nesteroff, *The Comedians: Drunks, Thieves, Scoundrels and the History of American Comedy* (New York: Grove Press, 2016), p. 291.
38. Anna Quindlen, 'Catch a Rising Comic at Four Showcases', *New York Times*, 8 December 1978, pp. C1, C27.
39. Nesteroff, *The Comedians*, p. 305.
40. Robert Klein quoted in Nesteroff, *The Comedians*, p. 299.
41. Wayne Federman and Andrew Steven, *The History of Standup*, podcast audio, June 2019, www.thehistoryofstandup.com/s02/01-holy-city-zoo.
42. Nick De Semlyen, *Wild and Crazy Guys: How the Comedy Mavericks of the '80s Changed Hollywood Forever* (New York: Crown Archetype, 2019).
43. Yael Cohen, *We Killed: The Rise of Women in American Comedy* (London: Picador, 2013), pp. 209–236.
44. J Finley, 'From Awkward to Dope: Black Women Comics in the Alternative Comedy Scene', in Julie Webber (ed.), *The Joke Is On Us: Political Comedy in (Late) Neoliberal Times* (Lanham, MD: Lexington Books, 2019), pp. 221–244.
45. Viveca Greene and Ted Gournelos (eds), *A Decade of Dark Humor: How Comedy, Irony, and Satire Shaped post-9/11 America* (Jackson: University Press of Mississippi, 2011).

COMEDIANS' INSIGHTS

The Audience You Attract

Edward Aczel (UK)

Better a bit left field.

Maria Bamford (USA)

I think people with mental health interests, creative types and mistakenly (when an old headshot of me in my 20s is marketed) the poor people who have just 'come out for a good time'. I am not a good time.

Angela Barnes (UK)

It's really hard to quantify your audience. I'd say I appeal mostly to people in their thirties and older. People that watch TV as well as YouTube, or listen to the radio etc. Though I've found that younger women identify with my stance on voluntary childlessness – I think there aren't many women over forty talking about their life without children. Though I'm sure many girls look at me as a vision of their nightmare future, and that's fine too! I think more recently that I've attracted an audience through speaking openly about ADHD too. So many people with a neurodivergence, myself included, feel that they are different and find it hard to be like their peers – so we are attracted to watching people that might think like we do. My friend told me that I was a hit with her thirteen-year-old daughters' friends because I had gone viral on TikTok. I had absolutely no idea that a routine of mine was on TikTok and doing well! I could have been cashing in on all that pocket money!

Jo Brand (UK)

Predominantly women, men who have a sense of humour and are not thin-skinned misogynists, and gay men and women.

Nathan Caton (UK)

I get an audience from my Radio 4 work – which is usually a slightly older, white middle-class audience. But then I get an audience from *Mock the Week* or *Live at the Apollo* – which is a younger crowd. So in summary, I think I attract a diverse audience. But I don't mind. As long as they're laughing then it's all good.

Jo Caulfield (UK)

I've no idea. There's no set age group. But I do see groups of women dressed up for a night out, with a 'Fuck it, we just want to have a few drinks and have a good time' attitude. Cyndi Lauper should write a song about it.

Tanyalee Davis (Canada/USA/UK)

I feel very fortunate because being an 'autobiographical' comedian my act transcends gender, race, geographical barriers that some acts have.

Alexis Dubus (UK), Who Performs as Marcel Lucont (France)

I actually seem to attract quite a broad spectrum, and with the Marcel shows the French stereotype translates all over the world. Whether people realise it's a character or not, I think a wide range of people enjoy being presented with everything they love to hate about the French.

Andy Erikson (USA)

Silly people of all ages. People who enjoy squirrels and inside jokes. I like nerds of all ages.

Alex Farrow (UK)

Philosophy fans.

Richard Herring (UK)

I seem to have a crowd that most comedians envy. They are smart and listen and know enough about comedy to get the good stuff and not tolerate (too much) rubbish. They are not a pushover but are generous if they like something. It's quite a wide range of ages and types of person as they have come to me from many different projects, but they are mainly around my age, more male than female and work in IT!

Bec Hill (Australia/UK)

Nerdy men who own cats. Not exclusively, but in the Venn Diagram of nerd fans, male fans and cat-owning fans, the intersection is surprisingly large. I'm not complaining, mind. My entire audience fits within an even bigger intersection titled 'lovely people'.

Robin Ince (UK)

People who might slightly be in the outside of things – age-wise I get fourteen-year-olds and ninety-year-olds – they are usually inquisitive. I often talk to many of them after shows and they can sometimes share candid stories.

Milton Jones (UK)

It's a real mixture. I've done a lot on Radio 4, but also other TV shows like *Mock the Week* which have a younger demographic. So sometimes whole families come united by a love of nonsense perhaps (although often they bring one person with them who has no idea why everyone else is laughing).

Jackie Kashian (USA)

Mostly readers. It's nice.

Athena Kugblenu (UK)

People who want to do better. Radio 4 listeners. Twitter followers.

Beth Lapides (USA)

I always think of it as a psychographic more than a demographic, but open-minded and introspective, kind of arty, smart, LGBTQIA, recovery and discovery.

Stewart Lee (UK)

Guardian-reading men and their families.

Elf Lyons (UK)

Anyone whose favourite space as a kid was the library or Blockbusters. That is basically my audience.

Andrew McClelland (Australia)

Often my crowd is a little older and possibly a bit conservative, so I always have some lefty political stuff in there as well in an attempt to reach out to those who don't want politics in their comedy and think I'm a safe bet.

Aditi Mittal (India)

Anyone that will pay good money to buy a ticket to watch me.

Al Murray (UK), Who Performs as the Pub Landlord (UK)

I often get this question about my audience and I get people saying, 'Don't you realise who's in your audience, that they don't get the joke?' The thing is, I don't know who's in my audience in the same way that no other comedian does either. No one knows who's coming to their show or, actually, why they're laughing. You think, 'What, are you saying you're better than them? Are you saying you're smarter than they are? Are you looking down on my audience?' When I get asked that question, the smart-arse answer I give is, 'Well I've been to more of my shows than anyone else. I think I've got a clearer idea of who they are.' I mean last night, for instance. Night before last, we were in Dundee. 'Cos I do find out who they are, you know. I've got that barometer. We had a gravedigger and his wife, worked for the council. We had a guy who was a biotechnician in the NHS. We had a couple of lorry drivers. And they get a real drubbing in the current show. We had a retired teacher. People bring their teenage boys as well. Because I think they come for the thrill of the rudeness. I don't know anything more about them than that. I think this is an unknowable question in a way.

Sander Õigus (Estonia)

Stand-up is pretty new in Estonia so basically everyone. But the people at the shows tend to look like me, bearded men in their thirties. Probably because similar people relate to each other easier.

Anuvab Pal (India)

Actually, this is how I imagine an ideal couple who might like this kind of comedy. He is English and works in a global think tank/finance research division advising British businesses as they invest around the world. She is British of Indian origin and works for an offshoot of the UN. They've lived in Scandinavia, New York, Mumbai, and Singapore. Currently they live in Primrose Hill. OK, I might be talking about a specific couple that come to my shows.

Lucy Porter (UK)

My comedy was reviewed as 'middle-aged, middle-class and middle of the road'. Which I don't think the reviewer intended as a compliment, but it absolutely was spot-on. I mean I mostly play to people who look and sound like me. The brilliant comedians, the geniuses, they transcend boundaries of class and age and anything else you can think of, race and religion. But I have not done that! I mean I love my audience and I do think that I'm like them but a little bit weird. So it's like watching themselves but in a parallel universe where they did something different in their twenties and they've ended up here. So maybe that's the appeal, I don't know.

Rod Quantock (Australia)

Loyal, increasingly old (like me), politically, socially, and environmentally conscious and often active.

Joe Wells (UK)

Guardian reader types, sometimes other autistic people.

Nigel Williams (UK/Belgium)

I seem to attract all ages but mainly thirty-five upwards, an audience that is news savvy and politically up to speed.

Bilal Zafar (UK)

At one stage, I think it was mainly middle-class people that go to see live comedy in arts centres and at the Edinburgh Fringe. Over the last two years, I've been able to gain an online audience through Twitch, where I do surreal comedy streams. Now it feels like I have a much wider range of people because people can watch Twitch for free and has allowed to me reach an audience of people that I feel are more like myself. I definitely notice that Muslims come to see my shows, possibly because there are so few Muslim comedians in the UK. At the moment it seems to be a real mix of people.

CHAPTER 3

Where Stand-Up Happens
Morten Nielsen

Introduction

On 22 March 2022, American stand-up comic Adrienne Iapalucci made her first performance in Denmark as one of three openers to the famous New York-based stand-up comic Louis CK, in a sold-out Royal Arena. As a multifunctional space built for large-scale cultural and sporting events, the Royal Arena in Amager, Copenhagen has a capacity for up to 17,000 seated spectators and houses a number of smaller stages and venues that makes it possible to run 60–80 events each year. Although New York-based Iapalucci is a hugely talented stand-up comic, she usually performs in smaller venues with the audience close to the stage. In the huge Royal Arena, most of the audience enjoyed the show by watching two giant video screens on each side of the stage. In 2017, Iapalucci was 'passed', that is, accepted as a regular performer, at the legendary Comedy Cellar comedy club in lower Manhattan, New York, and has performed there often on a nightly basis ever since while also doing regular shows in many of the city's other comedy venues and bars and on tour across the country. Iapalucci has appeared on season 2 of Netflix's stand-up comedy series *Degenerates*, she posts jokes and humorous commentaries almost daily on various social media, and co-hosts *Vadge*, a weekly podcast series, with fellow stand-up comic Sarah Tollemache.

It may be argued that Adrienne Iapalucci's wide range of performance activities and use of differently scaled outlets and modes of artistic expression is an apt indicator not only of how stand-up comedy operates but also of the sites and localities where it happens today. At the outset, stand-up comedy can be considered as a spoken performative art form with a clear demarcation between performer and audience, which aims to make the latter laugh.[1] Traditionally and still today, stand-up comedy is mainly performed live from a stage from where the comic engages in public communication by speaking directly to the audience about well-known issues and themes in a surprising and – hopefully – humorous way. Still, as indicated by Iapalucci's portfolio, even if the conventional stage-based performance setting remains dominant and probably will continue to be so for the foreseeable future, stand-up comedy now happens across a wide range of spaces, venues, localities, outlets, and formats. So, for example, in a process that was intensified but certainly not prompted entirely by the Covid-19 lockdowns, the art of stand-up comedy is rapidly moving into the digitally mediated world of podcasts, streaming services, and various forms of social media. As a striking parallel to the considerable impact that network radio comedy had on vaudeville shows a century ago, new forms of digitally mediated stand-up comedy pose crucial and critical challenges to the form, content, and, indeed, spatiality of the hugely popular art form. For can we actually speak of stand-up comedy if it no longer happens in a public venue where an audience can react immediately and intuitively to the humorous utterances of the performer? Is it actually a joke, we could ask, if we don't hear it when and where it is being uttered?

This chapter examines the locations – performance venues, physical spaces, virtual outlets – in which stand-up comedy in the USA takes place. After discussing the different types of venues in which stand-up has existed historically – such as theatres, nightclubs, bars, clubs, music venues, and arenas – it moves on to explore contemporary comedy clubs in New York City. Particular emphasis is given to the organisation of the venues and shows, the performance conventions they incorporate, and how their spatial and aesthetic properties as venues shape the work of the comics who play them.

Historical Overview

Vaudevillian comedy is generally considered as the precursor to stand-up comedy.[2] Growing out of the raucous *varieté* shows that were popular during the latter part of the nineteenth century, vaudeville houses presented their audiences with slightly more family-friendly shows that included a motley group of performers, such as singers, dancers, contortionists, jugglers, animal acts, comedy quartets, and acrobats. One recurrent act in vaudeville shows was the comedy monologist, who may be considered as an incipient version of the later stand-up comic.[3] The monologist performed at the front of the stage between the main curtain and the footlight at the same time as the stagehands changed scenery. As a show-filler that served the practical purpose of enabling a smooth transition between the different acts, the monologist was essentially left without stage props to support the performance and would instead address the audience directly by telling jokes.

While some vaudeville-like venues already existed, the opening of B. F. Keith's Boston-based theatre in 1894 constituted the beginning of the vaudeville era in US show business, which lasted until around 1925. In collaboration with Edward Franklin Albee, another showbiz mogul, Keith came to define and even name the entertainment format that is today known as vaudeville. During its heyday, Keith–Albee were uniquely dominant and controlled the majority of the many vaudeville houses that existed across the country.[4] The size of the vaudeville houses varied significantly, ranging from small venues with a few hundred seats, to medium theatres that could hold a thousand people, to the larger palaces with room for 5,000 audience members.[5] Although popularity grew rapidly during the early years of the century and the show business of vaudeville came to constitute a unique branch of entertainment where future stars could hone their craft, both physical and working conditions were questionable. The vaudeville houses were poorly built and maintained and the performers had little or no possibilities for securing their positions and rights. At the turn of the century, W. C. Fields worked as a comic and would later recall this period as 'the most miserable (time) of my life. I would never have gone through with it if I had known what it was going to be like ... mental torture is too high a price to pay for anything.'[6]

From the mid-1920s, American show business became 'wired for sound'.[7] Many venues began to integrate electronic speaker systems, which also meant that performers, such as the comedy monologists, could speak in calm and soft voices, enabling the intimate relationship with an audience that we have come to know as a key facet of contemporary stand-up comedy. But the technological innovations invariably accelerated the demise of vaudeville. Network radio was quickly becoming a widely used mass medium that was only surpassed in popularity by motion pictures. The new technologies that made it possible to experience the biggest stars in show business from the home, together with the devastating consequences of the stock market crash in 1929, meant that the vaudeville era was over.

History has proven that comedy survives even during the worst of times – often accompanied by alcohol. When the Prohibition was lifted in 1933, the comedy scene soon moved from the illegal speakeasies into legitimate although Mob-run nightclubs. Similar to the earlier *varieté* and vaudeville shows, the line-up for a nightclub show would consist of several acts, such as dance bands, a speciality act, and a comic. Some clubs would have a purpose-built show stage, while in other venues the dance floor was used as performance area, meaning that audience members and comics would be only a few inches from each other. To comics such as Don Rickles and Jackie Gleason, this unique performance environment allowed them to hone their craft as masters of improvised 'insult comedy'.

From the 1930s until the end of the 1960s, stand-up comedy performed by comics in sharp and elegant tuxedos took place not only in alcohol-drenched nightclubs run by the Mob but also in presentation houses (or movie theatres), as part of a live bill preceding the showing of a feature film, as well as at hotels. Located some ninety miles from Manhattan, the Catskill Mountains were a holiday resort area that was popular especially among Jewish families. Many nightclub and former vaudeville comics found seasonal work at hotels in the area where they were expected to be an integral part of the non-stop entertainment schedule.[8] In parallel but in a completely different social universe, African American comics performed mainly to African American audiences. The Catskill Mountains were colloquially known as the 'Borscht Belt' (or the Jewish Alps), while African American theatres, cabarets, and nightclubs across the country were lumped together under the term the 'Chitlin' Circuit', deriving its name from the soul food dish chitterlings.[9]

Throughout the 1950s and 1960s, nightclubs and hotels continued to function as the primary venues for the art form that was about to become known as stand-up comedy. But alongside the comedy conformity of the quick-witted one-liner comics that populated stages across the country, a new and spontaneous form of comedy was emerging in smaller venues, clubs, and coffee houses that both accommodated and appreciated looser and less formal comic performances.[10] In 1950, two local beatniks called Eric Nord and Enrico Banducci opened the hungry i in San Francisco, a small basement club where folk singers, poets, and comics performed in front of a bare brick wall.[11] The now iconic aesthetic image of a comic standing in front of an exposed brick wall was born then and there. This stripped-down performance style would soon be further developed when the comic Mort Sahl started to perform at the hungry i in 1953. Wearing an unassuming red sweater vest, his performances fundamentally challenged the already then clichéd nightclub conformity by insisting on a deeply personal and politically charged style of comedy.[12]

The generational divide led to permanent social and cultural fissures across most Euro-American societies during the latter part of the 1960s also had a significant impact on the performance and experience of stand-up comedy. Prominent forms of stand-up comedy that spoke to the older generations continued to exist as cheerful and even comforting radio and

TV entertainment as well as in nightclubs and hotels. But to some parts of the younger generations who were riding the tidal waves of significant societal change, the predictable uniformity of such comedy was representative of everything they wanted to tear down. Like the sandblasted brick wall in the hungry i, these segments of the younger generations wanted to rid contemporary popular culture of its surface ornamentation in order to explore something that was imagined as more honest and personal. In 1962, Pip's opened in Brooklyn and the following year, the Improvisation Café (soon known as the Improv) opened in Manhattan. Both clubs were unique in being the first to book only stand-up comics, but it was the Improv that came to embody the performance aesthetics that has defined stand-up comedy ever since.

Located in a former Vietnamese restaurant, the Improv was initially an unassuming coffeehouse with no alcohol licence that seated only seventy-four people. Budd Friedman, who ran the venue together with his wife, Silver, imagined that it would serve as a late night café and possible impromptu performance venue for their show business friends after they had performed elsewhere in the city.[13] Similar to the hungry i, Friedman had stripped the bare brick wall behind a small stage where he had also set up a speaker system with a microphone beside an upright piano. In contrast to other venues in the city, the layout of the club happened to allow for a separation of bar and showroom, which appealed to the many struggling comics who were longing for a space to socialise with their peers. Friedman soon recognised the untapped entertainment allure of centring solely on stand-up comedy. Despite lacking prior expertise, he quickly assumed the role of auditioning comedians and putting together the evening's line-up. Entrusting their fate to an inexperienced booker soon became a daily source of anxiety for numerous fledgling comedians, who often found themselves replaced either by more prominent headliners or at Friedman's discretion if he deemed the audience's laughter insufficient.

Friedman's accidental innovation was to offer comics and audiences a performance venue that reeked of artistic coolness and youthful spontaneity. It was essentially a surprisingly cheap business model that was built around the showcase of (unpaid) new talent but without the hubbub of elegantly and easily digestible Borscht Belt-style entertainment packaged for expensive hotels. Obviously it did not take long for other entertainment entrepreneurs to jump on the stand-up comedy bandwagon and within the following decade, Friedman's unique comedy concept began to duplicate itself on a larger scale. In 1972, Catch a Rising Star opened on New York's Upper East Side and the Comedy Store opened on Sunset

Boulevard in Los Angeles. Both comedy clubs copied the entertainment formula that Friedman had invented some years earlier but they were significantly more successful in attracting larger audiences while also streamlining the method for showcasing new talent. Mitzi Shore, the legendary owner of the Comedy Store, considered her comedy club a 'college of comedy' for aspiring comics, who were given the opportunity to develop their individual styles in a creative and progressive environment.[14] This descriptor also implied, however, that none of the comics were getting paid and that Mitzi would single-handedly decide who would get the prime spots and who would be assigned the less attractive time-slots late in the night. Still, although the pay was meagre (or in most cases absent), other privileges were available to comics performing at or hanging out around the comedy clubs. As stand-up comedy grew in popularity, comics were increasingly viewed as rock stars with the accompanying assortment of screaming fans, drugs, and sex.[15]

The Improv and the Comedy Store had proven that stand-up comedy provided a profitable business model for new performance venues, which had a potential for reaching a nationwide and possibly even a global audience. Realising that a new consumer market was ready for the taking, in 1975, HBO aired its first comedy special, which not only introduced a new format for performing and experiencing stand-up comedy but also indicated that a new comedy boom was underway. During the following years, hundreds of new comedy clubs mushroomed even in smaller towns, which made it possible for more comics to make a living from their art form. Many new comedy clubs were established in defunct music venues, restaurants, theatres, and discos from the principle that only certain things were required in order for a performance venue to function properly: a liquor licence, a deep talent pool, a functioning sound system, a microphone, and tables and chairs.[16] During an intense period of time that lasted roughly from the mid-1970s until the early 1990s, stand-up comedy was the ideal form of entertainment for the growing audiences who wanted carefree amusement. It was perfectly designed for a few hours of noncontroversial distraction and it was easily accessible either live at comedy clubs, pubs, and restaurants or from the growing number of broadcasted TV shows and comedy specials.

Paradoxically, the massive popularity of stand-up comedy was one of the main factors that eventually led to the boom going bust in the early 1990s. In order for comedy clubs to maintain a full programme, mediocre comics were allowed to perform and the quality of the live shows began to suffer. Comics seemed to be everywhere and as a consequence, it became harder to distinguish good stand-up comedy from bad. Considering that it was now possible also to enjoy the biggest comedy stars on TV, the enthusiasm for live comedy declined and, as a consequence, many club owners ended up filing for bankruptcy. With the closing of the legendary comedy clubs that started the comedy boom, the Improv and Catch a Rising Star, it became clear to both performers and club owners across the country that the market had become oversaturated.[17] In order for stand-up comedy to survive, then, it had to find new formats and venues for reaching its audience.

Almost like a frustrated teenager no longer accepting the conservative platitudes of an arrogant older generation, the alternative comedy scene in the early 1990s arose as a confrontation with the 'brick-wall conformity' of the era's stand-up comedy stars,[18] who had allegedly been partially responsible for the entertainment business going bust. Rather than negotiate their way towards getting stage time at comedy clubs, which willingly accepted even mediocre local acts with little or no sense of artistry, many younger comics preferred instead to produce their own shows in rooms which had rarely, if ever, been used as venues for stand-up comedy shows. Comic Patton Oswalt describes the change of scenery to John Wenzel in his book *Mock Stars*: 'The Largo was a music club. The Diamond Club was a music club … The whole thing was that we were taking it out of comedy clubs and doing it anywhere else we could – coffee shops, bookstores, whatever. It was the same thing in New York with the Luna Lounge and the Time Café'.[19]

As indicated here by Oswalt, alternative comedy had to be seen in relation to the music industry and its categories of 'alternative music' and 'indie music'. If you went to a reasonably equipped record store during the early 1990s, it was under this catch-all category that you would find popular but initially somewhat unorthodox bands, such as Nirvana and Pearl Jam. In the attempt to liberate themselves from the restrictions of conventional comedy, the new 'alt comics' would often perform alongside or even go on tour with bands, whose status and legitimacy was predicated on being in (real or, more often, purely staged) opposition to the dominant and market-driven musical trends of the day.

Stand-Up Comedy Venues in New York City Today

Stand-up comedy has gone through a boom period since around 2008, significantly prompted by new-found performance possibilities on online social media platforms and the availability of a massive amount of recorded comedy specials and shows on cable TV and streaming services. As in the 1970s, the popularity of comics has skyrocketed and stand-up comedy is now experienced by many as a legitimate form of commentary on the politics of the world.[20] New York's stand-up comedy scene is again bustling with plenty of opportunities for a range of comedic voices – from no-nonsense one-liner comics to conceptual experimentalists – to be heard in performance venues that may or may not be specifically designed for entertainment purposes. The main performance spaces for stand-up comedy are unsurprisingly the comedy clubs that only have comics on the bill. The large majority of comics working in New York City today aim to get 'passed' at one of the primary comedy clubs, which means that they will be offered spots there and, equally importantly, get paid for doing so. There are still new stand-up comedy clubs being opened but the major ones that are most sought both by performers and audience remain those that have been part of the city's entertainment industry for several decades, such as Caroline's, the Stand, New York Comedy Club, the Comic Strip Live, and especially the Comedy Cellar in MacDougal Street, Greenwich Village (Figure 3.1).

Originally a music venue, the Cellar only became a comedy venue in 1981 when comic Bill Grundfest suggested to its original owner that he might perform in the then somewhat uninviting and dark basement.[21] The popularity of the Cellar really exploded in 2011, when Louis CK (who was probably the most well-known and most respected comic in the world at the time) shot the opening credit for his FX series *Louie* in the staircase leading down to the venue, and also included a small section of his acts there as part of each episode. The Cellar is a relatively small venue which seats only 150 people. As popularity grew, its current owner, Noam Dworman, decided to expand his comedy empire by taking over the Fat Black Pussycat and Village Underground located around the corner. With the three different venues, it is now possible to run anything from ten to fifteen daily shows, each with six to seven comics on the bill. To many comics, the particular attractiveness of the original Comedy Cellar in MacDougal Street as a performance venue is the layout of the main room. The stage is raised a few inches off the floor and is located on the long side of a rectangular room facing the audience members, who are seated on chairs around tables. According to comic Sean Patton, it is the acoustics of the Cellar's Macdougal Street room that makes it so special as a performance venue: 'It has a low ceiling so the laughs hold and don't float away. Because of the low ceiling, laughs bounce off the back wall making it possible for good comics to create a wave of laughter that goes on and on. It's really cool when that happens.'[22]

Where Stand-Up Happens   75

Figure 3.1 A guest walks into the Comedy Cellar in Greenwich Village as arts venues reopen on 2 April 2021 in New York City
Photo: Alexi Rosenfeld / Contributor / Getty Images Entertainment / Getty Images.

For the large majority of working New York comics, it is a crucial and ongoing challenge to get as much stage time as possible. Comedy clubs offer tightly packed and carefully curated shows to their audiences but they are only on rare occasions ideal places for comics without years of experience to try out new material. In order for comics to test new jokes on an audience, they do so-called open mics, which are shows where anyone can perform, or less formal bar shows where the audience has not paid specifically to be entertained by stand-up comics. There are open mics on all weekdays throughout the city, some in established comedy clubs but most in other venues, such as backrooms in bars and restaurants, bookstores, and music shops. Most open mics are run by one or two comics who host the shows and make sure that all performers stick to the allotted time, which may vary from three to ten minutes, depending on the format of the show and the number of comics who have signed up to do a set.

To many up-and-coming comics, doing an open mic can be a gruelling experience of performing to a room full of struggling peers, who are there not only to work on the delivery of new jokes but often also to challenge their own stage fright and subjective capacity for tackling a possible no-laugh response. Still, despite having to constantly face one's own performance weaknesses, even comics with several years of experience aspire to 'hit more mics' in order to hone their craft and eventually get passed at the comedy clubs.

Bar shows can be organised by the owners (or staff) or, equally likely, by comics responsible for providing a solid line-up of performers while also hosting the show when there are several comics on the bill. Performing in a bar, pub, or restaurant is often slightly more challenging than doing shows in comedy clubs or trying out new material at an open mic. Audiences have rarely been asked to be entertained by stand-up comics insisting on having everyone's full attention for an extended period of time. And whereas comedy clubs deliberately design the performance setting and sound system to enhance the audience's experience of the show, in bars and restaurants, conditions are often less than optimal without stage lighting (let alone a stage!), adequate acoustics, and decent sound systems that would make it possible for everyone in the room to hear what the comics have to say. To make up for the less than ideal working conditions, bar shows tend to offer more stage time than is usually the case in comedy clubs and at open mics. Faced with audiences that may or may not be able to keep their focus on the performer, comics can stretch out and experiment with the format and structure of their jokes and try out longer bits and stories.

Many comedy shows are held in multipurpose venues that host a range of events and arrangements. Both located in Brooklyn, the Bell House and Union Hall are live venues that are widely known for having independent comedy shows with up-and-coming and leading comics. Building on the tradition of the alt comics from the 1990s and onwards, several of these comedy shows deliberately experiment with formats that do not follow the conventional set-up–punchline structure. At the Bell House in Gowanus, Brooklyn, for instance, local comic Ian Fidance hosted for several years the monthly show *Picture This*, where animators interact with comics to produce collective free-floating associations out of drawings and spoken words. Either the comic starts talking or the animator starts drawing and from there, the performance is built by their images and words held together by the improvisational proficiency and dialogic openness of both interlocutors. Until his move to

Los Angeles a few years ago, comic Kyle Ayers hosted the irregular *First Comes Love* show at Union Hall in Park Slope, Brooklyn. Based on the surprisingly huge number of responses to a fake advert asking for porn movie scripts, Ayers used local comics to act out the scripts on stage in front of an audience.

Performance venues that host stand-up comedy shows also serve as vital information hubs for comics looking for possible spots. Comedy clubs with separate bar areas enable comics to socialise during shows, discuss the challenges of getting more stage time, and possibly pick up information about available spots in other clubs or bars in the city. With the growing popularity of stand-up comedy, the most sought-after comics often perform in several shows at different venues on the same night. On any given weekday, comics therefore frantically move between venues to get to the next show that they have been booked on and, if not, then to an open mic that they signed up for.

While even the most experienced and popular New York-based comics perform in venues that have no more than 500 seats, some have managed to secure spots at significantly larger shows.[23] When Adrienne Iapalucci and fellow comics Daniel Simonsen and Raanan Hershberg opened for Louis CK at the Royal Arena in Copenhagen, they underlined that stand-up comedy has moved into the biggest live performance venues, not just in the USA but globally. In New York and many other larger urban areas in the USA, the upscaling of stand-up comedy shows to larger venues has largely followed the comedy boom that started around 2009. Hence, whereas only three comics managed to sell out Madison Square Garden before 2009, three comics did so between March 2014 and March 2015 and each multiple times.[24] Elsewhere in the city, in 2017, Dave Chappelle had a sixteen-night residency at the Radio City Music Hall selling a total of 93,715 tickets. While Sharon Lockyer here speaks about the stand-up comedy scene in the UK, her argument is also applicable to the US: 'Stand-up comedy is now a staple ingredient of arena programs and sits comfortably alongside music events and family entertainment, which traditionally have been the mainstay of arena programs.'[25]

Many comics who perform in larger theatres and arenas agree that such venues invariably have an impact on both the form and content of their act. Audiences at large arena events come equipped with expectations of experiencing performances of the highest quality that will somehow speak directly to them. In order to make a joke work in front of an audience of several thousand people, the tendency is therefore for comics to present their material in a clear and easily digestible manner.[26]

Finding New Performance Spaces

When Covid-19 hit in March 2020, entertainment businesses and performance venues could immediately feel the impact of a global ban on physical public life. From one day to the next, working comics, producers, and managers of comedy clubs, bars, and general performance venues had to rapidly rethink their business strategies in order to survive in a new and radically transformed social environment. Within the first year of the pandemic, several strategies were introduced in order to allow for physical live shows, such as outdoor performances on rooftops, patios, and backyards organised informally and shows in parks and parking lots managed by comedy clubs. As aptly described by Zinoman, during this period, despite the questionable legality, performing live in New York was 'like selling beer during the Prohibition; It's outlawed and everyone's doing it'.[27] Performing in a public park was a challenge to many comics whose art form is predicated on being able to actively use the acoustics and spatial organisation of conventional performance venues. Lacking the low ceiling and sound system of most comedy clubs, some jokes could not be heard and would die out and it was usually impossible to establish the (staged) dialogue between performer and audience. Performing in parking lots was even more challenging. Audiences would sit in their cars and flash the headlights or honk their horns as a sign of positive feedback, distracting many comics, especially during the first shows organised in these somewhat awkward performance venues.

The pandemic has had a significantly negative impact on the comedy business with clubs shutting down, shows being cancelled, and careers being ruined or put on hold. As is often the case, however, huge crises also carry the potential for new innovations prompted by an imminent need for radical change in order to survive, whether physically, socially, or economically, in a new and potentially more unstable environment. The extended lockdowns forced comics and comedy clubs to find ways of performing and generating income without the use of physical performance venues. While some were (and still are!) reluctant to make the move, many traditional comedy clubs gradually intensified their digital presence alongside entirely digital comedy clubs and shows. Venues experimenting with new approaches include the Nowhere Comedy Club, which tries to recreate a club atmosphere online by allowing you to see audience members in small boxes on the screen next to the comic; the Bramble platform, created by the Brooklyn Comedy

Collective, which enables audience members to move through different performance venues in a virtual theatre and interact with other people (appearing as avatars); and the InCrowd Comedy show, which has comics performing in front of a wall of screens of audience members watching from home.[28]

Despite the exciting and innovative ways of experiencing and performing stand-up comedy which were conceived as a response to lockdowns, the digitalisation of the art form and its performance outlets was well on its way long before the global pandemic. Rodney Dangerfield is credited for being the first comic to have a personal website,[29] but Dane Cook emerged as the main front-runner in terms of realising the potential of the internet in reaching new audiences and generating revenue at the same time. In the early 2000s, Cook created a now legendary MySpace page where he marketed his comedy while spending an extensive amount of time interacting directly with his growing fan base, which eventually made it possible for him to sell out arenas without ever having had television exposure, something that was then considered a necessary requirement.[30] During recent years, comics have increasingly turned to social media for trying out and experimenting with new jokes. YouTube is now used by comics as an outlet to release self-produced specials and to upload shorter clips that may get buried on personal websites. With the introduction of Twitter in 2006, comics found an ideal digital laboratory for testing their material before using it in live shows. With a limit on 140 characters, joke-writing became a question of linguistic concision and of figuring out exactly what themes work on audiences with a constantly declining attention span. More recently, TikTok has opened up new avenues for stand-up comedy to reach a wider and also younger audience. Sarah Cooper, a New York-based comic, became an overnight sensation during the lockdowns by lip-syncing speeches by Donald Trump, which led to her signing a contract for a Netflix special and a CBS sitcom.

However, not all comics are excited about moving shows online. Felicia Madison, the booker for West Side Comedy Club, complained in 2020 that online comedy is like having sex without an orgasm, so 'why bother?', and comic Dave Chapelle argued that comedy without an audience is like a 'swim meet without water'.[31] Livestreamed comedy shows cannot replace the live experience of comics making jokes a few inches from their audience. But it does seem that online comedy has managed to draw sizeable audiences, many of which are now habitually buying tickets to shows that are experienced from home.

Conclusion

Since its birth in riotous *varieté* shows, stand-up comedy has happened in a range of different performance settings, from the often-chaotic vaudeville houses to elegant nightclubs, informal coffee houses, specialised comedy clubs, huge stadiums and arenas, and, most recently, online comedy outlets. During this intense and often turbulent period of booms and busts, the staging for a stand-up comedy performance has remained minimal, often with a chair and a microphone as the only props. To comics, such as Adrienne Iapalucci, that joyous explosion of laughter remains the primary objective of stand-up comedy but, as we have seen, it impacts greatly on both the performance and experience of the art form whether it happens in a dimly lit comedy club, in an online comedy show, or on the huge stage of the Royal Arena. There is therefore no doubt that the setting in which the stand-up comedy act is happening has a significant impact on both the comic's performance and the audience's experience of it. Everything from lighting and heating to the acoustics and spatial layout of the venue, and even the behaviour of staff and audience members, are integral factors in creating the optimal conditions for the flow of energy to combust into laughter.[32] Each venue format invites the comic to develop particular forms of comedy. Performances in small and intimate bar shows are fundamentally different from comedy clubs, which again cannot be compared to stadiums and huge arenas. The explosion of new digital outlets and formats is a reminder that performance settings are not simply the neutral framing for comics to enact their art form. It is integral to and partly responsible for the making and experience of stand-up comedy.

Notes

1. Ian Brodie, *A Vulgar Art: A New Approach to Stand-Up Comedy* (Jackson: University Press of Mississippi, 2014), p. 14.
2. Rebecca Krefting, *All Joking Aside: American Humor and Its Discontents* (Baltimore: Johns Hopkins University Press, 2014), p. 38.
3. Wayne Federman, *The History of Stand-Up: From Mark Twain to Dave Chapelle* (Beverly Hills, CA: Independent Artists Media, 2021), p. 16.
4. According to Kliph Nesteroff, there were 5,000 vaudeville theatres at the beginning of the twentieth century. Kliph Nesteroff, *The Comedians: Drunks, Thieves, Scoundrels and the History of American Comedy* (New York: Grove Press, 2015), p. 1.
5. Nesteroff, *The Comedians*.
6. Nesteroff, *The Comedians*, p. 4.
7. Federman, *The History of Stand-Up*, p. 27.

8. Phil Berger, *The Last Laugh: The World of Stand-Up Comics* (New York: Cooper Square Press, 2000), pp. 11–12.
9. Mel Watkins, *On the Real Side: A History of African American Comedy from Slavery to Chris Rock* (Chicago: Lawrence Hill Books, 1999).
10. Gerald Nachman, *Seriously Funny: The Rebel Comedians of the 50s and 60s* (New York: Pantheon Books, 2003).
11. According to some accounts, it was actually Nord who first started the hungry i before selling it to Banducci in 1951. See Dennis McLellan, 'Enrico Banducci, 85; Owned hungry i Nightclub', *Los Angeles Times*, 16 October 2007.
12. James Curtis, *Last Man Standing: Mort Sahl and the Birth of Modern Comedy* (Jackson: The University Press of Mississippi, 2017).
13. Budd Friedman, *The Improv: An Oral History of the Comedy Club That Revolutionized Stand-Up* (Dallas: BenBella Books, 2017).
14. Richard Zoglin, *Comedy at the Edge: How Stand-Up in the 1970s Changed America* (New York: Bloomsbury, 2008), p. 147.
15. William Knoedelseder, *I'm Dying Up Here: Heartbreak and High Times in Stand-Up Comedy's Golden Era* (New York: Public Affairs, 2009).
16. Federman, *The History of Stand-Up*, p. 82.
17. Stephen Holden, 'The Serious Business of Comedy Clubs', *New York Times*, 12 June 1992, pp. C1, C22.
18. Nesteroff, *The Comedians*, p. 336.
19. John Wenzel, *Mock Stars: Indie Comedy and the Dangerously Funny* (Golden, CO: Speck Press, 2008), p. 153.
20. Nicholas Holm, *Humour as Politics: The Political Aesthetics of Contemporary Comedy* (London: Palgrave Macmillan, 2017).
21. Andrew Hankinson, *Don't Applaud: Either Laugh or Don't (At the Comedy Cellar)* (Melbourne & London: Scribe, 2021).
22. Sean Patton interview, New York, 13 March 2017.
23. The current popularity of stand-up comedy has undoubtedly allowed for an unprecedented number of comics to perform in stadiums and larger arenas but there are previous examples as well, most notably Steve Martin, who performed to an audience of 500,000 in larger venues in fifty cities across the USA during his 1977 tour. In February 1990, Andrew Dice Clay was the first comic to sell out Madison Square Garden, and in the early 2000s, at the height of his popularity, Dane Cook managed to do the same in a number of American arenas and stadiums.
24. Jesse David Fox, 'How the Internet and a New Generation of Superfans Helped Create the Second Comedy Boom', *Vulture*, 30 March 2015.
25. Sharon Lockyer, 'Performance, Expectation, Interaction, and Intimacy: On the Opportunities and Limitations of Arena Stand-Up Comedy for Comedians and Audiences', *The Journal of Popular Culture*, Vol. 48, No. 3, 2015: p. 588.
26. Lockyer, 'Performance, Expectation, Interaction, and Intimacy', p. 591.
27. Jason Zinoman, 'Live Comedy Is Back in New York! But Outdoors. Is This a Good Thing?', *New York Times*, 26 August 2020.

28. Jesse David Fox, 'I Was Afraid of Virtual Comedy Shows – Until I Went to One', *Vulture*, 30 September 2020.
29. Federman, *The History of Stand-Up*, p. 113.
30. Nesteroff, *The Comedians*, p. 351.
31. See Jason Zinoman, 'Can You Make Money in Live Comedy Right Now? Some Producers Say Yes', *New York Times*, 20 April 2020; and Jason Zinoman, 'Does a Comedian Really Need an Audience?', *New York Times*, 3 June 2022.
32. Sophie Quirk, 'Containing the Audience: The "Room" in Stand-Up Comedy', *Participations*, Vol. 8, No. 2, 2011: p. 228.

Further Reading

Auslander, Philip, *Liveness: Performance in a Mediatized Culture*, 2nd ed. (Abingdon and New York: Routledge, 2008).

Brodie, Ian, *A Vulgar Art: A New Approach to Stand-Up Comedy* (Jackson: University Press of Mississippi, 2014).

Double, Oliver, *Getting the Joke: The Inner Workings of Stand-Up Comedy*, 2nd ed. (London: Methuen, 2014).

Friedman, Budd, *The Improv: An Oral History of the Comedy Club That Revolutionized Stand-Up* (Dallas: BenBella Books, 2017).

Lockyer, Sharon, 'Performance, Expectation, Interaction, and Intimacy: On the Opportunities and Limitations of Arena Stand-Up Comedy for Comedians and Audiences', *The Journal of Popular Culture*, Vol. 48, No. 3, 2015: pp. 586–603.

Mintz, Lawrence E., 'Standup Comedy as Social and Cultural Mediation', *American Quarterly*, Vol. 37, No. 1, 1985: pp. 71–80.

Rutter, Jason, 'Rhetoric in Stand-Up Comedy: Exploring Performer–Audience Interaction', *Stylistyka*, Vol. 10, 2001: pp. 307–325.

Wenzel, John, *Mock Stars: Indie Comedy and the Dangerously Funny* (Golden, CO: Speck Press, 2008).

Zoglin, Richard, *Comedy at the Edge: How Stand-Up in the 1970s Changed America* (New York: Bloomsbury, 2008).

CHAPTER 4

Recorded Stand-Up from Radio to Netflix
Brett Mills

While stand-up comedy may usually be thought of primarily in terms of live performance, it has a significant and successful existence across a wide range of media, such as radio, television, film, and online. These media each have their own conventions and norms, and stand-up therefore must respond to and align with these. The key issue here is the matter of liveness. Stand-up comedy is usually thought of as a form of cultural performance in which a performer carries out their act in a place and time shared with the audience of that performance. Stand-up is a live form, and that liveness is embedded within every aspect of its text and reception. This is not to deny the rehearsed and structured nature of stand-up; the most common form of it involves months of writing and rehearsal as the comedian works towards a structured performance. To say that stand-up is live is not to suggest that it arises only from that moment of liveness, for it is not a result of that performer-place-time-audience interaction alone. That moment instead imbues that which is rehearsed with a specificity, in which the specifics of the venue, or the audience, or the performer contribute to a performance that is akin, but not identical, to every other iteration of that show.

This liveness is embedded in the pleasures of stand-up comedy, meaning audiences are aware of, and can take pleasure in, the 'being there' of that specific performance which can never be fully recreated. Similarly, for comedians the pleasure – and perhaps dread – of stand-up is the unknowability of each performance prior to its taking place, and the labour of the comedian involves successfully working with the particularities of *this* performance in which the show they have developed and likely delivered many times before mutates as they are performing it, necessitating 'a long history of connection between comedy and improvisation'.[1] Also fundamental is that such factors, and their impact, are often inexplicable; it is not as if this performer, with this audience, in this venue, in these contexts, constitutes a rigid formula that will produce precisely the same experience each time. Thus a foundational pleasure of stand-up comedy is this very unknowability of outcome. The excitement of the live cultural experience – for comedian and audience – is the notion that the performance they took part in was a moment impossible to recreate.

This represents a significant problem for recorded stand-up. Recorded media is not live, and is instead a representation of a moment that has passed. A fundamental purpose of recorded media, such as photography and film, is the capturing of moments so they can be preserved as evidence of the past, serving as historical documents that evidence a moment took place. Contemporary societies use such technology precisely for evidential purposes, including historical moments such as wars, the use of CCTV in criminal proceedings, and individuals using camera phones to record family events and holidays. In doing so these technologies are used as evidential tools in a manner akin to the use of culture prior to their development, for painting has a long history of being understood as, and employed for, the purposes of evidence, stretching all the way back to cave-paintings. Thus a variety of cultural forms have been repeatedly used to 'capture' moments, and the study of history would be impossible without such records. But this means that while these artefacts may well have been produced at the time they intend to depict, they are immediately representations of the past, instantly a record of 'then' rather than 'now'. This invites a particular relationship between the text and its audience, who are invited to see the text in an evidential manner, a portal into a time, and a moment of which they are not a part, presenting 'an event that actually happened'.[2]

There is, then, a problematic contradiction that needs to be overcome when media are used to record stand-up comedy. That is, the key pleasure of stand-up is its liveness, the situated specificity of this particular performance, which cannot be recreated and which is a co-creation between performer and audience. Recorded media is instead about the past, fixing an event into a text which is not about liveness but instead about history, and whose pleasures rest on the access they give to that past. Furthermore, recorded media gives audiences access to a performance at which they were not present, allowing it to be consumed years after it took place. This means there are two audiences for recorded stand-up: the one present at the performance, and the one watching it as a recording after the fact. This latter audience is diffuse, spread across time and geography and thus not the communal, collective body present at the live event. For stand-up, where the social aspect of audiencehood is so important, the unknowability of the audience for the recording is a real problem, for a performer has no control over where or how or with whom this recorded event will be consumed. Taking stand-up – intrinsically a live event – and turning it into a recorded text is thus not a straightforward act, and the history of recorded stand-up can be seen as a continuous attempt to overcome this problem.

That said, there are components of recorded media that offer a reformulated version of the liveness that is so essential to stand-up comedy. Television, for example, for much of its early period, was wholly live, because the technology for recording material was not fully developed. So while we may now think of television as primarily a recorded medium, this is a more recent characteristic, and not necessarily embedded within its technology. As Philip Auslander notes, at its inception, '[t]elevision's essence was seen in its ability to transmit events as they occur, not in a filmic capacity to record events for later viewing'.[3] The word 'television' means being able to see at a distance; its attraction was and remains its ability to enable people in one place to see things happening in another place at the same time as those present. In doing so, television creates a live audience in multiple spaces, offering a sense of 'being there' to those who are elsewhere, and inviting audiences in a variety of places to understand themselves as part of a larger, technologically generated community. When watching live stand-up – or any other live event – on television, the distant audience is not physically present but is temporally present, encountering the performance at the same time as the immediate audience, thereby enabling one key component of the liveness upon which stand-up thrives. Television's 'essential properties as a medium are *immediacy* and *intimacy*',[4] with 'immediacy' functioning as a form of distanced liveness. But 'intimacy' is important too; it is not the same as presence, but invites audiences to understand their engagement with the material on offer in a manner that belies the spatial disparity between performer and viewer. That intimacy can be achieved through the ways in which stand-up is shot, as close-ups and editing enable audiences to see performers much more closely than may the case for the audience present in the live venue. But intimacy is also tied to ideas of collectivity and communality, especially as television – despite newer technologies expanding places in which it can be accessed – remains a medium largely consumed in the home.[5] Television addresses its audience personally, with newsreaders and chat show hosts often speaking directly to camera, directing their communication to audience members they cannot know but who are invited to understand themselves as being addressed as a community of individuals. This mirrors the address of the stand-up comedian at a live gig, where the performer–audience intimacy is a conflation of the individual and the mass. There is, then, a congruence in the mode of address for stand-up as a form and television as a technology, in which liveness is transmuted in 'immediacy' and 'intimacy' which, while not the same, enables the medium to approximate some of the experiences and pleasures of the stand-up gig 'proper'.

Other recorded media work in similar ways, though each medium attunes this relationship in particular ways as a result of the specifics of its technology. Radio, like television, enables audiences to encounter moments from afar as they happen, functioning as a multi-site audience brought together by technology. Radio lacks images, but this enables a different kind of 'intimacy' centred on the voice alone, making the sense of being spoken to directly even more powerful. Online streaming platforms such as YouTube and Twitch, and video-conferencing programmes such as Zoom and Skype, have been exploited by stand-up comedians in recent years because they offer the same kinds of live event possibilities of broadcasting technologies such as television and radio. As Marilyn Tofler points out, these streaming platforms have been 'shown to be successful in reaching both a wide local and international audience'.[6] But they have an added advantage: where television and radio are largely one-way media, these newer technologies enable performer–audience interaction that is akin to, but not the same as, that in live gig venues. Performers can see and hear audience reactions; audience members can see other audience members, thereby creating a sense of community among geographically distant individuals; and performers and audience members can interact, either directly through talking to one another or through chat rooms in the platforms. Fundamental to this development are the possibilities of approximating notions of liveness and co-presence, which are seen as so vital to the pleasures of the stand-up gig, and it is noticeable that, when new technologies are developed, it is these aspects which stand-up comedians first experiment with, and it is those technologies' abilities – or lack of such abilities – that means they succeed or not as tools for stand-up comedy. There has been experimentation with using cinemas for similar live events; for example, the final date of Ross Noble's *Nobleism* UK tour in 2007 took place in Liverpool but was broadcast live to forty-three cinemas across the country, with a potential audience of 10,000 people. Yet this remains a one-off, and cinema has not become a normalised site for live comedy in the ways in which other technologies have. This is probably because the sense of intimacy and community is harder to imply across multiple cinema audiences, but also because the cinema is not a place which is culturally associated with liveness. It is, then, the centrality of liveness that has driven the relationship between stand-up and technologies of recorded media throughout their history.

This history shows that what we now understand as the conventions and norms of comedic entertainment in recorded media actually have their origins in earlier forms of live entertainment. After all, when radio and television were invented, and broadcasting as a form of communication technology enabled corralling large numbers of disparate people into a communal audience for the first time, no one really knew how to make these media work and what would be successful on them. Where cinema could draw on theatre for its presentational conventions, the very geographical disparity, plus the implication of liveness, meant radio and television had no direct precedents that could offer a model for their use. Thus the early years of television were resolutely experimental, with programme-makers looking largely to 'existing forms – radio, film, music hall, theatre, literature – to create its own unique range of programme fare'.[7] For broadcast entertainment, the only sources that could be drawn from were vaudeville in the USA and music hall in the UK. There was resistance to this; John Reith, the first director general of the BBC and the man responsible for formulating the conception of 'public service broadcasting' which still largely persists to this day, asserted that 'to have exploited so great a scientific invention for the purpose and pursuit of entertainment alone would have been a prostitution of its powers'.[8] Nevertheless, forms of comedic entertainment were a staple part of the BBC's output from its very inception, and these largely functioned as little more than broadcast versions of music hall and vaudeville acts, with the intention of approximating the pleasures inherent in those live, theatrical experiences. So on the BBC's first night of television broadcasting, on 2 November 1936, the first proper programme to be shown, following an opening ceremony and a news bulletin, was called *Variety* and consisted a multiple short entertainment acts akin to the music hall. The first comedians to appear on television are described in the listings magazine *Radio Times* as 'Buck and Bubbles', who are 'versatile comedians who dance, play the piano, sing, and cross-chat'.[9] Other comic performers who presented their acts on the fledging broadcasting system in its first few months include Sutherland Felce ('Conjuror and Comedian'), Walker and Smarte ('Comedy Jugglers'), Russell Swann ('Conjurer and Comedian'), and Sherkot ('Silent Comedian').[10] A BBC press release at the time indicates that for such programming, 'Informality and brightness will be the keynotes',[11] and programme-makers were keen to explore how these new technologies could best be used to disseminate the vaudevillian and music hall 'spirit' such performances offered.[12]

Recorded media was also seen as a threat to existing forms of live comedic entertainment, and the early years of broadcasting consisted of ongoing negotiations, agreements, and boycotts between the BBC and live venues. In the early days of radio in the UK in the 1920s, live broadcasts from music halls were banned, because organisations dedicated to ensuring the ongoing commercial success of live venues were concerned that broadcast comedy would steal their audiences.[13] Many performers who may have wanted to break into the new media and reach national audiences found that their contracts forbade them from doing so. Throughout the 1920s the BBC worked with industry organisations and trade unions in an attempt to come to an agreement allowing them access to existing venues and performers. Where those agreements were reached, they remained extremely limited in scope. Theatre owners' and performers' organisations felt that broadcasting had no possibility of 'enhancing the value of the artist'.[14] On the other hand, the BBC thought radio broadcasts of performances were not a threat to the stage because they lacked the visual element which theatre audiences would still be willing to pay to experience. Given that live stand-up and its recorded version now have a symbiotic relationship – to the extent that an appearance on recorded media can have significant positive impacts on a stand-up's subsequent live revenue – the animosity that underpinned recorded and live media organisations in the 1920s might be seen as quaint and small-minded. But it can instead be more productively read as indicative of the idea – which persists today – that the live version of comedy is the more true, authentic version, which deserves to be preserved. After all, comedians of the time could instead have simply moved to broadcasting, seeing the potential for larger audiences and therefore more commercial success. But clearly there was an assumption that something is lost culturally and societally should live comedy cease to exist, to be replaced by its broadcast version. The irony, of course, is that the BBC at the time appeared to agree with this view, given that it broadcast versions of live performances intended to approximate that live experience as closely as possible within the limits of available technology. While this was born out of necessity, for broadcasting was yet to have any conventions or heritage of its own that it could draw from, it also indicated broadcasters' reverence for the forms of culture that already existed and the valuable purpose of bringing that culture to national audiences. Embedded in recorded media of broadcasting, then, is an awareness of the importance of factors fundamental to stand-up, and the history of broadcasting from its very inception can be seen as an ongoing project of approximating these via technologies of record.

We can therefore understand recorded stand-up as a form of translation from one medium to another. The desire to find a way to emulate liveness was, in the USA, a simple consequence of geography. For a large country spread across multiple time zones, it has never been practical to repeatedly perform programmes live for each region. Instead, programmes would be performed live on the East Coast, and recordings of these were then shown in time zones further west, with the verisimilitude of liveness.[15] Liveness, then, while typically understood as a factual component related to temporality, was reshaped by broadcasting into a visual style that could be employed even within recorded programmes. When consuming comedy on broadcasting there is no real way for an audience to know whether what they are encountering is actually live: a stand-up audience can assess this through the simple factor of audience–performer co-presence. It is for this reason that when television broadcasts actual live events – such as sporting events or on-the-spot news reporting – a caption saying 'live' often appears on-screen; the extra indicator is required because what may look live isn't necessarily so. Television comedy's success in 'fooling' critics and audiences into thinking programming is live is demonstrated by the fact that the sitcoms *I Love Lucy* (CBS 1951–1957) and *The Honeymooners* (CBS 1955–1956), both of which experimented with new camera and recording technologies in order to find ways to develop an aesthetic of liveness, were successful enough that recorded episodes of the former were sometimes misleadingly labelled by newspapers as 'live'.[16] For recorded media, then, liveness is a textual element rather than a performative truth.

The sitcom is a useful format for examining how this aesthetic of liveness came into being, as well as the ways in which recorded media has drawn on and reshaped stand-up comedians and their acts. After all, the genre itself developed out of a desire to find ways to draw on comedians' personalities and acts while also capitalising on the regularity and episodic nature of broadcasting. The BBC developed early radio sitcoms such as *Band Waggon* (BBC Radio 1938–1940) and *It's That Man Again* (BBC Radio 1939–1949) as an attempt to create 'entertainment of a … "personalized" kind which could have a permanent niche in the listeners' week'.[17] Both featured comedians already successful on stage, and both originally had a revue format featuring short sketches and recurring characters. It was over time that programmes such as these evolved into featuring longer sections which were more narratively driven, telling comedic stories of recurring characters in recognisable situations. The sitcom's potential for multiple episodes and episodic storytelling was – and is – not possible in stand-up's usual live format, which functions as single, one-off event. Sitcom is a genre only possible in serialised broadcasting, resulting from the interplay of the pleasures of comedy that had been honed via live performance and the possibilities of television and radio.

That the sitcom is indebted to stand-up remains evident, for there are conventions of the genre that persist decades after the genre came into being. First, performers and writers of sitcoms frequently come from a stand-up background; one of the markers of recognition for a stand-up is that they are offered their own sitcom. Contemporary examples include Aziz Ansari's *Master of None* (Netflix 2015–2021), Mae Martin's *Feel Good* (Channel 4/Netflix 2020–2021), Aisling Bea's *This Way Up* (Channel 4 2019–2021), Lee Mack's *Not Going Out* (BBC1 2006–), and Larry David's *Curb Your Enthusiasm* (HBO 2000–2024), but this convention can be traced back to the origins of the genre in series such as *The George Burns and Gracie Allen Show* (CBS 1955–1958). A recurring trope of such programming is a performative elision between the main character in the programme and their off-screen stand-up persona, which itself often alludes to the 'real' person offstage, resulting in a complex 'textual persona',[18] in which the performer's 'individuality' is a key appeal.[19] One of the key ways this is evident is that many sitcoms are named after their stars, who share their first name (and sometimes their whole name) with the character they play; for example, *Ellen* (ABC 1994–1998), *Roseanne* (ABC 1988–1997, 2018), and *Miranda* (BBC2/BBC1 2009–2015). In some cases, stand-ups play identically named stand-ups in sitcoms, with sections of their routines incorporated into the programmes and springboards for episodes' narrative elements; for example, *Seinfeld* (NBC 1989–1998) and *Kelly Monteith* (BBC2 1979–1984). The latter series also contains another trope which is also apparent in *It's Garry Shandling's Show* (Showtime 1986–1990), *Sean's Show* (Channel 4 1992–1993), and *Mrs. Brown's Boys* (RTÉ1/BBC1 2011–); characters breaking the fourth wall and talking directly to the programme's audience, mirroring stand-up comedians' acknowledgement of, and direct address to, their audiences. Such conventions, which are common in broadcast comedy, are much rarer in non-comic programming, where realist conventions require the appearance of verisimilitude and performers to play someone other than themselves. In these ways, the sitcom can be understood as a form of recorded stand-up, with some programmes making those stand-up elements more explicit than others. But it also demonstrates the extent to which, over a century after broadcasting began, contemporary television comedy conventions persist in drawing on, and recreating, elements derived from stand-up and which continue to define contemporary stand-up.

Stand-up's pleasures and conventions inform other recorded media too. For example, sketch shows and variety shows continue the tradition of offering audiences a wide range of performers adopting a variety of comic characters and styles, loosely packaged together as a coherent programme of entertainment composed of 'mini-climaxes' of punchlines and humorous moments.[20] An example would be *Saturday Night Live* (NBC 1975–), which was conceptualised as 'blending original cutting-edge comedy with the unpredictability of live TV, which consciously harked back to the most innovative variety series from the medium's first generation – *Your Show of Shows* [NBC 1950–1954]'.[21] Here the liveness of stand-up comedy is retained in the form of live broadcasting, offering up 'unpredictability' as a pleasure akin to that at live comedy gigs (even though such unpredictability actually takes place within extremely rigid regimes of 'comprehensive premeditation'[22]). The importance of this live aspect is signalled in the programme title, which uses the word as a persistent indicator of the now-ness of the series. Where recorded media is not live, it often instead aims at a similar form of contemporaneity through programme titles. So where *Saturday Night Live* not only signals its liveness but also the very day and time when that liveness is taking place, satirical programmes such as *The Daily Show* (Comedy Central 1996–), *The Now Show* (BBC Radio 4 1998–2024), and *Last Week Tonight* (HBO 2014–) have titles that indicate their focus on the present or near-present. All of these series feature stand-up comedians and sections that function as if they were stand-up routines, even if their content is much more rigidly structured and delivery may take place in formats not typical for stand-up (e.g. from behind a desk). All of these series are also satirical, adopting a 'silly meets serious' approach by finding humour in recent events while simultaneously offering serious and in-depth comic analyses of politics and society.[23] It is notable that there is a preponderance of comic responses to contemporary events in recorded media, and programmes are developed for precisely this purpose. But it also functions as a reformulation of liveness, in which programmes that are not actually live still serve to indicate their fundamental relationship with the contemporary. This also shows how comedy's pleasures often arise from a kinship between performer and audience, such that even if they are not in the same time and place, the topics up for comic analysis relate to a shared, contemporary world.

This shared world of performer and audience is evident in another trope common in comedic recorded media, which is the inclusion of the audience in the text. This can happen in a variety of ways. The most common is that the audience is heard, via laugh-tracks that are recorded instances of actual audience laughter in response to comic moments, or the (much rarer) addition of 'canned' laughter onto comedic texts. Most of the shows cited earlier are performed in front of actual, live studio audiences, recreating the performer–audience spatial relationship typical in stand-up comedy. It is worth noting the oddness of this: television drama, for example, is not usually performed in front of an audience, even if it can be understood as a development of the kinds of drama found for centuries in theatre which did have an audience present. Throughout its development recorded comedy has retained the audience, when most recorded media has understandably abandoned it. And that audience's presence functions as a fundamental part of the text, with the audience watching that media at home able to hear the laughter and clapping of the audience who were physically and temporally present when the comedy took place. Audiences are also often seen; many programmes open with shots of the studio audience, clapping as the programme is introduced, and it is not unusual for the viewing audience to see the studio audience even before they have seen any of the programme's actual comic stars. As such, this depiction of the audience 'confirms the categorisation' of this piece of recorded media as comedic.[24] The existence of a studio audience also has implications for the aesthetics of such media and the ways in which the comedy is performed. While cameras and studios make possible the construction of complex and visually interesting geographies of narrative space, the presence of a studio audience instead severely limits the possibilities on offer. Everything must be performed to that audience, who function as a fourth wall to which all must be visible and comprehensible. Performers must face that audience, resulting often in odd and unnatural forms of staging when multiple performers are required to carry out dialogue. Performers leave odd pauses in dialogue, giving time for long laughs to die down. The apparatus by which production occurs, and the very functionality of all that is taking place, is incorporated into the text in ways that would be understood as unnatural or artificial for many other kinds of recorded media, so that, as Judith Roof points out: 'The comic event is always aware of itself.'[25] To this end, much recorded media of stand-up comedy incorporates the audience into its representational strategies, with a concomitant limitation on possibilities of visual experimentation understood as a necessary trade-off. The result is that audiences watching this comedy alone at home are invited to feel part of a community, a technological recreation of the collective act of audiencehood, which is fundamental to stand-up comedy.

The importance of this audience–performer aesthetic is evident in that, as Karin van Es and Judith Keilbach point out: 'Nowadays even digital media

platforms make their claim to live through services such as Facebook Live, YouTube Live, Snapchat Live Stories and Periscope.'[26] Where platforms such as YouTube remain overwhelmingly dedicated to recorded material, their experimentation with liveness indicate how important the here and now remain for culture. That recorded stand-up which is not consumed by individuals at the same time as others – as is the case for most broadcast media – somehow undercuts the comedic experience is evident in Netflix's engagement with stand-up material. Initially set up as a company that delivered VHS tapes and DVDs to consumers, its movement into making its own programming and distributing these via online streaming required Netflix to examine new audience–broadcaster relationships, which remain in flux. The most significant effect Netflix and other streaming services are understood to have had on consumption is their employment of the 'binge model',[27] where audiences are invited to watch multiple episodes of serialised programming in a short time rather than waiting for weekly instalments, as was the case in 'traditional' forms of broadcasting. But streaming does not work for stand-up, because these are typically one-off specials which are consumed in a manner identical to that usual for formats that preceded streaming. It is therefore no surprise that Netflix has announced its intentions to explore the possibility of live broadcasting, with stand-up named as one of the genres it sees as having potential within a live mode.[28]

The particular pleasures associated with liveness and stand-up have had a timely piquancy and urgency in the last few years given that pandemic-related social distancing restrictions meant that in many countries online spaces became the only place where large numbers of people could gather for stand-up gigs. Many performers established comedy nights on platforms such as Zoom, selling entry codes for access in an attempt to find alternative funding streams to replace those no longer possible in traditional venues. That the live audience remains of significance to comedy is shown by the fact that similar formats were adopted by traditional broadcasters for programmes that had hitherto had live audiences. So panel comedy shows such as *Mock the Week* (BBC1/BBC2 2005–2022), which had previously been recorded in front of a live studio audience, recreated this performer–audience relationship via a Zoom audience. The audience's reactions were recorded and included as part of the broadcast, mirroring the laugh track that would usually have been recorded from the in-studio audience. Indeed, *Mock the Week* made *more* play of its audience–performer relationship in this online format than it had done previously, for where it had in the past rarely engaged with studio audience members, in the Zoom version the presenter, Dara Ó Briain, routinely singled out individual viewers, making comments on their clothes, behaviour, or homes. Here Zoom appeared to encourage an active engagement with, and display of, the intimacy and immediacy of recorded comedy in a manner that far exceeded its previous formulation.

But what does recorded stand-up look like when it has no audience nor any access to one? Again, pandemic-related restrictions give an indication. The stand-up comedian Bo Burnham's Netflix special *Inside* (2021) took place entirely within a shed in the garden of Burnham's house, as he grappled with both the loneliness of lockdown and the purpose of comedy within a world that had made the contexts necessary for stand-up to work impossible. It has been described as a 'Zeitgeist-chasing musical comedy made alone to an audience of one'.[29] While it is clear the programme has been made for a viewing audience, it is shot and performed as if the audience is instead a voyeur, eavesdropping on private moments as the comedian engages in gratuitous bouts of introspection. It indicates the double-play that stand-up comedy engages in, where the comedian's talk hovers between dialogue and monologue. But is also indicates the complications – and possibilities – the recording of stand-up offers comedy, precisely because of the ambiguities about audiencehood, especially in a text such as this, which does not include an audience as part of its content. That liveness, immediacy, intimacy, and the performer–audience relationship are paramount to recorded stand-up comedy can be shown in that it takes a global lockdown for them to be abandoned, and the result is considerable angst for the comedian and their material.

Notes

1. Tobyn Demarco, 'Improvisation and Stand-Up Comedy', *The Journal of Aesthetics and Art Criticism*, Vol. 78, No. 4, 2020: p. 419.
2. Frank Boardman, 'Evaluating Stand-Up Specials', *The Journal of Aesthetics and Art Criticism*, Vol. 78, No. 1, 2020: p. 59.
3. Philip Auslander, *Liveness: Performance in a Mediatized Culture*, 2nd ed. (Abingdon and New York: Routledge, 2008), p. 12.
4. Auslander, *Liveness*, p. 14, emphasis in original.
5. For example, in the UK statistics show the majority of television is still watched in the 'traditional' way, on a television set, at home. See Ofcom, *Media Nations: UK 2021* (London: Ofcom, 2021), p. 6.
6. Marilyn Tofler, 'Australian-Made Comedy Online: Laughs, Shock, Surprise and Anger', *Continuum: Journal of Media and Cultural Studies*, Vol. 31, No. 6, 2017: p. 829.

7. Richard Paterson, 'Drama and Entertainment', in Anthony Smith (ed.), *Television: An International History*, 2nd ed. (Oxford: Oxford University Press, 1998), p. 57.
8. J. C. W. Reith, *Broadcast over Britain* (London: Hodder and Stoughton, 1924), p. 17.
9. Radio Times, *Radio Times*, 53 (683), p. 88.
10. Radio Times, *Radio Times*, 53 (690), p. 95.
11. Quoted in Asa Briggs, *The History of Broadcasting in the United Kingdom, Volume 2, The Golden Age of Wireless* (London: Oxford University Press, 1965), p. 607.
12. Ian Wilkie, 'Vaudeville Comedy and Art', *Comedy Studies*, Vol. 4, No. 2, 2014: p. 219.
13. Briggs, *The History of Broadcasting in the United Kingdom*, p. 77.
14. Briggs, *The History of Broadcasting in the United Kingdom*, p. 78.
15. Albert Abramson, *The History of Television, 1942 to 2000* (Jefferson and London: McFarland and Company, 2003), p. 49.
16. Abramson, pp. 49, 66.
17. Briggs, *The History of Broadcasting in the United Kingdom*, p. 118.
18. Lorenzo Logi and Michele Zappavigna, 'Impersonated Personae: Paralanguage, Dialogism and Affiliation in Stand-Up Comedy', *Humor*, Vol. 34, No. 3, 2021: p. 349.
19. Marianna Keisalo, 'Perspectives of (and on) a Comedic Self: A Semiotics of Subjectivity in Stand-Up Comedy', *Social Analysis*, Vol. 62, No. 1, 2018: p. 117.
20. John Limon, *Stand-Up Comedy in Theory, or, Abjection in America* (Durham, NC: Duke University Press, 2000), p. 9.
21. Gary R. Edgerton, *The Columbia History of American Television* (New York: Columbia University Press, 2007), p. 306.
22. Espen Ytreberg, 'Premeditations of Performance in Recent Live Television: A Scripting Approach to Media Production Studies', *European Journal of Cultural Studies*, Vol. 9, No. 4, 2006: p. 426.
23. Amanda Martin, Barbara K. Kaye, and Mark D. Harmon, 'Silly Meets Serious: Discursive Integration and the Stewart/Colbert Era', *Comedy Studies*, Vol. 9, No. 2, 2018: pp. 120–137.
24. Liz Guiffre, 'From *Nanette* to Nanettflix: Hannah Gadsby's Challenge to Existing Comedy Convention', *Comedy Studies*, Vol. 12, No. 1, 2020: p. 33.
25. Judith Roof, *The Comic Event: Comedic Performance from the 1950s to the Present* (New York: Bloomsbury, 2018), p. 95.
26. Karin van Es and Judith Keilbach, 'Keeping Up the Live: Recorded Television as Live Experience', *View: Journal of European Television History and Culture*, Vol. 7, No. 13, 2018: p. 65.
27. Mareike Jenner, *Netflix and the Re-Invention of Television* (Basingstoke: Palgrave, 2018).
28. Peter White, 'Netflix Exploring Live Streaming for First Time: Plans to Roll Out for Unscripted Series and Stand-Up Specials', *Deadline*, 13 May 2022, https://deadline.com/2022/05/netflix-live-streaming-1235023539/.

29. Jason Zinoman, 'Bo Burnham's *Inside*: A Comedy Special and an Inspired Experiment', *The New York Times*, 1 June 2021, www.nytimes.com/2021/06/01/arts/television/bo-burnham-inside-comedy.html.

Further Reading

Auslander, Philip, *Liveness: Performance in a Mediatized Culture*, 2nd ed. (Abingdon and New York: Routledge, 2008).

Edgerton, Gary R., *The Columbia History of American Television* (New York: Columbia University Press, 2007).

Limon, John, *Stand-Up Comedy in Theory, or, Abjection in America* (Durham, NC: Duke University Press, 2000).

Paterson, Richard, 'Drama and Entertainment', in Anthony Smith (ed.), *Television: An International History*, 2nd ed. (Oxford: Oxford University Press, 1998), pp. 57–68.

COMEDIANS' INSIGHTS

A Particular Performance Technique You Use in Your Act

Edward Aczel (UK)

Finding a way to make the audience laugh in unexpected places.

Tom Ballard (Australia)

In recent years I've been using a lot of shouting and exaggerated performance to drive my stuff home. I've been channelling a lot of anger at the state of politics and the world, and for whatever reason really upping the ante and force of my delivery has really helped to sell what I'm banging on about and make the stuff funnier.

Maria Bamford (USA)

I switch voices for fun but also to increase the chance of people listening. My natural voice – from what I've been told – sounds like a squeaking balloon.

Daphna Baram (Israel/UK)

'Making the room one' is the most useful thing I have learned. Encircling the room in my gaze and making sure everybody in it is included even if I do not address them specifically.

Angela Barnes (UK)

A technique I do sometimes employ is a good old-fashioned rant. But the key is to build jokes along the way in a rant. Mark Steel is of course the king of this. If you're going to bring anger onto stage, you have to remember that it has to be funny. There has to be punchlines. Sometimes the humour can come from a rant about something that really isn't worth the energy of ranting over.

Jo Brand (UK)

When I first started comedy, I knew because of my appearance that I would get a lot of flak from the audience before I'd even opened my mouth – so a technique I often used while the audience (particularly late show Comedy Store, Jongleurs or The Tunnel or any rowdy, posse audience) shouted abuse, I'd just stand there totally still half smiling at them and looking unconcerned. In other words boring them into silence until they got fed up with their somewhat limited (owing to alcohol ingestion) repertoire. It worked 95 per cent of the time.

Jo Caulfield (UK)

I'm happy to be the butt of my own jokes. You can't take the piss out of other people and ridicule them until you've allowed the audience to laugh at your own stupidity. It gives balance. It makes us equal. Once an audience has laughed at me, I can make them laugh at themselves.

Lou Conran (UK)

I don't necessarily have a technique, my performance is generally based on reaction and action.

Tanyalee Davis (Canada/USA/UK)

Since I am only 3'3" tall I use my physicality my gestures and movements to accentuate my jokes.

Tiernan Douieb (UK)

Being as friendly and unthreatening as possible, so I can con the audience into listening to me joke about how awful everything is.

Alexis Dubus (UK), Who Performs as Marcel Lucont (France)

I love using silence, to build tension, to set a mood and to land a punchline at just the right moment.

Andy Erikson (USA)

Sometimes when I forget my jokes, I pretend to be a cat until I remember my jokes.

Mary Gallagher (USA)

To always address something happening in the room, in this moment, with this audience, with this show, happening here and only now.

Justin Herman (USA)

I like to use pacing and momentum to influence the response to a punchline, and then I like to break that rhythm for misdirection on the next joke.

Bec Hill (Australia/UK)

I use a technique I developed which I call 'Paper Puppetry'. It's a bit like a cross between a flipchart presentation and a pop-up book. I've used it to tell simple stories and jokes, but the most popular use for it has been to demonstrate misheard lyrics. Each piece takes weeks – sometimes months – to make; from initial concept to storyboarding, constructing, and colouring. But I enjoy the process and it's all worth it when I get to perform it.

Harry Hill (UK)

Change the subject very quickly – leading the audience away from the previous gag somehow stimulates a laugh.

Matt Hoss (UK)

I do a lot of crowdwork as a compère, and I always repeat what the audience member has said to make sure the entire audience has heard it via my microphone.

Tom Houghton (UK)

Self-deprecation. My act is spoofing my privilege. I need to use self-deprecation to puncture that or else it just comes off as arrogance. It's also a great way of dealing with would-be hecklers. Basically just say the things they might say about me myself before they get the chance.

Charmian Hughes (UK)

I make deliberate eye contact with audience members – they are my existential confidantes.

Robin Ince (UK)

The older I get, the less technique I think I have. The main technique is just to let everything come pouring out while telling the negative voices to shut up, they'll have plenty of time to talk after the gig.

Radu Isac (Romania/UK)

I mostly talk about things that people already have strong opinions on. This way I know I have their attention.

Milton Jones (UK)

I play an exaggerated version of myself to try and create stupid cartoons in people's heads. If it works people laugh at my daftness.

Brian Kiley (USA)

Because my act is very joke oriented, I try to draw them in with the set-up, pause to build the tension and then, hit them with the punchline. I think of it as having a secret that they want to hear.

Beth Lapides (USA)

Stream of consciousness. I know there's something I want to talk about, and I know where I'm going to enter maybe, I might know the emotions that my mind to find words.

Stewart Lee (UK)

Silence.

Laura Lexx (UK)

This is something someone else pointed out to me that I do, but it's the technique of making sure any conversation I'm having with an audience member is referred back to the rest of the crowd so they (a) hear it all and (b) feel involved.

Trevor Lock (UK)

Notice what is happening in the audience.

Pope Lonergan (UK)

Comedians regularly comment on the fact I alternate between standing and kneeling while onstage. (And, in my mind, I'm gonna hold on to the delusion that I invented this – that I invented kneeling.) This wasn't a conscious 'technique' intended to elicit a certain response from the audience. It was just something I did, almost like a nervous tic. But I've since realised transitioning from standing to kneeling quietens the room and prepares people for storytelling, for intimate disclosure, for 'campfire confessional'. It makes people lean in and become more receptive to a routine with a slower tempo.

Elf Lyons (UK)

Dares. I give myself dares. To keep it different. You don't want to get used to saying things the same repetitive way each night – otherwise it starts to feel like you are exhaling ash into the audience. You need to feel always slightly frightened, as if you are balancing on the precipice of something unknown. So – I give myself dares. Eg: do it in French / pronounce no vowel the same way twice / you 'have to be sexy' / you have to 'scare the audience'. It gives me a focus – and then, once I tell the audience and bring them in on the gag it creates a whole other comic level of play.

Tom Mayhew (UK)

Sometimes, it's fun to not say anything, and just react to what the room does.

Jimmy McGhie (UK)

Oooh well pausing is something you eventually discover. Also dealing with hecklers with patronising insincere kindness, like when talking to an elderly relative.

Aditi Mittal (India)

Being funny.

Al Murray (UK), who Performs as the Pub Landlord (UK)

The aspect of what I do I'm known for is the crowdwork I do. Improvised crowdwork, as well. And the reason I worked so hard on getting that right was when I first started doing the character in the cabaret circuit – because no one does characters, they do themselves – you've got to find a way of putting across the fact that you're a character. It's really important, because otherwise it turns into a piece of theatre. The fourth wall goes up. And, you know, immediately the audience can start disconnecting from you and thinking, 'Well, why's a publican onstage?' or, 'Why's Alan Parker Urban Warrior onstage?' Or, 'Why's this bloke who says he's a postman [onstage]? What's going on, right?' I think from acting is the idea that action defines character, so what you do tells the audience who you are. So the simplest way to get across what the character was like was to have him talk to people. And then show his point of view. Rather than do a joke that demonstrated his point of view, show his point of view in action, literally in action with other people. So that's really where the motivation for doing it came from.

Sander Õigus (Estonia)

It's hard to name a technique but maybe mirroring the audience and matching their energy is an easy and universal thing to bring out. Whatever the type of material I'm doing, this is always an integral part.

Anuvab Pal (India)

I often try to think of a joke in terms of a scene. And I play out the scene almost as a conversation, and then pepper it with funny lines. So if I'm talking about the British in India and I'm trying to make it funny, I'll think about the first British person meeting the first Indian person as he gets off a ship in 1609, and then have them chat, in my head.

Lucy Porter (UK)

I have learned how to whisper forcefully in order to control a loud audience. Ian Coppinger told me ages ago. I was so embarrassed that it had never occurred to me independently. But I went out and tried it, like, that very week and never looked back. It's a whisper but not a kind of tentative or timid whisper. If you whisper, people think you've got something interesting to say and they lean in. As long as you don't do it too often. You only get away with it once. So you've got to save it like the nuclear option. You have to deploy it when it's really needed. But you do it, they lean in and then you of course immediately, you have to be so confident in what you're going to say. And it is the point where you keep your absolute killer one-liner, and deploy it then.

Rod Quantock (Australia)

I am never conscious of technique.

John-Luke Roberts (UK)

I like to make eye contact: if something's not working, it often turns out I've just forgotten to look the audience in the eye. Eyes? Eyes.

John Scott (UK)

To help things look spontaneous, I pretend to be pausing for thought.

John Simmit (UK)

I go out and have a conversation with my antenna turned up for how it's being received.

Nigel Williams (UK/Belgium)

Going off on a tangent and asking an audience member to remind me where I was when I get back to her/him as if it's a storyline I have to get back to. Acting like there is no logical order to the gig, and yet making the circle round at the end.

PART II
Interpretation and Meaning

CHAPTER 5

Stand-Up Comedy and Gender

Ellie Tomsett and Rosie White

Introduction

In this chapter we consider how gender has shaped the evolution of stand-up comedy, in relation to industry practices and the content of comic material. We focus on the history and complexities of gender and stand-up comedy in the UK – however, many of our observations may be applicable to live comic performance from wider global contexts.

Gender is a fundamental framework through which we experience the world but our understanding of it varies across time, in different cultures and contexts. Judith Butler describes gender as 'a practice of improvisation within a scene of constraint', arguing that it is always done 'with or for another, even if that other is only imaginary'.[1] Her work has shaped the understanding of gender in the late twentieth and early twenty-first century because it acknowledges how we are all trying to 'do' gender according to the social models our cultures offer. Butler inadvertently links the 'improvisation' of gender identity to the practice of stand-up comedy – like performers, we are working with an audience, on a particular stage, and that dynamic is at once liberating and constrained. The difference is that we can never leave the stage. Wherever we identify on the gender spectrum, the way we are perceived by others in relation to our gender has a huge impact on our lives. How we are treated and the way we present ourselves to the world are all informed by gender identity.

Feminism is an umbrella term for a range of political debates but at its root is a belief that gender is a primary source of inequalities: as Nivedita Menon comments, 'when one "sees" the world like a feminist [...] it is rather like activating the "Reveal Formatting" function in Microsoft Word. It reveals the strenuous, complex formatting that goes on below the surface of what looked smooth and complete.'[2] Gender affects the way audiences respond to stand-up comedians because stand-up comedy involves 'a person on display in front of an audience'.[3] It is an embodied form – the skill contained within the physical presence of the performer. As such it is vital to consider how that body on display within stand-up performance will be interpreted through a gendered lens. In this chapter we draw your attention to the gendered 'formatting' of stand-up comedy. We begin by discussing the gendered development of stand-up regarding spatial and social injustice, before considering how comedy content addresses gender.[4]

Cultural Context

The *context* of comedy inevitably informs its *content*. Within UK and US culture there are many gendered stereotypes around the inability of women to be funny. For a masterclass in these sexist stereotypes we can turn to Christopher Hitchens, whose infamous *Vanity Fair* article, 'Why Women Aren't Funny' (2007), ascribes women's lack of humour and men's command of it to a 'natural' dynamic where men are forced to employ comedy to attract women. This bizarre account of comedy and gender demonstrates the inherent misogyny of such claims. How those attitudes are attached to racism and homophobia is made evident in Hitchens' proposal that: 'there are some impressive [funny] ladies out there. Most of them, though, when you come to review the situation, are hefty or dykey or Jewish, or some combo of the three.'[5]

The idea that 'women can't be funny' has been vociferously challenged in recent years, yet underlying assumptions at the root of these stereotypes are very much alive and well. These stereotypes have ramifications for women's everyday lives and also for women who want a career in stand-up.[6] Expressions of 'surprise' that women are capable of being funny are, even now, articulated by audiences directly to women comics with startling regularity, both in person and online.[7] This is despite the fact that in recent years a wider range of comedians who identify across the gender spectrum are joining and finding success within the industry.[8] The demand that women in comedy constantly comment on their experience 'as a woman' places an additional burden on them which their male contemporaries do not experience. Male comics are not asked how they feel 'as a man' in the industry. This dynamic has a material effect on women and non-binary comedians regarding access to spaces and paid work.

Not all women are feminists, and not all feminists are women. Women in stand-up who identify as feminist do however encounter negative attitudes from audiences and fellow performers. Feminists as 'humourless killjoys' is an enduring stereotype but Sara Ahmed's celebration of the 'feminist killjoy' reclaims such gendered language, demonstrating how refusing to go along with the 'joke' has its own power.[9] Ahmed instructs women to embrace the 'killjoy' position, killing the joy of those who seek to perpetuate harm by repackaging sexism, racism, and homophobia as humour.[10] Performers such as Roseanne Barr in the USA, or Jo Brand and Linda Smith in the UK, turned the joke around in the 1980s; their comedy worked to address the patent idiocy of gender roles, often by adopting the role of the bad-tempered feminist.[11]

In the present context many forms of popular feminism are evident within stand-up comedy, yet women's issues are often depoliticised or individualised rather than recognised as systemic. Some contemporary stand-up is more about individual experience rather than overtly political debate. Katherine Ryan's routines address the challenges of motherhood or her time working at Hooters. She addresses the latter as a 'family restaurant', which gets an instant roar of laughter as the audience recognise a brand famous for capitalising on young women wearing revealing uniforms. Luisa Omielan's shows mine narratives around her complex dating and sex life; in one routine she enumerates all the things she contributes to the 'relation-ship boat' while her boyfriend contributes nothing apart from naming their 'relation-ship' as 'Noncommittal'. These routines focus on personal self-improvement narratives but note ongoing inequalities between men and women. This occurs within a cultural context which often assumes feminist gains have been made and are secure despite significant continued inequities, such as gender pay gaps, access to abortion as healthcare, and unequal care burdens.

The predominantly personal stand-up narrative may be understood as a response to negative stereotypes about women's rights activists as overly 'woke'. Such attitudes congeal around feminist debates which identify structural inequalities. Dismissive framing of feminism and feminists is part of contemporary right-wing discomfort with growing popular awareness of racial and gender discrimination. Making feminists the butt of the joke (from the 1900s to the twenty-first century) is an attempt to undermine the campaigns for gender equality, because they challenge existing hierarchies. Within this complex and challenging social environment, women and non-binary people have attempted to infiltrate the male-dominated profession of stand-up comedy.

Performance and Industrial Contexts

As an art form reliant on public speech, stand-up was conceived and developed within male-dominated spaces. The right to express an opinion in public spaces has been predominantly afforded to (white) men.[12] Inequalities regarding where women can and cannot go, and what they are sanctioned to do in particular spaces, has shaped stand-up comedy. Early venues for comedy, such as nineteenth-century music halls, hosted mixed-bill events showcasing a range of acts: jugglers, magicians, singers, and dancers as well as comedy performers. Women have been present during all periods of stand-up's development from music hall onwards, but they were a small minority.[13] Just as the uproarious music halls became more family-friendly 'variety' venues in the late nineteenth century, so stand-up moved from theatres to working men's clubs in the mid twentieth century. Working men's clubs were private venues managed by committees and founded in nineteenth-century industrial towns and cities. They provided a space in which men gathered to drink and talk, watching entertainment that offered light relief after a long working day. Women did not gain equal rights in working men's clubs until 2007; before that they could join as 'lady members', without any voting rights. Nevertheless, women comics such as Marti Caine were performing in these spaces.

During the 1960s and 1970s, when working men's clubs were a primary venue for comedy, women stand-ups' work was far tougher because women were a primary source of humour as 'the wife' or 'the mother-in-law'. Remnants of this were visible in the comedy of television stand-ups from this era such as Les Dawson, whose comic material depicted his mother-in-law as silent and sexless. Femininity, in the clubs, was traditionally depicted as grotesque and monstrous. It is difficult to perform and take command of a space, as is necessary in stand-up, when a key part of your own identity (your gender) has been publicly disparaged by the compère, the other acts, or vocal audience members. This is of course compounded further when gender intersects with other aspects of identity such as race and ethnicity, sexuality, disability, and social class.[14] In working men's clubs, as in many venues, barriers to participation were embedded in the physical spaces themselves for anyone whose gender, race, ability, and/or sexuality were not considered the 'norm'.

During this era comedians performed on bills interspersed by women entertaining the audience by stripping. Women in stand-up had to work hard to be *heard as well as seen*; to move past default objectification by their audiences. Costumes for women working within these and subsequent comedy performance spaces became part of the dynamic. Some women felt that they had to cover up their bodies to avoid objectification, a dilemma faced by many women in male-dominated industries. When the predominant form of inclusion for women within any space is as sexual objects, then the challenge of working outside of an objectified framework becomes more difficult. In the late 1970s, when comedy venues began to appear in UK city centres such as London and Manchester, it did not magically fix the problem. Women were still considered a novelty act, a rarity that needed to be interspersed across a programme to ensure variety. Women were rarely booked in the same line-up as each other for fear of having 'too many' on the bill. These issues continued into the 2010s: a 'one is enough' tokenistic approach to booking women and sexist introductions from compères, as well as concerns about being sexualised by an audience, remained part of the problem for women performers.[15]

As the twenty-first century has entered its second decade, women and non-binary comedians in the UK began to establish their own comedy venues in order to ensure a safe space for the material they created.[16] Audiences may seek out these alternative spaces to avoid mainstream venues which facilitate popular misogyny, both by continuing to book acts that trade in outdated sexism, racism, and/or homophobia but also through continued targeting of stag and hen parties via marketing that relies on gender stereotypes.[17] Just as social traits are gendered, so the physical space of comedy performance is often allocated on gender lines. This means that significant work is done by women and minority groups to create live comedy spaces which are inclusive – for performers on stage *and* their audiences.

We now turn to stand-up comedy as an industry and a livelihood. Comedy is a complex subsection of the creative industries and there is a significant gap between opportunities for paid work at grassroots level compared to the kind of money and prestige afforded to those at the highly commercial top end. Interventions which support wider participation in stand-up comedy from women and non-binary comics almost universally occur at the entry point to the industry. One example is the UK Women in Comedy Festival in Manchester, established by promoter Hazel O'Keefe in 2013, an initiative which seeks to address gendered disparities in comedy. Most of the Women in Comedy Festival to date has been volunteer-led and unfunded, indicating divisions within the industry regarding gender and power which replicate wider social dynamics.

In his exploration of industry gatekeepers at the Edinburgh Festival Fringe, Sam Friedman notes that those in positions of power, such as the scouts and commissioners who function as tastemakers of UK comedy, are commonly from very similar backgrounds, most notably in relation to social class. He argues that the social background of people in these positions has a significant impact on the way they engage with comedy and, through their work, replicate notions of comic taste: 'Had these scouts themselves come from more diverse social backgrounds, it is possible that they might have been more inclined to direct their own "expert" taste towards a more diverse imagined audience.'[18] The ability to appeal to a relatively narrow group of people enables a stand-up comedian to move from performing live in smaller venues to the wider audiences afforded by radio and television. The homogeneity of those involved in enabling women comics to move between live and mediated forms is concerning. A key aspect of Friedman's findings was the persistent notion of a marketable 'T-Shirt Comic'. This kind of comic is defined as 'young, white, attractive, male comics such as Jack Whitehall and Russell Howard, who were described [by his tastemaker interviewees] as "safe" and "inoffensive"'.[19]

This concept of a commercial comic is inherently gendered. More women and non-binary comics are now beginning to appear in mediated UK comedy, such as established TV stand-up and panel shows such as *8 Out of 10 Cats Does Countdown* (Channel 4 2012–), *Would I Lie to You* (BBC 2007–), or *Live at the Apollo* (BBC 2004–). Although this responds to calls for more gender diversity on-screen, it often means that the young male 'T-Shirt Comic' has simply been replaced by an attractive, young, white woman, or 'Tea-Dress Comic'. The integration of these Tea-Dress Comics in the mid-2010s (such as Rachel Parris, Ellie Taylor, and Cariad Lloyd) has challenged the male dominance of these televised spaces, but only though presenting a respectable middle-class whiteness that in turn replicates forms of racial exclusion. This is not a critique of the specific comics themselves but rather of the structures and organisations within which they work. Booking practices that address intersectional aspects of diversity are still notably rare in the UK comedy industry.

Gendered Topics for Humour

Just as the contexts of stand-up performance are gendered, so the content of stand-up routines has been shaped by gender dynamics. Much of this can be understood in terms of the superiority theory of how humour works; that *we* are laughing at *you* because *you* are not part of *our* culture or social group. In this sense stand-up may be addressed to a particular social group, forcing even those in the audience who are not in that group to join in the laughter or be seen as humourless, as 'not able to take a joke'. In this regard comedy can be a way to put 'other' people in their place by demarcating what is 'normal' or 'common sense'. This can entail cruel forms of humour, using language not usually acceptable in mainstream performance, and accommodating prejudices such as sexism, racism, homophobia, and transphobia.

The most infamous British example of this type of comedian is Bernard Manning, a working-class Lancashire stand-up comic who worked his way through the northern club circuit in the 1950s and 1960s, appearing on television in the 1970s.[20] His routines were honed in working men's clubs and translated into mainstream family entertainment in shows such as *The Comedians* (Granada 1971–1993), which made him a star. The 'blue' sexual aspects of his work did not make it to television, but the sexist aspects did, with many jokes featuring 'the wife' or 'the mother-in-law' as a grotesque punchline. The following example of a performance at his own club in 1994 gives a sense of how Manning worked. He is a large man, standing behind a microphone:

> [American accent] As WC Fields used to say, the only reason they invented alcohol was so that ugly women could get a fuck. [Pause as audience laugh. Looks down at a woman in the front row] I bet *you've* supped some fucking stuff in your time … [Pause, laughter] Fucking brewery![21]

The joke positions women as monstrous, disgusting, sexually rapacious, and complicit. The direct address to the woman in the audience demands that she be the butt of the joke and laugh for him; it is a power play. Performing to a packed club with a largely white audience of men and women, Manning controls the room. His timing is leisurely and apparently relaxed, with pauses as the audience laugh, building each joke. There is craft here but it is reliant on a discourse which renders women, gay men, and anyone who is not English or white as 'fair game'. This is what Andy Medhurst has termed 'togetherness through offensiveness', in his analysis of one principal example of the continuing appeal of such comedy, Roy Chubby Brown.[22] Like Brown, Manning is deliberately shocking, as were many of his peers on the club circuit. Despite all the swearing the humour does not immediately appear malicious; said with a smile, the woman in the front row appears to be laughing too. This stand-up is about community, specifically a white, working-class northern community that by the 1990s was already nostalgic for its own past.

Manning's 'World Famous Embassy Club', which he opened in 1959 in north Manchester, was his stage when television rejected him – not on the grounds of sexism but rather because of his racist jokes, which also brought down younger comedians such as Jim Davidson. In 1996 Freda Burton and Sonia Rhule won a racial harassment case against Manning, who targeted them during a Round Table event at the Pennine Hotel in

Derby where they were employed as waitresses: 'After he had directed a number of sexually and racially explicit comments at them, some of the guests started to harass them. "Nobody came to help us, and nobody stopped it," said Ms Rhule.'[23] The case demonstrates how such comedy is essentially a form of bullying but also how the tide was turning against this type of stand-up. However, this stand-up style did not die in the 1990s; it continues in the work of 'outsider' comics such as Roy Chubby Brown and in the early comedy club work of contemporary stars such as Jimmy Carr. Carr, who writes his own material, presented himself as radically different from his peers in the twenty-first century by employing similar strategies to Manning and Brown, specifically by directing a stream of misogyny at particular women in the audience during early live shows. This tactic, which marketises controversy, is still evident in the recent uproar about Carr's Netflix special, *His Dark Material* (2021).[24] Sexist comedy is an easy win for a young comic on the live circuit and during the late twentieth century it was a marketable commodity: 'most [working men's club] comics used prepackaged jokes with a wide circulation. The point was not radically to change the audience's perceptions but to get a reflex response. [...] Misogyny, along with racism and homophobia, was an easy way.'[25] Yet the dynamic of stand-up does not remain static for long. Even as a market for misogyny continued, there was the emergence of a new 'alternative' comedy scene in the early 1980s.

It would be tempting to believe that this was a radical shift in the form, but this is too simple. There had been women performing stand-up and making fun of gender long before the 1980s.

Comedy by Women on Gender

The women who made a living 'on the halls' in the nineteenth and early twentieth century often came from working-class backgrounds, dealing in humour that was unprintable in the polite press. Their wit and saucy personae had to manage audience hecklers, which were part of the entertainment and a key skill of their trade. Some big stars, such as Marie Lloyd (1870–1922), made a fortune from music hall performances, and Lloyd moved herself and her family into the wealthier London suburbs. This did not necessarily make them feminist forerunners; nor were they necessarily lauded by their middle-class sisters. Virginia Woolf, watching Marie Lloyd on stage, wrote that she was 'a born artist – scarcely able to walk, waddling, aged, unblushing. A roar of laughter went up when she talked of her marriage. She is beaten nightly by her husband. I felt that the audience was much closer to drink & beating & prison than any of us.'[26] Woolf's distance from Lloyd – as a 'respectable' middle-class woman – is evident in this passage, but there is also some sympathy regarding the audience Lloyd managed so expertly.

Music hall was a bear pit, and some women were able to make a good living in it, but they were not regarded as *properly* feminine; they had to jettison that respectability to make their performance work. Music hall comedy afforded women the opportunity to inhabit a variety of personae, in the tradition of 'character comedy'. Jenny Hill (1848–1896) and Nelly Power (1854–1887) were early stars of the form. Vesta Tilley (1864–1952), Ella Shields (1879–1952), and Cissie Loftus (1876–1943) emerged during the classic era that straddled the late nineteenth and early twentieth centuries. Florence Desmond (1905–1993) tracked that music hall tradition into twentieth-century variety theatre shows. Tilley, Power, and Shields were male impersonators; Loftus and Desmond were primarily impressionists; and Jenny Hill, 'The Vital Spark', performed as a working-class girl, 'down-trodden but defiant'.[27] It was difficult to *just* be a woman on stage and Lloyd was one of the few who managed to approach this. Her stage persona was a carefully crafted extension of her own working-class femininity, combining innuendo with an extraordinary command of the audience. T. S. Eliot called her 'the expressive figure of the lower classes', a title which, together with Woolf's earlier comment, indicates her fame and cultural reach, as well as her designation as distinctly Other to middle-class society.[28] Lloyd's famous opponent was the chairwoman of the Purity Party, Laura Ormiston Chant, who attempted to censor Lloyd's lyrics only to find that she herself was branded a prude and a hypocrite for understanding the implications of lyrics such as 'a little of what you fancy does yer good'.[29] Marie Lloyd imbued her songs and repartee with sexual implications that placed women's desire to the fore in a manner that scandalised polite society; she was notably absent from the Royal Command Performance at the Palace Theatre, London, in 1912. This first Royal Variety show marked a cleaning up and acceptance of music hall traditions as family entertainment. Lloyd performed that night under a bill advertising 'Every Performance by Marie Lloyd Is a Command Performance by Order of the British Public'.[30] Frances Gray argues that Ormiston Chant and Lloyd were coming at the same problem from different directions – sexual exploitation and abuse of women.[31] They both addressed the politics of sexuality and the female body in the public sphere. That *problem* of the female body on a comedy stage continues, through glamorous, quick-witted comedians who worked the working men's club circuit, such as Ellie Laine and Marti Caine, to breakthrough female acts on the 'alternative' circuit, such as double act Dawn French and Jennifer Saunders, or Jo Brand.

The left-leaning alternative comedy clubs which emerged in the late 1970s and early 1980s in London and other cities across the UK should have offered a less aggressive forum for women but most accounts indicate that this was not the case.[32] Dawn French and Jennifer Saunders were aware that they were initially included in the Comic Strip line-up because their male colleagues 'were desperate for women'.[33] When the Comic Strip troupe progressed from live shows at the club in Soho to more profitable work on television, French discovered that she and her female comedy partner were being paid half as much as their male colleagues.[34] While male alternative stand-ups performed routines which critiqued sexism, their behaviour offstage did not always align with onstage politics; many male comics still failed to acknowledge their own privilege. The content of women's stand-up was frequently distinct from their male counterparts on the alternative circuit because they had to deal with gender issues, whether navigating the audience's reactions to a woman doing comedy or the desire to address feminist politics in their act. Sexual politics was such a common topic on the 1980s alternative circuit that listings magazines described some performers as 'sex pol comedy'. Jo Brand was once listed as a 'sex pot comic', due to a misprint.[35]

Jenny Lecoat found success as a stand-up in early alternative comedy but quickly grew frustrated with being pigeonholed as a feminist comedian, finding that she was confined to a new stereotype.[36] Morwenna Banks and Amanda Swift, writing in the late 1980s as the alternative circuit was becoming the mainstream, comment on this transition as a necessary shift: 'We should encourage the idea that the art that women produce can become great art and not just great women's art. We need feminism to make women's experience visible, but having done that, we must accept that a woman artist may choose her material – and may emphasize being a woman, or may not.'[37] That choice is still not automatically on offer to women in stand-up; overcoming standard social prejudices regarding femininity continues to hamper stand-up performers on stage and within the industry. Some comics on the circuit in the early 1980s, such as Helen Lederer and Pauline Melville, crafted routines which satirised femininity and played with stereotypes about feminists.[38] Alternative comedy offered women in stand-up a little more room to manoeuvre regarding the types of venue that were available and the topics that could be addressed, because the routines were designed for a younger and more liberal audience than the working men's club circuit. It also presented new pressures, however: to present appropriate political material, remain feminine and feminist, and *still* be women in what is regarded as a men's profession. This was most visible when the alternative comedy which began in small back rooms of pubs began to transition to more profitable mainstream media. *Friday Night Live* (formerly *Saturday Live*, Channel 4 1985–1988) was designed to showcase the new comedy of the era but the figures who forged long-standing careers were mainly male comics such as Harry Enfield, Rik Mayall, and Adrian Edmondson. The show's producer, Paul Jackson, had already fostered an all-male stable of alternative stars in *The Young Ones* (BBC2 1982–1984). Many of the women who emerged on the alternative comedy circuit in the 1980s simply disappeared; some moved into production and writing.

One of the most enduring figures to emerge from the alternative stand-up circuit is Jo Brand (Figure 5.1). Now established as a television favourite, appearing on comedy panel shows such as *Have I Got News for You* (BBC 1990–) and hosting *The Great British Bake Off: An Extra Slice* (BBC 2014–2016; Channel 4 2017–), she first began working as a stand-up in the London comedy clubs that sprang up to surf the success of the Comedy Store. Her first set in 1986, at a charity show in a Soho club, was curtailed by a heckler who chanted 'Fuck off you fat cow' from the moment she got onstage to the moment she left it. She later discovered that he was another comedian on the alternative circuit who 'had a reputation for being somewhat anarchic'.[39] Brand's account of her transition from nursing to comedy recounts the strategies she employed to counter such relentless attacks. She called herself the Sea Monster, a nickname she had been gifted by a friend which served to make her more anonymous but also marked her out as not-human and therefore not a female stand-up. Her costume in those early sets – baggy clothes, Doc Martins, and wild hair – also registered as androgynous, shielding her body in a manner which made some people assume she was a lesbian. This self-presentation, crossing the boundaries of gender and sexuality, demonstrates a strategy for survival in an arena which could often be gladiatorial, privileging masculine aggression. Brand sidestepped this by delivering her routine in a bored monotone and carefully choosing her venues.[40] At the same time, her early routines focused on jokes about her weight, pre-empting vicious hecklers and employing self-deprecation to disarm the audience. As she gained experience her delivery gained nuance, becoming more relaxed and naturalistic.

Figure 5.1 Jo Brand. *The Peoples Assembly Presents: Stand Up against Austerity.* Live at the Hammersmith Apollo, London, 2014
Photo: Andrew Aitchison / Contributor / Corbis Historical / Getty Images.

Such strategies trace a line from the music hall to contemporary feminist stand-up; throughout this history women on stage have employed verbal wit, cross-identification and costume, together with often surreal and unexpected humour. It seems logical that much of the comedy produced by women in the inhospitable arena of stand-up might be unexpected; mining their own experience for jokes and observational humour, women provide a different perspective to much mainstream male stand-up comedy. This can be transformed into surreal personae, such as Brand's Sea Monster, and deft political observation, as with comedians such as Bridget Christie. Christie, like Brand, employs low-key delivery, but combines this with off-kilter, occasionally manic, character performance. The most famous of these is perhaps her early show, *A.Ant* (2010), in which she appeared in a homemade ant costume and addressed the inequities of working as an ant (i.e. a woman) in live comedy: 'Through the character of A.Ant, Christie managed to tackle some really provocative and political points about female comedians, including the preconceptions of an audience, the seemingly relentless "are women funny" debate, and the sexism still rife on the circuit.'[41] Gender is often (wrongly) assumed to be a 'women's issue' because Western societies are designed around white middle-class cisgender men, so that anyone who deviates from this 'norm' is framed as 'other'. 'Not having to think about' your identity, whether it is gender, race, class, or ability, is a privilege and this is what Christie exposes through *A.Ant*.

Christie's work has continued to address gender politics, through shows such as *A Bic for Her* (2013), *Ungrateful Woman* (2014), and *What Now?* (2018). In addition to using character comedy to address gendered power dynamics, as with the work of clown Elf Lyons and sketch artist Lolly Adefope, women and non-binary comics are increasingly focused on overt body positivity and intersectional identities (such as Sofie Hagen, Mae Martin, Luisa Omielan, Sophie Duker, Suzi Ruffell, Desiree Burch, and Jordan Gray).

Conclusion

In this chapter we have explored how stand-up comedy has been, and continues to be, shaped by privilege. The gendered nature of the spaces of live comedy performance, as well as the content of comic material, have collectively created a hostile environment for women and non-binary comedians while affording space to white men. In the 2020s there is a popular assumption that gender equality within the comedy industry has been achieved, often due to the hyper-visibility of a few predominantly white, middle-class women comics. Where a surface level of change has occurred, this is the tip of the iceberg; it is literally the bit we can see. Structurally, below the surface, the industry still has a long way to go in terms of being inclusive to those from all genders.

At the height of 2017's #MeToo movement, comedians (nationally and internationally) were among those implicated in the sexual abuse and harassment of women in the entertainment industries. In the UK comedy industry that abuse of power is an enduring issue, and power remains mostly with white, middle-class men. Campaigns such as Get Off! Live Comedy have recently been established to prevent sexual harassment through campaigning, support, and resources for producers and promoters.[42] Yet the extent of gender inequity is evident if we follow the money. At the top of the industry, where economic rewards for playing stadiums or arenas are significant, men remain much more visible than women; examples of comics who do very well from stadium work include Russell Howard and Michael McIntyre. Sarah Millican is one of the few women comedians in the UK who has a similar level of visibility, but she does not do stadium shows and cannot rival male stand-ups such as Peter Kay who in 2013 topped the *Mirror*'s 'comedy rich list' with an alleged income of £32.8 million; Millican came in at number 9 with £2 million.[43] Women and non-binary comedians continue to be overwhelmingly confined to the grassroots of the industry where remuneration for creative labour is often insufficient to develop a sustainable career and their precarity leaves them more vulnerable to exploitation and harassment.[44]

It is important to remember that *women were present* at all stages of the development of stand-up comedy, despite the heteropatriarchal environments they have faced. Ever resourceful, to survive within these environments women comedians developed a range of rhetorical and performance strategies to address the gendered power imbalances they experienced on and offstage. These strategies are used to downplay, obscure, or mitigate a gendered reading of their personas by audiences. In a better world it would not be necessary for this kind of gendered power negotiation to occur in any arena, because it places additional pressures and responsibilities on women and non-binary comics to solve a problem within a system they had no role in creating. Gender remains a significant aspect of societal interaction so that acknowledging, playing with, or subverting audiences' gendered expectations within stand-up performance continues to be a necessary and enduring feature of the form.

Notes

1. Judith Butler, *Undoing Gender* (New York: Routledge, 2004), p. 1.
2. Nivedita Menon. *Seeing Like a Feminist* (Haryana, India: Zubaan and Penguin Books India, 2012), p. vii.
3. Oliver Double, *Getting the Joke*, 2nd ed. (London: Bloomsbury, 2014), p. 19.
4. Our use of the words man and woman (without qualifier) within this chapter should be read as inclusive of trans men and trans women, although we acknowledge the additional barriers trans people face.
5. Christopher Hitchens, 'Why Women Aren't Funny', *Vanity Fair*, 1 January 2007, www.vanityfair.com/culture/2007/01/hitchens200701.
6. Regina Barreca, *They Used to Call Me Snow White ... But I Drifted: Women's Strategic Use of Humor* (Hanover: University Press of New England, 1992).
7. Ellie Tomsett, *Stand-Up Comedy and Contemporary Feminisms: Sexism, Stereotypes and Structural Inequalities* (London: Bloomsbury, 2023).
8. Canadian comic Mae Martin provides an example of a successful non-binary comedian working in the UK, Jes Tom provides a US example.
9. https://feministkilljoys.com.
10. Sara Ahmed, *Living a Feminist Life* (Durham, NC: Duke University Press, 2017).
11. Frances Gray, *Women and Laughter* (Charlottesville: University of Virginia Press, 1994), pp. 133–160.
12. Judith Baxter (ed.), *Speaking Out: The Female Voice in Public Contexts* (Basingstoke: Palgrave Macmillan, 2006).
13. Sam Beale, *The Comedy and Legacy of Music Hall Women 1880–1920* (Cham: Palgrave, 2020).
14. Kimberlé Crenshaw, 'Mapping the Margins: Intersectionality, Identity Politics and Violence against Women of Color', *Stanford Law Review*, Vol. 43, No. 6: pp. 1241–1299.
15. Tomsett, *Stand-Up Comedy and Contemporary Feminisms*.
16. Sophie Quirk and Ed Wilson, 'New Alternative Comedy: Productive Crises c.2005-Present', in Oliver Double and Sharon Lockyer (eds), *Alternative Comedy Now and Then* (Cham: Palgrave, 2021), pp. 267–288.
17. Ellie Tomsett, '"Less Dick Jokes": Women-Only Comedy Line-Ups, Audience Expectations and Stereotypes', in Double and Lockyer, *Alternative Comedy Now and Then*, pp. 239–265.
18. Friedman, *Comedy and Distinction*, p. 161.
19. Friedman, *Comedy and Distinction*, p. 152.
20. Gray, *Women and Laughter*, pp. 134–137.
21. Bernard Manning, *Bernard Bites Back* [online video] (Time Artistes Production, Ashton Under Lyme: 1993), www.youtube.com/watch?v=GlKxLuBxozE.
22. Andy Medhurst, *A National Joke: Popular Comedy and English Cultural Identities* (London and New York: Routledge, 2007), pp. 187–203.
23. Alison Clarke, 'Abuse on the Premises: The "Bernard Manning" Case Means Firms Cannot Turn a Blind Eye to Harassment', *The Independent*, 13

November 1996, www.independent.co.uk/news/uk/abuse-premises-1352192.html.
24. 'Jimmy Carr Sparks Fury with Holocaust Joke in Netflix Special', *BBC News*, 5 February 2022, www.bbc.co.uk/news/entertainment-arts-60261876.
25. Gray, *Women and Laughter*, p. 135.
26. Medhurst, *A National Joke*, p. 79.
27. Morwenna Banks and Amanda Swift, *The Joke's on Us: Women in Comedy from Music Hall to the Present* (London: Pandora Press, 1987), pp. 2–5.
28. Banks and Swift, *The Joke's on Us*, p. 43.
29. Gray, *Women and Laughter*, pp. 122–123.
30. Banks and Swift, *The Joke's on Us*, p. 48.
31. Gray, *Women and Laughter*, pp. 123–124.
32. Banks and Swift, *The Joke's on Us*, pp. 25–28.
33. Dawn French, *Dear Fatty* (London: Century, 2008), p. 255; Jennifer Saunders, *Bonkers: My Life in Laughs* (London: Viking, 2013), p. 51.
34. French, *Dear Fatty*, p. 268; Saunders, *Bonkers*, p. 57.
35. Thanks to Oliver Double for this insight.
36. Banks and Swift, *The Joke's on Us*, p. 31.
37. Banks and Swift, *The Joke's on Us*, p. 39.
38. Banks and Swift, *The Joke's on Us*, pp. 31–34.
39. Jo Brand, *Look Back in Hunger: The Autobiography* (London: Headline, 2009), pp. 317–318.
40. Brand, *Look Back in Hunger*, p. 321.
41. Ellie Tomsett, 'Twenty-First Century Fumerist: Bridget Christie and the Backlash against Feminist Comedy', *Comedy Studies*, Vol. 8, No. 1, 2017: p. 59.
42. See https://getofflivecomedy.co.uk/ (accessed 26 April 2023).
43. 'Comedy Rich List: Peter Kay Tops List of UK's Richest Comedians', *Mirror*, 26 May 2013, www.mirror.co.uk/3am/celebrity-news/comedy-rich-list-peter-kay-1911365.
44. Tomsett, *Stand-Up Comedy and Contemporary Feminisms*.

Further Reading

Barreca, Regina, *They Used to Call Me Snow White ... But I Drifted: Women's Strategic Use of Humor* (Hanover: University Press of New England, 1992).
Beale, Sam, *The Comedy and Legacy of Music Hall Women 1880–1920: Brazen Impudence and Boisterous Vulgarity* (Cham: Palgrave Macmillan, 2020).
Gilbert, Joanne R, *Performing Marginality: Humor, Gender and Cultural Critique* (Detroit: Wayne State University Press, 2004).
Gray, Frances, *Women and Laughter* (Charlottesville: University of Virginia Press, 1994).
Mizejewski, Linda and Victoria Sturtevant (eds), *Hysterical: Women in American Comedy* (Austin: Texas University Press, 2017).

Tomsett, Ellie, *Stand-Up Comedy and Contemporary Feminisms: Sexism, Stereotypes and Structural Inequalities* (London: Bloomsbury, 2023).
Willett, Cynthia and Julie Willett, *Uproarious: How Feminist and Other Subversive Comics Speak the Truth* (Minneapolis: Minnesota University Press, 2019).
Wood, Katelyn Hale, *Cracking Up: Black Feminist Comedy in the Twentieth and Twenty-First Century United States* (Iowa City: University of Iowa Press, 2021).

CHAPTER 6

Stand-Up Comedy and Sexuality

Joanne Gilbert

'I had a hard time coming out to my dad 'cause he's Muslim. Now he expects me to get like ten wives – that's a lot of wives. [laughter]'[1] With this joke, Canadian lesbian stand-up comic Sabrina Jalees brings the house down, delighting her audience with a punchline that simultaneously paints her Pakistani father as an enlightened supporter of her gender identity and as a strict adherent to stereotypical Muslim gender norms. In twenty-seven words, Jalees performs her marginality, deftly deploying her comic material to create an incisive and entertaining cultural critique. Standing onstage, eliciting laughter from a room of strangers, Jalees is empowered not only economically (earning a living by telling jokes) but also rhetorically, using lesbianism (the very feature that marginalises her) to punch up or make fun of the dominant culture. Her material subverts the patriarchal power dynamic, playfully calling it into question while foregrounding her sexuality onstage. It is precisely this ability – to disarm through amusing – that distinguishes humour from other rhetorical forms. And humour's function as an 'anti-rhetoric' uniquely equips it to advance agendas and simultaneously disavow its own potency, rendering even the most acerbic critique 'just a joke'.[2]

Although they are considered taboo topics in polite conversation, historically, sex and sexuality have been staples of comedic discourse at least as far back as the Middle Ages, when fools kept by kings amused the court with explicit sexual and scatological references.[3] Indeed, knaves, clowns, and court jesters performed 'naughty' material sure to amuse their audiences, paving the way for their contemporary analogues, today's stand-up comics. Within the long and storied tradition of stand-up comedy, comics from marginalised groups have performed important rhetorical work, using their material in service of cultural critique.[4] Rhetorical postures such as the confrontational 'bitch', the suggestive 'bawd', and the neutral 'reporter' that do not entail comics putting themselves down tend to be prevalent among lesbian comics.[5] As they engage audiences with material that seeks to redress power imbalances, whether through subtle jabs such as Jalees's 'wives' bit or more blatant attacks, lesbian comics create awareness and identification, enlightening their audiences through humour. This chapter provides an analysis of contemporary LGBTQ comics, focusing on the rhetorical functions of LGBTQ stand-up comedy. Specifically, it examines the acts of ten gay, eight lesbian, and two trans comics, revealing the way this discourse educates audiences about LGBTQ culture, critiques homophobia/transphobia, and creates identification and empowerment for performers and audiences alike.

Humour as Education

Beyond its formal function of eliciting laughter, the first rhetorical function of humour evident in the work of LGBTQ comics is to educate their audiences through material ranging from comedic stories to well-placed one-liners. Typically, comics using this strategy focus on language and cultural norms. For example, when discussing her childhood, lesbian comic Fortune Feimster asserts: 'I was considered to be a tomboy back then – which was a more appropriate term for future lesbian. [laughter, applause, and shouts]'[6] Similarly, trans comic, Nori Reed shares that 'I am trans-fat [laughter] … which everyone knows is the most dangerous kind. [laughter] If you're not laughing, you're being transphobic – and also fat-phobic. [laughter]'[7] And devoting significant stage time to consideration of language, gay comic Drew Anderson regales his audience with a story about getting high with his mother, recalling: 'She just looked at me right in the face, and she was like, "Drew, come on – are you a top or are you a bottom?" [laughter and applause] And … I was like, "Mom – I'm actually *verse* [laughter and support] which means sometimes I'm on top, and sometimes I'm on the bottom." And she just paused and looked at me and was like, "So you're a bottom?" [laughter and applause]' Anderson also focuses on language when he discusses the terms gay men use to describe themselves sexually:

> Gay men really like to put ourselves into categories specifically – you know, you've got all the positions – top, bottom, verse – ya know, and then you get into all the animals … bear, seal pup … otter … if I had to describe myself within the gay community, it would be an old golden retriever [laughter] … laid back, slow moving, *gorgeous*, [laughter] loves cock.[8] [laughter]

Finally, lesbian comic Sydnee Washington explains that she is 'femme,' noting: 'Femme means that I dress like I want men to talk to me – but I don't. [laughter]'[9] In these instances, LGBTQ comics illustrate the ability of humour to inform by amusing. Through their discussion of labels used to describe their gender identities and sexual preferences, these performers educate their audiences while eliciting laughter and creating community.

Another way LGBTQ comics educate is by performing material that focuses on norms within LGBTQ culture. Gay comic George Civeris maintains that 'Pride is obviously ... really important ... for all of June this year, I only bought clothing from companies that use LGBT-friendly sweatshops. [laughter]' Later, commenting on this and other actions, he adds: 'Hypocrisy's a very big part of gay culture, so – if you call me out on it – that's hate speech [laughter] ... . I don't think your activism is fully intersectional unless it includes the liberation of multinational conglomerates [laughter and shouts] ... . No matter what gender my kids are, I'm raising them as brands. [laughter]'[10] Playfully explaining the importance of Pride month to the LGBTQ community, Civeris provides a wry commentary on 'woke' culture in general. Employing a similar rhetorical tone, trans comic Jes Tom acknowledges,

> I'm not a lesbian – I just hate men [laughter] ... . I am a non-binary transgender person, which means I am trans, but I don't identify as a punk musician or a spoken word artist. [laughter] As a non-binary transgender person, I feel most affirmed by cis confusion, [laughter] so if anybody didn't get that, thank you – I feel seen. [laughter and applause][11]

Poking fun at trans norms such as alignment with the punk and spoken word scene, Tom makes light of the 'confusion' cis people exhibit when negotiating trans identities as well as of the faux-therapeutic discourse used to communicate empathy, 'I feel seen'.

Ridiculing other norms, lesbian comic Robby Hoffman discusses moving to Los Angeles from Toronto with her girlfriend, noting: 'We packed up a van – moved cross-country – lesbians, obviously. [laughter] I will say the only thing dykier than two lesbians going cross-country together in a van is two lesbians going cross-country in a van with their *cat!* [laughter] ... We brought the cat 'cause I've been a lesbian ten years, and I gotta up the *ante.* [laughter]'[12] Gay comic Josh Sharp also uses norms as a focus, describing his role as a groomsman in a wedding:

> I was emailed ... the instructions on wardrobe and it was a grey suit from Jos A. Bank, and I said, 'Well, there's lines I cannot cross, [laughter] ya know – I suck dick for fun – I can't own anything from Jos A. Bank. Come now. [laughter and support]' So I was like, 'Here's what's gonna happen ... I'm not going to do that, but I'll wear something that to your untrained straight eye feels like I'm wearing the same thing, but I'll know what it really is which is, it won't be grey – it will be slate [laughter] ...

it'll be very expensive, and a Dominican man on the Lower East Side will have tailored it to make my ass look incredible, ya know? [laughter]' So *that* was how I handled that ... trial – that was my act of rebellion – and resistance.[13]

Deftly deploying the stereotype of the gay fashionista, Sharp both instructs his audience regarding the norm, and offers a subtle critique of those who default to this stereotype.

Similarly subtle is the way Sabrina Jalees educates her audience through normalisation. Considering the one disadvantage of her sexual orientation, Jalees bemoans:

> The only thing that sucks about being a lesbian is in order to have a baby that looks half like me and half like my wife, I need my brother's sperm [laughter] .... I want my brother's sperm so that my wife does a handstand, I do a layup, and just pfft – baby! [laughter] ... The gayest move in the WNBA – done! [laughter]

Jalees's buoyant, matter-of-fact delivery normalises this type of artificial insemination, ultimately both teaching her audience and affirming her identity. Although it is impossible to know whether comics actively seek to educate their audiences through performance of material dealing with language and norms unique to LGBTQ culture, audiences are educated regardless of performers' intent. Indeed, the humour of LGBTQ comics educates audiences while providing a subtle critique of both conservative and liberal attitudes towards the LGBTQ community.

Humour as Cultural Critique

The second rhetorical function of LGBTQ humour is to offer blatant – sometimes scathing – critique of homophobic/transphobic culture as it manifests both intentionally and perhaps unwittingly. In this regard, the distinction between the victims (those who appear 'one down') and butts (the actual targets of ridicule) of jokes is key to understanding the subversive potential of comedy-as-cultural critique, and is entirely dependent upon audience identification and interpretation. Although most audiences fail to distinguish between victims and butts – likely because they can be identical – such differentiation is essential to humour serving as more than mere entertainment. The following examples illustrate the relationship between victims and butts of jokes. In her 2020 Netflix special, *3 in the Morning*, lesbian comic Sam Jay upbraids cis women who reject trans women, asserting:

> I hate women that don't embrace trans women ... They're real women ... they're contourin', they're waxin' [laughter] ... they're doin' everything you do ... . We need these super bitches – are you stupid? [laughter] These are our *X-men*. [laughter, shouting, and applause] The world is about to change for us. Get fucking excited! [applause] This is a Goddamned blessing! [laughter and applause][14]

Exhibiting characteristics of the bitch posture, a rhetorical stance that is typically aggressive and confrontational, Jay condemns transphobic sentiment. Although she cloaks the sentiment in comedy, Jay clearly condemns transphobia, and lets her audience know it, rendering victim and butt one and the same.

Discussing the Pulse nightclub shootings in Orlando, gay comic George Civeris provides a counterpoint to Jay's material, mocking the uber-woke rhetoric promulgated by LGBTQ allies. Civeris notes:

> Some people would ... write like, 'Ya know, let's not politicize this tragedy. Ya know, it doesn't matter what race or gender or sexual orientation the victims were or – what happened to them [laughter] – or where it happened [laughter] ... we just need to pray [titters] ... for these genderless, flesh-colored blobs [laughter] who may or may not have experienced some event [laughter] ... in the politically neutral space of congregation. [laughter]'[15]

Offering a pointed critique of both the lip service associated with allyship and the default to prayer intrinsic in the evangelical movement, Civeris offers his audience a victim and butt who again, appear to be the same.

This is not always the case, however; for example, gay comic Josh Sharp openly chides his putatively straight audience, telling them, 'I'm here tryin' to do me, and then I have to get on a plane and fly to the Midwest, and watch y'all dance to "Moves like Jagger," – it's an affront during Pride month. [laughter]' Invoking the stereotypical belief that straight people can't dance, Sharp inserts a dig at the Midwest as well, a region generally thought to be more straightlaced than its coastal counterparts. Although his critique is levied at straight culture, making that culture both victim and butt, Sharp – as a representative of gay culture consumed with appearances – can be construed as a snarky diva, another butt of sorts.

Asian-American, trans comic Jes Tom takes a milder approach, discussing the first time they met their girlfriend's parents:

> I got to meet her parents recently ... I was nervous because they're a little on the conservative side – they don't love the whole queer thing. But she has two older siblings who are both in long-term relationships with white people. And her last relationship before me was a long-term relationship

with a white person, so I walked in, and they were like, 'This is *fine*. [laughter and applause]' I was like, 'I'm a comedian,' They were like, 'Don't say *that* [laughter] – when you are silent and still, you're almost a nice Chinese boy. [laughter]'

In this bit, Tom may be the victim of the joke, but the true butts are the hapless Chinese parents, steeped in traditional values that prevent them from perceiving Tom's intrinsic attributes. Clearly, Tom launches a broader cultural critique, lampooning conservative values.

The context of meeting a significant other's parents for the first time plays a role in several comics' cultural critique through their deft depiction of the fear undergirding stereotypes. Lesbian comic Erin Foley, for instance, describes her conservative, Catholic mother's fear:

> I knew she had this like crazy stereotype in her mind of what my girlfriend was gonna look like, right? Like her worst fear in life is like we'd come home for a holiday, and we'd roll into the driveway in this Ford monster truck. [laughter] And my girlfriend'd get out, ya know, she'd climb out of the truck, and be like, 'Hey Mrs. Foley, my name's Jackie – I'm shagging your daughter. [Spits] [laughter] Oh wow … you got a great house here – it looks real nice. Whoa – hold up – I notice some shingles are loose on the roof. [laughter] Let me go to my truck and get my caulking gun and toolbelt and fix that up for ya. [laughter and applause]'[16]

In this bit, Foley's girlfriend might be the victim being mocked through stereotypical description, but clearly, homophobes and all those who subscribe to such stereotypes are the true butt.

Trans comic Nori Reed is more direct, noting: 'Some people assume I'm kinky … the kinkiest thing about me is I go to Whole Foods [titters] … you give them all your money, they treat you like shit, [laughter] and you bag your own groceries [laughter] … thank you, Daddy. [laughter]' In this joke, Reed both renders ridiculous the notion that all trans people are kinky and playfully insults Whole Foods and its customers, critiquing the natural food culture at large. Consequently, while Reed is the victim, closed-minded conservatives (e.g. those who assume all trans people are kinky) are one butt and health-conscious consumers the other.

Although it is not common for contemporary LGBTQ comics to use self-deprecation in their acts, occasionally they make fun of themselves by mocking their communities. Bob the Drag Queen, for example, maintains: 'Gay guys – we are pigs, we are disgusting. Just because you're gay doesn't mean you stop being fucking nasty as Hell! [titters] … We trade dick pics like trading cards. [laughter]'[17] Interestingly, this particular rhetorical tone – one that casts gay men as both victims and butts – is reminiscent of the popular 'men are pigs' material performed by a number of heterosexual male and female comics as well. Critics such as Michelle Colpean and Meg Tilly warn that humour such as Bob's that traffics in stereotypes risks succumbing to 'weak reflexivity' or 'pseudosatire', as its presentation of ironic discourse devoid of critical commentary risks reproducing rather than dismantling dominant ideologies.[18] Although their discussion focuses on race, Colpean and Tilly's concern can be applied to all marginalising features. A counterpoint to this perspective, however, is the distinction between humour, whose primary goal is to entertain, and polemic, whose primary goal is to attack.

In this vein, Tasmanian lesbian comic Hannah Gadsby uses and ultimately rejects self-deprecation in their groundbreaking show, *Nanette*. Towards the beginning of their performance, Gadsby, whose work has been widely hailed as transformative, confesses, 'I don't think I'm very good at gay. [laughter] I'm not the only one who thinks that [laughter] ... I've been getting a bit of ... negative feedback of late from my people, the lesbians. [laughter]'[19] Later, they ask, 'Do you know what I reckon my problem is? I'm not lesbian enough! [titters]', and follows with the punchline, 'I mean, I keep my hand in [laughter and applause] – bit of lesbian content there [laughter] – I'll be sprinkling it throughout the show. [laughter]' Wondering aloud, 'What sort of comedian can't even make the lesbians laugh? [hesitant laughter]', they respond, 'Every comedian *ever*. [extended laughter and applause]' Through the mild self-deprecation they use, Gadsby constructs self as victim and the lesbian community as butt. By making fun of themself, Gadsby does what many marginalised comics do – they beat the dominant culture to the punch. Research on in-group/out-group distinctions regarding audience interpretation and response to humour affords some insight into the reason for this strategy, suggesting that audiences tend to reject 'punch-down' humour when it is performed by members of the dominant group.[20] As a member of a marginalised group, however, Gadsby's self put-downs engage and amuse an audience familiar with this strategic use of self-deprecation.

Humour as Empowerment

The third and final rhetorical function of humour in the acts of LGBTQ comics is empowerment, specifically that achieved by creating a sense of identification with comics among audience members. Although identification is key to the success of any stand-up comedy, marginalised comics in general, and LGBTQ comics specifically, are strategic about using their experience to empower themselves and their audiences. Not only do they critique the culture at large but they also highlight their own empowerment. Foregrounding sexuality, LGBTQ comics use two strategies that focus on their own actualisation: they speak truth to power, upending hierarchies through humour that at times becomes overtly polemical; and they share their coming-out stories, using humour to describe a pivotal point in their lives. Hannah Gadsby's compelling use of the first strategy is a unique admixture of self-deprecation and polemic as they 'use[s] the style to critique the style.'[21] Confessing to their audience that 'I built a career out of self-deprecating humour … and I don't want to do that anymore', Gadsby shifts from joking to disclosing truths about their life. They ask, 'Do you understand [extended applause] … what self-deprecation means when it comes from somebody who already exists in the margins? It's not humility – it's humiliation', and explain, 'I put myself down in order to speak, in order to seek permission to speak. And I simply will not do that anymore – not to myself or anybody who identifies with me. [extended laughter and cheering] And if that means that my comedy career is over, then so be it.' Gadsby's decision to reject further self-deprecation is a critical moment in both this performance and their career as they move from sharing their coming out as a lesbian early in the performance to disclosing incidents that left them traumatised.

Throughout *Nanette*, Gadsby becomes angrier and more confrontational, sharing a story of being beaten by a homophobic male, and asserting, 'I'm *incorrectly female – I'm incorrect* – and that is a punishable offense'. Ultimately, in their most passionate declaration, after disclosing two other incidences of brutalisation – molestation and rape – they warn, 'There is *nothing stronger* than a broken woman who has *rebuilt herself*.' These powerful lines elicit cheers and thunderous applause, as though the audience is aware that '[w]omen performing stand-up enact a kind of female empowerment that seldom corresponds to their lived experience as women or as comics'.[22] Finally confiding, 'I don't want my story defined by anger', Gadsby implores the audience, 'Please help me take care of my story', inviting them to share responsibility for ensuring that marginalised voices are heard.

Clearly, Gadsby's audience is galvanised in its support, an ideal situation for any performer. However, the more narrowly defined an audience for humour is, the more ideologically aligned performer and audience will be and the more likely it is that humour will become polemical.[23] This raises questions about the role of humour in general: is it necessarily the job of humour to call people to action? Should humour be deployed to change audience opinion? Are we expecting too much from stand-up comedy? After all, these are the *jokes*, folks! Labelling *Nanette* 'a feminist-queer metacommentary on comedy', Rebecca Krefting notes that Gadsby's departure from the traditional stand-up form 'has prompted some to question whether *Nanette* counts as comedy at all'.[24]

Although Gadsby is certainly unique in their presentation, offering a performance that seems more like a one-person show than traditional stand-up (and this is echoed in their 2020 Netflix special, *Douglas*, in which they discuss living as a person with ADHD and autism), other LGBTQ comics occasionally infuse their acts with political commentary or even rants. For example, in a bit that becomes increasingly political, after discussing her coming-out experience, Fortune Feimster exhorts her audience, 'The best gift that you guys as parents can give your kids is to accept them for who they are, [support, shouts, and extended applause]' and follows this with the punchline, 'It is honestly the best gift – that and cash. [laughter and applause]' Performing even more explicitly political material, gay Black comic Alex English discusses a Queer/Trans/Black Lives Matter protest where everyone was masked, asking, 'Do you have any idea how fantastic it feels to finally navigate a queer space without recognizing somebody I fucked? [laughter]' English maintains his aggressive tone, asserting, 'I refuse to date a white dude that doesn't have privilege … hooking up with a white guy that doesn't have privilege is like dating an empty ATM. [laughter]'[25] Like Feimster, he caps off a political bit (several jokes on a particular topic) with a punchline, but in this case he punches up.

Bob the Drag Queen is more blatant about speaking truth to power, exulting, 'This is best time in the world to be queer!' Revelling in his gender identity, Bob proclaims:

> Being queer is the best fucking thing ever to happen to me … . Everyone knows nowadays you can't say anything [shouts] remotely sideways about queers … . If you even slightly inconvenience a queer person on TV, [titters] one hundred male ballet dancers will show up outside your fucking job [laughter] and pas de bourrée until you come downstairs and apologize! [laughter, shouting, support, and applause]

Also discussing identity, Sam Jay departs from her comic material when she declares, 'It's OK to be uncomfortable, it's OK to be confused, it's not OK to act like people shouldn't have the same rights as you – that's what's *not* OK! [shouts and applause]' And in a playful take on political humour, gay comic Jaboukie Young-White assesses his appearance and announces, 'On a one to ten scale, I don't think I could model – but I could definitely end a Republican senator's career. [shouts, laughter, and extended applause]'[26]

Most important is the way LGBTQ comics use their coming-out stories as both a means of creating identification and a source of empowerment for themselves and their communities. By engaging in 'affective alliance building',[27] this material helps comics connect with their audiences. Sam Jay begins her discussion by sharing, 'I didn't think I didn't like dicks – I just thought, you know, keep sucking these dicks – concentrate, work harder! [laughter] Focus on the dicks you're sucking – visualize [laughter] – you'll fucking get there! [laughter]' Following this joke, she becomes introspective, asserting, 'That's why representation matters, Man. It does – it matters. You need to see yourself in the fucking world.' Returning to jokes, she notes, 'I'm from Boston, Bro. We didn't have Black dykes ... . [laughter] We had white dykes and they drove Subarus and they had long armpit hair. [laughter] And I was like "No ... [laughter] that's not what I am [laughter] – I'm not that". [laughter]'

Fortune Feimster also describes the need for representation:

> I became a debutante for my mom and then I was presented to society in what they call a 'coming-out party. [laughter and applause]' It just happened to be the *wrong* coming-out party. [laughter] It would be quite a few years before I realized that I was gay – which is *bonkers* because I have had this haircut since I was five years old. [laughter and applause] My hair knew I was gay – *I* didn't [laughter] ... . I look back at that time in college and I couldn't believe that I wasn't out. But honestly, it wasn't like I was in the closet, and I was hiding – I just didn't see myself represented in the world. Back then ... there was no YouTube, there was no *Will and Grace*, no *Frozen* [laughter] – nothing that I could relate to. Turns out representation matters. [shouts, support, and extended applause]

Consistently employing a lighter rhetorical tone than either Jay or Gadsby, Feimster addresses the same issues but in a more playful manner. Focusing on the moment she came out, she recalls, 'I say out loud for the first time in my entire life, I go: "Oh. My. God – I'm *gay!*" [laughter, shouts, support, and extended applause] And I came to that conclusion from watching a Lifetime movie! [loud laughter and applause]' Feimster remembers telling her brothers, acknowledging:

> I'm so nervous. I'm like ... 'Guys ... I've gotta tell you something ... I'm gay.' And my brothers go, 'Duh.' ... [laughter and applause] And I said, 'Well, just out of curiosity ... what made you think I was gay this whole time?' And one of my brothers goes, 'Well, once when you were 7, you got hit with a soccer ball, and you yelled, 'Ow – my dick! [extended laughter and applause]'

When they first describe coming out to their mom, Hannah Gadsby notes, 'My mom is very funny', explaining that:

> Her response to me coming out when I first told her that I was a little bit lesbian [laughter] ... 'Oh Hannah [laughter] – why did you have to tell me *that*? That's not something *I* need to know! [laughter] I mean, what if I told you I was a *murderer*? [laughter]' ... It's a fair call – murderer, [laughter] *murderer* – you would hope that's a phase. [laughter, applause, and whistles]

Later in the performance, after telling the audience that they are quitting comedy, Gadsby discloses, 'When I came out of the closet, I didn't have any jokes. The only thing I knew how to do ... was to be invisible and to hate myself.' They add, 'It took me another ten years to understand that I was allowed to take up space in the world, but by then, I'd sealed it off into jokes like it was no big deal.' As discussed earlier, Gadsby offers a performance that is only part stand-up comedy; when revealing their pain, they are dead serious, and the audience reacts accordingly. For Gadsby, and to an extent for Jay, the shift from humour to angst allows audiences to identify in deep and significant ways. The opportunity to share outrage and anguish with their audiences empowers these comics in a way that solely telling jokes does not.

Even in joke form, however, coming-out stories create identification and empowerment. For instance, deploying the same trope used by Feimster of being the last to know, Erin Foley confides:

> Apparently, for a long ... chunk of time, I had no idea I was gay, but everyone else knew [laughter] – which was awkward ... [laughter and applause] They were like, 'Erin, we were waiting for you to be comfortable, talk about it, come out on your own time ... ' – which was supercool, but I feel like if someone had given me a little push in that direction, [titters] it would have saved me ten years of horrible dates with men and low self-esteem, but whatever! [laughter]

Similarly, gay comic DeWayne Perkins recalls:

> I came out when I was 17, but I knew that coming out risked losing people that were close to me ... . I was too afraid to tell my sisters in person, so I just sent them a group text, and all it said was, 'Hey Guys – I'm gay.' Then one of them wrote back, 'Yeah – that makes sense. [laughter]' Then I wrote back, 'What is that supposed to mean? [laughter]' Then she wrote, 'You wear a lot of cowboy boots in the summer.' ... [laughter] I was so mad 'cause I was expecting them to abandon me. I was gonna use that trauma to create art in the future. [laughter][28]

And gay comic John Early shares: 'I think my parents first knew I was gay when I was five years old ... they used to take me to Vanderbilt University basketball games … at the women's games, I'd be sobbing … [crying] "It's just fucking incredible to see women coming together like this … [applause and laughter] – fighting for a common cause if that makes any fucking sense." [laughter] That's how they knew.'[29]

A final trope used frequently in LGBTQ comics' coming-out stories is one featuring the discomfort and negative reactions of family. Sabrina Jalees recalls, 'I wanted to come out to my Muslim family for a long time, but my dad was always like, "Shhh – keep it a secret, Man. [laughter] Secrets are *cool*." [laughter] I was like, "Dad, I'm married now – what's your five-year plan with this secret?" [laughter]' Gay comic, Solomon Georgio reveals:

> I came out when I was 18 – back in the year 2000, ya know, before it was cool. [titters] I told my parents I was gay … . They're both … very traditional African immigrants, so I don't recommend doing that. [laughter] Write them a letter – they can't read [laughter] … . My dad got very upset – I don't know whether it was because I told them I was gay or that I sang the entirety of 'Papa Don't Preach' immediately afterwards [laughter] … . But he got very mad, and he said the most clichéd thing you can say in that situation. He said, 'God hates gay people. [titters]' I was like, 'Tight [laughter] – I'm an atheist. [laughter, shouts, and applause]'[30]

Another description of parental anger comes from gay, Asian-American comic Joel Kim Booster who tells his audience, 'as Christian as my parents are, they did not take it super well when I came out of the closet – mostly because I did not come out of the closet. They read my journal when I was 17.' He further explains, 'It was rough because at that point in my life, my journal was less of like an introspective thoughts and dreams journal, and more of just a Buzzfeed list of guys' dicks I was sucking … [laughter]'[31] And Jaboukie Young-White remembers:

> I ended up coming out to my family not too long ago … My dad probably took it the hardest at first. My dad was like, 'Oh my God, I can't believe my son is gay – I could have a stroke, I could have a heart attack.' And I was like, 'You're being such a fucking queen right now. [laughter and applause] It's kind of my *moment* – and you're hogging the spotlight, so fall back. [laughter]' … The funniest thing that my dad said though … he was like … 'You ask your son to go mow the lawn, and he just decides to be *gay*. [laughter and applause]' And like, I wanted to be mad, but that's *exactly* what happened, [laughter] honestly. [shrieks, loud laughter, and applause] He asked me one too many times, and I was like, 'I'm gonna go suck a *dick* [laughter] … I fucking *hate* it here! [laughter]' My mom was the polar opposite though … . She texted me and she was like, 'I love my gay son. [laughter]' And then she started saying shit like, 'I don't know – maybe *I'm*

gay. [laughter, shrieks, and applause] I love my friends. [laughter] Me and Sandra have a great relationship – maybe we can make something work – I don't know. [laughter]'

Finally, Black lesbian comic Wanda Sykes offers a brilliant comparison in this now-classic bit:

> It's harder being gay than it is being Black. It is because there's some things [applause] ... that I had to do as gay that I didn't have to do as Black. I didn't have to come out Black! [thunderous laughter and applause] I didn't have to sit my parents down and tell them about my Blackness. [laughter] I didn't have to sit them down – 'Mom, Dad – I gotta tell ya'll something [laughter] – I hope you still love me [laughter] – I'm jus' gonna say it [titters] – Mom, Dad – I'm Black. [laughter]' [In her mother's voice] 'What? What did she jus' say? [laughter] Oh Lawd, Jesus – she didn't say Black Lawd, did she say Black?' 'Mom I'm Black.' 'Oh no Lawd Jesus [laughter and applause] ... anything but Black, Jesus [laughter and applause] – give her cancer, Lawd, give her cancer [laughter and applause] – anything but Black, Lawd. [laughter]' ... 'Mom ... I'm Black ... that's just how it is.' 'No – you know what – you been hangin' around Black people [laughter and applause] ... and they got you thinkin' you Black [laughter] – they twisted your mind. [laughter]' ... 'No, Mom ... I'm Black – that's just ... how it is.' 'What did I do? [laughter] What did I do? [laughter] I knew I shouldn't have let you watch *Soul Train* ... . [thunderous laughter and applause]'[32]

Because Sykes is neither confrontational nor threatening in her rhetorical style, she can lambast homophobia through this parodic coming-out story. Comics such as Sykes are successful precisely because audiences perceive their onstage and offstage personas to be one and the same.[33] Whether they are, in fact, the same is irrelevant; the perception that a comic is exclusively performing autobiographical material helps audiences trust the performer and, consequently, laugh appreciatively at material they perceive to be true.

Clearly, LGBTQ comics use their coming-out stories to create identification and empowerment, critiquing both overt and unconscious homophobia along the way. This rhetorical function of LGBTQ humour is critical as it creates a space within which performer and audience connect and, through laughter, create a community of shared values. Coming out stories matter in this context because not only do they provide an opportunity for this type of connection but they also enable comics to personalise the political – to offer audiences a discourse that simultaneously advances agendas and entertains, creates awareness, and amuses – a feat only humour can accomplish.

The rhetorical functions of humour in the performances of contemporary LGBTQ comics – to educate audiences about LGBTQ culture via discussion of language and norms, to critique homophobic/transphobic culture by both mocking and enacting stereotypes, and to create identification and empowerment by speaking truth to power and sharing coming-out stories – are key to understanding how humour enables marginalised voices to be heard. By providing a context for performing their marginality, humour allows LGBTQ comics to foreground their sexuality and to lampoon the dominant culture, all in the service of a good laugh.

Notes

1. Sabrina Jalees, *Comedy Central Stand-Up* [online video], www.youtube.com/watch?v=fS4ZNTELU9k.
2. Joanne R. Gilbert, *Performing Marginality: Humour, Gender, and Cultural Critique* (Detroit: Wayne State University Press, 2004), p. 12.
3. Chapter 2 of my book, *Performing Marginality*, provides a history of stand-up comedy; see specifically p. 44.
4. Situating contemporary stand-up comics within this historical tradition, *Performing Marginality* focuses on five rhetorical postures female comics assume onstage: the kid, the bawd, the bitch, the whiner, and the reporter. Of these, the bawd is the type most associated with blatant sensuality and sexual suggestiveness. Trafficking in material that ranges from innuendo to graphic description, the bawd intimidates audiences through her overtly sexual demeanor.
5. Joanne Gilbert, 'Lesbian Stand-Up Comics and the Politics of Laughter', in Peter Dickinson, Anne Higgins, Paul Matthew St Pierre, Diana Solomon, and Sean Zwagerman (eds), *Women and Comedy: History, Theory, Practice* (Lanham, MD: Farleigh Dickinson Press, co-published with Rowman & Littlefield, 2014), pp. 185–197.
6. Fortune Feimster, *Sweet and Salty* [online video] (USA: Netflix).
7. Nori Reed, *All Jane Comedy Festival* [online video], www.youtube.com/watch?v=AjjjRYSyj4o.
8. Drew Anderson, *Comedy at the Knitting Factory* [online video], www.youtube.com/watch?v=DkKDYYwodOU.
9. Sydnee Washington, *Comedy Central Stand-Up* [online video], www.youtube.com/watch?v=MXP7wsIWlJw.
10. George Civeris, *Comedy Central Stand-Up* [online video], www.youtube.com/watch?v=CD3Itv73zCs.
11. Jes Tom, *Open Flame at Littlefield* [online video], www.youtube.com/watch?v=vy1TuPo_B3Y.
12. Robby Hoffman, *Just for Laughs Toronto* [online video], www.youtube.com/watch?v=mL8rZf2fZYY.

13. Josh Sharp, *Comedy Central, This Week at the Comedy Cellar* [online video], www.youtube.com/watch?v=3YTgq5hRndY.
14. Sam Jay, *3 in the Morning* [online video] (USA: Netflix).
15. George Civeris, MoveOn.org, Facebook [online video], https://m.facebook.com/watch/?v=10153795917405493&_rdr.
16. Erin Foley, *Comedy Central Stand-Up* [online video], www.youtube.com/watch?v=Vyc-64QzP-k.
17. Bob the Drag Queen, *Comedy Central Stand-Up* [online video], www.youtube.com/watch?v=smOaqKhs_k4.
18. Michelle Colpean and Meg Tully, 'Not Just a Joke: Tina Fey, Amy Schumer, and the Weak Reflexivity of White Feminist Comedy', *Women's Studies in Communication*, Vol. 42, No. 2, 2019: pp. 162, 164.
19. Hannah Gadsby, *Nanette* [online video] (USA: Netflix).
20. S. Katherine Cooper, 'What's So Funny? Audiences of Women's Stand-Up Comedy and Layered Referential Viewing: Exploring Identity and Power', *Communication Review*, Vol. 22, No. 2, 2019: pp. 91–116.
21. Rebecca Krefting, 'Hannah Gadsby: On the Limits of Satire', *Studies in American Humour*, Vol. 5, No. 1, 2019: p. 94.
22. Rebecca Krefting, 'Hannah Gadsby Stands Down: Feminist Comedy Studies', *JCMS: Journal of Cinema & Media Studies*, Vol. 58, No. 3, 2019: pp. 167, 165, http://search.ebscohost.com/login.aspx?direct=true&db=a9h&AN=136582423&site=ehost-live.
23. William Howell, 'Judgments, Corrections, and Audiences: Amy Schumer's Strategies for Narrowcast Satire', *Studies in American Humour*, Vol. 5, No. 1, 2019: pp. 70–92.
24. Discussing Gadsby's awareness that male comics can use anger without anyone questioning whether they are doing comedy, Krefting asserts that 'men's anger counts as humour, while women's humour counts as anger'. Krefting, 'Hannah Gadsby: On the Limits of Satire', p. 100.
25. Alex English, *Comedy Central Tight Five with Ilana Glazer* [online video], www.youtube.com/watch?v=4Ru_73OZ7I4.
26. Jaboukie Young-White, *Comedy Central Stand-Up* [online video], www.youtube.com/watch?v=o_vDg_xaIVk.
27. Adam Carter, '"Essex Girls" in the Comedy Club: Stand-Up, Ridicule and "Value Struggles"', *European Journal of Cultural Studies*, Vol. 22, No. 5: p. 771.
28. Dewayne Perkins, *Comedy Central Stand-Up* [online video], www.youtube.com/watch?v=TGXS5rjuy-c.
29. John Early, *Comedy Central Stand-Up* [online video], www.youtube.com/watch?v=h-IPM2qZGoE.
30. Solomon Georgio, *Comedy Central Stand-Up* [online video], www.youtube.com/watch?v=9jZWeDlWuOI.
31. Joel Kim Booster, *Comedy Central Stand-Up* [online video], www.youtube.com/watch?v=IzYJCqD117A.
32. Wanda Sykes, *I'ma Be Me* [online video] (USA: HBO).

33. Joanne Gilbert, 'Laughs Last: Gender, Power, and Comic Identity', in Louise Peacock (ed.), *A Cultural History of Comedy in the Modern Age* (London: Bloomsbury Academic, 2020) pp. 87–111.

Further Reading

Gilbert, Joanne R., *Performing Marginality: Humor, Gender and Cultural Critique* (Detroit: Wayne State University Press, 2004).
Gilbert, Joanne, 'Laughs Last: Gender, Power, and Comic Identity', in Louise Peacock (ed.), *A Cultural History of Comedy in the Modern Age* (London: Bloomsbury Academic, 2020), pp. 87–111.
Gilbert, Joanne, 'Lesbian Stand-Up Comics and the Politics of Laughter', in Peter Dickinson, Anne Higgins, Paul Matthew St Pierre, Diana Solomon, and Sean Zwagerman (eds), *Women and Comedy: History, Theory, Practice* (Lanham, MD: Farleigh Dickinson Press, co-published with Rowman & Littlefield, 2014), pp. 185–197.
Hennefeld, Maggie, Annie Berke, and Michael Rennett, 'In Focus: What's So Funny about Comedy and Humour Studies? Introduction', *JCMS: Journal of Cinema and Media Studies*, Vol. 58, No. 3, 2019: p. 138.
Krefting, Rebecca, 'Hannah Gadsby Stands Down: Feminist Comedy Studies', *JCMS: Journal of Cinema & Media Studies*, Vol. 58, No. 3, 2019: pp. 165–170.
Krefting, Rebecca, 'Hannah Gadsby: On the Limits of Satire', *Studies in American Humour*, Vol. 5, No. 1, 2019: pp. 93–102.
Willett, Cynthia and Julie Willett, *Uproarious: How Feminist and Other Subversive Comics Speak the Truth* (Minneapolis: Minnesota University Press, 2019).

CHAPTER 7

Laugh No Limit
Black Stand-Up Comedy

J Finley

Historical and Cultural Context of Black Stand-Up Comedy

The African American comic tradition is traceable to the Middle Passage, the journey taken by enslaved Africans on slave ships from the African continent to the Americas from the seventeenth to the nineteenth century. The Middle Passage represented a break from past cultural and social systems, yet enslaved Africans transformed elements of old and new ways of using language, stories, and other cultural expressions, forming what would become the distinctive traditions of African American humour. Black people in the USA have forged a unique and dynamic humour that has functioned to keep spirits lifted under the harshest of conditions.

Early African American humour functioned as a method of cultural formation, an in-group way of communicating based on the specific needs and experiences of the enslaved community, and was often incomprehensible to outsiders. Enslaved people employed Black folk humour, steeped in Black linguistic practices, to orally transmit social values and history, to entertain and educate the community, and to open space for resistance to racial oppression in ways that did not overtly threaten white people. The in-group quality of Black folk humour that emerged during the period of enslavement also enabled Black people to experience embodied joy and the social pleasure of connection engendered in the community of laughter.

Black folk humour is the foundation of contemporary African American comedy, including elements such as trickster tales in which animal characters are given human qualities in stories that mask Black resistance to oppression, and sometimes even fleeting moments of comedic revenge at the expense of the dominating class. Black folk humour also employs everyday Black cultural expressions, especially African American vernacular English and body language, such as the rolling of the eyes. Ritual insults have been a fundamental form of Black humour, from children 'playing the dozens' to hip-hop artists engaging in rap battles and roasts, which are playful rituals of insult humour where the person with the most devastating insult wins. Each of these elements incorporates the act of signifyin(g), the most fundamental trope of African American cultural expression, which means to take the language or expression that is available and transform its meaning by way of embellishment, metaphor, and/or simile.[1] Signifyin(g) has historically worked to create an in-group Black identity, a sense of pleasure rooted in the collective laughter of those in the know.

The subtleties of in-group Black humour, along with ideas about enslaved Africans as natural entertainers, helped cement the popular image of the enslaved people as happy, docile clowns who were content with being enslaved. In public discourse during the early nineteenth century, Blackness came to be synonymous with the clown, and the Black comic mask that had been a private tool for survival and resistance for enslaved people – playing the fool – became a source of derision and ridicule in American popular culture. The image of the happy, laughing slave, embodied in the smiling 'Sambo' caricature, or the buffoonish 'Zip Coon' who was fast-talking and free but too ignorant to understand his abject condition, became deeply entrenched stereotypes and reinforced to white slaveholders (and the beneficiaries of the ideology of white supremacy) the idea that slavery was a beneficial and necessary social and economic system.

Black(face) Minstrelsy

Though the origin story of blackface minstrelsy is a site of contestation, scholars agree that the quintessentially American genre has roots in the working-class enclaves of mid nineteenth-century northern American cities, especially New York City. For example, the most popular, but apocryphal, narrative of blackface's birth holds Thomas D. Rice, a white stage actor, as the originator. Around 1828, Rice purportedly saw a physically disabled Black man singing and performing a dance as he worked: 'Wheel about and turnabout and do just so, every time I wheel about I jump Jim Crow.' Fascinated by the strange performance and eager to make a name for himself, the story goes that Rice bought the man's clothes, memorised the song and dance, and began to exaggerate and imitate the performance on stage for white audiences.

However, scholar W. T. Lhamon, Jr has convincingly shown that it was the relative interracial intimacy between white and Black people, both in everyday life and in the popular entertainment venues they patronised together in theatre culture between the USA and the UK, that created the opportunity for blackface minstrelsy to flourish and thrive. As Lhamon notes: 'Rice and his audience found the seeds of blackface in transactions of fascination among Africans and Europeans circulating in the Atlantic, sharing gestures within unequal and exploitative political situations that were continually changing.'[2] The profane, rowdy atmosphere of the performances delighted and entertained the audiences so much that by the 1840s, blackface minstrelsy had become America's favourite pastime. White actors used burned cork to black their faces and exaggerated stereotypical features associated with Blackness (large red lips and bugged-out eyes), cementing the image of Black people as strange, funny, folksy, ignorant – the 'coon' image.

The image of the shucking-and-jiving Black person that began circulating in the nineteenth century became a mainstay of American popular culture. Before the Emancipation Proclamation in 1863, very few Black people had gained access to the stage, but with freedom creeping closer, Black comics emerged in their own versions of minstrelsy performances around 1855, and even though they were already Black, they also wore burned cork on their faces. Many Black minstrelsy troupes became popular, and even though their performances of degrading stereotypes were often as derogatory as those of white minstrels, Black comics had become part of the fabric of American popular culture, and performing gave hundreds, if not thousands, of African Americans new opportunities for travelling and economic mobility that had been denied them during slavery. Blackface minstrelsy made comedy and musical performance a viable career option for Black people in the late nineteenth and early twentieth centuries.

The TOBA Circuit and the Apollo Theatre: Modern Black Stand-Up Comedy

In the early twentieth century, Black audiences, especially in the South, were turning out for performances put on by all-Black revues. This caught the attention of white club owners, specifically, F. A. Barrasso, the Memphis businessman who founded the Theatre Owners Booking Association, or TOBA. More popularly known as 'The Chitlin' Circuit', Black performers would travel around the South (and later the North), performing to all-Black audiences. Crucially, these venues afforded new opportunities beyond 'playing the coon' like the minstrel shows, and the Chitlin' Circuit was a hotbed for the development and professionalisation of Black folk humour. Important stand-up comics who launched their careers here include Jackie 'Moms' Mabley, Slappy White, Butterbeans and Susie, Pigmeat Markham, Nipsey Russell, and a host of others who would emerge in the 1940s and 1950s. TOBA comedy was geared towards working-class Black people who were familiar with the tones, rhythms, and styles of Black folk humour.

The Great Depression took away the economic base of the Chitlin' Circuit in the South and many venues closed because patrons could no longer afford leisurely entertainments, and the centre of Black comedy shifted to the North – Harlem in New York City in particular – and its crown jewel was the Apollo Theatre. Well-known acts performed there, but Wednesday was always amateur night, where the prize for winning was one's very own weeklong show. The influence of the sensibility of the Chitlin' Circuit was noticeable at the Apollo, as performers began to infuse their humour with social and political critique, often directed at Southern racism. The master of ceremonies of the shows had the opportunity to address the audience directly, prefiguring the more contemporary style of stand-up comedy where performers spoke directly to their audience instead of performing skits. Jackie 'Moms' Mabley, whose career spanned six decades until her death in 1974, was one of the first Black comedians to speak directly to her audience in the monologue style of stand-up comedy that is recognisable today, often targeting Southern racism or using her grandmotherly persona as a foil to talk about more taboo topics. Mabley often targeted racism in the South, joking, 'Now they want me to go to New Orleans ... It'll be Old Orleans 'fore I get down there. The Greyhound ain't goin' take me down there and the bloodhounds run me back, I'll tell you that.'[3]

The Rise of Contemporary Black Stand-Up Comedy

By the mid-1950s, a societal push for racial integration was gaining traction in the USA, but comedy remained segregated. White comics such as Lenny Bruce and Mort Sahl began addressing more serious themes in their performances, taking on politics, government, and race and speaking to their audiences without theatrical pretence. At this point, satire became part of the American stand-up comic tradition. Black comics such as Godfrey Cambridge and Nipsey Russell followed their lead and performed to mixed audiences, dressed in suits and ties, speaking Standard English, and avoiding old tropes of Black folk humour to project more updated images of Black people into popular culture. Other Black comics preferred to perform for a Black, working-class audience and steeped their routines in vernacular language and cultural touchstones. Comics such as Mabley, Redd Foxx, and LaWanda Page were raunchier and more irreverent on the stage. What both groups of Black comics shared, however, was a leaving behind of the coon, or 'Sambo' stereotype, and characters that conformed to racist expectations of Black behaviour and speech.

In January of 1961, Dick Gregory became the first Black comic to headline a stand-up show for a white audience, in the Playboy Club of Chicago. Although he talked about American racism, his humour was non-threatening, and he used irony and satire to make his routines palatable to white audiences. Gregory opened the door for others, such as Bill Cosby, whose non-racial and innocuous story-based routines became wildly popular among white audiences.[4] Also in the 1970s, Clerow 'Flip' Wilson came up from the ranks of the Chitlin' Circuit to become the first Black man to host a variety show on a major television network.

Originally following in the footsteps of Bill Cosby, Richard Pryor went on a tour of the late night shows. After a trip to Berkeley, California, and exposure to Black Nationalism and the countercultural movements of the late 1960s (through his friend and fellow stand-up comic Paul Mooney), Pryor became politically conscious about white supremacy and anti-Black racism. At that point, he rejected the Cosby-esque sanitisation of Black humour for white consumption. Instead, Pryor infused his performances with Black urban street slang, and embodied the street savvy Black man, satisfying America's desire to see Black comedians perform authentically Black language, culture, and style. With a mercurial rise to fame and fortune in the mid-1970s, Pryor was a trail-blazer who paved the way for the next several generations of Black stand-ups who would emulate his unapologetic, irreverent, and hyper-masculine style.

The mantle of the pre-eminent Black comic was passed on to Eddie Murphy in the early 1980s. He was heavily influenced by Pryor's irreverence and machismo and was also a gifted impersonator and sketch comic. Like Murphy, Whoopi Goldberg's ascent to fame was helped along by her character work in her stand-up routines, and she touched on taboos such as abortion and colour prejudice among African Americans that broke barriers for women, along with Black comics. Murphy and Goldberg constructed comic personae with wide appeal that were still identifiably Black – this facilitated their crossing over to become entertainers and actors, and not stand-up comics alone. The 1980s saw a boom of Black stand-up comedians performing in all-Black comedy clubs across the nation, from Los Angeles to New York. Among those who made names for themselves as professional comics were Robert Townsend, Arsenio Hall, Marsha Warfield, the Wayans family, Danitra Vance, Robin Harris, Damon Wayans, Sinbad, and Thea Vidale.

Hip-Hop Comedy: The 1990s and 2000s

The 1990s transformed Black stand-up comedy. Black people were on television and in films more than they had ever been before, all-Black comedy clubs were booming, and hip-hop culture was becoming mainstream. *Def Comedy Jam* (HBO 1992–1997) established a crucial link between hip-hop culture and Black comedy. The show was created by Russell Simmons, the co-founder of the record label Def Jam Recordings, associated with some of the most influential hip-hop artists of the era, such as Public Enemy, LL Cool J, Method Man, and Foxy Brown. Hip-hop artists were often shown sitting in the audience on *Def Comedy Jam*, foregrounding the connection between the genres. Along with *Comic View* (BET 1992–2008), Black stand-up performances were characterised by subjects of embodied pleasures, irreverent socio-political critique, explicit, unapologetic Black language, and a mood of fun. For example, talking about the Rodney King beating at the hands of the LAPD, Eddie Griffin made light of the incredibly serious situation, joking on *Def Comedy Jam* about King receiving a multi-million-dollar settlement for the beating he endured. 'I'm *looking* to get fucked up [laughter]', Griffin quipped. 'Whoop my ass gimme my cash! [laughter and applause]'[5] These showcase programmes had an urban working-class sensibility and gave young Black stand-ups a platform on which to display their talent and speak their truths. Household names such as Martin Lawrence, Chris Rock, Dave Chappelle, Adele Givens, Tracy Morgan, and Bernie Mac got their big breaks there. Despite its popularity, this brand of urban Black comedy was not without its detractors. Critics complained that it harked back to minstrelsy and reinforced stereotypes of Black people as ignorant, lazy, hypersexual buffoons.

Despite criticisms, several Black stand-up comics managed to cross over to the mainstream and appeal to a larger audience during the 1990s. Chris Rock became a comedy superstar during the 1990s with his HBO comedy specials that gained him international acclaim and recognition as one of the American comedy greats. Rock's comedy was unapologetically Black in language, style, and themes. He gained mass appeal because of how his biting satire and political critiques not only targeted white racism but also poked fun at the contradictions and problems within Black communities and Black culture. 'Wealth is empowering', Rock jokes in *Never Scared*, his HBO special from 2004. 'Wealth can uplift communities from poverty, ok? A white man gets wealthy, he builds Wal-Marts and makes other white people have some motherfucking money. A brother gets rich, he buys some motherfucking jewellery, ok? [laughter and applause]'[6] Chris

Rock's comic persona popularised an old convention of Black humour, which was the tendency towards revealing truths about American society and Black culture that were uncomfortable, but in an entertaining way.

Dave Chappelle followed Chris Rock's success in the late 1990s and 2000s, using his stand-up comedy to talk about race and racism in the USA. Like Rock, Chappelle also poked fun at aspects of Black culture that he perceived as contradictory, foolish, or outrageous. Chappelle targeted hip-hop culture and simultaneously revealed inconsistencies while also celebrating the art form with his keen skills as a mimic and broad knowledge of the culture. In one iconic bit that turned into a full sketch, Chappelle imitates Atlanta rapper Lil' Jon. 'His music gets me so AMPED! [applause].' A video of Lil' Jon appears where the rapper repeats his tagline 'Okay! What?!' Chappelle jokes, 'That's all he says in the whole song! [laughter and applause] "Yeaah!" [laughter] Okaay! [laughter] That's all he ever says in any song! [laughter]'[7] Chappelle's success landed him one of the most lucrative television show series in history on the *Comedy Central* network, which he turned down.

Laugh No Limit: Black Stand-Up in the Afrofuture

Today, Black stand-up comedy is as diverse as the Black population in the USA. Black comics have been uniquely positioned to use the stage to not only sooth away the pain and tragedy of what it has meant in certain periods of American history to be Black, but also to ruminate on and reveal the possibilities of what Blackness can mean. Comics such as Kevin Hart and Hannibal Buress have made their professional careers through comedy focused on their personal insecurities. Wanda Sykes' experiences as a lesbian and mother are a testament to the different Black experiences contemporary Black comics bring to the stage. Black comedy has been a foundation upon which to reveal realities of Black life and make those realities accessible and entertaining to an increasingly global audience.

Audiences have typically expected Black comedians to entertain and amuse them, often at the expense of reinforcing stereotypes that reify racist, homophobic, or misogynistic tropes that have been used as tools of marginalisation. Or Black comedians have been expected to use comedic material that leaves little room for imagining Black experiences outside of those sanctioned in pop cultural discourse, or to express individual and collective ideas of liberation that do not conform to established narratives of the long Black freedom struggle. However, the consumption of Black stand-up has expanded, and spectators have become more attuned to and accepting of more nuanced, elastic ideas of who Black stand-ups can be, from the quirky and depressed, to the awkward and surrealist. Moreover, what they can discuss onstage is no longer required to adhere to traditional stylistic, topical, and historical discourses of Blackness and 'the Black experience'. Yet Black stand-up material has remained a site for amusement and pleasure, resisting forms of domination, a technique for seeking comedic revenge, and a place where Black people engage in ritual forms of play.

In the twenty-first century, stand-up comedy has become a technology enabling contemporary Black comics to orient themselves and their audiences towards something resembling liberation. Blackness is constructed by individuals and collectives through historical narratives, contemporary stories, and jokes about what it means to be Black within a given geographical, cultural, and historical context. Cultural institutions such as stand-up comedy are powerful sites for the circulation of these discourses, both in terms of the perpetuation of stereotypes and beliefs about the meanings and function of Blackness, and the expansion and transformation of them. Stand-up comedy is a site for those discourses to be upheld and challenged, sometimes simultaneously. Indeed, stand-up is a site where contemporary Black comics create unfettered worlds, where not all Black people are understood as a monolith.

Contemporary Black stand-ups are neither strangers in a strange land, nor are they aliens. They are the Afrofuture. The term Afrofuturism was first used in 1994 by cultural critic Mark Dery in the essay 'Black to the Future: Interviews with Samuel R. Delany, Greg Tate and Tricia Rose', where he described it as 'speculative fiction that treats African American themes and addresses African American concerns in the context of twentieth-century technoculture – and more generally, African American signification that appropriates images of technology and a prosthetically enhanced future.'[8] Afrofuturism refers to an imaginative aesthetic and critical orientation towards subversion that, as critic and scholar Ytasha Womack puts it, 'combines elements of science fiction, historical fiction, speculative fiction, fantasy, Afrocentricity, and magic realism with non-Western beliefs'.[9] Afrofuturism has typically been a framework for discussing literary genres, visual art, and musical expression, but is yet to be brought to bear on stand-up comedy. Contemporary Black stand-ups, however, are indeed engaging in Afrofuturistic expressions. The Afrofuture envisioned in contemporary Black stand-up is ultimately about fantasies of transcendence. It is not merely about tearing down and rebuilding; it is about insistent, intentional departure from this world, and the transportation from it is stand-up comedy. The remainder of this chapter considers contemporary Black stand-up comedy in the USA, looking at the range of styles and approaches within it, paying specific attention to the development of its Afrofuturistic qualities. In other words, what does it mean for contemporary Black comics to imagine another (or other) worlds through stand-up comedy? How do they engender new ways of understanding a future where anti-Blackness and the affects it conjures is not always the framing factor of Black life?

The relatively high presence in the past five years of hour- and half-hour-long stand-up specials from Black comics on streaming platforms such as *Netflix* and *Comedy Central*, where innovative styles and approaches to the art form shine through, is a sign that the limits of Black stand-up are expanding. Indeed, contemporary Black stand-up can be characterised by a more variable range of themes and comedic material, and many of these comics have become popular because of the global appetite for more generous and diverse representations of stories about Black people and Black life, which is why I draw on *Netflix* as my primary archive of contemporary Black stand-up, even though it is widely available across a wide terrain of pop cultural platforms, both live and mediated. Themes of subversion of racialised norms, irreverence to authority, the centrality of the Black body, and a sense of communal joy continue to feature in contemporary stand-up. Nonetheless, elements of resistance have given way to comedic approaches that centre *imagination*; fleeting moments of revenge are superseded by the materiality of *the emancipated Black body*; a sense of *contentment and personal growth* are foregrounded, ephemeral pleasures looming still; and rituals of play produce *Afrofuturistic otherworlds* where difference matters, disabused of its regulatory power to rank and marginalise.

Ditzes and Weirdos

Netflix released sixty-three mostly hour-long stand-up comedy specials between 2020 and 2021, and around 20 per cent featured Black comedians, a somewhat high proportion relative to the Black population in the USA, which hovers at around 14 per cent. Like most of the Black women comics featured in *Netflix*-produced comedy specials, Nicole Byer's *BBW (Big Beautiful Weirdo)*, debuting in December 2021, was tagged as 'raunchy and irreverent'. Yet she is an outlier in that she can also be found under the label 'quirky', a description she shares with no other Black woman stand-up featured on the streaming platform. Afrofuturism, according to Ytasha Womack, 'is the perfect space for those who don't fit in', a quality the genre shares with contemporary Black stand-up.[10] *BBW* opens with

Byer seductively walking out on a stage clad in a faux-fur cheetah print coat, caressing her breasts before throwing it open to reveal a cheeseburger print negligee. Her manicured nails grip a pole, and Byer swings around it in a strip-tease performance as the title, *BBW* flashes in pink neon across the screen. Byer's smile is coy and playful, beckoning one to *look* at her, also daring you to look *away*. She twerks and writhes her full figure, dropping down in a full split with ease; finally, her body spirals so quickly it is thrown onto the stand-up stage. Exhausted, she rolls over, 'I guess I should go do my show now'.

The subtitle of Byer's special *(Big Beautiful Weirdo)* signifies an Afrofuturistic will to visualise and enact an unlimited Black subjectivity. Old ideas are reimagined such that a BBW, typically indicating one is a 'big, beautiful woman', or 'big, black woman', marked in pop cultural discourse as both corporeally and sexually excessive, made knowable by embodiment – can also suggest unknowability, strangeness, and being 'quirky' at the same time. Byer embraces this comedic ambiguity and makes use of it to put her audience in the position of imagining Black women's subjectivity as something that can come to be known in the process of the stand-up experience – something that can be imagined anew, even layered (literally) with that old sauce. Byer's sexy cheeseburger arrival is absurd and pointed. As John Limon claims: 'A theory of stand-up comedy is about what to do with your abjection.'[11] She completely inhabits the hegemonic imagery associated with large Black women – excessive from every angle – yet she also draws comedic distance from them in the farcical way she presents them. One cannot be abject, as big, Black women many times are rendered, if one is agentive in the re-presentation of that abjection.

'What a treat, what a dream!' she exclaims to an adoring audience. The dream of this statement is more substantial than a triumphant throwaway; it is an invocation for the crowd to come with her *in that dream* as her imagination unfurls to reveal and transgress boundaries of Blackness. Byer's 'quirkiness', framed by comedic ambiguity and absurdist imagery, makes way for the obliteration of respectability through which Black bodies are often disciplined into suffocating compliance – forced to be covered, to speak in certain ways about certain topics, or risk having one's voice and perspective silenced. The central motif of *BBW* is the realisation of the liberated Black body, and part of what that means is to engage the audience with what that means specifically *for her* such that they might imagine what Black liberation could mean more broadly. Many times, it means accessing and embracing a component of her personality – 'ditziness' – a trait rarely associated with Black womanhood. Byer expertly plays the role of the ditz.

Her voice is nasal and frenetic and she often draws her words out and giggles for comic effect. This performative animation is the centre of her ditz persona. 'I'm excited to be doing this here in New York Cityyy! [Applause] It's the city where I started doing comedy. It is the city where I dropped a piece of pizza, cheese side down [laughter]', Byers jokes, 'and then ate it! [laughter and applause]' she giggles. 'It's also a city where I fucked a cab driver. [laughter] And was fingered by another. [laughter]' At another point Byer considers her anger and astonishment that the only white people who *did not* check in on her at the height of the Black Lives Matter protests in 2020 were the white men she'd slept with. She reveals, 'But I do like fucking white dudes. [laughter] I like to fuck 'em so hard their ancestors cry. [laughter and cheers]' She smiles and does a half curtsy. 'I got another one. [laughter]' There is something humorous in these acts of self-disclosure. There are certainly elements in the humour of revenge, where whiteness is comically disarmed.

Yet Byer's acknowledgement that she 'like[s] fucking white dudes' also signals a sense of liberation from the archive of suffering under which Black women are always sexual objects for white men's enjoyment. Black women are imagined in this bit as sexual subjects whose liberated bodies can fully engage with the pleasures (and absurdities) of interracial sex. There is a 'willing vulnerability'[12] in play in contemporary Black stand-up comedy through which the Black imagination can be the vehicle for connection between performer and audience, perhaps ultimately leading to social transformation. The Black ditz character Byer inhabits enables her to embrace and enact her weirdness. To be 'weird' is often to be an outcast or misfit, and that style of Afrofuturistic Black humour reaches towards a future where Blackness and Black experiences are extraordinary, enigmatic even. According to Womack: 'Imagination, hope and the expectation for transformative change is a through line that undergirds most Afrofuturistic art, literature, music, and criticism … It's a view of the world.'[13] This suggests that Black stand-up comedy has always been Afrofuturistic, and to punctuate her set, Byers closes, 'Honestly, this last year and a half has been pretty shitty, but I think we're all gonna be okay.'[14]

Eric Andre's 2020 *Netflix* special, *Legalize Everything*, is labelled 'absurd, raunchy, and goofy' – descriptions the set lives up to. The opening scene pans to a shot of revellers enjoying Bourbon Street in New Orleans. Sirens blaring, a police cruiser turns wildly onto the street. The door flies open

Laugh No Limit: Black Stand-Up Comedy

Figure 7.1 Eric Andre performs onstage during the Beach Goth Festival at The Observatory on 22 October 2016 in Santa Ana, California
Photo: Scott Dudelson / Contributor / Getty Images Entertainment / Getty Images.

and several empty beer bottles crash to the ground. Andre staggers inebriated out of the vehicle as an astonished crowd, presumably made up of real people, looks on. He grabs a giant blue bong from the passenger seat. 'I stole this from the evidence room', he tells a couple of cackling Black men. 'Legalize it', he says, before taking a hit. Walking through the streets in police uniform, he smokes marijuana and offers onlookers magic mushrooms, cocaine, and pills – much to their amusement and bafflement. Naked from the waist down, Andre screams, 'LEGALIZE EVERYTHIIIIING!' as the words scroll across the screen and he walks through the audience to mount the stage.

Legalize Everything's introduction sets an absurdist, even hedonistic tone with the call to presumably legalise all sorts of drugs and indulgences; however, one could read that call to 'legalize everything' as something much more serious, especially considering the politico-racial zeitgeist of 2020s US culture. Andre is a mixed-race man (Figure 7.1), at one point calling himself 'Blewish,' as his mother is Jewish, his father Haitian. In a deeply vulnerable way, Andre imagines a state of freedom for Black bodies. Kodwo Eshun makes a connection between Afrofuturistic production and conditions of constraint in which many Black cultural producers find themselves. 'Afrofuturism studies the appeals that black artists, musicians, critics, and writers have made to the future,' Eshun argues, 'in moments where any future was made difficult for them to imagine.'[15] He is of course free to be vulgar, but Andre also visualises what it means for a Black person, who is more disposed to dying at the hands of the state than other groups, *to live* even in the face of structures of force and domination that may destroy them. Andre makes that fantasy of freedom literal in the narrative arc of the opening scene, which can be read as a veiled call for Black liberation – a world where Black people do not have to live in fear of the state, even while engaging in deliberate acts that butt up against disciplinary structures. Arriving onstage, Andre lifts his shirt displaying his chest and stomach, a move signalling vulnerability and lack of fear. Perhaps Andre's 'willing vulnerability' in this moment is a gesture inviting the audience to hear him out about what liberation could mean, however goofy and absurd the style of delivery.

Like Nicole Byer, Eric Andre embraces the strange and his material is unapologetically weird. He deadpans his bizarre bodily desires and deeds. 'I like acid … but every time I drop acid, I jerk off to anime [laughter].' He asks the audience, 'What's the most high you've ever been in public?' at which point he descends into the first row and breathlessly, intensely mounts a man, pretending this is indeed *his* highest moment, to the audience's delight. There is an air of irreverence in Andre's set in which he fully embodies and accepts his eccentricity. Thinly veiled in this approach, though, is a deeply progressive political commentary, a fascinating study of the subversive power of Black humour and the way it takes on new modes of expression in historical and cultural context. Amid feverish jokes about the pleasures and challenges of recreational drugs and anal sex, Andre also calls out and sends up systems that marginalise, dehumanise, and abuse Black people. 'Dude, Papa John got fired from *Papa John's*! [laughter] OK, so Papa fucking John's was dropping the N-bomb at work like it's 19-diggety-six. Like he's Ty Cobb in the dugout. [light chuckles]' Andre traverses time to engross his audience in a story about the afterlives of slavery.

Luring the audience in with some American popular culture nostalgia from the 1990s, Andre gets ready to deliver some of his most searing material:

> Did you guys ever watch the show *Cops*? [cheers] Is it just me or is reggae the most inappropriate music they could have picked [laughter] to open up the show *Cops*? [laughter] You can't slap reggae [pause] over police brutality footage, [laughter] and call it a day … The intro to *Cops* was like [angrily

shouting] 'You're under arrest, you unarmed, innocent black teenager! Boom! [strikes the air]'

Andre breaks into faux reggae singing 'welcome to the island of peace and purity', before yelling once again, 'Kiss my boots, you disenfranchised, transgender prostitute! Bam! [kicks the air]' More faux reggae singing is interspersed with a comedic rant that brings Andre's political commentary to a head. '[Forcefully gruff] This is a system invented by rich, white, Christian heterosexual businessmen. And if you don't match that description,' Andre screams, pointing to his fantasised subject, 'then it is my job to subjugate and oppress you, motherfucker! For I am your judge, jury and executioneeeer! [laughter and applause]'[16]

For a full ten seconds, Andre mimics the gunshots of a semi-automatic weapon in a bit that manifests the existential threats to which those on the margins are constantly subject. The crowd applauds and laughs throughout this fantasy of annihilation, pausing only in the moment of tension brought on by Andre's eventual silence. 'Under the sea, Ba-dum, badum! [laughter]' Exhausted, in a cloud of approving laughter and cheering, Andre wipes sweat from his face and falls to the ground for a moment of respite. Andre lent his body to this scene, not only as a comedian who was making the joke but as the Black man who is particularly vulnerable to those blows and gunshots. The juxtaposition between the spectacle of state violence and the innocence conjured by the famous tune from *The Little Mermaid* surfaces a not-so-veiled articulation of what it means to be unfree and, conversely, the meaning of freedom. The imaginative world Andre erects presents Blackness as unlimited, unafraid, and, like much of the comedy before it, invested in the cause of Black liberation. Andre's offbeat style – like the trickster tales of long ago – can elide its ethical orientation, which is ultimately its utopian vision. If utopias manifest the ability to 'articulate a common future',[17] as Jill Dolan argues they do, and if Afrofuturism enables Black artists to 'use the Black imaginary to racialize the long-running discussion of utopia and dystopia',[18] it is reasonable to conclude that Andre's routine is Afrofuturistic and imagines a future 'that's more just and equitable, one in which we can all participate more equally, with more chances to live fully and contribute to the making of culture'.[19]

Exploding Time and Space

Leslie Jones' hour-long special, *Time Machine*, debuted on Netflix in 2020. As she ascends the stage, she greets the crowd and acknowledges to herself, 'I made it ... I am white people famous.' The entirety of Jones' set is shot through with an Afrofuturistic ethos, bringing the audience along on a journey of personal growth that characterises contemporary Black stand-up, and forcing a confrontation with our relation to time and space. 'Afrofuturists are constantly recontextualizing the past in a way that changes the present and the future', maintains Womack.[20] The 'time machine' that is Jones' primary comedic hook functions as a mode of self-discovery and means of personal and collective transcendence of external and internal forces through which Black women can be marginalised and represented in various states of unfreedom. Jones time travels through the various stages of her life – her twenties, thirties, forties – to her present fifties to give the world an insight into the process of ageing and what that means specifically for urban, Black, working-class women. She grows old, and we come along for the ride. 'I turned 52 this weekend. [applause] Damn right!' Jones performs a celebratory dance. 'Y'all know I don't care, I got my knee brace on the outside. I don't give a fuck. Y'all think I'm finna mess up the rest of my meniscus for you motherfuckers? [laughter] This is maturity. That's what this is. [laughter]' Irreverence bubbles to the surface, yet we can also read Jones' framing of her own advancing age as a device through which the audience might grapple with what it means for Black people to live, to learn, and to *become* who they are – a process that centres the living Black body, the becoming Black person in a world replete with imagery and facts of Black proximity to early death.

Seated on her stool near the end of her set, sweat dripping from the intensity of it, Jones peers out to her audience, 'I have to say that this is fucking awesome. [applause]' She sighs a deep breath and smiles. 'So overwhelmed. It's so crazy where my life is right now', she continues, becoming more serious.

> The hard work does pay off ... but I'mma tell you in my twenties I was so troubled in my twenties. I was like, 'Fuck, man.' You know, I was having fun, partying and shit, but I was scared for my future. I didn't know what the fuck I was gonna do. I knew I was funny but I just didn't know what to do. Sitting at the same bus stop everyday, going to the same shitty job, and terrible shoes, just fucked up life ... [laughter] And I look at myself now, and I go, 'I wish I had a time machine', like, to go back to tell the 20-year-old self, 'Hey, it's gon' be ok.' And when I see it, it's such a beautiful story.

Jones is consciously vulnerable, creating a mood of sincerity and openness. She goes on to envision the journey back to Compton and the confrontation and conversation she has with her younger self. 'I'm the 51-year-old Leslie, and I'm here to tell you, everything's going to be ok.' She offers advice to the young Leslie on relationships and romance, health and self-care, and her career. She offers her younger self affirmations: that she does have a story to tell, and that once she works hard, she will become a successful comedian. Through this conversation, we engage with Jones as a Black woman *becoming*, in a continuous oscillation between past and present, not merely a flattened stereotype who can be known or understood by way of who she appears to be.

Equally striking is the way Jones imagines the future. Arriving back in the present, Jones says she is afraid. 'What's gon' happen to me in the future … am I okay in the future? Now I wanna take the time machine to the future and see the 91-year-old Leslie.' In this far-off otherworld, Jones has the audacity to have been allowed to grow old. Pointing a futuristic firearm, old Leslie confronts her younger self, 'I was expecting you. Get your fucking ass back to your fifties and have a good life, man. [applause] Enjoy your fucking self, dude.' Old Leslie calms her younger anxieties and provokes something beyond comic relief; like the end of Byer's set, there is a mood of contentment.

The anxieties of being a Black woman trying to make it are lifted, or at least made manageable, to the point that Jones imagines herself wise and content in old age – this mood of contentment, even within deep conditions of economic and political constraint, is an Afrofuturistic theme that is pervasive in Black stand-up today. Jones quickly descends to the present. 'So what's the lesson?' Jones is now more serious than she has been. 'You can't fix the past. You can't see the future. Might as well live in the present and have some faith. [applause and cheering]' The time travel excursion Jones conjures demonstrates that living in the present reaches towards the future, a future where Black life is valued and Black people have the capacity to *become*. For 'to "imagine" is to create a fantasy – however realistic – and to "become" is to make that fantasy into reality – however fantastic … imagining and becoming [are] essential to Afrofuturist texts that seek to re-present reality through subversive reclamations of history'.[21]

Conclusion

The global circulation of Black stand-up comedy by way of mediated technological formats (social media and streaming platforms, in particular) has vastly broadened the circulation of Black comedic material, with fewer gatekeepers than have typically limited the distribution of Black stand-up, meaning that a more varied set of styles and techniques have entered the mainstream. The twenty-first century has seen a shift, and it seems like Black stand-up comics are using the stage as a liberatory site of contestation where they play with and on the limits of old tropes and styles to generate laughter, offering new perspectives on the meaning of Blackness and contemporary life in the neoliberal, late capitalist moment. They bring pleasure, positivity, critical perspective, flair, flourish, and humanity to the world in a way that was inconceivable for most of the Black humourists on whose shoulders they stand. By using humour to get to the heart of anti-Blackness and the disciplined body, Black comics offer up collective moments of liberation that move beyond the ephemeral adage, 'laughing to keep from crying', normalising 'kaleidoscopic blackness' through performance.[22] Contemporary Black stand-up is the vehicle for imagination. It is here we can see the function of Black humour ripple between the humour of resistance that will always be necessary in a world characterised and structured by racial hierarchy, and the humour of Black imagination, stretching limits to reach beyond the order of things towards something more, better, and perhaps inconceivable outside the comic frame.

Notes

1. H. L. Gates, Jr., *The Signifying Monkey: A Theory of African-American Literary Criticism* (Oxford: Oxford University Press, 1988).
2. William T. Lhamon, *Raising Cain: Blackface Performance from Jim Crow to Hip Hop* (Cambridge, MA and London: Harvard University Press, 1998), p. 156.
3. Mel Watkins, *On the Real Side: A History of African American Comedy from Slavery to Chris Rock*, 2nd ed. (Chicago: Lawrence Hill Books, 1999), p. 392.
4. As readers are likely aware, dozens of allegations of rape and sexual assault have been lodged against Bill Cosby, going back to the 1960s, and he was convicted of sex crimes in 2018 and sentenced to ten years in prison. Not only do these allegations make it difficult to engage with his past comedic art, but the picture of the man painted by his real-life actions could not be in starker contrast with the upstanding family man that is at the heart of his comic persona.
5. Eddie Griffin, *Def Comedy Jam*, season 1, episode 8 (Home Box Office, 1992).
6. Chris Rock, *Chris Rock: Never Scared* (Home Box Office, 2005).
7. Dave Chappelle, *Chappelle's Show*, season 2, episode 6 (2003).
8. Dery, Mark, 'Black to the Future: Interviews with Samuel R. Delany, Greg Tate, and Tricia Rose', in Mark Dery (ed.), *Flame Wars* (Durham, NC and London: Duke University Press, 1994), p. 180.
9. Ytasha L. Womack, *Afrofuturism: The World of Black Sci-Fi and Fantasy Culture* (Chicago: Chicago Review Press, 2013), p. 9.
10. Womack, *Afrofuturism*, p. 11.
11. John Limon, *Stand-Up Comedy in Theory, or, Abjection in America* (Durham, NC and London: Duke University Press, 2000), p. 8.
12. Jill Dolan, 'Performance, Utopia, and the "Utopian Performative"', *Theatre Journal*, Vol. 53, No. 3, 2001: pp. 455–479; 459.

13. Womack, *Afrofuturism*, p. 42.
14. Nicole Byer, *BBW (Big Beautiful Weirdo)* (Netflix, 2021).
15. Kodwo Eshun, 'Further Considerations of Afrofuturism', *CR: The New Centennial Review*, Vol. 3, No. 2, 2003: pp. 287–302; 294.
16. Eric Andre, *Legalize Everything* (Netflix, 2020).
17. Dolan, 'Performance, Utopia, and the "Utopian Performative"', p. 455.
18. Clayton D. Colmon Jr., *On Becoming: Afrofuturism, Worldbuilding, and Embodied Imagination* (PhD thesis, University of Delaware, 2020), p. 3.
19. Dolan, 'Performance, Utopia, and the "Utopian Performative"', 455.
20. Womack, *Afrofuturism*, p. 158.
21. Colmon, *On Becoming*, p. 5.
22. Danielle Fuentes Morgan, *Laughing to Keep from Dying: African American Satire in the Twenty-First Century* (Champaign: University of Illinois Press, 2020).

Further Reading

Limon, John, *Stand-Up Comedy in Theory, or, Abjection in America* (Durham, NC and London: Duke University Press, 2000).
Maus, Derek C. and James J. Donahue (eds), *Post-Soul Satire: Black Identity after Civil Rights* (Jackson: University Press of Mississippi, 2014).
Morgan, Danielle Fuentes, *Laughing to Keep from Dying: African American Satire in the Twenty-First Century* (Champaign: University of Illinois Press, 2020).
Watkins, Mel, *On the Real Side: A History of African American Comedy from Slavery to Chris Rock*, 2nd ed. (Chicago: Lawrence Hill Books, 1999).
Womack, Ytasha L., *Afrofuturism: The World of Black Sci-Fi and Fantasy Culture* (Chicago: Chicago Review Press, 2013).
Wood, Katelyn Hale, *Cracking Up: Black Feminist Comedy in the Twentieth and Twenty-First Century United States* (Iowa City: University of Iowa Press, 2021).

CHAPTER 8

Jewish American Stand-Up Comedy

Debra Aarons and Marc Mierowsky

The British comedian, author, song writer and public commentator David Baddiel has one word in his Twitter bio: 'Jew'.

Behind this single word lies a rich history, one that has ancient roots, not all of them humorous. However, in considering a history of stand-up comedy, the label which Baddiel uses to encapsulate his public persona points directly to a tradition of comics, whose performance of their Jewishness enabled stand-up to emerge from the vaudeville hall and the Borscht Belt, becoming as it did less a form of joke telling than a potent, satiric form of social critique intimately associated with the comic. Calling himself 'Jew' is Baddiel's *shtick*. Deriving from Yiddish's Germanic roots, the term literally means 'a small piece' or 'play', a piecemeal item or odd character. In the hands of early twentieth-century vaudeville and Borscht Belt performers, it came to stand for a kind of humorous patter linked to the generalised character of the joker, the *tummler*, the needler. During the 1950s and 1960s the term took on a wider meaning in English, thanks to a set of performers – Lenny Bruce, Mort Sahl, and Shelley Berman chief among them. No longer simply a 'gimmick' or 'gag', a person's *shtick* became a 'manner' or 'style', not a repetitive set of jokes but part of a fully formed persona.[1]

In this chapter we trace the emergence of a particularly personalised *shtick* – a deeply ingrained and disproportionately Jewish phenomenon – from the closed world of the Borscht Belt to the wide-reaching socially critical comedy of today. Our focus is primarily on Bruce and Sahl. The performances of these comedians reveal some essential issues that have continued to shape the development of stand-up – what can be said, who can say it, under what circumstances, and why? These are questions of licence, but in the routines of Bruce, Sahl, and their contemporaries, they reflected the position of the Jew in North American society. Drawing connections between the comic sensibilities of these performers and those exhibited in the contemporaneous literary personae adopted by Phillip Roth, our aim is to outline a distinctively Jewish comic style adept at pushing the limits of what could be said on stage. This style is characterised by a 'neurotic' fixation on mind as well as body, and an awareness of one's status as a pariah, an outsider looking in. Exposing the persona's own foibles to reveal society's ills was the mantra of this style. Its lasting impact on the history of stand-up can be traced through Joan Rivers to a newer wave of Jewish stand-up comics that includes in its ranks Larry David, Sarah Silverman, and Marc Maron.

The Borscht Belt

By most accounts, the history of Jewish stand-up in America begins in the vaudeville hall but comes into its own in the Borscht Belt. Also known as the Jewish Alps, the Bagel Circuit, or the Sour Cream Sierras, this string of resorts in the Catskills Mountains in upstate New York was given its most famous moniker by Abel Green, an editor at *Variety*. Green's joke is a riff on the American habit of labelling regions as belts – think the Rust Belt or Bible Belt – and the sour beetroot soup popular with eastern European Jews that flowed like a stodgy Red Sea across the summer resorts of the Catskills.[2] Served as often as twice a day, and always with copious amounts of other fare, Borscht came to stand in for one of the prime attractions of these resorts: food. The other, as its series of humorous names witnesses, was entertainment – comedy being front and centre.

The Catskills had been popular with Jewish holidaymakers since the late nineteenth century. The heyday of the Borscht Belt, though, was in the period between the 1920s and 1960s, when as many as 500 resorts, hotels, and bungalow colonies catered to the budgets of a large section of American Jews. The demand for these resorts was born of both discrimination and opportunity. Especially at the beginning of the period, Jews were excluded from mainstream clubs and hotels. As a group, however, they were experiencing an unprecedented period of upward social mobility. What emerged with the creation of their own holiday destination was a distinctly Jewish environment.

According to novelist Mordecai Richler, the clientele of Grossinger's, one of the larger Catskills resorts, was made up of the generation between 'the *luftmenschen* – tailors, cutters, corner grocers – so adored by Bernard Malamud' and the 'confident college boys' of Philip Roth's early fiction, who just happen to be Jewish. This transitional generation of Jews comprised the 'unlovely spiky bunch that climbed with the rest of middle-class America out of the Depression into a pot of prosperity'. Their fixation on financial stability, on their health, on the marriage prospects of their children embarrassed the younger generation and those more assimilated to America. For Richler, this cultural cringe was redeemed by the sense 'of self-ridicule' that pervaded Grossinger's, a 'consummate kibbutz' 100 miles north-west of Manhattan.[3]

Not everyone was in on the joke. But there was certainly an openness to humour and ridicule in the entertainment that the resorts offered, if not always a sense of ironic detachment. Entertainment was a crucial selling point for the resorts, providing one way they differentiated themselves from the competition – a fact we can pick up from a routine by the comedian Freddy Roman (born Fred Kirschenbaum):

> This fellow checks into a hotel with his wife. He goes to breakfast, goes to Simon Sez, eats lunch, lays around in the pool, rows on the lake, plays softball, eats dinner, goes to the early show, then goes to the late show, then goes to the coffee shop. Finally, at four in the morning, the wife says 'Let's go to bed'. 'Why?' he asks. 'Who's appearing there?'[4]

The often highly structured daily activities put on by Borscht Belt hotels and resorts have been depicted in films such as *Dirty Dancing* (1987), television shows such as *The Marvelous Mrs. Maisel* (2017–2023), and novels such as Roth's *The Professor of Desire* (1977). Patrons were treated to song, dance, reviews, games, lectures, and music. Mac Kinsbrunner, resident manager of the Concord, rationalised the frenetic pace of the holidays: 'people don't come to the mountains for rest any more ... they want *tummel*'.[5] In Yiddish *tummel* means noise, and the resorts employed people as *tummlers*. The *tummlers* would mingle with the guests, tell humorous stories, encourage them to participate in activities, stand up on stage and play a musical instrument, sing, and tell jokes. (This was how Mel Brooks and Jackie Mason got their start in comedy, as did many others destined to become celebrities.) Their patter acted as both social lubricant and running commentary, as we see in the steady stream *shpritzed* (sprayed) by Lou Goldstein, a *tummler* at Grossinger's. After a guest calls out for Goldstein to tell the joke about 'the two goyim [Gentiles]', the *tummler* responds:

> 'We don't use that word here. There are people of every faith at Grossinger's. In fact, we get all kinds here. (All right, lady, sit down. We saw the outfit.) Last year a lady stands here and I say to her, What do you think of sex? Sex, she says, it's a fine department store'. Goldstein announced a horseshoe toss for the men, but there were no takers. 'Listen here' he said, 'at Grossinger's, you don't work, You toss the horseshoe but a member of our staff picks it up. Also you throw downhill. All right, athletes, follow me.'[6]

Jewish American Stand-Up Comedy 161

The idea that Grossinger's attracted 'all kinds' is immediately satirised as the *tummler* needles a lady for what he deems to be too conspicuous a display of consumption. This then allows him to repeat a stock joke on 'Saks/sex', the humour of which lies in the same stereotype of the acquisitive Jew and the misinterpretation of a Yiddish accent. Encouraging participation in the horseshoe toss, the *tummler* manages to hit two targets of his own, parodying the perceived lack of Jewish athleticism and his guests' need for relaxation and luxury. It is the safety of the in-group that allowed such jokes. There was little social distance between *tummler* and guests. The back and forth between them trampled over the smouldering ruins of a fourth wall, making the performance intensely interactive.

This ease of interaction between comic and audience extended from the poolside entertainments to the more formal Saturday night revues, which at the larger resorts often boasted world famous performers. Because of their familiarity with all sorts of entertainers, and their lack of respect for the status of those whom they considered they had paid for, the Borscht Belt audiences developed a reputation for heckling. Demanding audiences let the comics know when they thought a joke didn't hit, or when it perhaps went too far. Mel Brooks once said 'the Catskills made my life. I will never forget those tough Jewish audiences. If you could make them laugh, you could conquer the world.'[7] Jewish comics such as Don Rickles, Shelley Berman, Totie Fields, and Rodney Dangerfield, even after they achieved wider fame, were still expected to cater to these largely Jewish audiences. Their routines were smattered with Yiddish and other in-jokes. Choosing to switch into another language or to intersperse one language with the vocabulary and inflections of another can signal particular meanings for different audiences. It can serve to include or alienate audiences. Specifically, this use of Yiddish amid a discourse primarily in English helped comics to bond with the audience culturally. When Jewish comics played to Jewish holidaymakers in the Borscht Belt they would sometimes deliver the set-up of the joke in English and the punchline in Yiddish. This allowed those who understood the joke to feel a sense of belonging, exclusivity, and collusion, while making it incomprehensible to the uninitiated.[8]

On the whole the jokes told were of and to a community that, while remaining on the national margins, was nevertheless upwardly mobile. There were already recurrent jokes in the vaudeville hall about the clash of cultures, as well as clashes within the culture between older immigrants and greenhorns (or later arrivals). But the most common Borscht Belt routine was made up of one-liners. Typical fare included mother-in-law jokes, jokes about demanding wives, how to make money, how to get on in the world, new class snobbery, triumphs of the smart, clever tricks, and putting one over a fool. The delivery was fast paced, joke after joke. Very often the jokes were written by people who did not themselves tell them but sold them on to comedians. There was little individuality to distinguish one joke teller from another. Mostly the personality represented on stage was the generic joke teller, a man, in suit and tie, essentially interchangeable with another – almost nothing was revealed about the person telling the joke. As Gerald Nachman puts it: 'They were efficient but anonymous joke merchants.'[9] And yet the *shtick* of the quick-fire joke teller took on an unmistakeably Jewish aspect. With Rodney Dangerfield and Jackie Mason, the Yiddish-inflected accent rang loud. But even when slightly softened, as in the case of Henny Youngman, the preponderance of Jewish comics both relied on and helped push an historical association of Jews and humour.

Youngman, known as the fastest and brightest of the one-liner comics, produced, for instance, the following routine:

> Married 41 years ... went back to Chicago where we got married ... had the same suite of rooms ... only this time *I* went in the closet and cried.
> [laughter]
> A lot of people say, 'How do you stay married for 41 years?' Here's the secret, my wife and I go to a romantic restaurant twice a week ... a little candlelight ... a little wine. She goes Tuesdays I go Fridays.
> [laughter and applause]
> My wife hates housework. I bought her an electric iron, an electric dishwasher, and electric drier. She said too many gadgets around, she had no place to sit down. What did I do? Bought her an electric chair.
> [laughter and applause]
> You must compromise. You must compromise when you're married. She wanted a fur coat; I wanted an automobile. We compromised. Bought her a fur coat we keep in the garage.
> [laughter]
> She found a furrier who does his own breeding. Crossed a mink and a gorilla. Got a beautiful fur coat but the sleeves are too long.
> [laughter]
> I gotta mother-in-law. I gotta tell you. She raises parrots. She raised a four-hundred-pound parrot. The parrot says 'polly want a cracker'. 'NO'.
> [laughter]
> ...
> Say two guys meet, 'What's the latest dope on Wall Street?' He says, 'My son'.
> [laughter]
> ...

A little old man gets hit by a car. The cop props him against the wall, covers him up with a blanket. He says, 'You're comfortable?' He says, 'I make a nice living'.
[laughter and applause][10]

This is light-hearted parody of what the audience can identify as a typical married Jewish man, though it is never explicitly said. The well-worn interpellation is taken on, but so too is the self-mockery that is a part of this identifiably Jewish American persona (one that is also seen in Jewish-British, and other Anglo-spheres in which Jews have jockeyed for position and track). The tried and true jokes about the aspirations of the Jewish housewife, the henpecked husband, the desire for material comfort, and the ambition to be noticed and admired are all fairly standard Jewish jokes.[11] Freud in *der Witz*,[12] writing in *fin de siècle* Vienna, notes all these tropes and admits that he himself is not immune to them.[13] So their origin is not necessarily American, but they have developed a very particular American flavour. Although anti-Semitism still flourished in America, and Jews continued to be regarded as different, they began to claim their difference and exploit it for its comedic value. Their difference and self-perceived outsider status gave them a convenient vantage point from which to comment on themselves and on others. Jews were able to rise to social heights not even fantasised about in central and eastern Europe, where many of their parents and grandparents had come from. As we see in Roth's novels about New Jersey in the 1940s and 1950s, Jews of the second generation had an American childhood, watching and playing baseball, attending senior proms, and living in their nuclear families in neighbourhoods where they coexisted (not always amicably) with Gentiles. They knew, however, that they were different and acquired ways of living with their difference within the mainstream. These generations lived through two world wars and the Depression, and their consciousness of being both Jewish and American evolved accordingly, flourishing in trepidation. Youngman's routine shows that he was acutely aware that the ability to shift one's focus away from material considerations was a luxury. For Jewish immigrants who had made their way financially, being 'comfortable' was a matter of pride and achievement. This is a sharp reminder that in the WASP (White Anglo-Saxon Protestant) mainstream at the time, talking about money was regarded as vulgar; for Youngman's audience money was a source of not very well-hidden pride.

The man who is at once a hapless victim of social mores and yet, in playing the fool, adapts their inconsistencies to his advantage (he and his wife going to romantic dinners separately) is in the tradition of the *schlemiel*, 'the Jew as he is defined by the anti-Semite, but reinterpreted by God's appointee'.[14] The jokes are impersonal but we can discern in this routine some embryonic features of modern stand-up. The sense of in-group safety, of self-parody, of material fixation, of desire for status is all pervasive but, at the same time, we see Youngman punching out and up to the dominant culture, to the perceived society in which this kind of wealth is a driver.[15] The manner and style of stand-up towards the tail end of the Borscht Belt era starts to become more identifiable with the persona of the joke teller. The practice of storytelling, and the embrace of an individuated persona, is seen to become more prominent. Interaction with audiences, always present and often robust, becomes more individualised as some of the Borscht Belt comedians strain outwards towards wider audiences (as did Don Rickles and Mel Brooks) and become less interchangeable.

Shtick often involved talking around a single topic, approaching it from all angles, finding the humour in it, even when the subject of the joke or anecdote was tragic. The man who survives a car accident and even in such dire circumstances misinterprets the denotation of 'comfortable' is a key instance. At the same time the *shtick* of Yiddish comedy was self-reflexive and deeply invested in playing with the language of humour, the manipulation of meaning, with displays of verbal dexterity that relied on the uniquely humorous accommodations and flexibilities that came with the importation of Yiddish words, syntax, and prosody into English.[16]

In charting the move from the Borscht Belt to the rebel comedians, the Jewish comics of the new wave, we see how this verbal brilliance gains new force as people such as Bruce turned it both in on themselves and out towards politics, sex, and religion, moving as they did away from the realm of the joke, towards the practice of satire.

Sick Jews and Rebel Comedians

An anonymous 1959 article in *Time* magazine identified a disturbing new trend in American comedy – a trend that was 'a symptom of the twentieth century's own sickness … partly social criticism laced with cyanide, partly a Charles Addams kind of jolly ghoulishness, and partly a personal and highly disturbing hostility towards the world'. The gags of this new wave 'come so close to real horror and brutality', the writer noted, 'that audiences wince even as they laugh'.[17] The article names these comics the 'sicknicks' and includes among their rank: Shelley Berman, Mike Nicholls and Elaine May, Tom Lehrer, Jonathan Winters, Lenny Bruce, and Mort

Sahl. Not all of them were equally sick, but all were doing new things with sketch comedy and stand-up.

Sahl is the earliest; Bruce, according to the critic, is the sickest.

Sahl was arguably the first comic to offer political stand-up from a well-thought-out world view. Sahl began performing in San Francisco, at the hungry i, the club that had the brick wall background that has become something of an architectural synecdoche for stand-up. Sahl didn't tell jokes. He read the paper, commented on the headlines, and from there offered freewheeling, bitingly satirical comments on politics. He took aim at J. Edgar Hoover, the feared director of the FBI, at Eisenhower, and at Senator Joe McCarthy whose hearings before the House on Un-American Activities Committee were the scourge of progressive politics and media.

In one routine he quips:

> Joe McCarthy doesn't question what you say so much as your right to say it [a reversal of Voltaire's dictum] ... For a while, every time the Russians threw an American in jail, the Un-American Activities Committee would retaliate by throwing an American in jail, too ... . Maybe the Russians will steal all our secrets, then they'll be two years behind.[18]

Sahl's act may seem fairly tame by modern standards. But the critique of American institutions was certainly dangerous and risqué in the early years of the Cold War. More than this, though, is that his performances develop a new sort of form. At its most basic level, Sahl moves from the conventional series of jokes to the kind of monologue that remains the prevailing form of modern stand-up. In this new form, Sahl opens up the topics available for comedic interrogation: politics, the military, patriotism. In the process he manages to hone the edge of socially aware comedy, harking back to a rich satiric tradition – where no subject is taboo – in order to raise stand-up comedy as a serious force for social critique. This new style was so marked that many of the Borscht Belt old guard objected to the fact that Sahl was not performing so much as talking about the news. He also wrote his own material – material that in content and delivery became inextricably bound to his persona as a political satirist.

Jeremy Dauber notes that Sahl's focus on real world issues and questions 'moved a kind of Jewish comic sensibility – one where every aspect of behavior was scrutinised under the microscope – onto the stand-up stage. Or, as Sahl put it: "I don't have any kinship with a Jewish background ... If the role of the Jew is to rock the boat and to be inquisitive – intellectually curious, that is – fine. Classic role".'[19] The idea of the Jew as critic, as pariah looking inwards from the social outskirts, was a crucial factor in shifting the perspective of stand-up. So too was the well-known and stereotyped Jewish obsession with psychoanalysis, of looking from the self even further in, a tradition formalised by Freud and adopted by Jewish intellectuals in the coastal cities of North America. While Sahl examined the behaviour of those in public life, his fellow sicknicks turned to themselves. Berman, whom the *Time* writer describes as having a 'face like a hastily sculpted meatball', found material by 'spelunking in his psyche'.[20] He examined for satiric gain his childhood, living above his father's delicatessen on the West Side of Chicago:

> ... an exclusively Jewish neighbourhood. Here we thrive, lowering real estate values.
> [audience laughs]
> And here we are moderately happy because we don't know from such things and we couldn't help it anyway
> [muffled laughter]

When young Sheldon (Berman's full name) wants $100 to go to acting school, he turns to his parents:

> Whenever I've had a problem in my young life, I've always gone directly to my mother. My mother has always had the same wonderful, consistent maternal advice
> [Imitates Mother's Yiddish Accent]
> 'Talk to your father'
> [audience laughs]
> So I called home
> ...
> [Imitates Father's more pronounced Yiddish accent]
> 'Alright bigshot, how you? Eh listen ... before you say another word I have a request to make from you: go to Hell. You know why go to hell so don't play act with me, actor.'[21]

There's a clear parallel between Berman's stage persona as a son of the second generation defying parental expectations to pursue acting and Alexander Portnoy, Roth's novelistic persona in *Portnoy's Complaint* (1969). In both cases a comic monologue on childhood and domestic themes raises the fully fledged character of the speaker to a position where he can be simultaneously the highly personal butt of the joke and the critic who excoriates the conditions that placed him in this horrifying but humorous position in the first place.

The comic best able to blend this intense fixation on self – body and mind – and outsider critique of twentieth-century America was Lenny Bruce (Figure 8.1). As we have argued elsewhere, Bruce consciously

Figure 8.1 Lenny Bruce at the Jazz Workshop, 1961
Photo: San Francisco Chronicle/Hearst Newspapers /
Contributor / Getty Images.

adopted a Jewish persona as an adult, honing it as a way to situate himself as 'the Other'.[22] Whereas Sahl sought to be the satirist speaking as an everyman – his only professed connection to Jewish tradition being his pariah status and disputatious spirit – Bruce opted to play 'Jewish'. In the process he brought the dirtier jokes of the Borscht Belt, the *shmutzik*, to the comedic mainstream, complete with the Yiddish inflections of vocabulary, syntax, and highly identifiable mannerisms. He used terms such as *emmis*, meaning 'honestly', as discourse markers. It was from his self-styled position as a 'dirty Jew' that Bruce critiqued mainstream society. He drew on his own life, his parents' divorce, his addictions, his sexual adventures, and his arrests, exaggerating and adapting aspects of his biography to craft a stage persona that allowed him both insight and distance. By holding to his identity as a Jew he could express 'an out-group sensibility with which to attack mainstream attitudes and behaviours, playing out the absurdity of the hypocritical practices he derided'.[23]

Like Sahl, Bruce did not consider himself to be an entertainer, and indeed the older guard of Borscht Belt comedians didn't consider him to be much of an entertainer either. His construction of himself as Jewish was, indeed, a construction, a persona distilled and sharpened by the ongoing collaboration with his mentor Joe Ancis. Like Sahl, Bruce thought that being Jewish was a mindset, just as much as it was a cultural practice. His approach to performance deviated from the old school style of joke telling. Rather than telling jokes, he adopted an informal lecture style. He set up scenarios and then riffed on them. In one he compares Kennedy and Truman to Nazi war criminal Adolf Eichmann:

> What will Kennedy look like as a war criminal?
> [muffled laughter]
> Adolf Eichmann. Have *Rachmones* [Yiddish for a combination of mercy, compassion, forgiveness, and empathy] for Adolf Eichmann.
> [Imitating Eichmann] 'My name is Adolf Eichmann and ze Jews came everyday and thought zey go to ze showers ... The mothers were quite ingenious. Mothers would take children and hide them in bins of clothing. We found the children ... put them in the chambers. I sealed them in. I watched through the portholes ... They made soap out of all [the Jews] ... My defence, I was a soldier ... Do you people think yourselves better? Because you burn your enemies at long distances with missiles? Without ever seeing vhat you have done to zem? ... Hiroshima auf wiedersehen.'
> [back in his own voice]
> If we had lost the war they would have strung Truman up by the balls.[24]

Bruce intersperses his imitation of Eichmann with Yiddish phrases. The incongruity works to point out the hypocrisy of his audiences as Bruce juxtaposes the crimes committed against his people (the Jews) with the crimes committed by his people (Americans). Eichmann's infamous defence that he was a soldier following orders is daringly and shockingly put in the same breath as the military expediency that justified Truman's dropping of the atom bomb on Hiroshima and Nagasaki. All the while the audience sits in silence.

Some of the more well-known disquisitions were on the difference between Jewish and Goyish (gentile), as well as using the form to disembowel and then blow up contemporary uses of language. Bruce set himself up as a Jeremiah, excoriating his audiences. (He addressed those who came to his shows as if they were complacent onlookers to society's injustices, an act of interpellation designed to activate their consciences so as to shake them from this complacency.) They were as much a part of his performance on any given night as he was. At his best, he was responsive to the mood and events of the day and reacted to the society he saw through his alienated and hypersensitive lens. Although framed in the form of a lecture, his delivery was jagged, as he speedily free-associated references to jazz, politics, racism, sex, drugs, and hypocrisy.

Bruce took himself seriously as a social critic. In another time, he might have been considered a prophet, in others a public intellectual. It was with Bruce that the rhythms of stand-up comedy, vulgar discourse, and a predilection for rubbing against sensitive private issues came to be regarded as a contribution to public intellectual discourse. As his reputation grew, Bruce set the terms of the comic–audience interaction, often concentrated and confronting. His choices of topic and language were intended to shock, disgust, and dismay. As we have put it in other work, 'his creativity and ingenuity, charged by his electrical wit, transformed the discourse from jokes and patter to shocking needling diatribes, engendering trepidation as well as laughter'.[25] Bruce crafted a style to match a persona: verbal dexterity showed his brilliance; he was fearless in his topic choice, using mannerisms and expressions from Yiddish, from the rhythms of clashing modal jazz; he styled himself a hip, cosmopolitan, knowing Jew.

Bruce's oft-expressed view was that comedy is not entertainment. He believed the calling of the comedian was to tell the truth. 'Today's comedian has a cross to bear that he built himself. A comedian of the older generation did an act and he told the audience, "This is my act". Today's comic is not doing an act. The audience assumes he's telling the truth. What is truth today may be a damn lie next week.'[26] He saw truth as contextual and personal.

'My only challenge was to tell my truth, man ... figure out what I had to say. These days, it's not enough to boost that roomful of strangers. The young comic spends all their time trying to sound different from the million other jokesters grabbing for the mic.'[27] Bruce's comic philosophy echoes Steve Allen's observation that 'satire is tragedy plus time'.

Bruce's style is difficult to capture in writing. One reason was that Bruce was not particularly good with a microphone – he was careless, and quick, and the sound technology did not always keep up with his pace and style, nor with the practice he called *shpritzing* – of spraying the audience with observations and harangues in rapid succession. In his 1965 concert at Berkeley, Bruce reflected on his famous *Religions Incorporated* routine, *shpritzing* the Catholic church and its history of acquisitiveness and in the process spraying LBJ (Lyndon Baines Johnson) by drawing attention to his lack of sophistication *contra* JFK (John Fitzgerald Kennedy):

> A genius religion. Three years ago I was wondering, I used to do a bit, four years ago, Religions Incorporated, so my view at that time was here's a rich church, Catholicism, next door is poverty, so it's hypocrisy. Obvious view. So I started digging, digging, reading really getting into it, and I realized, the reason for the baroque Church, the grand Church in the poverty neighborhood, is that, what the Church is is a school, it's a method of instruction. And people who have no understanding, who need instruction, don't know about philosophy, they can only understand material things. So a raggedy ass guy won't go into a raggedy ass temple.
> [audience laughs]
> 'I live in a shithouse, why'd I gotta go in one for?'
> [audience laughs]
> But if you show him something nice he can understand then you can instruct him. So the ecumenical council really are geniuses and they make some tremendous moves. So I figure there's a group looks to undermine them. Somebody talked Lyndon Johnson's daughter into converting. That sent the religion back two-thousand years. That dress she had on, she looked like a Guatemalan slave. Real Philomena at the wedding there, with it's, terrible, looked like a National Geographic picture.
> [audience laughs and claps][28]

The political, religious, and philosophical references give the bit the patina of learning. Bruce's biographers, Albert Goldman and Lawrence Schiller, catch something of the effect this style:

> When Lenny starts to spritz, interspersed with the hip jargon, riding along the bops and beats of his Broadway-Brooklyn tachycardic speech pattern, are allusions to big sounds like Stravinsky, Picasso, Charlie Parker, José Limon and James Joyce. Jazz, existentialism, analysis, peyote cults and California. He's concerned about the racial scene and the man in the White House and the economy, the way the country is changing. He has philosophy, an attitude. Speaks from experience, done an awful lot of reading.[29]

Goldman and Schiller go on to cast doubt on the amount of reading Bruce actually did. But it is notable that Bruce positioned himself through such urbane and apparently learned allusions as a serious critic, a scourge to the status quo, akin to the line of musicians, philosophers, artists, and writers who went before him in the intertwined pursuits of artistic innovation and free expression.

Jewish Comedy and Modern Stand-Up

The history of modern stand-up is not an exclusively Jewish one but there is unavoidable evidence of a preponderance of Jewish performers in this sphere. There are of course too many to mention, but we touch on those whom we think of as most embodying the tradition we have traced across this chapter, heralded by Sahl and Bruce.

Joan Rivers, whose career in stand-up lasted from the 1950s until her death in 2014, is probably the most well-known and long-standing Jewish female stand-up. She did not blanch from being a woman in a time when women stand-ups were few and far between. Her stand-up exploited prevailing views about female desirability, beauty, youth, a desire for material goods and wealth, and an upper-middle-class Jewish sensibility. She created and totally embraced a persona which was loud, neurotic, and devastating in its attacks on herself. A performer with exquisite timing and bold wit who lacerated her targets, she loved her audiences even as she railed at them. She combined the witty one-liners beloved of the Borscht Belt with scathing self-analysis, succeeding in lashing out at the values of the day while apparently embracing them. Her early remark, 'Women should look good. Work on yourselves. Education? I spit on education! No man ever put his hand up a girl's dress looking for a library card',[30] punctures the idea that women could be valued for their brains. This is part of the paradox of Rivers' comedy. She fixated on women's looks to expose the overly prominent value they held in male-dominated society without ever saying that they should not be valued. In this piece of advice, Rivers is serious that women need to make themselves as physically attractive (to men) as possible – she's on record throughout her life as committed to this idea, as she embraced cosmetic surgery, beautiful and elegant clothes, and an expensive and aesthetic lifestyle. But when she says, 'I spit on education!' she presumably does no such thing; quite the opposite. Her critique is that in the world she feels part of, brains are optional, sexual attractiveness is compulsory, for a woman's success. In many respects, at the time in which Rivers was speaking, that seemed to be true. Female comedians with notable exceptions, such as Phyllis Diller who deliberately worked against this ethos, were well advised to make their appearance as palatable to governing norms as possible. Rivers' legacy of exposing neurotic personal fixations and castigating the values of the time in which she lived is, much like Bruce's, enormous, opening the door for more recent edgy female comedians, such as Sarah Silverman. For them, being Jewish is not a matter of religion or culture, nor something that is incidental, but rather an intellectual disposition to critique, mock, and savage. Licenced by their identity as women, they break taboos about women and their bodies and claim the right to do so as theirs.

Showing the indelible influence of Sahl (who died in 2021), Marc Maron (b. 1963) is an American Jewish stand-up performer, known for his searing political commentary and scorching self-loathing, which he airs publicly. As a recovering alcoholic and drug addict, Maron, when sober, analyses the worst of his excesses. His political critique is sharp, relentless, and sometimes iconoclastic; as he often says, 'Left wing, right wing, I am wingless and tired of trying to fly. Here comes the ground.' Maron has been active on stage, television, and radio and has for some years had his own much vaunted podcast, *WTF with Marc Maron*, which allows long-form interviews. Politically, Maron speaks his own truth, no matter how unpopular with friends, relatives, and audiences. In this way he bears the torch long carried and finally set aside by Mort Sahl. His relentless self-examination and emotional flagellation is up there with the best of Bruce and Woody Allen.

Returning to the type of the *schlemiel*, we find Larry David (b. 1947), the creator and writer (with Jerry Seinfeld) of *Seinfeld* (NBC 1989–1998) and apparently the model for the character George Costanza. David was also the writer and main character actor in *Curb Your Enthusiasm* (HBO 1999–2024). David inhabits the role of the main character, who is based on himself except, as David says, as he'd be like in real life if he lacked social awareness and sensitivity. To write the character, of course, requires extremely finely tuned social awareness and sensitivity, which is what makes the character such a luminous persona. This is David's self-critique: it is thoroughgoing and merciless. The *schlemiel* is fully embodied, in his physicality, his behaviour, and his language. The awkwardness and embarrassment of this hapless small Jewish man returns us to the wisecracks of the Borscht Belt, filling in the outlines of a character with petty grievances, foibles, and insecurity, one uncomfortable in his milieu and even worse off in the wider world. This is the comedian ill at ease in society, a way of critiquing the cultural environment by integrating the *shtick* as a fully formed comic persona with a consistent world view.

Notes

1. *The Oxford English Dictionary* first records this second definition of *shtick* as a 'manner, style' in 1965, *OED*, s.v. 2. Though the *OED* is hardly the sharpest tool with which to gauge changes to Jewish culture, this shift in meaning reflects an expansion in the possibilities of *shtick* that, as we argue here, had a formative effect on the emergence of modern stand-up.

2. Jeremy Dauber, *Jewish Comedy: A Serious History* (New York: W. W. Norton, 2017), p. 157. For a general history of the Borscht Belt, see Stefan Kanfer, *A Summer World: The Astonishing History of the Jews in the Catskills* (New York: Farrar Straus Giroux, 1990).
3. Mordecai Richler, 'The Catskills: Land of Milk and Money', *Holiday Magazine*, July 1965.
4. Quoted in Dauber, *Jewish Comedy*, p. 158.
5. Richler, 'The Catskills: Land of Milk and Money'.
6. Richler, 'The Catskills: Land of Milk and Money'.
7. Cited by Eddie Portnoy in *Professional Jokers: Jewish Jesters from the Golden Age of American Comedy* [online video], www.youtube.com/watch?v=gq1A4i-lefI.
8. *Stand-Up America* (BBC2, 22 February 2003), 22.25.
9. Gerald Nachman, *Seriously Funny: The Rebel Comedians of the 1950s and 1960s* (New York: Pantheon, 2009), p. 22.
10. *Catskills Jewish Comedians Compilation* [online video], www.youtube.com/watch?v=zFl5__YQDQI.
11. See Devorah Baum, *The Jewish Joke* (Cambridge: Pegasus, 2018).
12. Sigmund Freud, *Jokes and Their Relation to the Unconscious* (Leipzig and Vienna: F. Deutike, 1905) Edited and translated by J. Strachey, published in English (New York: W. W. Norton, 1960).
13. See also Elliott Oring, *The Jokes of Sigmund Freud: A Study in Humor and Jewish identity* (Maryland: Rowman & Littlefield, 2007) in which he discusses the major types in Freud's Jewish joke collection, including *The Schnorrer* (The Sponger) and *The Shadchen* (The Matchmaker) as well as *The Ostjuden* (the Eastern European Jews, who were regarded as outsiders and unclean).
14. Ruth Wisse, *The Schlemiel as Modern Hero* (Chicago: University of Chicago Press, 1971), p. 6.
15. There is a trope of Jewish jokes starting in the 1960s which mock Jews who try to pass in WASP country clubs and are inevitably exposed by some or other deeply Jewish mannerism.
16. Linguists working on English have identified this type of syntactic and prosodic structure. It has been given the name 'Y movement' where Y is the initial for Yiddish. Often what people call a Yiddish accent denotes a certain type of syntax and prosody, which is uniquely identifiable.
17. 'Nightclubs: "The Sicknicks"', *Time Magazine*, 13 July 1959.
18. Quoted in Nachman, *Seriously Funny*, p. 61.
19. Dauber, *Jewish Comedy*, p. 86.
20. 'Nightclubs: "The Sicknicks"'.
21. Shelley Berman, *Outside Shelley Berman* [record] (USA: Verve Records, 1960).
22. Debra Aarons and Marc Mierowsky, 'Obscenity, Dirtiness and Licence in Jewish Comedy', *Comedy Studies*, Vol. 5, No. 2, 2014: pp. 165–177.
23. Aarons and Mierowsky, 'Obscenity, Dirtiness and Licence in Jewish Comedy', p. 171.
24. Lenny Bruce, 'War Criminals' on *The Historic 1962 Concert when Lenny Was Busted* [CD] (USA: Viper's Nest, 1998).

25. Aarons and Mierowsky, 'Public Conscience', p. 156.
26. John Cohen (ed.), *The Essential Lenny Bruce* (New York: Ballantine Books, 1970), p. 110.
27. *The Lenny Bruce Interview*, Jill Bourque's 'How We First Met and Stage Time with Steven Alan Green', *Jewish Journal*, 7 April 2013.
28. Lenny Bruce, *Berkeley Concert* [record] (USA: Bizarre).
29. Albert Goldman and Lawrence Schiller, *Ladies and Gentlemen, Lenny Bruce!* (New York: Penguin Books, 1991), p. 43.
30. Joan Rivers on *The Tonight Show*, with Johnny Carson (CBS, 1986).

Further Reading

Aarons, Debra and Marc Mierowsky, 'Obscenity, Dirtiness and Licence in Jewish comedy', *Comedy Studies*, Vol. 5, No. 2, 2014: pp. 165–177.

Baum, Devorah, *The Jewish Joke* (New York and London: Pegasus, 2018).

Cohen, John (ed.), *The Essential Lenny Bruce* (New York: Ballantine Books, 1970).

Dauber, Jeremy, *Jewish Comedy: A Serious History* (New York: W. W. Norton, 2017).

Freud, Sigmund, *Jokes and Their Relation to the Unconscious* (Harmondsworth: Penguin, 1976).

Goldman, Albert and Lawrence Schiller, *Ladies and Gentlemen – Lenny Bruce!!* (New York: Penguin Books, 1991).

Kanfer, Stefan, *A Summer World: The Astonishing History of the Jews in the Catskills* (New York: Farrar Straus Giroux, 1990).

Nachman, Gerald, *Seriously Funny: The Rebel Comedians of the 50s and 60s* (New York: Pantheon Books, 2003).

Oring, Elliott, *The Jokes of Sigmund Freud: A Study in Humor and Jewish Identity*, 3rd ed. (Lanham, MD: Rowman and Littlefield, 2007).

Richler, Mordecai, 'The Catskills: Land of Milk and Money', *Holiday Magazine*, July 1965.

Time Magazine, 'Nightclubs: The Sicknicks', 13 July 1959.

Wisse, Ruth R., *The Schlemiel as Modern Hero* (Chicago: University of Chicago Press, 1971).

Wisse, Ruth R., *No Joke: Making Jewish Humor* (Princeton: Princeton University Press, 2013).

CHAPTER 9

Stand-Up Comedy, Disability, and Social Justice
Sharon Lockyer

Introduction

Since its inception, stand-up comedy has changed, and continues to change, artistically, socially, politically, and economically. One of the most interesting and rapid shifts in live stand-up over the last two decades is the increase in the numbers of disabled comedians performing. Disabled comedians are now active in stand-up in a number of different countries including the UK, the USA, Australia, Canada, Japan, India, and Russia.[1] Disabled comedians have also been recipients of prestigious comedy industry awards.[2] In addition to global stand-up comedy tours by disabled comedians such as Adam Hills, Francesca Martinez, and Tanyalee Davis, some disabled stand-up comedians have also achieved mainstream media success.[3]

The increasing number and presence of disabled stand-up comedians in live and mediated comedy have begun to attract academic attention. While some of this work has involved interviewing disabled stand-up comedians about their experiences, and other studies have explored the content of performances, this research is united in its interest in the function and impact of such comedy, beyond its purpose to entertain.[4] For example, my analysis of the lived experiences of disabled comedians performing on the live stand-up comedy circuit in the UK reveals two main ideological motives for performing comedy as a disabled person. The first is to take control of the comic material and audiences and the second is to use comedy to affirm disability.[5] Research on stand-up comedy performed by disabled comedians in the USA has found that in addition to being entertaining, this comedy can fulfil numerous functions, including challenging and reversing negative assumptions about impairments and disabilities, acting as a coping mechanism and as a vehicle for social change.[6]

This chapter contributes to and extends this existing literature by closely examining the performances of disabled stand-up comedians from the UK. Specific attention is given to the ways in which stand-up performed by disabled comedians may be viewed as a form of social justice comedy through analysis of the techniques used, and themes explored, in the performances.

Contextualising Comic Constructions of Disability

When discussing comic constructions of disability, it is useful to make a distinction between the diverse ways in which comedy can be related to disability. Some researchers make a distinction between 'disability humour' and 'disabling humour'.[7] Disability humour is humour created and presented by a disabled person or where disability is the main focus of the humour. Disabling humour ridicules and demeans disability. Many of the historical ways in which disability has been represented in comedy has involved the latter form, where disability is comedically constructed in a negative and derogatory manner, and where non-disabled people laughed *at* disabled people.[8] Analysing comic constructions of disabled people across the twentieth century, Haller and Ralph argue that such constructions have passed through four phases. Phase one saw disabled people presented in freak shows and mental impairments were associated with idiocy. Phase two included non-disabled people making jokes about disabled people and limitations of impairments were highlighted. In phase three, disabled people had ownership of the comedy, corresponding to 'disability humour' – which is interpreted as a liberatory form of artistic expression.[9] Phase four saw disabled people being centred in the comedy, but disability was not the main focus of the comedy, and disability was normalised and presented as part of being human.[10] Phases three and four offer possibilities for comedy to challenge social barriers and negative attitudes and to facilitate positive understanding of disability.[11] In my interviews with disabled comedians performing on the live comedy circuit in the UK, I observed how disabled comedians were using their stand-up to move disabled people from comedy targets to the makers of comedy in order to challenge disablist stereotypes and restrictive cultural representations and expectations of disabled people.[12] The increased prominence of disabled stand-up comedians in live stand-up may accelerate such transformative possibilities. Such challenges to disablist stereotypes and negative cultural representations and expectations are possible as the meanings of disability are not fixed. Disability is sometimes referred to as a 'floating signifier' as its meaning is not a fixed or static fact, but constantly shifts and changes over time and across cultures.[13] This proffers the possibility that comedy can be used as a tool in the quest for social justice surrounding disability by positively shifting its meaning and conceptualisation.

Stand-Up Comedy and Social Justice

Social justice is underpinned by a number of principles, including equal opportunity, inclusion, cooperation, and equal access.[14] In recent years there has been growing interest in comedy studies in assessing the social and political impact of stand-up and exploring the ways in which it may be a tool for social and political change.[15] In their extensive analysis of the role of stand-up in social justice issues and challenges in the USA, Borum Chattoo and Feldman argue that 'comedy may be in the midst of its newest golden age of experimentation and influence' on a global scale.[16] They refer to this era as a 'new era of social justice comedy' and point to a number of factors to justify this categorisation, including the convergence of news and entertainment in contemporary media and communications, increased opportunities to consume and share comedy in the digital age, erosion of trust in government and 'traditional' media, and a 'post-9/11 sociocultural moment' where interest in and demands on social justice have been reignited by social movements, including the Movement for Black Lives and #MeToo.[17] They argue that comedians, who they refer to as 'social justice influencers', can contribute to social change by explicitly requesting solutions to societal issues, reconstructing problems that are presented in the news, centring identity and discriminatory practices, and revealing taboos.[18] They offer a taxonomy of comedy's effects on social change, arguing that comedy can contribute to social justice debates and challenges in four ways. It can draw attention to specific issues and causes, reduce audience resistance to opinions, erase social barriers, and generate debate.[19] Other researchers similarly interpret stand-up comedy as a significant rhetorical vehicle for social transformation as comedians can articulate how society should be rather than how it is.[20] These contemporary debates suggest that there may be social justice potentials for disability comedy, for example, using it to advocate for disability equity, for participatory and representational inclusion, and for equality and freedom from discrimination and prejudice.

Collecting and Analysing Stand-Up Comedy by Disabled Comedians

To explore the social justice potential and impact of stand-up by disabled comedians, I examined the specific techniques used, and themes explored, in performances by Laurence Clark and Rosie Jones (Figure 9.1), who are both British stand-up comedians, actors, and writers with cerebral palsy.[21] Since 2003, Laurence Clark has regularly performed solo shows at the Edinburgh

Figure 9.1 Rosie Jones performs live on stage at the Henham Park during the Latitude Festival in Southwold, Suffolk
Photo: SOPA Images / Contributor / LightRocket / Getty Images.

Festival Fringe. He won *Shortlist* magazine's Funniest New Comedian in 2007 and was a finalist in the Amused Moose awards at the Edinburgh Festival Fringe. He has also performed as part of the Abnormally Funny comedy troupe, has appeared on a range of television programmes including *Newsnight* (BBC1) and *We Won't Drop the Baby* (BBC1), and has written for a variety of publications. Rosie Jones was a finalist in the Funny Women Awards in 2016, first performed at the Edinburgh Festival Fringe in 2017, took her first one-hour solo show to Edinburgh in 2018, and embarked on her first UK tour in 2023. She has also appeared on a range of television comedy programmes including *The Last Leg* (Channel 4) and *8 Out of 10 Cats* (Channel 4), starred in her own television programme *Trip Hazard: My Great British Adventure* (Channel 4), and has written for a range of other television programmes. Textual analysis was used to explore the comic discourses, techniques, style, and themes present in Clark's and Jones' stand-up comedy performances, considering both their verbal and visual aspects.[22]

Stand-Up Comedy as Disrupting Disability Stereotypes and Cultural Representations

Laurence Clark's The Best Fake Charity Collection Buckets

Laurence Clark's live stand-up comedy shows often combine a conventional stand-up comedy style delivery (e.g. a single performer taking centre stage) with slide projections and video clips. Clark's *The Best Fake Charity Collection Buckets* (2011) is a good example of such performance style.[23] The performance is based on Clark's quest to raise money for ridiculous charities, with each charity in the sketch becoming increasingly ludicrous. The video sketches are played to a live audience. Clark contextualises the charity bucket sketches for the live audience by explaining from the outset:

> A while ago I was on holiday in South Africa. And I was waiting at a bus stop, minding my own business, and suddenly I heard this jingling sound. When I looked down at the sunhat resting on my lap someone had thrown coins in. [limited laughter] So, me being me, I thought, I could have some fun with this. [laughter] So, I would go around London with my very own charity collection buckets. [laughter] I wanted to test what would be the most ludicrous fake charity causes that I could get money for from the British public. [laughter] And boy was this fun. [laughter]

A video recording is then played to the live audience on a large screen positioned behind and above Clark on stage. The recording shows Clark using his wheelchair on a London street, holding a bucket with the first fake charity – 'PAY OFF MY MORTGAGE' – emblazoned on the bright orange charity bucket. Clark enthusiastically shakes the fake charity bucket so the loose change in the bucket jangles while he repeatedly says, 'pay off my mortgage', as the live audience laughs. Passers-by continually drop money into the bucket with one patting Clark on his arm as they walk away. This enthusiastic response comes despite Clark's comments to the passers-by, 'No sir, you really don't want to pay off my mortgage, you don't want to do that, really', and, 'No you don't want to do that', and, 'No, no, no!' as Clark pulls the bucket away. One contributor responds with, 'Yes I do!', as the live audience laughs.

Throughout the performance Clark introduces each fake (and increasingly obscure and ridiculous) charity to the live stand-up comedy audience before playing the next clip. Following the 'PAY OFF MY MORTGAGE' charity, five others are included: 'PLEASE DON'T PUT MONEY IN HERE. AS I WILL GET A CRIMINAL RECORD IF YOU DO'; 'THIS IS A SCAM – sucker'; 'I AM NOT A CHARITY CASE'; 'KILL THE PUPPIES'; and 'TOP UP HEATHER MILLS £24.3M SETTLEMENT'. The causes are all supported by passers-by (except for the last), despite Clark providing explanations that they are fraudulent as money is dropped into the bucket. Through such performances, Clark draws attention to the problematic ways in which some people ignore or make assumptions about wheelchair users and/or make assumptions about the individual's expressed wants, needs, and desires – patronisingly thinking that they know what is best.

A key part of the fake charity collection bucket sketches is Clark's critique of the charity model of disability. This model views disabled people as victims of their impairments and in need of pity.[24] Disabled people's situations are viewed as tragic and disabled people are seen as 'different' via the charity model. Some disabled people have a negative view of this model as it depicts disabled people as dependent and helpless and in need of care, which can lead to problematic stereotyping.[25] Clark signals his critique of the model from the outset through careful framing of the sketches by recalling his experience of coins being thrown into his sunhat when on holiday in South Africa. Through the strategy of creating fake charity collections, Clark resists the perception of disabled people that underpins the charity model of disability and encourages those audience members present in the live stand-up comedy show, and in the charity bucket clips, to do the same. Resisting this model serves to highlight how some disabled people live independently, are far from helpless, and are live fulfilling and happy lives – distant from the pitying view of disability.

In addition to ridiculing and critiquing the charity-inducing view of disability, which is often held by non-disabled people, the interactions that Clark has with members of the public in the sketches reveal other problematic ways in which he is perceived and treated. During the 'KILL THE PUPPIES' clip an elderly man walks past Laurence. The man's attention is attracted by the charity bucket that Clark is holding, and the man walks over:

MAN: Why do you want that?
CLARK: Why do I want this? Umm.
MAN: A cripple, are you, of some sort?
CLARK: Umm, yes, I'm a cripple, you could say.
MAN: I see. Palsy? Is that it?
CLARK: I have cerebral palsy, yes.
MAN: I see. Well, there you are. [Man throws coins into the bucket, audience groans]

This interaction demonstrates how language is a significant location of socio-political concern surrounding inequality and oppression.[26] There is tension in the conversation over the word 'cripple'. This word is rarely used in contemporary British society due to its offensive potential. Clark's hesitation through the use of 'Umm' signals his reluctance to say the word (and perhaps his surprise that this word has been used). Clark's statement, 'yes, I'm a cripple, you could say', acknowledges that while others might use such a term, he would rather not. Clark's correction of the man's use of the shortened and dismissive 'Palsy' to 'cerebral palsy' again challenges the man's use of language. This challenge is extended further by the caption inserted over the sketch before the man says, 'A cripple, are you, of some sort?' The caption, presumably added by Clark, reads '(indecipherable old man mumblings)', which serves to ridicule the man and weaken what he says next – the offensive and derogatory word – and the dismissive tone adopted by the man.

Clark's strategic use of video clips in the live stand-up comedy performance may be more impactful than simply retelling stories of the interactions. Watching the video clips allows the stand-up comedy audience to witness, first-hand, how Clark is treated. Researchers analysing the process of using traumatic personal experiences as stand-up comedy material refer to 'authenticating strategies' which stand-up comedians choose to use in order to convey to audiences that they are referring to their real-life lived experiences and not simply creating stories for comic effect.[27] Clark's deliberate use of video clips can be viewed as an 'authenticating strategy' as they *show* Clark's actual lived experiences of being a disabled person in contemporary Britain, actually showing the interactions with non-disabled people, rather than simply describing them. Witnessing the troubling encounters, while Clark is physically present, centre stage in the room, draws the audience physically and socially close to Clark, which may facilitate a deeper shared, and critical, appreciation of the hostility and unfair treatment experienced by disabled people.

Rosie Jones' Funny Women Final

Rosie Jones' *Funny Women Final* performance was part of the Funny Women Awards 2016 Final show.[28] During the performance, Rosie treats the audience to a number of jokes and anecdotes related to her lived experiences. In the early part of Jones' stand-up comedy performance, she says that, 'Being disabled is amazing. [audience cheers] It is. [audience cheers] You can dribble on people you don't like. [laughter]' Jones then follows this up by saying, in a disingenuous tone, 'Oh I can't help it [laughter]', and then returning to her own credible voice to say, 'I can. [laughter and applause]'. This early joke serves to simultaneously challenge the view that having a disability is negative (as Jones says it 'is amazing') and also to counter the stereotypical view that some disabled people lack control of their bodies – as Jones commands when, where, and who she dribbles on, in addition to commanding the performance stage. Stand-up comedy allows Jones to define who she is, what she can do, and how she would like to be understood by audiences. Self-definition is 'central to counter-acting objectification and dehumanisation of the "other" and shifting specific identities from the object to the subject of comedy'.[29] This joke may be described as 'charged humour', which is used to refer to comedians who tell jokes that deliberately confront inequality and exclusion and critique what is regarded as 'normal'.[30]

Towards the end of Jones' performance, Jones shares her experience of being a disabled person at work: 'At work I'm the only disabled person, which means the disabled toilets are used for one thing. It's for everyone else to shit in. [laughter] You've all done it. [laughter] You have. [Jones points to an audience member in the front row, audience laughter]' Jones then recounts how she deals with situations where she needs to use the disabled toilet when it is engaged. While she is waiting for her non-disabled work colleague to finish, Jones explains how she waits 'silently, I can even hear them shit [laughter]', and how she deliberately 'wees' herself, 'so when they come out of the toilet they are not only greeted by a disabled person, they're greeted by a disabled person and their puddle of piss. [laughter]'

Jones explains how she then looks at her colleague and then looks 'down at my wee for a long time and I say, "You did this [laughter] – happy now?" [laughter]' This comic narrative makes use of what is sometimes referred to as the 'comedy of recognition' where audiences reproduce disablism and laugh because they recognise themselves in the joke.[31] Jones' direct address to the audience – 'You've all done it' – coupled with the accusation that one of the (presumably non-disabled) members of the audience has used a disabled toilet, can encourage the audience to reflect on their own problematic behaviour. This 'comedy of recognition' serves to reposition non-disabled audience members who have used disabled toilets as deficient or impaired in their thoughts and behaviour towards disabled people. The climax of this comic story – 'You did this – happy now?' – also serves to shame non-disabled people who use disabled toilets, making non-disabled people responsible for the disabled person who has been waiting to use the disabled toilet creating a 'puddle of piss'. This inverts the way in which disabled people are often stigmatised and made to feel shame about their disability – in this instance it is non-disabled people who are stigmatised and made to experience shame.[32]

This comic narrative also subverts dominant cultural representations of disability. Mainstream representations of disabled people often focus on what disabled people lack, or are not, and therefore imply that there is a deficiency or deficit.[33] In Jones' retelling of the story, it is non-disabled people using disabled toilets who are deficient due to their lack of recognition and consideration of disabled people, thus reversing dominant tropes in disability representations. Such inversion relates to Bakhtin's theory of carnival where socio-political hierarchies are reversed, albeit temporarily, through humour and laughter.[34] In this instance, although Jones describes how she 'wees' herself (which might ordinarily convey an inability to physically control her body), she has physical and moral power, as it is the non-disabled person who is at fault for using the disabled toilet. Furthermore, through the narration of this experience, carefully constructing the scene and informing the stand-up comedy audience about what she does in this situation, Jones exploits non-disabled people's false perceptions of her and turns the disabling attitudes and behaviour back onto people who hold those views and behave in such a way. The impact of this critique is further extended as it relates to a basic bodily function that both disabled and non-disabled stand-up comedy audience members can relate to, thus creating a sense of intimacy and empathy as a reflection of shared human experience.[35]

Jones' use of the 'comedy of recognition' corresponds to the intentions of performing comedy expressed by some disabled stand-up comedians. In my research, I found that in addition to the primary function of entertainment, some disabled stand-up comedians interpreted their comedy as having a series of secondary functions.[36] These functions related to the diverse ways in which the comedy can deepen audience understanding of disability. Using 'comedy of recognition' may have a significant role to play in facilitating and extending this understanding about problematic disablist attitudes and behaviour, which may encourage social transformation of disability. Research on the manipulative and influential potential of stand-up comedy has shown that comedian influence can continue beyond the stand-up comedy performance and have longer-term social impact.[37] In addition, the use of 'comedy of recognition' by disabled comedians suggests that comedy has the potential to move beyond the play frame into the serious frame to promote critical thought, disrupt disabling stereotypes, norms, and expectations, and influence change.[38]

On the Limits of Stand-Up Comedy, Disability, and Social Justice

The textual analysis of Clark's and Jones' stand-up comedy performances has illustrated how the carefully constructed themes covered, and techniques employed, may have serious potential as they challenge negative stereotypes surrounding disability, criticise the hostile interactions that disabled people experience from non-disabled people, including the problematic language used to refer to disabled people, and invert socio-political hierarchies. As such, Clark's and Jones' performances may be seen as contributing to Borum Chattoo and Feldman's 'new era of social justice comedy'.[39]

That said, it is important to acknowledge the limits to stand-up comedy's social justice potential due to the complexities involved with the form. The capacity of stand-up comedy by disabled comedians to facilitate critical thought and social change is dependent on audiences recognising that, in addition to being entertaining, comedy can challenge and critique – for instance, recognising that in some cases they may be the target of the joke. Given the complexity of comedy, which plays on ambiguity and interpretive diversity, and also polysemy, where jokes can have multiple meanings, there is the increased potential for the intent of a joke or comic narrative to be interpreted in a different manner by the audience than that which is intended by the stand-up comedian.[40] Unlike serious discourse, comedy offers different ways of interpretation and these ways may be in opposition to each other.[41] Therefore, comic attempts to critique hierarchical relations, to challenge disabling views that some audience members may hold, and to critique dominant discourse surrounding disability, may, for some comedy audience members, be interpreted as supporting and strengthening those relations, views, and discourses. This has been referred to as the 'Alf Garnett Syndrome' where the target of the comedy (such as racism and sexism) is celebrated by some audience members.[42] Future research could fruitfully explore how audiences respond to, interact with, and respond to disabled comedians in order to complement, and extend, our understanding of the social justice potentials of stand-up comedy in relation to disability.

Notes

1. For example: UK – Abnormally Funny People, Chris McCausland, Francesca Martinez, Laurence Clark, Liz Carr, Lost Voice Guy, Rosie Jones, and Tim Renkow; USA – Asperger's Are Us, Comedians with Disabilities Act, Drew Lynch, Josh Blue, and Preferred Parking Comedy Tour; Australia – Adam Hills, Imaan Hadchiti, Steady Eddy, and the late Stella Young; Canada – Angelo Schiraldi and Tanyalee Davis (grateful thanks to Nadia Desroches for introducing Angelo Schiraldi's work); Japan – Hawking Aoyama (grateful thanks to Joaquin Aras for highlighting Hawking Aoyama's comedy); India – Nidhi Goyal and Sundeep Rao; Russia – Sergei (Sergeich) Kutergin.
2. For example, Francesca Martinez won the Daily Telegraph Open Mic Award at the Edinburgh Festival Fringe in 2001 and Tim Renkow won the Amused Moose Laugh Off at the Edinburgh Festival Fringe in 2014.
3. Jack Carroll was runner-up in *Britain's Got Talent* in 2013 (ITV), Drew Lynch was runner-up in *America's Got Talent* in 2015 (NBC) and Lost Voice Guy won *Britain's Got Talent* in 2018 (ITV). There have also been numerous appearances of disabled stand-up comedians on the BBC's flagship stand-up comedy programme, *Live at the Apollo*, including Adam Hills, Chris McCausland, Francesca Martinez, Jack Carroll, Lost Voice Guy, Tanyalee Davis, and Tim Renkow. Lost Voice Guy, who won the BBC New Comedy Award in 2014, co-wrote and stars in the semi-autobiographical BBC Radio 4 sitcom, *Ability* (2017–2021), and this is currently in development as a television sitcom (see British Comedy Guide, 'Ability' (2022) www.comedy.co.uk/tv/ability/). Tim Renkow created the BBC THREE television comedy series *Jerk* (2019–2021) and, since Spring of 2022, Chris McCausland has hosted the Radio 4 panel show, *You Heard It Here First*.
4. Examples of studies focusing on the experiences of disabled comedians include: Shawn Chandler Bingham and Sara E. Green, *Seriously Funny: Disability and the Paradoxical Power of Humor* (Boulder, CO: Lynne Rienner Publishers, 2016); Sharon Lockyer, 'From Comedy Targets to Comedy-Makers: Disability and Comedy in Live Performance', *Disability & Society*, Vol. 30, No. 9, 2015: pp. 1397–1412. Examples of studies focusing on the content of performance by disabled comedians include: Cassandra Hartblay, 'Welcome to Sergeichburg: Disability, Crip Performance, and the Comedy of Recognition in Russia', *The Journal of Social Policy Studies*, Vol. 12, No.

1, 2014: pp. 111–124; Nicola Martin, 'A Preliminary Study of Some Broad Disability Related Themes within the Edinburgh Festival Fringe', *Disability & Society*, Vol. 25, No. 5, 2010: pp. 539–549; D. Kim Reid, Edy Hammond Stoughton, and Robin M. Smith, 'The Humorous Construction of Disability: "Stand-Up" Comedians in the United States', *Disability & Society*, Vol. 21, No. 6, 2006: pp. 629–643.
5. Lockyer, 'From Comedy Targets to Comedy-Makers'.
6. See Reid, Stoughton, and Smith, 'The Humorous Construction of Disability'.
7. Reid, Stoughton, and Smith, 'The Humorous Construction of Disability', p. 631.
8. Tom Shakespeare, 'Joking a Part', *Body & Society*, Vol. 5, No. 4, 1999: pp. 47–52.
9. By Reid, Stoughton, and Smith, 'The Humorous Construction of Disability', p. 629.
10. Haller and Ralph, 'John Callahan's Pelswick Cartoon and a New Phase of Disability Humor'.
11. Haller and Ralph, 'John Callahan's Pelswick Cartoon and a New Phase of Disability Humor'.
12. Lockyer, 'From Comedy Targets to Comedy-Makers', p. 1400.
13. See Reid, Stoughton, and Smith, 'The Humorous Construction of Disability', p. 631, who draw on Stuart Hall, *Representation: Cultural Representations and Signifying Practices* (Thousand Oaks, CA: Sage, 2002).
14. See Sally M. Hage, Erin E. Ring, and Melanie M. Lantz, 'Social Justice Theory', in Roger J. R. Levesque (ed.), *Encyclopedia of Adolescence* (New York: Springer, 2011), pp. 2794–2801.
15. For example, see: Jennalee Donian, *Taking Comedy Seriously: Stand-Up's Dissident Potential in Mass Culture* (Lanham, MD: Lexington Books, 2019); Rebecca Krefting, *All Joking Aside: American Humor and Its Discontents* (Baltimore: Johns Hopkins University Press, 2014); Matthew R. Meier and Casey R. Schmitt (eds), *Standing Up, Speaking Out: Stand-Up Comedy and the Rhetoric of Social Change* (New York and London: Routledge, 2017); Sophie Quirk, *Why Stand-Up Matters: How Comedians Manipulate and Influence* (London: Bloomsbury, 2015).
16. Borum Chattoo and Feldman, *A Comedian and an Activist Walk into a Bar*, p. 5.
17. Borum Chattoo and Feldman, *A Comedian and an Activist Walk into a Bar*, p. 18.
18. Borum Chattoo and Feldman, *A Comedian and an Activist Walk into a Bar*, p. 8.
19. Borum Chattoo and Feldman, *A Comedian and an Activist Walk into a Bar*, p. 13.
20. Meier and Schmitt, *Standing Up, Speaking Out*, p. xxiv. Such research can be seen as adopting the 'critical humour studies' approach to research advocated by Lockyer and Pickering. The 'critical humour studies' approach focuses on both how comedy relates to, and differs from, other types of discourse and what is unique to comedy as a communication mode. See Sharon Lockyer and Michael Pickering, 'You Must Be Joking: The Sociological Critique of Humour and Comic Media', *Sociology Compass*, Vol. 2, No. 3, 2008: pp. 808–820.

21. Purposive sampling was employed to collect relevant stand-up comedy performances by disabled comedians. Purposive sampling refers to an approach to data collection where the research aims and questions determine what is studied and analysed. The current research aims, coupled with my previous research on disability and comedy, and familiarity with disabled comedians' performances facilitated the purposive sample.
22. Textual analysis facilitates understanding and analysis of how people from different cultures make sense of things, including their sense of self and how they are positioned within culture and society. See Alan McKee, *Textual Analysis: A Beginner's Guide* (London: Sage, 2003), p. 1.
23. See the 'clips' section on Laurence Clark's website: www.laurenceclark.co.uk/clips/.
24. Marno Retief and Rantoa Letsosa, 'Models of Disability: A Brief Overview', *HTS Teologiese Studies/Theological Studies*, Vol. 74, No. 1, 2018: p. 6.
25. Retief and Letsosa, 'Models of Disability', p. 6.
26. As argued by Beth Haller, Bruce Dorries, and Jessica Rahn, 'Media Labelling versus the US Disability Community Identity: A Study of Shifting Cultural Language', *Disability & Society*, Vol. 21, No. 1, 2006: p. 70.
27. See Oliver Double, 'Tragedy Plus Time: Transforming Life Experience into Stand-up Comedy', *New Theatre Quarterly*, Vol. 33, No. 2 (2017): pp. 143–155.
28. See the 'video' section on Rosie Jones' website: https://rosiejonescomedy.com/video/.
29. Lockyer, 'From Comedy Targets to Comedy-Makers', p. 1403.
30. As used by Krefting, *All Joking Aside*, p. 2.
31. Hartblay, 'Welcome to Sergeichburg'.
32. See Erving Goffman, *Stigma: Notes on the Management of Spoiled Identity* (London: Penguin, 1963); and Michelle R. Nario-Redmond, *Ableism: The Causes and Consequences of Disability Prejudice* (Hoboken, NJ: Wiley Blackwell, 2020).
33. See Anita Silvers, 'The Crooked Timber of Humanity: Disability, Ideology, Aesthetic', in Mairian Corker and Tom Shakespeare (eds), *Embodying Disability Theory: Disability and Postmodernism* (London: Continuum, 2002) p. 237.
34. Mikhail Bakhtin, *Rabelais and His World* (Bloomington: Indiana University Press, 1984).
35. Susan Seizer, 'On the Uses of Obscenity in Live Stand-Up Comedy', *Anthropological Quarterly*, Vol. 84, No. 1, 2011: p. 214.
36. Lockyer, 'From Comedy Targets to Comedy-Makers'.
37. Quirk, *Why Stand-Up Matters*.
38. See Kate Fox, 'Humitas: Humour as Performative Resistance', in Krista Bonello Rutter Giappone, Fred Francis, and Iain MacKenzie (eds), *Comedy and Critical Thought: Laughter and Resistance* (London: Roman & Littlefield, 2018).
39. Borum Chattoo and Feldman, *A Comedian and an Activist Walk into a Bar*, p. 18.

40. See Simon Weaver, *The Rhetoric of Racist Humour: US, UK and Global Race Joking* (Farnham: Ashgate, 2011).
41. As argued by Michael Mulkay, *On Humour: Its Nature and Place in Modern Society* (Cambridge: Polity Press, 1988).
42. Michael Pickering and Sharon Lockyer, 'Introduction: The Ethics and Aesthetics of Humour and Comedy', in Sharon Lockyer and Michael Pickering (eds), *Beyond a Joke: The Limits of Humour* (Basingstoke: Palgrave Macmillan 2009), p. 18. Alf Garnett was the main character in the 1960s and 1970s BBC sitcom, *Till Death Us Do Part*. Garnett was a racist bigot, but audiences were split between those who were laughing 'at him' and those laughing 'with him'.

Further Reading

Bingham, Shawn Chandler and Sara E. Green, *Seriously Funny: Disability and the Paradoxical Power of Humor* (Boulder, CO: Lynne Rienner Publishers, 2016).

Borum Chattoo, Caty and Lauren Feldman, *A Comedian and an Activist Walk into a Bar: The Serious Role of Comedy in Social Justice* (Oakland: University of California Press, 2020).

Hartblay, Cassandra, 'Welcome to Sergeichburg: Disability, Crip Performance, and the Comedy of Recognition in Russia', *The Journal of Social Policy Studies*, Vol. 12, No. 1, 2014: pp. 111–124.

Krefting, Rebecca, *All Joking Aside: American Humor and Its Discontents* (Baltimore: Johns Hopkins University Press, 2014).

Lockyer, Sharon, 'From Comedy Targets to Comedy-Makers: Disability and Comedy in Live Performance', *Disability & Society*, Vol. 30, No. 9, 2015: pp. 1397–1412.

Lockyer, Sharon, '"It's Really Scared of Disability": Disabled Comedians' Perspectives of the British Television Comedy Industry', *The Journal of Popular Television*, Vol. 3, No. 2, 2015: pp. 179–193.

Lockyer, Sharon and Michael Pickering, 'You Must Be Joking: The Sociological Critique of Humour and Comic Media', *Sociology Compass*, Vol. 2, No. 3, 2008: pp. 808–820.

Martin, Nicola, 'A Preliminary Study of Some Broad Disability Related Themes within the Edinburgh Festival Fringe', *Disability & Society*, Vol. 25, No. 5, 2010: pp. 539–549.

Meier, Matthew R. and Casey R. Schmitt (eds), *Standing Up, Speaking Out: Stand-Up Comedy and the Rhetoric of Social Change* (New York and London: Routledge, 2017).

Reid, D. Kim, Edy Hammond Stoughton, and Robin M. Smith, 'The Humorous Construction of Disability: "Stand-Up" Comedians in the United States', *Disability & Society*, Vol. 21, No. 6, 2006: pp. 629–643.

CHAPTER 10

Stand-Up Comedy and Offence
Simon Weaver

Introduction

Offensiveness is a key issue in contemporary public discourse, especially in relation to media content. Stand-up comedy has provided an important site for discussions of offensiveness, both inside of performances and in the commentary on comedy in other forms of popular media. This chapter provides a brief summary of some well-known examples of stand-up comedy that are embroiled in debates on offensiveness, before engaging in a discussion of what constitutes offensive stand-up comedy. It theorises the discursive work that offensive stand-up comedy does in contemporary contexts through concepts of rhetoric, the performative, and symbolic violence, arguing that the offended other is an essential component of much offensive stand-up comedy. Comedy and harm are discussed and an explanation of what researchers have described as the impact of humour and comedy is given. Throughout the chapter, the points made are elaborated with extracts from British stand-up comedian Ricky Gervais' Netflix special *Supernature* (2022), especially through an analysis of jokes made by Gervais about transgender people. These and other jokes are examined alongside the disclaimers used in the stand-up comedy performance.

A cursory observance of social discourse on offensive stand-up comedy might conclude that there are two broad camps, arguing with each other over the nature of stand-up comedy, on what it means to be offended, and what should be done by or to those that offend others. This can be encapsulated with concerns over issues of offensiveness, identity, and protected characteristics on one side, and protecting free speech and pushing the boundaries of 'acceptable' discourse on the other. This is a binary that has taken on a clear political dimension, as a discourse that is used and recreated in politics, especially with the emergence of right-wing national populisms across Europe and the USA. These populisms are primarily built on and describe cultural differences between groups, rather than economic differences or inequalities,[1] and thus contribute to notions of a 'culture war'.[2] Stand-up comedy has a central role in these social discourses because it is a cultural form or art that deals specifically with cultural taste, values, and beliefs, which are the materials of difference in the current populist zeitgeist, with the addition of an inbuilt emphasis on expressing those topics through laughter and, at times, ridicule and disgust. In these conditions, stand-up comedy has the potential to provide an aestheticised entertainment politics of cultural difference that situates offensiveness at the boundaries of cultural groups.

In relation to cultural discourse, it is often assumed that news media whip up scandals by picking up a joke told by a particular comedian and reframing it to maximise shock value. There has also been concern expressed by comedians about an increasing tendency for audiences to vocally object to material they find offensive or politically disagreeable. The chapter critically assesses Mary Douglas' statement that when a joke is judged to be 'in bad taste, risky, too near the bone', controls are 'exerted either on behalf of hierarchy as such, or on behalf of values which are judged too precious and too precarious to be exposed to challenge'.[3] Offensive stand-up comedy may be intrinsically tied to power relations and hierarchy in society, but the values and meanings expressed or ridiculed in stand-up comedy may also be precious and precarious because of their position in hierarchies of power. The impact that power can have on social identities, and the targeting of some identities with symbolic violence, is evaluated through stand-up comedy.

Stand-up comedy and offence are discussed in this chapter through an engagement with the work of the British stand-up comedian Ricky Gervais, in particular his Netflix special *Supernature* (2022), which contains jokes about transgender people. As well as being a stand-up comedian, Gervais is a comedy writer, producer, and actor. He came to prominence for co-writing and acting in the situation comedies *The Office* and *Extras*, where he played the lead characters. Gervais moved into stand-up comedy in 2001. Between 2003 and 2009, four high-profile stand-up comedy shows followed. Each show led to the release of a commercially successful DVD, although Gervais' stand-up comedy received a mediocre critical reception.[4] Gervais' next two stand-up comedy shows, *Humanity* (2017) and *Supernature* (2022), both became Netflix specials. Two of the earlier shows, *Fame* (2007) and *Science* (2009), received criticism for containing jokes about rape.[5] His first Netflix special, *Humanity* (2017), received criticism for jokes about transgender people.

Offensive Stand-Up Comedy, Ridicule, and 'Punching Down'

Offensiveness is not a new phenomenon and it has, historically, formed a stock component of comedy. Aristotle wrote in 360 BC that Greek comedy contained malice and that 'the man with malice will turn out to be happy at his neighbour's misfortune'.[6] Offensive comedy is often interpreted as malicious or cruel by joke targets and audience groups, which suggests there is a connection between the early observations on superiority and comedy and the generation of offence. In 1804, Jean Paul Richter observed that '[f]or a *situation* or an *action* to be ridiculous, we must see in the comic subject not only a true contradiction with the external but a fictive internal contrast'.[7] Offensiveness is often generated when aspects of identity are labelled ridiculous, when the joke target is presented as holding discursively incongruous positions on identity characteristics, or when aspects of an identity are presented as a fiction. This resonates with jokes about transgender people from Ricky Gervais:

> And now we understand things more, we're more tolerant. We're – I think it's going too far the other way, though, because now *nothing's* mental. You can't find summat that someone's – Nothing is considered mental. *Everything* is a syndrome or an addiction or a preference, right? I could have my legs removed – have wheels put on, identify as a pram, right – [laughter] And if you say I'm mental, you're a bigot, right? [audience laughing] Now – That's a bit hack, that joke, now, isn't it? 'Oh, I identify as a thing, then.' It's a bit old-fashioned, but I'm gonna leave it in to annoy people, right? Because that's the bit that'll offend people. Same as *Humanity*. I talk about AIDS, famine, cancer, the Holocaust, rape, paedophilia, but no, the one thing you mustn't joke about is identity politics. The one thing you should never joke about is the trans issue, right. 'They just wanna be treated equally.' I agree. That's why I include them. [Laughter and applause][8]

In this extract, Gervais constructs humour around the idea of transgender identification as a fiction, which aligns with the definition of ridicule offered by Jean Paul Richter. This constructs the transgendered person as the ridiculous object of laughter. Gervais then adds to the definition of the identity as fiction and ridiculous by discussing offence. Here, Gervais uses the notion of being an equal opportunity offender and inclusive of transgender because it is included in his routine. Despite this disclaimer, the joke relies on a diminution of identity and thus a humour of superiority. Offensive stand-up comedy is dependent on the diminution of the othered identity, but it is also developed and continued by the offended other because such comedy derives its power from explicitly pre-empting and ridiculing the offence it will cause. The offended other is then locked into a cycle of ridicule when they protest and the offence itself provides symbolic material for the further generation of ridicule.

In line with the description Gervais gives of the reception of his transgender jokes, there is evidence that humour and comedy can generate more than just laughter and that this too is connected with reactions of offence towards comedy. Nancy Bell explains, in relation to humour, 'that the range of responses is much broader than simply laughter'.[9] Unlaughter (or not laughing) is one such response and can be used to communicate 'a lack of appreciation of, or perhaps offense at, the joke'.[10] Unlaughter might be either conscious or unconscious and Bell outlines how unlaughter or serious responses, which includes offence, are more likely to be generated by 'aggressive forms of humor that contain a negative, if playful, message'.[11] Irony and jocular abuse are also identified by Bell as particularly prone to the signalling of unlaughter.[12] Highlighted in this discussion are the old connections between comedy, ridicule, and offence, which are fuelled through the incongruities of identity, context, and discourse, and provoke a range of responses from receptive laughter to unreceptive unlaughter. Bell's research emphasises that laughter is not the only response to humour and implies that it is an attempt to evoke a power relationship in discourse to assert a 'proper' response to humour.

Examples of stand-up comedy demonstrate that claims of offensiveness can be connected with very different issues, perspectives, and discourses but that all maintain political importance and are further politicised through the controversies that develop around them. In 1964, the US stand-up comedian Lenny Bruce was convicted of obscenity because of language used in his stand-up comedy. Bruce had used language judged to be obscene in a number of performances and had been arrested on three separate occasions. Similar uses of profanity appeared in the stand-up comedy of Richard Pryor, in the late 1960s, without intervention by US law enforcement in what was a changed cultural context ushered in by the ending of US censorship, the influence of a liberal Supreme Court under Earl Warren, and an emerging social permissiveness. More recently still, contemporary British comedians have courted controversy and faced claims of offensiveness from different groups and individuals. In 2010, Frankie Boyle, in his Channel 4 stand-up comedy and sketch show, *Frankie Boyle's Tramadol Nights*, told a rape joke (that included themes of incest and disability) about the celebrity Katie Price and her disabled son. The programme received a number of complaints and Ofcom, the UKs broadcast media regulator, ruled that the joke had broken rules in relation to harm and offence for not providing 'adequate protection for members of the public from the inclusion in such services of harmful and/or offensive material' and for not ensuring 'that material which may cause offence is justified by the context'.[13] Channel 4's defence that it was 'absurdist satire' was rejected by Ofcom, who noted that 'simply because humour is absurd or surreal does not, in itself, lessen its potential to offend'.[14] This example reminds us that in the UK, broadcast comedy does not operate in a 'free speech bubble'. More broadly, it suggests that claims of offensiveness are not necessarily a misreading of comedy or hyperbolic in relation to culturally accepted modes of discourse, and can be legally reinforced. The stand-up comedian Jimmy Carr has also received criticism for rape jokes in a number of stand-up comedy shows and most recently in *His Dark Material* (2021), a high-profile Netflix special. The show also contained a joke about the murder of the Roma people in Nazi concentration camps that received widespread criticism for offensiveness in media and political discussion.

Both Frankie Boyle and Jimmy Carr have been described through the idea of a 'new offensiveness', which was coined by the *Guardian* comedy critic, Brian Logan, in 2009.[15] For Logan, examples of contemporary comedy resonate more with the 'offensiveness' of older, 1970s and 1980s stand-up, with the material of Bernard Manning and Jim Davidson, than with the politically correct or satirical style of the alternative comedy movement. Here, 'new' is taken to refer to a re-emergence rather than the invention of a particular form of offensive comedy. That said, neither Manning nor Davidson used rape as a stock joke content in their stand-up comedy. Hunt discusses how Boyle and Carr often use rape as a subject and argues that 'Jimmy Carr, for example, seems more confident with rape than race as a stand up'.[16] He highlights how Boyle's female targets are often those who do not display dominant femininity.[17] Both Carr and Boyle defend their comedy as 'ironic' or 'satiric'.[18] Explored in more depth later, Ricky Gervais has used similar joke content and methods of defence or disclaimers. The US stand-up comedian Dave Chappelle, like Gervais, has received criticism and accusations of offence for jokes about LGBTQ+ people, particularly in the Netflix specials *Sticks & Stones* (2019) and *The Closer* (2021).

Such examples of stand-up comedy that offend are often discussed in social discourse through loose concepts of 'punching up' and 'punching down', or targeting those with more or less power, status, and capital than the comedian or that of the identity group of the receptive audience. Interestingly, the concepts of punching up or punching down are also discussed by a number of these comedians (see, e.g., Dave Chappelle in *The Closer* (2021)), and disclaimers are created around the ideas that layer the notion of punching down with comic incongruity and ambiguity. This is done by Ricky Gervais in *Supernature* (2022):

> But now there's so much outrage, and we hear about it, and it's taken seriously, you know? There's Oxbridge comedians writing for the posh papers, the rules of comedy, they're laying it down, laying down the law. Right? And it's all stuff like, erm, 'Comedy should punch up. You should never punch down. You should never punch down.' Sometimes you've gotta punch down, like if you're beating up a disabled toddler. [laughter] Know what I mean? If you punch up, you'll miss the little cunt, and he'll win. [laughter] You know. I like that joke 'cause it highlights the difference between metaphorical punching down in jokes and actual [laughter] punching down. But people nowadays want you to believe that words are actual violence, right? Now, you laughed at a joke about beating up a disabled toddler. No one got hurt. If I'd have actually dragged out a disabled toddler [laughter] and started beating him up, you wouldn't laugh, right? [laughter] That's why I dropped that bit. [laughter]

This example sees Ricky Gervais ridicule the notion of punching down through evoking a populist position that sees punching down as something that is pushed by various comedy elites, and that it is a strategy for critiquing comedians like him who are not a part of that elite group. Gervais then goes on to argue that people who use the concept of punching down do not understand language and mistake it for 'actual violence'. This is a further disclaimer – equal opportunity offending is acceptable because language is not harmful. This position, as a disclaimer, ignores or misunderstands the performative component of language. The philosopher of language J. L. Austin explains that in performative language, 'the uttering of a sentence is, or is a part of, the doing of an action'.[19] In applying this to offensive comedy, and as language connects with the generation of emotion, or encourages emotional reaction or affect, we can assert that to say offensive words is *to be* offensive, that offensive language is so because it is performative.

The Characteristics of Offensive Stand-Up Comedy

Defining the characteristics of offensive stand-up comedy, or offensive comedy more generally, is not an easy task. Offensive comedy is hotly debated and some, such as Ricky Gervais, deny its existence, or at least argue that particular examples of offence are not genuine. It is reasonable to assume that a range of responses can be generated by stand-up comedy, in addition to laughter.[20] It is also reasonable to assume that when offence is generated by stand-up comedians, there is the generation of emotional hurt, or that there is an affective response to the comedy by the individual that produces negative emotion – such as emotional distress – rather than amusement or laughter. The idea that offensive stand-up comedy might be harmful is addressed later. It is, however, arguable that a negative emotional or affective response, or offence, at stand-up comedy, is not enough to render criticism of it valid. It is also arguable that not all claims of offence are genuine. When it occurs, offence is intrinsically linked to the moral values and taboos of a culture, or group within a culture, and these change across time and space (or context). For example, many, but not all, would now argue that Lenny Bruce was mistreated and did not produce unacceptable comedy in 1960s America. Challenges to offensive stand-up comedy need to be (and often are) accompanied by a wider description of how stand-up comedy produces meanings that are socially and politically problematic or offensive.

It is widely recognised that humour, comedy, and jokes can function as rhetorical devices and have the potential to form convincing communication.[21] This is because of the identical structure of humour and rhetorical devices such as metaphor or metonym, which have a family resemblance with incongruity. It is possible to connect the rhetoric of comedy with symbolic violence, the concept from the French sociologist Pierre Bourdieu that describes the process by which groups accept that their *habitus* – or life-world – is less significant or valuable than others. Language plays a key role in convincing us of the value of a *habitus*. Malicious humour as rhetoric can be the enactment of symbolic violence, or at least an attempt at it.

When offence is generated from stand-up comedy that deals with protected characteristics, such as in examples of racist or sexist humour, the grounds for offence are clearer and the critique of stand-up comedy more straightforward. This activity has been much enhanced by scholars in the field of critical comedy studies. The ideologies that are being rhetorically strengthened and which are effective in generating hurt are generally, if not universally, accepted as socially problematic, and this is often recognised in law. Generated offence becomes more difficult to interpret in situations where offence is the outcome of stand-up comedy that describes protected characteristics that come into conflict with one another, where protected characteristics overlap, where the offence is generated because of aspects of identity that are not protected by law, where critique or satire of a topic is more socially acceptable (which could be because social mores have shifted, for example, in jokes about religion, religious figures or belief), or where the legal frameworks that censor speech on a particular topic are subject to contestation. This represents some of the liquidity or ambiguity of discourses of offensiveness, which are frequently contested. In practice, the act of defining offensive comedy is an ambiguous process for broadcast media organisations. Mills outlines the difficulties that regulators in the UK have faced in defining acceptable and offensive television comedy, which principally stem from the ambiguities of comedy itself. Mills cites audience research from the BBC's 2009 publication *Taste, Standards and the BBC* that lists 'strong language', trust in the comedian, and context as factors that impact on definitions of offensiveness in relation to television comedy.[22] Some writers have attempted to define the characteristics of offensive comedy. Jerry Palmer argues that three factors impact on the definition of offensive humour and comedy. These include the structure of a joke; the dynamics between the target of the joke, the audience, and the comedian; and the context of the joke.[23] These factors mirror the Aristotelian rhetoric triangle of speaker, audience, and content,[24] and thus connect with the processes of meaning generation in language use more generally. It is also evident that this work aligns with the guidance used by the BBC (as mentioned earlier). Of course, relationships between stand-up comedians and audiences, and the definitions of contexts, can be multiple, and joke structures and targets can also be ambiguous. This complicates further the analysis of offensive stand-up comedy.

Stand-up comedians have a range of potential responses to claims of offensiveness directed at them, which may mitigate such claims and/or extend controversies. Comedians may use existing social discourse and arguments to justify offensive content. This can be seen in many forms of offensive comedy, although in each case the arguments for offensiveness can be constructed with different normative frameworks. Comedians perform a number of rhetorical strategies around their comedy to prevent criticism and present a certain type of discourse, and employ a number of 'justification ideologies', one of which is 'the "I'm being ironic" narrative'.[25] Although there appears to be nothing new in the use of offensive material in British stand-up comedy, this strategy of justification or disclaimer was not used by the stand-up comedians of the 1970s and 1980s, such as Bernard Manning and Jim Davidson, who were far more likely to assert that their material was 'just a joke' and, for example, that their racist jokes did not reflect their true opinions.[26] We might say that where stand-up comedy used to be 'just a joke' it is now 'ironic offensiveness'. Ricky Gervais, in *Supernature* (2022), uses irony as a means of justifying his comedy:

Stand-Up Comedy and Offence 197

Okay, right. That was irony, okay? There's gonna be a bit of that throughout the show. See if you can spot it. OK? [laughter] Now – that's when I say summat I don't really mean, for comic effect, and you, as an audience, you laugh at the wrong thing 'cause you know what the right thing is. It's a way of satirising attitudes. Like that first joke, I used the old-fashioned sexist trope that women aren't funny. Now, in real life, I know there are loads of funny women. Like, um – [laughter] I did it again. Well spotted. Good. [laughter]

The labelling of the material as irony, as not meant, and of this being understood by the audience, is a description of the encoding and decoding process that forms a metalinguistic defence of the joke and a pre-empting of criticism. In Gervais' preferred reading, the audience encode the material as not meant, and all other encodings are illegitimate because they are misreadings. The use of disclaimers and denials are intrinsic components of the discourse of offensiveness itself, evidenced through the common placing of such explanations before or after accusations of offence or hurt in social discourse. Bennett distinguishes between sarcastic irony, satiric irony, both of which are more obvious, and blank irony.[27] He describes the latter as '[w]hat is being said is perhaps not meant – we can't be sure – but neither is it actively criticised',[28] and that '[t]he irony matters especially here because of what (if we take it literally) it is *about*'.[29] What is important in this discussion is that blank irony or satire may fail to develop a satirical or ironic reading, or may never have been intended to get there at all, through the construction of aggressive humour or ridicule. We could argue that Gervais' disclaimer is an example of sarcastic irony because the extract is signposted as irony, but it fits the definition of blank irony because the stereotype of women being not funny is not actively criticised.

Satire and irony that discuss a social problem or identity around which offence is possible, which does not sufficiently address that problem or identity, offers a polysemic discourse that can generate laughter and ridicule with the offended as the joke target. If blank irony/satire does not offer sufficient clues on the reversal of meaning, if intent is neither stated nor the humour obviously ironic, there remains no straightforward or coherent method for asserting that polysemy – or multiple possible meanings – is *not* the outcome. In the case of Ricky Gervais, there is no reversal of stereotype present in the comedy, and although the comedian may not actively believe the stereotype, there is no counterargument offered to undermine the stereotype. A defence of irony/satire, where the irony/satire is blank, is similar to the 'it's just a joke' disclaimer that has been extensively critiqued as a rhetorical device to defend against criticism.[30] Blank irony assumes a difference from traditional stand-up comedy, which was supposedly less reflexive or self-aware. It assumes a playing with offence and stereotype that is essentially not 'real' offensive comedy. Traditional British stand-up comedians, such as Bernard Manning, also displayed an understanding of the layers of comedy and seriousness, and were quick to add 'it's just a joke' to explain their material as not serious sexism or racism, or their acts as not the equivalent of their serious beliefs or behaviour.[31] Consideration of this sees the distinction between old and new break down. It also breaks down because stand-up comedians today use the notion of 'just joking' alongside the defence of irony. Gervais explains:

> But they know I'm joking about all the other stuff, but they go, 'No, no, he must be – no, he must mean that', right? Like – like a joke is a window to the comedian's true soul. It's just – that's just not the case. I – I'll take on any view to make the joke funniest. I'll pretend to be right wing. I'll pretend to be left wing. I'll pretend to be clever. I'll pretend to be stupid. Whatever makes the joke funnier, without prejudice. Okay, full disclosure. In real life, of course I support trans rights. I support all human rights, and trans rights are human rights. You know. Live your best life. Use your preferred pronouns. Be the gender that you feel that you are. But meet me halfway, ladies. Lose the cock. That's all I'm saying. [Laughter and applause]

In Gervais' disclaimer, prejudice is held in the mind or soul of the comedian and is something that is meant, rather than being a performative effect of linguistic utterances that do not require intentionality to have an impact. This defence is subject to further irony as Gervais asserts his 'true' position but then undermines and subverts it through a use of humour at the end of the extract. The joke is thus constructed around the seriousness of critiquing offensive comedy.

Is Offensive Stand-Up Comedy Harmful?

In contrast to some 'common sense' and audience notions that jokes are 'just jokes', there is evidence from psychology that humour can have an impact in relation to gender and that this is frequently not acknowledged by joke tellers and receptive audiences. This research aligns closely with a concept of symbolic violence and also adds evidence to the argument that offensive stand-up comedy is performative language engaged in an exchange that requires a receptive audience and an unreceptive joke target or other.

The effects of humour are explored in psychological studies that examine disparagement humour,[32] which has been defined as that which 'denigrates, belittles, or maligns an individual or social group'.[33] This clearly aligns with descriptions of what it is to suffer offence. Disparagement humour studies have discovered facts on the impact of disparagement humour, which include a focus on gender and humour. These findings can be viewed alongside a consideration of the polysemy of humour and comedy – that disparaging and non-disparaging readings may be possible from single instances of stand-up comedy and thus align with the idea of a receptive audience and an unreceptive joke target.

Most research on disparagement humour seeks to record the impact of certain humour types. Ford, Richardson, and Petit explain that evidence 'suggests that *instigating* disparagement humor might indeed foster prejudice against the targeted group'[34] – that joke tellers may be able to develop their own prejudice through disparagement humour. They go on to explain that '[i]t does not appear that *exposure* to disparagement humor promotes a negative disposition towards a targeted group',[35] but that 'disparagement humor functions as a releaser of existing prejudice'.[36] Therefore, disparagement humour will have a prejudicial affect for audiences that already express an amount of prejudice.[37] Another study suggests that 'men who are more sexist find sexist jokes funnier' and that it is through such 'disparaging humour' that sexism becomes normalised.[38] Similarly, research suggest that if someone has hostile sexist attitudes, exposing them to sexist jokes may increase discriminatory attitudes towards women.[39] Such evidence fits with the idea that stereotypes and negative images are recognised and accepted before they can be considered 'funny', but that other readings will occur for the non-receptive audience.[40] In relation to offensive stand-up comedy, it suggests that the offended may well have grounds for complaint based on the reproduction of problematic attitudes.

Thomae and Pina have researched the implications of disparagement humour for male groups. They find that 'sexist humor can serve men to establish positive distinctiveness through intergroup comparisons and reduce male in-group threat'.[41] It thus works on the cohesion of the exclusive male gender group and acts to critique relations with other groups – 'sexist humor can be the result of adherence to in-group norms and a perceived instability or illegitimacy of the intergroup hierarchy'.[42] Thomas and Viki argue that sexist humour 'appears to elevate the propensity to commit rape'.[43] (See Romero-Sánchez et al. for similar findings.[44]) Thus, they suggest, their results 'sound a note of caution towards the use of sexist jokes in social settings'.[45] Thomae and Pina also report research on the impact of sexist humour for rape proclivity and victim blaming:

Viki et al (2007) demonstrated that men reported the highest levels of victim blame for an acquaintance rape victim (as opposed to stranger rape victim) following the exposure to sexist (as opposed to non-sexist) jokes. Moreover, the men in this experimental condition perceived the seriousness of the rape as lower than the men in all other experimental conditions and recommend the lowest number of years for the perpetrator in a prison sentence.[46]

Further evidence suggests that jokes can have a negative impact on their targets. Ford et al. report the negative impact of sexist humour on women: 'we found that women (but not men) reported greater state self-objectification following exposure to sexist comedy clips than neutral comedy clips'.[47] They add: 'sexist humor causes women to engage in more body surveillance compared to neutral humor'.[48] This observation supports the idea that offensive stand-up comedy is a form of symbolic violence and as such has the potential to reinforce inequality between gender groups. There is evidence that gendered humour is not subject to the same level of criticism that other forms of offensive humour receive. For example, Woodzicka et al. show that sexist jokes are less likely to be labelled 'sexist' than racist jokes are likely to be labelled 'racist', and that sexist jokes are less likely than racist jokes to be labelled 'offensive'.[49] At present, disparagement humour studies have not focused on disparaging jokes about transgender people.

This research implies that if offensive stand-up comedy is to function as irony or satire – to be specifically political and *critical* of gender hegemony and violence – it needs to convince all genders that it is not offensive. This may be an impossible and paradoxical task as offensive stand-up comedy, I argue, *requires* the unreceptive audience or other and in many recent examples, includes that other in the building of jokes. This may also be a difficult task, from the outset, for a comedian such as Ricky Gervais, who as a white, male, middle-class comedian does not express any evident identity markers that allow for an *ethos* of counter-hegemonic gender critique to be assumed a priori. Gervais, in part, considers some of these objections and builds a further response to the offended other in *Supernature*:

> But these people are virtue signalling. They're trying to bring people down to raise their own status, and they say, 'It's 'cos no, we're protecting minorities.' Like – they're basically saying minorities haven't got a sense of humour, which is so patronising. And I get that as well, what it's like to be outnumbered. In this country, we're still only 5 per cent Black, 5 per cent Asian, 5 per cent LGBTQ, you know? Tiny numbers. Now, I'm a white, heterosexual multimillionaire, right? [laughter and cheering] Um – There's less than 1 per cent of us. [laughter] But – do I whine? No! Do I – [laughter] I don't mind. I just get on with it. 'Come on, Rick. Come on, Rick!

[laughter]' 'Just keep fi–' I'm like Rosa Parks, d'you know what I mean? I'm like – [laughter] Except I fought for the right to *never* have to take a seat on a bus, but – . [laughter]

Again, Gervais asserts the notion that he is an equal opportunity offender and that it is in fact those who do not tell jokes about minority groups that are discriminating and being 'patronising'. He does this through irony, through the idea that he is a minority, and the extract draws on the boastfulness that is a key component of Gervais' stand-up persona. Despite the irony, the discourse leaves in place the idea that all representation in stand-up comedy is equally positive and not connected to problematic social discourses or performative speech acts of offence. It also resonates with much of the discourse of older British stand-up comedy, which often depicted the white male comedian as picked on and as a minority in their own land.[50] Returning to the instability of telling jokes about other genders, the task is made more difficult when we consider that Abrams, Bippus, and McGaughey found that gender groups typically find jokes about their gender less funny than jokes about another gender.[51] Yet this could also aid the paradox of offensive comedy that *requires* the receptive audience that laugh and the unlaughter of the offended joke target.

The idea of 'cancel culture' is frequently discussed in popular media and discourse alongside the issues of offensive comedy described in this chapter. It is clear that offensive stand-up comedy in the UK is not subject to censorship when performed live, although there are legal boundaries that govern acceptable speech when all comedy styles are broadcast. It also seems to be the case that the idea of cancel culture is a trope that builds the triad of offensive stand-up comedy, receptive audience, and unreceptive other. The idea of a cancel culture gives the other of comedy a power that it does not possess, forges the comedian as a populist, anti-elitist performer, and maps directly onto the culture war narrative. This gives stand-up comedy a central place in social discourses that deal with cultural taste, values, and beliefs. In these conditions, stand-up comedy is an aestheticised entertainment politics of cultural difference actively engaged in drawing the boundaries between cultural groups. To return to Mary Douglas' statement that when a joke is seen to be 'in bad taste', controls are 'exerted either on behalf of hierarchy as such, or on behalf of values which are judged too precious and too precarious to be exposed to challenge', we can see that criticism of stand-up comedy that is judged offensive represents a response to the performativity of offensive speech acts. These responses are not always made on behalf of those in power and thus can attempt to 'punch up' towards the offensive comedian. It follows that although offensive stand-up comedy may be intrinsically tied to power relations and hierarchy in society, the values and meanings expressed or ridiculed in stand-up comedy may be precarious because of their position in hierarchies of power, the marginality of some identities, and the impact of symbolic violence on some identities. The sum of the argument and evidence provided in this chapter on the performativity of offensive stand-up comedy points towards the potential benefits of some capacity for censure of offensive comedy by stand-up comedians in relation to marginalised groups. However, because offensive stand-up comedy is a genre with a structure in which the offended other is essential, it seems inevitable that practitioners of it will ignore such censure.

Notes

1. Pippa Norris and Ronald Inglehart, *Cultural Backlash: Trump, Brexit, and Authoritarian Populism* (Cambridge: Cambridge University Press, 2019).
2. Simon Weaver, *The Rhetoric of Brexit Humour: Comedy, Populism and the EU Referendum* (London and New York: Routledge, 2021).
3. Mary Douglas 'The Social Control of Cognition: Some Factors in Joke Perception', *Man*, Vol. 3, No. 3, 1968: p. 366.
4. Newsnight Review, 'Ricky Gervais – Animals', *BBC News*, 13 January 2003, http://news.bbc.co.uk/1/hi/programmes/newsnight/review/2654105.stm.
5. Simon Weaver and Karen Morgan, 'What's the Point of Offensive Humour', *The Conversation*, 2017, https://theconversation.com/what-is-the-point-of-offensive-humour-76889.
6. Plato. '*Philebus* (360 BCE): The Basis of Comedy', in Magna Romanska and Alan Ackerman (eds), *Reader in Comedy: An Anthology of Theory and Criticism* (London and New York: Bloomsbury, 2017), p. 33.
7. Jean Paul Richter, 'On the Ridiculous' and 'The Comic in Drama (1804)', in Magna Romanska and Alan Ackerman (eds), *Reader in Comedy: An Anthology of Theory and Criticism* (London and New York: Bloomsbury, 2017), p. 161.
8. Ricky Gervais, *Supernature* (UK: Netflix, 2022).
9. Nancy Bell, 'Reactions to Humor, Non-Laugher', in Salvatore Attardo (ed.), *The Encyclopedia of Humor Studies*, Volume 2 (Los Angeles, London, New Delhi, Singapore, and Washington, DC: Sage, 2014), p. 268.
10. Bell, 'Reactions to Humor, Non-Laugher', p. 629.
11. Bell, 'Reactions to Humor, Non-Laugher', p. 629.
12. Bell, 'Reactions to Humor, Non-Laugher'.
13. Ofcom, 'Section Two: Harm and Offence', 3 March 2021, www.ofcom.org.uk/tv-radio-and-on-demand/broadcast-codes/broadcast-code/section-two-harm-offence.
14. Ofcom, *Ofcom Broadcast Bulletin*, No. 179, 2011, www.ofcom.org.uk/__data/assets/pdf_file/0028/46729/obb179.pdf.
15. Leon Hunt, 'Near the Knuckle? It Nearly Took My Arm Off! British Comedy and the "New Offensiveness"', *Comedy Studies*, Vol. 1, No. 2, 2010: pp. 181–190.
16. Hunt, 'Near the Knuckle?', p. 183.

17. Hunt, 'Near the Knuckle?', p. 185.
18. Josh Halliday, 'Frankie Boyle's Use of Racial Language Intended as Satire, Says Channel 4', *The Guardian*, 23 December 2010, www.theguardian.com/media/2010/dec/23/frankie-boyle-tramadol-nights.
19. J. L. Austin, 'Performatives and Constatives', in Paul Cobley (ed.), *The Communication Theory Reader* (Abingdon and New York: Routledge, 1996), p. 257.
20. Bell, 'Reactions to Humor, Non-Laugher'.
21. Simon Weaver, *The Rhetoric of Racist Humour: US, UK and Global Race Joking* (London and New York: Routledge, 2016).
22. Brett Mills, 'A Special Freedom: Regulating Comedy Offence', in Chiara Bucaria and Luca Barra (eds), *Taboo Comedy: Television and Controversial Humour* (London: Palgrave Macmillan, 2016), p. 214.
23. Jerry Palmer, *Taking Humour Seriously* (London and New York: Routledge, 1994), p. 164.
24. Aristotle, *The Art of Rhetoric* (London: HarperCollins, 2012), pp. 184–185.
25. Lloyd Peters and Sue Becker, 'Racism in Comedy Reappraised: Back to Little England?', *Comedy Studies*, Vol. 1, No. 2, 2010: p. 195.
26. Weaver, *The Rhetoric of Racist Humour*.
27. Joe Bennett, 'The Critical Problem of Cynical Irony: *Meaning What You Say* and Ideologies of Class and Gender', *Social Semiotics*, Vol. 26, No. 3, 2016: pp. 250–264.
28. Bennett, 'The Critical Problem of Cynical Irony', p. 256.
29. Bennett, 'The Critical Problem of Cynical Irony'.
30. Sharon Lockyer, 'Dynamics of Social Class Contempt in Contemporary British Television Comedy', *Social Semiotics*, Vol. 20, No. 2, 2010: pp. 121–138.
31. Stephen Dixon, 'Bernard Manning', *The Guardian*, 18 June 2007, www.theguardian.com/news/2007/jun/18/guardianobituaries.obituaries1.
32. Dolf Zillman, 'Disparagement Humor', in Paul E. McGhee and Jeffrey H. Goldstein (eds), *Handbook of Humor Research*, Volume 1 (New York: Springer, 1983), pp. 85–107.
33. Thomas Ford and Mark A. Ferguson, 'Social Consequences of Disparagement Humor: A Prejudiced Norm Theory', *Personality and Social Psychology Review*, Vol. 8, No. 1, 2004: p. 79.
34. Thomas Ford, Kyle Richardson, and Whitney Petit, 'Disparagement Humor and Prejudice: Contemporary Theory and Research', *Humor*, Vol. 28, No. 2, 2015: p. 171.
35. Ford, Richardson, and Petit, 'Disparagement Humor and Prejudice'.
36. Ford, Richardson, and Petit, 'Disparagement Humor and Prejudice'.
37. Katherine M. Ryan and Jeanne Kanjorski, 'The Enjoyment of Sexist Humor, Rape Attitudes, and Relationship Aggression in College Students', *Sex Roles*, Vol. 38, Nos. 9/10, 1998: pp. 743–756.
38. Miranda A. H. Horvath, Peter Hegarty, Suzannah Tyler, and Sophie Mansfield, '"Lights on at the End of the Party": Are Lads' Mags Mainstreaming Dangerous Sexism?', *British Journal of Psychology*, Vol. 103, No. 4, 2012: p. 455.

39. Manuela Thomae and Afroditi Pina, 'Sexist Humor and Social Identity: The Role of Sexist Humor in Men's in-group Cohesion, Sexual Harassment, Rape Proclivity, and Victim Blame', *Humor*, Vol. 28, No. 2, 2015: pp. 187–204.
40. Weaver, *The Rhetoric of Racist Humour*; Paul Butterfield, 'Comment on "Taking Humour (Ethics) Seriously, but Not Too Seriously"', *Journal of Practical Ethics*, 15 January 2015, www.jpe.ox.ac.uk/letters/comment-on-taking-humour-ethics-seriously-but-not-too-seriously/#more-340.
41. Thomae and Pina, 'Sexist Humor and Social Identity', p. 200.
42. Thomae and Pina, 'Sexist Humor and Social Identity', p. 200.
43. Manuela Thomae and G. Tendayi Viki, 'Why Did the Woman Cross the Road? The Effect of Sexist Humor on Men's Rape Proclivity', *Journal of Social, Evolutionary, and Cultural Psychology*, Vol. 7, No. 3, 2013: p. 264.
44. Monica Romero-Sánchez, Mercedes Durán, Hugo Carretero-Dios, Jesus L. Megias, and Miguel Moya, 'Exposure to Sexist Humor and Rape Proclivity: The Moderator Effect of Aversiveness Ratings', *Journal of Interpersonal Violence*, Vol. 25, No. 12, 2010: pp. 2339–2350; and Monica Romero-Sánchez, Hugoi Carretero-Dios, Jesus L. Megías, Miguel Moya, and Thomas E. Ford, 'Sexist Humor and Rape Proclivity: The Moderating Role of Joke Teller Gender and Severity of Sexual Assault', *Violence against Women*, Vol. 23, No. 8, 2017: pp. 951–972.
45. Thomae and Viki, 'Why Did the Woman Cross the Road?', p. 264.
46. Thomae and Pina, 'Sexist Humor and Social Identity', p. 198.
47. Thomas E. Ford, Julie A. Woodzicka, Whitney E. Petit, Kyle Richardson, and Shaun K. Lappi, 'Sexist Humor as a Trigger of State Self-Objectification in Women', *Humor*, Vol. 28, No. 2, 2015: p. 253.
48. Ford, Woodzicka, Petit, Richardson, and Lappi, 'Sexist Humor as a Trigger of State Self-Objectification in Women', p. 253.
49. Julia A. Woodzicka, Robyn K. Mallett, Shelbi Hendricks, and Astrid V. Pruitt, 'It's Just a (Sexist) Joke: Comparing Reactions to Sexist versus Racist Communications', *Humor*, Vol. 28, No. 2, 2012: pp. 289–309.
50. Weaver, *The Rhetoric of Racist Humour*, pp. 110–116.
51. Jessica R. Abrams, Amy M. Bippus, and Karen J. McGaughey, 'Gender Disparaging Jokes: An Investigation of Sexist-Nonstereotypical Jokes on Funniness, Typicality, and the Moderating Role of Ingroup Identification', *Humor*, Vol. 28, No. 2, 2015: pp. 311–326.

Further Reading

Bell, Nancy, 'Reactions to Humor, Non-laugher', in Salvatore Attardo (ed.), *The Encyclopedia of Humor Studies*, Volume 2 (Los Angeles, London, New Delhi, Singapore, and Washington, DC: Sage, 2014).
Bennett, Joe, 'The Critical Problem of Cynical Irony: *Meaning What You Say* and Ideologies of Class and Gender', *Social Semiotics*, Vol. 26, No. 3, 2016: pp. 250–264.

Hunt, Leon, 'Near the Knuckle? It Nearly Took My Arm Off! British Comedy and the "New Offensiveness"', *Comedy Studies*, Vol. 1, No. 2, 2010: pp. 181–190.

Lockyer, Sharon, 'Dynamics of Social Class Contempt in Contemporary British Television Comedy', *Social Semiotics*, Vol. 20, No.2, 2010: pp. 121–138.

Mills, Brett, 'A Special Freedom: Regulating Comedy Offence', in Chiara Bucaria and Luca Barra (eds), *Taboo Comedy: Television and Controversial Humour* (London: Palgrave Macmillan, 2016), pp. 209–226.

Pérez, Raúl, *The Souls of White Jokes: How Racist Humor Fuels White Supremacy* (Stanford, CA: Stanford University Press, 2022).

Peters, Lloyd and Sue Becker, 'Racism in Comedy Reappraised: Back to Little England?', *Comedy Studies*, Vol. 1, No. 2, 2010: pp. 191–200.

Weaver, Simon, *The Rhetoric of Brexit Humour: Comedy, Populism and the EU Referendum* (London and New York: Routledge, 2021).

Weaver, Simon, *The Rhetoric of Racist Humour: US, UK and Global Race Joking* (London and New York: Routledge, 2016).

Weaver, Simon and Karen Morgan, 'What's the Point of Offensive Humour?', *The Conversation*, 2017, https://theconversation.com/what-is-the-point-of-offensive-humour-76889.

CHAPTER 11

Stand-Up and Politics
Sophie Quirk

In the December of 2015, comedian Sofie Hagen opened the inaugural episode of *The Guilty Feminist* podcast with the words, 'I'm a feminist – *but* last time I met up with Deborah I was wearing a new top and every fifth minute I felt desperate for her to mention that I looked pretty. [laugh]'[1] Her co-host and fellow comic Deborah Frances-White laughed, crying 'is that true?!' before responding, 'I'm a feminist – but some days my life doesn't even pass the Bechdel test. [laughter]'[2]

Hagen left the podcast in the autumn of 2016. Frances-White has continued, joined by rotating co-hosts. She has become a significant voice in contemporary feminism; her achievements include a bestselling book and a Comedy Women in Print Game Changer award. The podcast achieved over 50 million downloads by 2018,[3] generated over 280 episodes by the time of writing in 2021, routinely fills large theatre venues for its live recordings, has scooped several awards, and has engaged its audience in activism, charitable donation, and volunteering on an impressive scale. Although based in the UK, it has engaged an international audience. The joke structure that opened the first episode – 'I'm a feminist but ... ', followed by the speaker's confession of a thought or act which they feel undermines their feminism – continues to open episodes to this day.

When we describe stand-up as 'political', we may mean a range of things. Some comedy is considered political because it talks about formal political structures such as government and its policies: for example, when *The Guilty Feminist* voices opposition to the UK's Police, Crime, Sentencing and Courts Bill,[4] or the abandonment of civilians in Afghanistan following the withdrawal of US and UK troops.[5] The term 'politics' may also describe the podcast's feminist and anti-hierarchical agenda. *The Guilty Feminist* further embodies a political position in the way that its stand-up components are arranged and presented, including in decisions about which comedians to stage, the podcast's emphasis on collaboration over combat and competition, and how comic licence is used and understood.

Stand-Up and Politics

Figure 11.1 (L–R) Jessica Fostekew, Deborah Frances-White, and Katie Melua attend a live podcast recording of *The Guilty Feminist* by Deborah Frances-White during the London Podcast Festival at King's Place, London, 26 September 2020
Photo: Dave Benett / Contributor / Dave Benett Collection / Getty Images.

The podcast is not solely – or even primarily – a stand-up comedy show. Structurally, panel discussion forms the main framework of almost all episodes. Frances-White and her co-host will typically perform a short stand-up set each but other kinds of act, such as music and poetry, are also frequently included. The podcast regularly features guests who are not comedians, and some episodes have had no stand-up segments at all. The intent is not only to be funny and entertaining but also to educate, inspire, and motivate listeners to engage in feminist activity for the benefit of themselves and others. All episodes will include jokes and laughter, but most engage a range of emotions such as joy, anger, and fear. Some discussions are truly harrowing.

Nonetheless, *The Guilty Feminist* is a platform for stand-up comedy. While most comedians can perform the same material numerous times to different audiences, Frances-White's is regularly broadcast to a loyal audience, so she must constantly create new writing.[6] She has calculated that this demanding format requires her to produce a whopping nine hours of stand-up material per year.[7] *The Guilty Feminist* has hosted events that look and feel more like live comedy shows, and has helped to build loyal and enthusiastic fanbases for the comedians that feature on it. Frances-White describes the podcast as her own, alternative business model in a comedy industry where the odds have historically been stacked against women.[8]

This chapter interprets *The Guilty Feminist* as way of presenting stand-up comedy in an innovative format, while acknowledging that the podcast offers other things as well. Frances-White's format provides particularly interesting example of how comedians' politics shape their practice because she has developed, and made public, a detailed political philosophy and has articulated how this underpins her stand-up. This is evident in her book, *The Guilty Feminist: From Our Noble Goals to Our Worst Hypocrisies*, and also in the many interviews that she has given where her feminism – and its impact upon her craft and creativity – are discussed. Frances-White does not produce the podcast alone: latterly, it has gained a support team and its producer, Tom Salinsky, has been acknowledged from the start as an important co-creator. His responsibilities include editing live material into podcast episodes, so he has significant influence over content. He is often mentioned, and sometimes heard, in his role as producer or as Frances-White's husband. He is clear, though, that the podcast ultimately represents her vision, saying, 'I defer any and all artistic decisions to Deb'.[9]

The podcast is used here as an example through which to explore how the politics of a stand-up performance are woven through every aspect of that performance, both in ways that are made visible and in ways that remain comparatively hidden. This chapter argues that the politics of stand-up comedy performances are embedded not only in their content but also in their form.

Deciding Whom to Stage

The vast majority of people to have featured on *The Guilty Feminist* are women. This forms one of the podcast's most visible, and obviously political, points of difference to mainstream platforms. Typically, it is Frances-White and her co-host who participate in the 'I'm a feminist but … ' joking segment and who deliver all of the stand-up comedy, and there have only been a few occasions where the co-host is a man. Frances-White has said: 'when I started the podcast … I mostly started it to wallow in my own oppression. What I've learnt about more than anything is my own privilege.'[10] She explains:

> [T]here are so many, many, many more marginalised women and people of minority genders than me ... there are many, many men who are far more marginalised than me, who are far more oppressed than me, who have far less voice than me, and so my feminism has become much more about closing power gaps ... and trying to fight injustice wherever it is, and sometimes it isn't along gender lines.

This means that Frances-White is constantly working to ensure that both she and her guests acknowledge hierarchies and oppression in an intersectional way, and the podcast books as diverse a range of minority and marginalised performers as it can. *The Guilty Feminist* provides a platform not only for women but for diverse, underrepresented voices.

The decision to reserve space for women and minority performers reflects a live controversy in the comedy industry. In recent years, some sections of the industry have engaged in efforts to diversify, giving more space to women and minorities. One of the most publicised examples is the BBC's edict that there must be at least one woman in the line-up for its TV panel shows, which form an important platform for comedians looking to achieve a foothold in public consciousness. This emphasis on diversity has received some backlash. Comedian Sara Pascoe explains:

> Comedy, because it's a live thing and people come to see *you* if they want to see you, for lots of people has to be meritocratic ... and, 'you do *not* get to skip the queue because you don't have a penis, because there's only one-in-twenty of you or because you've got [a] different racial background to me' .... I've met so many men who think women have stolen their careers, or brown people.[11]

One noxious effect of this attitude is that some comedians face the misinterpretation that their success is due to assistance from the very systems that have marginalised them, rather than their own merit. Sindhu Vee recalls being told that, although she is a good comic, it 'helps' to have '"a different" [Vee laughs] "racial perspective": I was like, dude, it is not helpful in any way that I'm Indian in *anything*. In some things it doesn't help *at all*.'[12]

Frances-White acknowledges that *The Guilty Feminist* can be a comparatively tough environment for male performers. Recording on Zoom during theatre closures resulting from the Covid-19 pandemic, Frances-White tells her cis-gendered, male co-host Richard Herring: 'if you came out onto the stage to do stand-up comedy at *The Guilty Feminist*, there would be people look at each other and go "oh. This is not what we've come for."'[13] Frances-White has observed that her male guests sometimes 'shrink a little and behave like the lone woman on a panel of men. They get nervous, take up less space, try harder than they need to.'[14] She elaborates: 'Every time without fail, the audience have warmed to the male guests we've had, and they've relaxed in turn and the show has been terrific ... but the microclimate that we've inadvertently created gives more power, space and assumption of brilliance to women.' Richard Herring reflects: 'in the last ten years, the comedy scene – certainly the comedy scene that I'm involved with – has changed enough that the audience wouldn't be weirded out by, you know, several women on a bill but definitely [Herring laughs] for most of the time I've been a comedian that would be [the case]'.[15] Herring's qualifier – 'the comedy scene that I'm involved with' – is an important one. Often, women on the comedy circuit face the same disadvantages as cis men encounter at *The Guilty Feminist*. In creating an environment where men are minoritised and particularised, the podcast is responding to a wider context where the opposite is much more common and likely to be read as 'normal'.[16]

Pascoe acknowledges the view that diversity drives subvert meritocracy, but offers an alternative narrative:

> I gig with a lot of men who think that they are better than me, and sometimes they have done gigs where they have done better than me. Now, in that narrative how unfair is the world? ... There are men who are in their 50s who used to *own* this career who can't get on television now – and it's true, they can't. And rather than them thinking, 'I should maybe try ... I should maybe stop with the homophobia or ... being horrible about fat people' – right? That is a really unfashionable kind of comedy and it's not going to get you on television. And rather than them thinking that's why they can't get on television they go, 'cause *you're* there. *Sitting in my seat.*'[17]

Pascoe asserts that, although there remains an audience for the type of comedy that she posits as outdated – 'if you want to go and see ... any type of comic, they still exist, no one's cancelled them, no one's shut them down' – the 'gigs that are flourishing are the most diverse. The ones that didn't diversify ... they died.' Frances-White concurs: 'You might think "oh, I'm a straight, white, cis man *(whines)* I'm not allowed to speak anymore." Yes you are ... Find something relevant to say that people wanna say at the moment, that's really in your heart to say, and find a unique way of saying it, or, you know, work on your craft ... and you will find your audience.'[18]

In this narrative, the diversification of comedy is posited not as the result of an anti-meritocratic ethos but rather as the product of meritocratic and commercial structures: more diverse comedy is marketable to the largest contemporary audiences. This candid co-option of capitalistic discourse reflects a political standpoint and a departure from former trends.

Stewart Lee explains how, in the early part of his career in the 1980s, 'under the shadow of an unattainable ideal of ideological purity, nobody, not bands or stand-up comedians or comic-book creators, wanted to be seen to "sell-out to the Man" by … achieving any level of commercial sustainability'.[19] These anti-commercialist credentials have, historically, been associated with progressive politics in comedy. However, these attitudes have supported some very poor and inequitable employment practices. In their study of comedians' working conditions, Nick Butler and Dimitrinka Stoyanova Russell note that 'the intrinsic rewards of creative work serve to obscure – and, at times, justify – highly precarious conditions of employment'.[20] In an informal, atomised, and competitive industry, comedians routinely endure 'emotionally distressing employment conditions',[21] being forced to project an image of diligence, commitment, and friendliness by, for instance, performing for free or enduring uncomplainingly when pay is late, insufficient, or inequitable. Oliver Double observes that, today, 'comedians start out by doing months or years of unpaid new-act nights', and that runs at the Edinburgh Festival Fringe – which are widely seen as an important part of comedians' career progression – 'might well leave them with massive debts'.[22] In addition, the live comedy circuit has been highlighted as a context in which harassment and abuse thrive.

Many comedians are recognising an urgent need to make stand-up comedy a safer and more equitable profession, leading to calls for increased professionalisation in the UK. The recent emergence of comedian-led industry bodies the Live Comedy Association and Get Off! Live Comedy respond to this. *The Guilty Feminist* also reflects this trend in its attitude to professionalisation. It is notable that the podcast engages in frank dialogue around pay and money. Frances-White openly discusses her business model: performers are paid from live ticket sales (which initially meant running at a loss) and, since the closure of theatres during the Covid-19 pandemic compromised this revenue, also through advertising and fan subscriptions via Patreon.[23] Up to summer 2021, *The Guilty Feminist* had themed no less than three whole shows around money, each of which emphasised that money is an important tool that should be exercised for political benefit. There is no hint of the idea that the pursuit of decent pay is in tension with the artistic or political ethos of stand-up comedy. The pursuit of fair pay and respectful working conditions are posited as important feminist behaviours.

Frances-White asserts that *The Guilty Feminist* and spaces like it have changed the industry such that powerful figures no longer assume that women comedians lack market appeal. By making the proactive choice to stage women and other marginalised voices, the podcast has demonstrated that there is a market for their work. Rather than hiding commercial aspects, the podcast recognises that open discussion of pay and conditions is a prerequisite of progress towards equitability and fairness. These decisions embody Frances-White's political ideals and have been effective as political action.

'Women Taking Up More Space': Collaboration

Traditionally, stand-up comedy has been seen as a highly combative environment. Ross Noble posits this as intrinsic to comedians' training:

> The success of a comic is judged instantly – if they laugh you're a hit, if they don't you're not. Also a fledgling stand-up must often learn their craft in pubs and clubs where their art is being judged … But it is this harsh critical environment that a truly brilliant stand-up must go through to equip them with the skills to develop and form them into a seasoned performer.[24]

Noble reflects a traditional narrative; not only is the comedy gig posited as a 'harsh critical environment', but the comedian's ability to negotiate this is presented as an essential and noble skill. It is combat that enables the comedian to become a 'truly brilliant … seasoned performer'. In addition, relations between comedians themselves are often described as highly and inevitably competitive. Mark Lamarr states: 'It really is the unspoken collective trait of the stand-up. We all think we're the best. You couldn't do it otherwise.'[25] Competition and combat have commonly been accepted – or even venerated – as an inevitable part of the comedian's life and craft.

Many comedians feel that this atmosphere is changing. By 2018, Sara Pascoe noted: 'lots of people [wrongly] think a live gig is going to be really nasty' and unwelcoming; Jarlath Regan agreed, citing this as 'the hangover of those old clubs, and that old vision'.[26] Aisling Bea perceives a cultural shift:

> From the outside looking in, I'd say during the nineties it felt like comedy was a lads' club for people who were quite competitive with each other: [puts on laddish voice] 'Yeah, yeah, no I was best on that gig. I smashed it, yeah, yeah, yeah' … But that's not sustainable for anyone's mental health … I think now, the new comedy isn't just … a place that's safe for women, it's a place that's safe for … anyone who's not, like, competitive or aggressive … It's like there's this whole community that we have that's just really warm and friendly and it just feels lovely.[27]

As Bea suggests, there are a number of stand-up spaces that aim to be less combative, instead encouraging a feeling of 'community'. *The Guilty*

Feminist presents its stand-up in a non-traditional format which emphasises supportiveness and collaboration. A conventional comedy night would introduce each act as a separate entity; for any performer to share their stage would be comparatively rare. At *The Guilty Feminist*, the stand-up segments are solo, but they are framed between sections of discussion. This emphasises dialogue over monologue and enables performers to celebrate (as well as tease) one another. Often, comedy bills have a hierarchy. The final act may be venerated as the 'headliner' with enhanced status and more stage time. The compère holds a position of particular authority: often the only act that gets to appear more than once, they are the visible administrator of the evening and wield significant influence in shaping audience expectation and atmosphere. They appear immediately before and after every act, saying a few words of introduction or response, so that they have the opportunity to shape the audience's interpretation of other performers. At *The Guilty Feminist*, Frances-White co-hosts, with each host introducing the other. These stand-up acts are presented as equals: both are hosts, each performing a set of equal significance. In stark contrast to Lamarr's comment, 'We all think we're the best. You couldn't do it otherwise', Frances-White states that she is often not the funniest stand-up on the podcast, and she is 'absolutely fine with that'.[28]

Frances-White is careful to stress the spirit of collaboration when talking about her supposed competitors, including those in the fields of feminism and podcasting. She consistently emphasises the value and achievements of *The Guilty Feminist*, but also stresses that it is not only this podcast but the wider network of valuable works and actions to which it belongs that is creating change. Asked whether she thinks she is the most powerful voice in UK female comedy, Frances-White refutes the idea in terms which emphasise the importance of collaboration over competition: 'I wouldn't like to do a rating system because I think there are many powerful voices in many different ways'.[29] She lists a number of women working in comedy, articulating what she sees as their particular influence, before concluding: 'I just feel like it's a landscape. And the idea of a power hierarchy doesn't really track with feminism.' She acknowledges that podcasts have emerged with features similar to her own, and says:

> If it's inspiring other women to find a voice and speak then that can only be a good thing ... Like, it's definitely inspired more women to podcast and if I didn't want that what kind of feminist would I be? ... To go, 'Oh no! ... There's only room for one feminist podcast!' Feminism is about women taking up more space. There are millions of male voices that are broadcast on official channels. The internet is a space with no gatekeepers. Women speak up, find your voice, speak on.

The podcast also builds supportive audiences. In conversation with fellow comedian Stuart Goldsmith, Frances-White says:

> *The Guilty Feminist* is a microclimate for success for women … It is a place where, when I say 'and tonight my co-pilot is … ' the audience act like they are at a rock concert … they freak out. And then you see those women come on to the stage. You can't not respond to being treated like a rockstar, you just get a bit bigger. And a few women have said to me ' … this must be what it's like to be a man in a regional comedy club' [White and Goldsmith both laugh] … the expectation of who we were hoping for … we were hoping for you. But it is actually a more powerful, tribal feel at *The Guilty Feminist*.[30]

The podcast employs a number of practices that seek to diminish the combativeness and competitiveness traditionally associated with stand-up comedy. These decisions are informed by Frances-White's politics: she sees competitiveness and combativeness as contrary to the collaborative and mutually supportive atmosphere that expresses feminist principles and supports intersectional, feminist aims. The decision to formulate the show as a podcast, released over the internet – 'a space with no gatekeepers' – creates an opportunity to form a model of production which eschews the hierarchies and commissioning structures of the mainstream comedy industry. The politics of the podcast's creator are woven through these fundamental aspects of its design and format.

Comic Licence: 'It's Not about Censorship, It's about What You Wanna Do'

Like *The Guilty Feminist*, Regan's *Men Behaving Better* is a comedian-led podcast with a mission to advance gender equality. In this case, the focus is on the role played by men. In an episode released in 2018, comedian Fin Taylor emphasises that what he will feel licenced to say 'in the context of a comedy show' is different to other places.[31] He has often courted controversy in his material, and this has included questioning the #MeToo movement (although he also expresses solidarity with it). He asserts:

> I take issue with the idea that everything is set in stone, and that consensus forms so quickly and … people can't even question it publicly without getting, sort of, shamed … So all I'm doing on stage is … kneading it like dough, like stretching it and making it stronger by going 'are you sure you believe … this? Are you sure you think this?' And that's enough to annoy some people but I think if you're kind of, mature enough, then you can appreciate that's what's happening.

Taylor's discussion of his work references common ideas about the physical and ideological space in which comedy takes place: the normal rules of polite discourse are suspended. The everyday norms and moral codes of a community can therefore be teased and subverted, and things that might normally be considered inaccurate or indecent can be articulated without risk of real punishment to the speaker. Taylor's emphasis on challenging consensus and disrupting the potential for uncritical, mob-like acquiescence reflects an attitude that is fairly common among comedians. For example, similar sentiments have been espoused by influential stand-up comedians who are known for political material, such as Bill Hicks and Stewart Lee.[32] It also echoes some dominant ideas in comic theory, one influential example being Mary Douglas' notion of the joker as an individual who has valuable freedoms, 'a privileged person who can say certain things in a certain way which confers immunity ... Safe within the permitted range of attack, he lightens for everyone the oppressiveness of social reality, demonstrates its arbitrariness by making light of formality in general, and expresses the creative possibilities of the situation.'[33] Taylor implies that if the audience cannot 'appreciate' the comedian's freedoms, then the audience is to blame. He brushes aside comedians' own responsibility to express a sense of right and wrong: 'I'm a comedian, so ... [my job] is sort of to provoke thought ... I don't claim to have any answers, I just ask a lot of questions. That's sort of the point of it really.'

Frances-White was also a guest on this episode of *Men Behaving Better*, and her response to Taylor's comments revealed important differences in her interpretation of comic licence:

> I hear the justification, 'well it's comedy' ... and 'we should be able to joke about anything'. And I think, 'well ... yeah we can joke about anything'; and they say, 'I reserve the right as a comedian, as my contract with the audience, to go anywhere, to go to dangerous places.' And I go, 'yeah, you *can* do that. But it strikes me as very colonial. In the same way that white men went to India with guns and smashed the place up – you can do that, they did do that, they definitely did that. But it's not your country.'

Frances-White admits that there is 'a validity in [sighs] playing in a play space and ... just having a thought experiment', and that every topic definitely has good jokes that can be made about it. However, if you are a comedian who has no direct experience of the subject, then 'they're not your jokes'. This does not mean that you cannot mention the topic, but rather that you should approach it with the respect and thoughtfulness that follows from an awareness of being in someone else's territory. Another way she posits of thinking about the colonising potential of comic material is to consider 'who's the punchline of the joke ... is [it] the powerful people who are oppressing and marginalising ... are you punching up [or] are you punching down?'

Taylor emphasises that his comic licence has built-in safeguards because the audience can reject jokes that overstep the mark. He states:

> I take issue with the fact that I'm wilfully tearing up sacred cows because I preview this stuff and ... an audience won't laugh at something that is just mean-spirited ... sometimes I go too far in the preview and have to rein it in and realise what I'm actually asking and there are some [consensuses] ... that are there for a reason. There are some that you should, sort of, play with and some that you shouldn't.

Taylor argues that material which truly oversteps the boundaries of reasonable licence will be rejected by audiences and cut from the show. Again, this is a commonly cited article of faith among comedians: the audience bears joint responsibility with the comedian – or perhaps sometimes has sole responsibility – for indicating where material oversteps the mark. Douglas similarly argued that audiences can act as arbiters: the joker is one who can safely challenge existing hierarchies but also works *within* consensus since they are restricted to the 'permitted range of attack':

> there are jokes which can be perceived clearly enough by all present but which are rejected at once ... Social requirements may judge a joke to be in bad taste, risky, too near the bone, improper, or irrelevant. Such controls are exerted either on behalf of the hierarchy as such, or on behalf of values which are judged too precious and too precarious to be exposed to challenge.[34]

Frances-White denies the efficacy of this safety mechanism. In her view, comedians 'absolutely can' make any jokes that they want to but the individual must decide how to use that privilege: 'It's not about censorship, it's about what you wanna do.'[35] She argues:

> If it's not funny, it's not harmful. Nothing not-funny in a comedy context is going to travel. The problem ... is if it is funny to some people, or to a significant amount of people. If the audience is really going for it, then that joke gets taken out into the world and it travels. And it's used as a weapon.

Her advice to comedians is:

> if you're not a very good comedian, you do not need to worry about the social impact of your comedy ... If you're a good comedian, or you intend to be a good comedian, then you have to worry because jokes have power when they're out in the world ... they can be used a missile to hurt and to alienate.

Frances-White's assertion that it is funny jokes – not bad ones – that can carry hurtful and harmful attitudes necessarily leads to the view that comedians should 'worry' about the ethics of their material. If the boundaries of comic licence cannot be trusted to ensure that harmful material is rejected, then the comedian must take some responsibility.

Frances-White is not unique in interpreting comic licence in this way: many comedians would agree. This interpretation of comic licence leads to the view that, on *The Guilty Feminist*, a code of ethics is both possible and desirable. The idea that comic licence can be trusted to regulate the appropriateness of the jokes told is rejected: we cannot assume that just because the present audience laugh the joke is doing no harm. The practice of joking within *The Guilty Feminist* still involves challenge and risk. As Frances-White explains:

> Most of the content is ad-libbed. I am trying to be bolder and more inclusive in my topics – both things requested by many of the listeners. Every week we are flirting furiously with disaster. I know I will definitely screw up and upset a bunch of people three of four times a year, and all I can do is listen, understand, apologise and learn for next time.[36]

Where offence is caused, the comedian engages in a process of reflection, and it is understood that they will be responsible for apologising where necessary. Indeed, Frances-White asserts that a process of apology and moving on is useful in itself: 'I've come to the conclusion that me accidentally stepping on a landmine, apologising and surviving encourages other people to find their voice and see that getting stuff wrong is survivable.' This is not a matter of submitting uncritically to those who take offence but of listening and being alert to the fact that complaints may be valid, and that remedial action may be needed. The opposite can also be true: 'sometimes an individual will take me to task for something that I then re-examine and decide to stand by. It's my voice and I don't have to capitulate to another's belief every time.' Frances-White listens to her audience's judgement – in the form of both her live audiences' reactions and online comments – so that they collaborate in deciding what is and is not acceptable, but their willingness to laugh at a joke is not seen as synonymous with that joke being reasonable. Her own judgement remains the final arbiter of what she wants to say.

Traditional notions of comic licence posit that comedy creates ideal conditions for creativity and social change because of its irreverence towards everyday rules and courtesies. So, it is easy to argue that if comic licence is curtailed, jokes will be both less funny and less politically effective.

Frances-White, however, sees comedy that is both funny and responsible as central to *The Guilty Feminist*'s political agenda. She identifies that the tone of much feminist discourse is gloomy and disheartening,[37] and sees the podcast's funniness as central to its ability to engage and inspire audiences. The particular joke form which forms the 'cold open' of each podcast episode – 'I'm a feminist but … ' – has an important role in practical feminism:

> our imperfections – we often think, 'well I'm the only one' … we find ourselves falling short of some, you know, ridiculous standard we've set ourselves … That can feel, then, like guilt, and guilt if held on to – if not exfoliated – turns into shame, and shame is luggage, you carry it. And then you think 'can I speak up in this meeting? Can I ask for more?' … If you're carrying this, sort of weight that, ' … I don't think I'm actually that good a feminist', it holds you back. Shame causes inactivity … you think 'I'm not able to say, because … I'm such a hypocrite.'[38]

Frances-White believes that the 'I'm a feminist but … ' joke form allows *The Guilty Feminist*'s acts and audience to 'exfoliate' those guilty moments: 'when you put that on the table, they're funny – they're really good comedy – but we also can either laugh at them and go "that doesn't matter", or, if it does matter, "let's work on it, let's … get beyond that".' In the two examples from Hagen and Frances-White given at the start of this chapter, the audience laugh in a way that is friendly and accepting, signalling recognition that such 'failings' can be part of a life that aims to be feminist. Frances-White expresses her surprise at Hagen's revelation ('is that true?!'); along with the audience's laughter, this establishes a mood in which hidden experiences can be shared and enjoyed, and guilty moments 'exfoliated'.

This approach makes productive use of the role of the joker as one who uses the freedom afforded by joking to '[lighten] … the oppressiveness of social reality, [demonstrate] its arbitrariness … and [express] the creative possibilities of the situation'. The joke form exists to expose, challenge, and heal the speakers' own foibles, along with the societal context that feeds them, and gains its power by creating recognition and sympathy among audiences; they express consensus around the need to laugh at, address, or move on from the incongruity. It also permits the operation of comic licence as a social good. The 'I'm a feminist but … ' joke form is overt in its intent to offer what theorist Lawrence E. Mintz called: 'a critique of the gap between what is and what we believe should be'.[39] It signals the start of an interaction that sincerely intends to close that gap.

Conclusion

The Guilty Feminist presents stand-up in an unconventional format: one that has been designed specifically to embody the political attitudes, and further the political aims, of its creator. It addresses politics in its choice of subjects, voicing opposition to governments and promoting a feminist agenda which opposes all forms of oppression and dominance. It also makes politicised decisions about whom to stage. In giving more space to women and other marginalised voices it has contributed to a shift in industry perceptions about which identities are 'marketable' to comedy audiences. It has developed a collaborative and mutually supportive platform for stand-up which resists some of the industry's competitive and hierarchical practices, and makes visible its own, more equitable employment practices. In its approach to comic licence, the podcast embraces risk and responsibility, seeing both as vital to good comedy. Above all, it adopts comedy as a political strategy to engage audiences and inspire political learning and political action.

The comedy industry, like any system, has politics and power dynamics. This is true even in those environments that consider themselves to be 'unpolitical', where inattention to politics can still cause political harms. Inequality and abuse have been enabled to thrive in many parts of the industry; jokes told and enjoyed with no thought of consequences can do damage. In *The Guilty Feminist*, we see that the politics of stand-up comedy is not just a matter of what is said but also of how it is staged. For those who make comedy, this implies a duty to be alert to the politics present in all decisions, artistic and logistical. Analysis of comedy's politics should likewise look beyond its subject matter, acknowledging that politics exists within form and context, as well as in the material delivered.

Notes

1. *The Guilty Feminist* [podcast], '1. Nudity with Shappi Khorsandi', 16 December 2015, https://guiltyfeminist.com/episode/?episode=1.
2. The Bechdel test is named after the cartoonist Alison Bechdel, whose comic strip *Dykes to Watch Out For* popularised a simple test establishing basic requirements for representation of women in movies: does it 'one … have at least two women in it … who, two, talk to each other about, three, something besides a man'? A surprisingly large proportion of mainstream movies fail this test. See Alison Bechdel, 'The Rule', *Dykes to Watch Out For*, 1985, www.npr.org/templates/story/story.php?storyId=94202522.

3. Deborah Frances-White, *The Guilty Feminist: From Our Noble Goals to Our Worst Hypocrisies* (London: Virago, 2018), p. xii.
4. See, for example, *The Guilty Feminist* [podcast], '252. EMERGENCY EPISODE – Noisy and Annoying', 3 May 2021, https://guiltyfeminist.com/episode/?episode=308.
5. *The Guilty Feminist* [podcast], '268. EMERGENCY EPISODE for the crisis in Afghanistan', 23 August 2021, https://guiltyfeminist.com/episode/?episode=325.
6. *The Guilty Feminist* [podcast], '251. Being a Super-Ally with Sophie Duker and Emma Dabiri', 26 April 2021, https://guiltyfeminist.com/episode/?episode=307.
7. *The Comedian's Comedian* [podcast], '289 – Deborah Frances-White', 22 April 2019, www.comedianscomedian.com/289-deborah-frances-white/.
8. *The Comedian's Comedian*, '289 – Deborah Frances-White'.
9. *You'll Do* [podcast], 'Feminism with Deborah Frances-White and Tom Salinsky', 14 April 2020, www.bbc.co.uk/programmes/p089cwgc.
10. Channel 4 News, *Ways to Change the World* [podcast] 'Series 5 – Episode 2: Deborah Frances-White', 29 May 2020, www.channel4.com/news/series-5-episode-2-deborah-frances-white.
11. *Men Behaving Better*, 'Why Is There #MeToo fatigue? What Can Be Done about It? (Sara Pascoe, Brett Goldstein and Sindhu Vee)', 20 October 2018, https://soundcloud.com/men-behaving-better/why-is-there-metoo-fatigue-and-what-should-be-done-about-it [emphasis original].
12. *Men Behaving Better*, 'Why Is There #MeToo fatigue?'.
13. *The Guilty Feminist* [podcast], '282. When's International Men's Day? special with Richard Herring, Nikesh Shukla and Will Hislop', 19 November 2020, https://guiltyfeminist.com/episode/?episode=282.
14. Frances-White, *The Guilty Feminist*, pp. 140–141.
15. *The Guilty Feminist*, '282. When's International Men's Day?'.
16. For more on this see: Ellie Tomsett, '"Less Dick Jokes": Women-Only Comedy Line-Ups, Audience Expectations and Negotiating Stereotypes', in Oliver Double and Sharon Lockyer (eds), *Alternative Comedy Now and Then: Critical Perspectives* (Basingstoke: Palgrave, 2022), pp. 239–265; Sophie Quirk, 'Comedy Clubs that Platform Marginalised Identities: Prefigurative Politics in Sophie Duker's Wacky Racists', *European Journal of Cultural Studies*, Vol. 25, No. 2, 2022: pp. 373–388.
17. *Men Behaving Better*, 'Why Is There #MeToo Fatigue?' (emphasis in original).
18. *The Comedian's Comedian*, '289 – Deborah Frances-White'.
19. Stewart Lee, *How I Escaped My Certain Fate: The Life and Deaths of a Stand-Up Comedian* (London: Faber & Faber, 2010), p. 6.
20. Nick Butler and Dimitrinka Stoyanova Russell, 'No Funny Business: Precarious Work and Emotional Labour in Stand-Up Comedy', *Human Relations*, Vol. 71, No. 12, 2018: pp. 1666–1686, p. 1667.
21. Butler and Russell, 'No Funny Business', p. 1682.
22. Oliver Double, *Alternative Comedy: 1979 and the Reinvention of British Stand-Up* (London: Methuen, 2020), p. 202.
23. *The Guilty Feminist* [podcast], '275. Fighting for Hope with Bridget Christie and guests Travis Alabanza, Holly Harrison-Mullane and She Drew the Gun', 11 October 2021, https://guiltyfeminist.com/episode/?episode=333.

24. Oliver Double, *Getting the Joke: The Inner Workings of Stand-Up Comedy*, 2nd ed. (London: Methuen, 2014), p. x.
25. Mark Lamarr in Oliver Double, *Getting the Joke: The Inner Workings of Stand-Up Comedy* (London: Methuen, 2005), p. ix.
26. *Men Behaving Better*, 'Why Is There #MeToo Fatigue?'.
27. *The Comedian's Comedian* [podcast], '148 – Aisling Bea: Live at the Edinburgh Fringe', 14 November 2016, www.comedianscomedian.com/148-aisling-bea-live-at-the-edinburgh-fringe/.
28. *The Comedian's Comedian*, '289 – Deborah Frances-White'.
29. *The Comedian's Comedian*, '289 – Deborah Frances-White'.
30. *The Comedian's Comedian*, '289 – Deborah Frances-White'.
31. *Men Behaving Better*, 'Separating the Man from His Work (with Deborah Frances White, Bronagh Waugh and Fin Taylor)', 28 October 2018, https://soundcloud.com/men-behaving-better/can-we-separate-a-man-from-his-work-with-deborah-frances-white-bronagh-waugh-and-fin-taylor.
32. Sophie Quirk, *Why Stand-Up Matters: How Comedians Manipulate and Influence* (London: Bloomsbury, 2015), p. 158.
33. Mary Douglas, 'Jokes', in Mary Douglas (ed.), *Implicit Meanings: Selected Essays in Anthropology*, 2nd ed. (London: Routledge, 1999), p. 158.
34. Douglas, 'Jokes', pp. 151–152.
35. *Men Behaving Better*, 'Separating the Man from His Work'.
36. Frances-White, *The Guilty Feminist*, p. 164.
37. *The Comedian's Comedian*, '289 – Deborah Frances-White'.
38. *The Comedian's Comedian*, '289 – Deborah Frances-White'.
39. Lawrence E. Mintz, 'Standup Comedy as Social and Cultural Mediation', *American Quarterly*, Vol. 37, Spring 1985: p. 77.

Further Reading

Douglas, Mary, 'Jokes', in Mary Douglas (ed.), *Implicit Meanings: Selected Essays in Anthropology*, 2nd ed. (London: Routledge, 1999), pp. 146–164.

Frances-White, Deborah, *The Guilty Feminist: From Our Noble Goals to Our Worst Hypocrisies* (London: Virago, 2018).

The Guilty Feminist [podcast] (2015–), https://guiltyfeminist.com/.

Quirk, Sophie 'Comedy Clubs That Platform Marginalised Identities: Prefigurative Politics in Sophie Duker's Wacky Racists', *European Journal of Cultural Studies*, Vol. 25, No. 2, 2022: pp. 373–388.

Tomsett, Ellie, '"Less Dick Jokes": Women-Only Comedy Line-Ups, Audience Expectations and Negotiating Stereotypes', in Oliver Double and Sharon Lockyer (eds.), *Alternative Comedy Now and Then: Critical Perspectives* (Basingstoke: Palgrave, 2022), pp. 239–265.

COMEDIANS' INSIGHTS

Your Writing Process

Edward Aczel (UK)

Come up with an idea, and repeat on stage – until it's funny.

Tom Ballard (Australia)

I write down any possible dumb idea I have – a joke idea, or just a topic or observation that angers/interests/amuses me – into a big files in 'Notes' on my phone as I go about my life. Then when it's time to write, I sit down and go through all those ideas and see if any of them are still appealing (or if I can even remember what the hell I was trying to get at). I'll then try to brainstorm around that idea, write it out word for word on my computer and try to (vaguely) memorise it before trying it out onstage at a new material night or low-pressure gig. I've worked with directors and writing buddies before, and they can be extremely helpful. Having another pair of eyes and ears who can tell you, 'No, that sucks' or 'I have no idea what you're talking about' or 'Drop that bit, you animal' is invaluable.

Maria Bamford (USA)

I just start talking and then repeating the same stories and premises over and over again until it's sixty minutes in length. I 'poop it out' and it's about volume – not quality. I can work on it forever, but I need to fill the hour first.

Angela Barnes (UK)

I can't write straight onto a laptop – it has to be freehand. I treated myself to a reMarkable last year – which is a device that really does feel like writing on paper – but it means I don't have my jokes and ideas in endless notebooks and scraps of paper. They are at least all filed logically on one device, and I can upload them to a laptop and share them electronically.

Jo Brand (UK)

Used to sit down with a blank sheet of paper. Never worked. For a long time now, as and when an idea occurred to me, I'd put it on my phone and then sit down later and try to organise it into something vaguely coherent.

Nathan Caton (UK)

I'll have a notebook with subject headers – topics that I know I wanna write about; it can be personal stuff/stories or things I've seen in the news etc. But I'll pick one topic and then brainstorm and see what comes to mind. When I first started doing stand-up I would write out every single joke word for word, but now I'll just have the main funny points I wanna hit and then go from there. I'll go to a new material night and then see what/how it comes out. Then after the gig I'll go over the set, which I'll have recorded and then refine the material to how I want it, or if the material didn't work I completely delete the recording and NEVER talk about it again!

Jo Caulfield (UK)

I have scribbled bits of paper stuffed in every pocket. Random thoughts. Words. Potential punchlines. I take those ideas on stage and let the energy of the audience dictate and direct where the joke goes. I do that between two bits of material that work, obviously.

Lou Conran (UK)

I MC a lot and that enables me to try stories, and in improvising I can add or takeaway from a particular story if it is getting a good reaction.

Tanyalee Davis (Canada/USA/UK)

I pretty much LIVE my comedy. I've had an extraordinary life so I tell the audience my expectations in a funny way.

Alexis Dubus (UK), Who Performs as Marcel Lucont (France)

I actually find I write best when I'm on the move, for initial ideas at least. Then I'll hone those ideas when sat down at my desk and also while on stage.

Andy Erikson (USA)

I like to watch game shows and get inspired by the questions and topics. I share my jokes on Twitter to get feedback as well. I love writing with other comics at coffee shops or at open mics.

Alex Farrow (UK)

My favourite is 'Tagging' – notebook out with a group of comics. Then adding new lines to each other's premises and punchlines.

Justin Herman (USA)

I try to ride moments of inspiration to fatigue and I try to force putting words to paper when I feel nothing. It's the trial and error in between those extremes, trying things on stage and rewriting where the real work gets done.

Richard Herring (UK)

In the old days I used to try to write the shows and then learn them and then improvise a little, but now I like to start with ideas which I explore on stage in preview shows. I sometimes have a blog or half an idea to work from – sometimes I might read it out – but I find the best way to get inspiration is in the white hot heat of performance, so increasingly I knock an idea around on stage for a few performances until I have it right. I work out where it's too long, where it needs an extra laugh and then move on to adjusting pace, tone, individual words until it gets funnier. I continue this right until the end of the life of the show. There are always ways to improve and I enjoy trying to perfect it every night. And find new avenues to explore even in a routine I've done a lot.

Bec Hill (Australia/UK)

I used to script all my solo shows (and recommend this for newbies, as it helps you understand what bits are and aren't necessary for a joke to work), but once I had a few solo shows under my belt and found my 'voice', I was able to loosen up. These days I tend to do new material nights with a bullet-point list of ideas with rough punchlines (either in my head or written down) and then just chat through them and see what lands. If something doesn't land, but I feel in my gut like it could be good, I'll rework it until it DOES land.

Harry Hill (UK)

Try to write every day, always have a notebook on me.

Charmian Hughes (UK)

Morning walking, let ideas come to me, notice things, let my imagination run – 'what ifs' and 'whys' – and then play with them and write them up when I get home.

Robin Ince (UK)

I make notes all the time on whatever blank paper I can find – I start from tiny germs of ideas scribbled down and then the 'writing' is done by making it up on stage.

Milton Jones (UK)

I am always on the lookout for words, images, and scenarios from real life that I can twist or exaggerate to cause misunderstanding in the world I create on stage.

Myq Kaplan (USA)

I always carry a digital recorder and record any seed of a thought that I think might eventually become a joke. When my recorder is full, I go back through and write the ideas out longhand in a notebook. When my notebook is full, I type the ideas out into my computer. Additionally, I do a lot of 'writing' while performing. I'll go on stage with some of these idea seedlings and see how they blossom. I guess the audience is the water? Or dirt? Or sunlight? That sounds nicer. The audience is sunlight! If I riff a new fun thought on stage, I will later record it into my recorder and the process begins anew. Springtime!

Jackie Kashian (USA)

I work on bits *on stage*. I have bullet points and, usually, one punchline. On stage I feel out the premise, expand on the premise, often contract on the premise. Try to make it as personal as possible – especially if the bit is about something *large* – like flying or food or social tropes.

Athena Kugblenu (UK)

I start with opinions.

Beth Lapides (USA)

Always. Noticing, thinking, remembering. Then wishing I had more time to write, remembering I have enough time to write, writing, moving on to other tasks, getting caught up in them, wishing I had more time to write.

Stewart Lee (UK)

Long sessions at laptop + chance improvisation on stage.

Elf Lyons (UK)

I imagine I am a child preparing for my birthday party. I don't think logically – about what is healthy to eat – I just think about all the sweet things I *like*. I don't think linear and start structuring a routine or show with a beginning, middle, and end with motifs and a clear thesis. I make a big buffet table in my mind and I cover it with comedy party food – all the routines/ideas/songs/jokes that make *me happy*. Even if they don't necessarily make sense *together* – like mash potatoes and jelly. *I have to prepare the same way a child would prepare for their party – no logic – just joy*. It has to start from a place of optimism. Even if the material is incredibly dark and intense.

Tom Mayhew (UK)

I think of an issue or cause that really matters to me, and shape my passion into punchlines.

Andrew McClelland (Australia)

Unlike a lot of observational stand-ups I know, whatever type of show I'm performing I write it out in full. Every word at it's best and leanest. It's rare that I actually speak every one of those words correctly, but I like to have the script in exactly the shape I'd like to perform it on opening night. Once the season begins many changes are made of course and the fat trimmed, but it's always nice to have that there as a record of the dream show at its opening.

Aditi Mittal (India)

The word process implies that there is order in my writing. I basically write till my self-hate and panic subside for an hour every morning.

Alfie Moore (UK)

Funny or interesting thought – research subject – notes on laptop – edit – try out on stage – re-edit or delete.

Martin Mor (UK)

Three finished jokes a day. (Usually topicals). Lots of research on topics that I want to cover.

Al Murray (UK), Who Performs as the Pub Landlord (UK)

When people ask me, 'Which do you prefer, writing stand-up or writing a book?', it's stand-up every time. The show I did last night, there's a bit in it that wasn't quite firing last night, so I'll change it round tomorrow. And you never have to finish it, you never have to sign off on it. You own the material forever, so if I want to do a joke from fifteen years ago because it feels like the minute to do it, I'll do that. The fluidity of writing it yourself, of writing stand-up, is the thing I really love about it. And it's the thing that makes me want to lie in a gutter about writing other stuff.

Sander Õigus (Estonia)

I write on stage, meaning I have some premises written down and then I work them at open mics until they turn into something or don't. The rush and adrenaline of being on stage produces way better material than sitting comfortably at home.

Anuvab Pal (India)

I often write in a block of conversation, much like a scene in a screenplay. I try to remove description and explanation straight to the audience, as much as I can, to let the conversation flow. And if I do need to say something to the audience, I try to make it ironic. I'm uncomfortable as a straight narrator. I'm trying hard to be an unreliable narrator.

Rayen Panday (Netherlands)

Most of it forms in my head, I hardly write anything down. I either have a conversation with friends or just thoughts that form and when I try it out on stage, afterwards I start to keep working on it in my head.

Rod Quantock (Australia)

I don't write – ever – I research a lot, jot down points and ideas and then talk them through making it up as I go with the audience. I record, review, and refine.

John-Luke Roberts (UK)

When it comes to putting a show together, what seems to work best for me is writing far too much – setting aside a couple of hours in the morning to write as many ideas and sentences and things-which-might-be-jokes down, then seeing what I laugh at when I read it later, and what an audience laugh at when I do it onstage.

John Simmit (UK)

Thoughts and observations come, get instantly put into my iPhone's Notes app for later reference (I used to have a notebook in the early days) … sometimes minutes before I got on. I still need to sort that out.

Mark Simmonds (UK)

I write down any wordplay I think of or spot in conversations. Once I have about ten, I'll sit down in a cafe and craft them into jokes.

Joe Wells (UK)

I usually start by asking myself, 'What's my opinion on this?' So I can start with an angle then build the jokes from there.

PART III

Performance Dynamics

CHAPTER 12

Audience

Ian Brodie

Stand-up comedy is performed in front of an audience. This point is both profoundly self-evident and profoundly important. To think of the audience as somehow incidental and to contemplate the comedian's words as if they were not to be performed live but instead for a different medium – most notably, to be read – is to miss the point. Comedians construct their material to best elicit the desired aesthetic responses – laughter being chief among them – from any given crowd that might be assembled before them. The audience's engagement is constitutive of the thing produced in that moment of performance, interpreting, challenging, encouraging, stressing, complementing, completing, and validating the embodied verbal performance of the comedian. Moreover, each audience member has a real-time experience of both that performance and the spontaneous reactive engagement of others in the same audience. This reactive engagement is not only retained but is essential to those instances where stand-up comedy enters recorded or broadcast media, as Brett Mills explores more fully in Chapter 4.

It is useful to consider the stand-up comedy audience in three different senses.

The Genus 'Stand-Up Comedy Audience'

First, there are people who might seek out opportunities to watch stand-up comedy, whether live or mediated, irrespective of whether they know the reputation of a particular performer. They have expectations for the genre and, however subjective and contingent, a grasp of some of its history, including notable performers and comic spaces, and thus have a certain fluency with the form. They are analogous to those who might go to an art gallery for purposes other than a particularly appealing exhibition. With stand-up comedy as a vernacular art form, this audience comprises much of its art world, the 'community of individuals prepared to see the world as the artist does through their statement'.[1] These audiences are the implied referents in such pronouncements as '[c]omedy audiences understand the tales they are told may well be fictitious, their only concern is that they are entertaining' and '[s]tand-up comedy audiences want to be challenged'.[2]

There are subtypes of this sense of audience: one can speak of 'British [stand-up] comedy audiences' or the 'stand-up comedy scene in Mumbai',[3] with expectations that the ostensibly global genre of stand-up comedy might be inflected with national and local socio-cultural perceptions of the politics of speech acts and the traditions of solo comedic verbal performance. Similarly, but informed by a sense of marginalisation from the dominant cultural industry rather than geography, 'Black comedy audiences' and 'Christian comedy audiences', as but two examples, have their own sets of expectations for performance. More specifically, particular venues are spoken of as having their own audiences, such as London's Comedy Store's audience[4] or Los Angeles's UnCabaret.[5] In this sense, 'audience' is essentially synonymous with both 'tradition' and 'market', yet the term emphasises the dynamism of interaction within stand-up comedy and lessens the implications of both conservatism and commodity value which the other terms might respectively imply.

There was a time, of course, when there was no stand-up comedy and thus no audience for it: it is possible to trace the emergence of audiences in new global settings in very recent history, such as India, France, South Africa, and Russia, all of which had solo comic non-musical performance traditions but nothing resembling the discursive form of what most would recognise as stand-up comedy. Typically, tentative scenes emerge when established international acts embark on global tours, when first- or second-generation emigrants return as performers, and – most significantly – when a shift in media distribution expands the potential reach of stand-up comedy performances, such as the expansion of satellite channels and, more recently, streaming platforms. Stand-up recordings teach a listener how to be a stand-up audience member, if only by the example of having a seasoned audience incorporated into the audio. Looking further back, and despite the varying opinions about precisely where and when stand-up comedy began, we can consider the contexts that allowed it: the invention of the public address system, the telephone, the radio, and the motion picture brought the discovery that amplified speech could use the same conventions as close, face-to-face speech and not have to be modified to accommodate for distance and competing sounds. This provided audiences with a fluency for naturalism and the expectations of its aesthetic possibilities, much as the way a murmured, crooning, gentle voice could become a viable mode of popular song. Within those conditions, something other than a monologue and other than a series of self-contained and formulaic jokes, by someone speaking as themselves and not as a character, and doing so in an uninflected voice, could be taken as a potential art form because an audience was prepared by something already like it.[6]

The Stand-Up Comedian's Audience

Second, there are the people who have developed an interest in the performances of a specific comedian or, thinking of the same group differently, the people a comedian has successfully cultivated as being interested in their performances. This group may not necessarily comprise a subgroup of the first sense: Hannah Gadsby, Tig Notaro, and Stewart Lee have attracted an audience who otherwise profess little to no interest in stand-up comedy in general. But for the most part, a person attracted to the genre discovers a performer they consider to be particularly adept and seeks out new performances while revisiting older ones. Because stand-up comedy is perspectival and frequently rooted in the communication of lived experience (albeit more with an end to eliciting laughter than to communicating ethnographic and biographic exactitude), the audience can come to know the comedian's history, biases, appetites, inclinations, and obsessions, much the way one knows the same of someone in one's immediate circle. This parasocial relationship is cultivated by the comedian as much through the onstage material as through other mechanisms of persona construction, in interview, podcast appearances, writing, or acting: new material benefits from its location within the accumulated and preceding collected work of the comedian. When the performance will be performing to 'their' audience – on their headlining tour or at the taping of an album or special – a comedian can presume familiarity. Conversely, when not performing for their specific audience – at an unannounced club performance, when appearing alongside a headliner, as part of a variety programme, or, of course, when the comedian is starting out and has no audience of their own – the comedian cannot make that assumption. It is for this reason that established performers will seek out opportunities to test new material away from an audience predisposed to like it.

Audiences in our first sense comprise the general economic engine of stand-up comedy as a popular art form, and audiences in the second comprise the long-term viability and financial security of the individual professional stand-up comedian. The ability to book television appearances and performance venues or to have recordings partially or fully underwritten by distribution companies is contingent on demonstrating an a priori demand, so there is an incentive to maintain and build an audience over and above the performative benefit of the parasocial relationship. The complex interplay of the transactional with the interpersonal, as framed through the assumption of 'truth' that is embedded in the vernacular understanding of stand-up comedy, is made most apparent at moments of an audience's sense of betrayal. As Phillip Deen writes: 'It is no coincidence that the conversation about [Bill] Cosby's character and comedy has focused on the audience members' feeling that they had been betrayed by someone they felt they knew.'[7]

These two senses of audience – the abstract group of people fluent with the named art form 'stand-up comedy', and a group of people, largely but not exclusively drawn from the first group, oriented towards the performances of a particular stand-up comedian – are necessary considerations operating in the background of the third sense of audience, the one that takes up the remainder of this chapter: the group of people present at any one stand-up comedy performance whose aesthetic responses complete the stand-up comedy text.

The Live Audience as Writing and Performance Partner

The 'work of art' as it relates to stand-up comedy, its 'primary focus of appreciation',[8] is live performance. Its liveness and the contributive presence of an audience are integral to any subsequent mediation of a performance, whether through broadcast or recording, in part or in whole. The words spoken on a stage, enlivened by tone, gesture, and cadence, come to fullest form when complemented by the ideally desired reactions of an audience. Although foremost among these reactions is laughter, booing, hissing, hooting, applause, gasps, verbal interjections, and even silences comprise immediate interpretative implications for any given utterance and in turn condition the meaning of the next one. The words and ideas that the comedian prepares for performance are clearly aimed at eliciting laughter and, while it can never be fully assured, and poor performances do happen, knowing the expectations of audiences in general (our first sense) makes for more reliable predictions for any given live audience.

The labour of stand-up comedy in terms of the preparation of material thus occurs as much with an audience in the way of editing and honing as may ever take place off the stage as deliberate composition. Many comedians, such as Marc Maron, frequently state that their 'writing' happens on the stage itself: the first effort at giving shape to a potential topic already occurs in the dialogic form of addressing thoughts to an audience. Subsequent reflection on the success of that performance guides the next effort at expressing the same topic to a different audience, and over time a form emerges that tends to successfully express that topic and garner the audience's desired response with sufficient frequency that the bit is in essence 'finished'. However, other comedians expressly state that they write their material in a literal sense: away from the stage, committing something to a page, working out an idea and a form, based on their already practised understanding of audiences. Nevertheless, this deliberately written material is soon thereafter performed in front of an actual audience to test whether it indeed receives the desired responses and to assess how it can be improved. Subsequent editing of prepared material may involve literal pen and paper revising, but inevitably it too entails testing before diverse audiences until such time as it is finished. In both instances, 'finished' implies a confidence in the material, not a closure: a proactive sense that it will more often than not encourage the desired response when brought before an anticipated audience.

Audiences may indeed be aware that they are part of this process of editing: venues in larger comedy scenes (such as London, New York, and Los Angeles) are often witness to established and famous comedians making surprise appearances, solo shows may be booked in preparation for taking a show on tour or a showcase event such as the Edinburgh Fringe, and a tour may in turn be understood as preparation for a recording. An audience member's understanding that they are present to earlier drafts of performances is largely predicated on their knowledge of the particular comedian's reputation and status. Confidence in one's a priori reputation may be the sole preserve of only a few comedians: even if there is a future, larger, more profitable audience in mind, the expectations for competent performance are always directed at the one immediately present and, for the vast majority of comedians, each performance is an exercise in cultivating a reputation, rather than the presumption of one.

The Live Audience as Negotiating Partner

As I have argued elsewhere,[9] stand-up comedy mirrors small-scale, interpersonal speech events where and when playful, ludic talk occurs. Folklorists and cultural anthropologists refer to 'small talk', 'shit talk', 'talking shit', occasions outside of the more structured and instrumental contexts of work and home, and outside of more conventionalised cultural performances, when people in some semblance of affiliation – friends, co-workers, neighbours, family – are gathered leisurely, and talk becomes a form of play, as an occasion where talk's phatic and aesthetic intents are as important as its informational intent. In such moments of talk, one person will draw focus (with tacit permission), and there is a switch from the back and forth of conversational talk to engage in a form that is tacitly recognisable, locally appropriate, and topically relevant to the talk that preceeds it. Focus is marked by body language and movement cues – the listeners orient themselves in the direction of the speaker (if only through glances and regular eye contact) and cede most of the talk to the teller. Focus is sustained through the ongoing goodwill and encouragement of the others present until such time as their point reaches its conclusion and focus is ceded, or, through insufficiently meeting expectations of competency, focus is withdrawn. Each person present is already in some form of relationship with the speaker defined by any number of social identity pairings (co-worker, family member, classmate, etc.): they bring their specific understanding of the person speaking into their evaluation of the performance person within that dyad, while now also assuming the pairing of listener and speaker. (We are more patient with a child or the recently bereaved when their performances do not otherwise meet our expectations.) Arguably, the right to maintain the adopted role of speaker is initially and provisionally extended by the others present and that role is regularly claimed.

Stand-up comedy is in essence the professionalisation of such talk. Each performance of stand-up comedy is a marked speech event. It occurs in venues, whether specialised or temporarily adapted, where the socially recognised category of stand-up comedy is said to be taking place: conversely, it occurs alongside other styles of expressive performance yet is singularly distinguished therefrom. To assert that what is to follow is a stand-up comedy performance and that the person is a stand-up comedian is to suggest that the performance and the person are to be initially evaluated within the expected criteria of those categories. Such a distinction is not merely pedantic: a different moment is being apprehended when we witness an actor playing a stand-up comedian delivering a stand-up comedy performance; we will evaluate it the way we evaluate a performance in a film (or television, or theatre), its success or failure dependent on the representation of stand-up comedy, secondary to its merits as a stand-up comedy presentation.[10] Similarly, when a stand-up comedian is doing a different speech act, from participating in an interview to a commencement address to a spoken comic essay directed to a camera, it will be evaluated according to the expectations of those speech acts, however much their identity as a stand-up comedian is a frame.

In live stand-up performance, focus is given to the performer not simply through eye contact and eschewing most talk but through the stage – however informally and temporarily the physical place may be considered such – and through amplification. The stage makes the distinction between performer and audience concrete, while the public address system provides the advantage of volume, reducing the sonic imbalance of one among many to the more equitable one among a few. The microphone and the stage have become visual shorthand for stand-up comedy performance.

The right to assume the role 'stand-up comedian' has been provisionally extended by the audience, through the apparatus of the venue, and continues to be granted so long as they meet the expectations of how the audience understands that role. Their embodied self (physical characteristics; dress), their voice (timbre; accent), and their semantic content introduce further markers that suggest additional pairings – mutual or complementary identifications (ethnicity, class, nationality, gender identity, sexuality, political affiliation, pop culture participation) – and serve to affiliate the comedian to the audience members, individually and as a collective, beyond but not entirely overshadowing their comedian–audience dyad. Irrespective of the many possible social identity pairings participated in by the comedian and any one audience member, the one that is most at the forefront is the pairing of stand-up comedian and stand-up comedy audience: indeed, it is the only *necessary* social identity pairing and may be the only one active at the onset of performance.

While the genre may be practically coterminous with small-scale talk, the speaker identifying this identity as 'stand-up comedian' invokes the expectation of 'professionalism': whether or not any money is given to the performer, there is often some money outlaid by the audience. As such, competency in the form and in meeting the expectations of the audience tends to trump the extension of goodwill based on other kinds of affiliation and fellow feeling. Furthermore, even if money is not an operative motivation, being a stand-up comedian implies performing material for a greater number of people, certainly beyond one's immediate circle, and increasingly outside of local contexts, shared referents, and stylistic expectations. Knowing how to quickly establish goodwill and fellow feeling when neither may be particularly forthcoming is integral to professional growth.

This moves towards our second sense of audience: the cultivation of both a reputation for competency in the art form and an identity beyond that of stand-up comedian which facilitates the next performance. By being 'known' the comedian skips past the initial hurdles of needing to prove affiliation and relevance and, emulating the small-scale ludic speech context again, is a person emerging from a group with established mutual social identity pairings to become the focus of a speech act that will already be assumed to meet competency expectations. Each performance before a live audience is also an additional step towards building 'their' audience.

The Live Audience and the Aesthetics of the Spontaneous

The aesthetics of the small talk speech act at the level of voice are also extended to stand-up comedy. The stylistic tone of stand-up comedy and its form is dialogue: an intensely one-sided dialogue, to be sure, but dialogue, nonetheless. It is propelled and sustained by an ongoing interaction with the audience. The comedian can venture into characterisation, enactment, and more stylised forms, much as we do in everyday talk, but they are discrete moments within the natural conversational mode.

There is a tricky conceit in stand-up comedy. Audiences are aware that, for the most part, and with all the provisos mentioned earlier, the words spoken by the comedian have been prepared in advance. At the same time, the aesthetics of stand-up lean towards a naturalness of talk, consistent with the ordinary voice, that connotes extemporaneity. Although the word monologue is often used in vernacular discussions of stand-up comedy, it is hardly ever monologic in that self-contained sense of a theatrical monologue: it is not marked as a discrete independent piece of verbal art that is performed essentially without variation, irrespective of context. Rather, it adapts to the moment of performance.

'Naturalness' (defined here as the notable absence of affectedness) and the conversational, non-monologic form further heighten the audience's sense that the talk arises more or less spontaneously. Extemporaneity does not preclude an absence of artistry: sociolinguistics and the ethnography of speaking point to 'breakthrough into performance', where talk enters a state of flow and is shaped – virtually self-consciously – on vernacular aesthetic principles ('ethnopoetics'). But words that 'sound prepared', as if following a script, break that sense of unaffectedness. This is not a new observation: in *The Book of the Courtier*, the early modern writer and diplomat Castiglione describes the twinned terms of verbal *sprezzatura* (nonchalance) and embodied *disinvoltura* (ease) which can be consciously adopted in social performances in order to make a display of exceptional ability seem unaffected, 'so as to conceal all art and make whatever is done or said appear to be without effort and almost without any thought about it'.[11]

The absence of the appearance of affectedness for most of the duration of the talk is in keeping with stand-up's vernacular origins. Small talk draws from immediate circumstances, slowly moving away from news of the day towards talk that is more pleasurable and discursive. An individual's contribution responds to and builds upon the talk that preceded it. Even if what is spoken is commonly known to be part of that person's active repertoire and not a spontaneous creation, what gets selected from that repertoire is deemed appropriate by its contiguity with what occurred previously. And it is never entirely separate from the conversation that occasions it: neither an imaginary fourth wall nor a lectern intercede, and talk is to and with, not simply at, the others.

The preparation of material in stand-up comedy, then, is the creation of discrete units (routines) that will sound emergent, to be performed before an audience as if they were either extemporaneous or, perhaps, to be selected from a range of possible items in a repertoire that 'just happen' to be appropriate to the immediate context. They are discrete enough that they are distinguishable and can be located in various orders alongside other routines to comprise a set: a unit in an earlier stage of development may be nestled between routines considered closer to their ideal form, so that an audience encounters the routine with their goodwill affirmed through a confident display and, should the newer material falter, have that goodwill subsequently restored through a similarly confident one.

Lastly, while it is useful to remember that the entirety of a performance has its own integrity, and assessing a particular routine within it should at least consider what comes before and after, it is also legitimate to consider each routine as a discrete entity. Evidence that they are still meant to 'work' beyond the context of the full performance is seen in recordings for dissemination, where routines become tracks on LPs or CDs, or chapters on DVD and Blu-rays, and appear alone on satellite or streaming radio services, or on YouTube, TikTok, or Instagram, entirely extracted from the full performance.

The Live Audience as Interlocutor: Crowdwork

The live stand-up comedy audience is not homogeneous yet often can function as a mass: the reaction of the plurality to one utterance can provide sufficient traction for the next, and competing reactions – male cheers versus female booing, for example – can be anticipated, putatively dividing the audience along simplistically contrasting social identities until a subsequent 'reconciliatory' utterance brings affiliation back.

At times, however, the stand-up comedian may actually address the audience seeking a response that does not comprise affect sounds but speech. Speaking to individuals and asking them questions can be used to display spontaneous wit (even if the wit comprises a standard repertoire of stock answers) and further demonstrate *sprezzatura*. For comedians whose live performances do not follow a specific unifying arc the conversation can encourage the performance of a routine from their repertoire. Conversely, audience interaction may constitute a particular circumscribed portion of an overall performance, an interval of spontaneity. (With the rise of TikTok as a promotional device, these encounters are often posted by the comedian themselves as demonstrations of their particular spontaneous wit: ironically, this has also led to sets comprising little prepared material and instead mainly efforts to engage the audience thus so that it can be filmed and posted online.)

'Crowdwork', the vernacular term for encouraging direct address, illustrates the stylistic overlap between small talk and stand-up. It suggests that there is an implicit conversation lurking beneath the performer and audience interaction and also strengthens the ostensibly non-hierarchical, peer-to-peer nature of the speech, drawing heretofore distanced people into further bonds of affiliation and familiarity. This may involve temporary ridicule and insult in a manner similar to small-group teasing relationships, only to have the tension from teasing absolved in subsequent conciliatory utterances. As an illustration, the Scottish comedian Liam Withnail posted the following interaction with an audience member ('Chris') from a show at the Frog and Bucket Comedy Club in Manchester:

Chris, what do you do my man?
[I, uh, work at a university]
You work at a *university*? Okay, a scholar, what do you do?
[I research]
You *research* at the university, okay, very good and uh
what do you research? I'm *desperately* trying to dig for some comedy gold here Chris [laughter]
You're making it very *f***ing* difficult with your one-word
| Please leave me the f*** alone | answers [laughter] but
I'm a *st*- I'm a *stubborn* man and I'm willing to stay here for the next hour and a half until we get something f***ing funny out of this conversation Chris so [laughter]
what, what do you research?
[I'm researching physics]
You're researching physics. You know what Chris?
One nil to you: I f***ing *give up* okay [laughter turning to applause]

I can't be arsed
Trying to make *physics research jokes*
At *half four* on a f***ing *Saturday* afternoon [laughter][12]

The Live Audience as Opponent: Heckling

All of the above could suggest a placid and wholly amicable relationship between the stand-up comedian and their audience, where reciprocity and collaboration are mutually agreed upon objectives oriented towards a common goal. But the language of professional stand-up comedians is often metaphorically violent, with talk of 'killing', 'slaying', 'leaving them dead' to indicate success, or 'dying' to indicate failure. Crowds are won or lost, where the polyvalence of the terms suggest not only the threat of a loss of focus but also a loss at some zero-sum encounter. Certain audiences and venues (returning again to our first sense of the term) may have expectations for such antagonism towards the comedian, and the apparatus of stand-up comedy – the naming of the event as such, the geography of the venue, the introduction, if any, by an emcee or compère – does not mean that the claim to the social identity of 'stand-up comedian' does not need to be immediately, rigorously, and diligently proven for the entire duration of the comedian's time on stage.

If crowdwork makes explicit the otherwise implicit dialogue of stand-up comedy performance through the comedian's solicitation of and direct engagement with specific voiced contributions from an audience, heckling is its counterpart, where an audience member briefly breaks the focus of the performance – heretofore given solely to the comedian by the collective audience and by the expectations of the art form – through an unsolicited contribution. Such an interruption can itself be quickly turned into crowdwork, and the comedian again demonstrates a confidence and facility with the genre by parrying effectively through both a display of wit and a subsequent smooth transition back to material. Specific comedians, such as Jimmy Carr or Jamie Kennedy, may have honed a reputation for confronting hecklers to the point where heckling is an anticipated part of the performance. The parrying is particularly effective when the comedian has managed to maintain the goodwill of most of the audience through demonstrating competency and relevancy: the heckler is not so much interrupting the speech from the stage as interrupting the conversation between the performer and the rest of the audience, choosing to draw focus to themselves and away from the performer, against the will of the rest of the room. In an April 2022 performance at De Montfort Hall in

Leicester, Jimmy Carr called for security after a heckler continually interrupted his performance:

Uh guys? Security guys?
Security guys hi? [light laughter]
[Heckler: *Security* you f***ing c***] [Ooh]
You seem, you seem like a very aggressive *man*
And we're at a *comedy* show
[Heckler: and this is what you're f***ing going to do with it?]
Yeah. Sure. [Cheers]
Hey listen, let's not be
let's not be, let's not be *those* people
We've *all*, all of us
We're not judgy people
We've all got f***ing *hammer*-drunk after work on a Friday
And woken up on a Saturday going | *oh my god*
I'm *king* of the *c***s* | [laughter]
It's *his* go *tomorrow* [laughter]
[Carr laughs]
Oh *well*, we'll wait for him to *go* [pause]
Oh this is *exciting isn't it*? [laughter]
[as heckler leaves, crowd chants 'Cheerio!' à la 'Here we go!' football chant][13]

The audience continued to support Carr against the heckler to the point where Carr 'defended' him, and the interruption to the flow of the performance was negotiated by the audience and Carr collectively until such time as he was removed and an equilibrium could be restored with an emphatic '*Okay*, back to the show!'

The heckler may not be specifically hostile to the performer: rather, they may be misconstruing the conventions of stand-up comedy as a specific type of ludic speech act and making assumptions on where and how focus is given and ceded. Attending a stand-up comedy performance as part of other activities – a hen (bachelorette) party being a classic example – can interrupt the otherwise collectively held assumption that focus is principally reserved for the person on the stage. Similarly, they may simply be disrupting the flow of talk from the stage by engaging in conversation directed elsewhere: to a seat partner, or to the other end of a phone call. It is a misconstrual of the comedian's conversational speech act as one of many permitted within this social space instead of the primary one, and flouts the expectations of attentiveness and relative silence of audiences at cultural performances in general. Nevertheless, whether the heckler is hostile or not, the venue, with or without the specific request of the comedian, may remove the heckler on the grounds of them being disruptive to the performance.

However, the disruption may arise not from a sole audience member but from a significant portion, where, fairly or not, the comedian is deemed to have insufficiently fulfilled the expectations of performance competency and, seemingly with the consent of the whole audience, or in the absence of a strong dissent, focus is pulled with no intent to restore it. The performance frame is broken, with the identity of stand-up comedian withdrawn from the performer. The most famous incident is Michael Richards at the Laugh Factory on 17 November 2006, and his failure to navigate a heckle by using racial epithets:

AUDIENCE MEMBER #1: That was uncalled for
RICHARDS: What was uncalled for? It's uncalled for you to *interrupt* my ass you cheap mother*f***er*
You guys have been talkin' and talkin' and talkin'
'I don't know I don't know I don't know'
[murmur from crowd]
What's the matter? Is this too *much* for you to *handle*?
They're going to *arrest* me for calling a black man a *n***er*?
[raised voices from crowd]
Wait a *minute*: where's he *going*?
AUDIENCE MEMBER #2: That was uncalled for you f***ing cracker-ass motherf***er
RICHARDS: *Cracker-ass*? You calling me cracker-ass n***er?
AUDIENCE MEMBER #2: F***ing white boy
RICHARDS: Are you threatening me?
AUDIENCE MEMBER #2: We'll see what's up
RICHARDS: Oh it's a big threat, that's how you get back at the *man*
AUDIENCE MEMBER #2: That was *real* uncalled for
RICHARDS: Wait a minute: he's not *going* is he?
AUDIENCE MEMBER #2: It's not *funny*, that's why you're a *reject*, never had no *shows*, never had no *movies*, 'Seinfeld' that's *it*
RICHARDS: Oh I guess you got me there, you're absolutely *right*
I'm just a *wash-up*, gotta stand on the *stage*
[people leaving en masse]
Oh you're *leaving* | we've *had* it we've *had* it |[14]

The performance frame was clearly broken, and any tacit expectations for the audience to remain attentive and contributing little more than affect sounds were no longer in play. Richards' 'you're absolutely right, I'm a wash up' was likely meant sarcastically yet appeared retroactively accurate: as the footage went viral Richards' standing as a somewhat beloved cultural figure and, for our purposes, his claim to the identity 'stand-up comedian' were immediately diminished, not only for those in attendance at the Laugh Factory but for audiences in all our senses of the word.

Conclusion

In all the foregoing, counterexamples surely come to mind: experiments with performances recorded before no audience; levels of preparation involving props and recorded effects that clearly undermine the conceit of unaffectedness and extemporaneity; the esteem among comedians for those who on occasion 'walk the room' (impel the entire audience to leave in disgust or contempt for their material while still delighting the other comedians present). However, defining a genre not as a set of absolute postulates and formal structures but as a set of expectations and orientations allows for the flouting of those expectations: the exceptions are notable because the audience is sufficiently conversant with the style, and the performer's words and delivery are constructed in anticipation of that fluency.

The work of art in stand-up comedy is the live performance: an ephemeral real-time occurrence of comedian and audience, where the former speaks words and the latter reacts. As the preparation intends reaction, and the audience intends to have reactions, the reaction is a necessary and fundamental part of the work of art. It indicates the connotative interpretation of the words while evaluating the success or failure of performance competency. In instances when that ephemeral performance is broadcast or recorded that reaction is included, and the mediated audience member experiences and interprets the performance as the combination of comedian and audience. When the cultural critic or the scholarly exegete considers the stand-up performance, it is incumbent on them to include the audience's reaction as part of the material being interpreted.

Notes

1. Arthur C. Danto, *The Transfiguration of the Commonplace* (Cambridge, MA: Harvard University Press, 1981), p. 207.
2. Ben Judge, 'Greg Fleet: Secrets and Lies', Fest, 6 August 2008, www.fest-mag.com/edinburgh/archive/greg-fleet-secrets-and-lies; Ryan Stout, 'Stand-Up Comedy Audience Want to Be Challenged', *Twitter*, 26 May 2018, https://twitter.com/StoutRyan/status/1000522292697350145/.
3. Sam Friedman, 'The Godfather, Part Two', *Comedy Studies*, Vol. 5, No. 1, 2014: p. 84; Aju James, 'Caste, Gender, and "Global Indian-ness": Spaces of Safety in Stand-Up Comedy in Global Mumbai', *Feminist Media Studies*, Vol. 22, No. 4, 2020: pp. 831–847, p. 831.
4. Sophie Quirk, 'Containing the Audience: The "Room" in Stand-Up Comedy', *Participations: Journal of Audience & Reception Studies*, Vol. 8, No. 2, 2011: pp. 219–238.

5. Jesse David Fox, 'The Birth of UnCabaret Was Just What Comedy Needed', *Vulture*, 27 January 2022, www.vulture.com/article/beth-lapides-uncabaret-good-one-podcast.html.
6. Stephen Davies, 'Defining Art and Artworlds', *Journal of Aesthetics and Art Criticism*, Vol. 73, 2015: p. 379.
7. Phillip Deen, 'Is Bill Cosby Still Funny? Separating the Art from the Artist in Stand-Up Comedy', *Studies in American Humor*, Vol. 5, No. 2, 2019: p. 292.
8. Andrew Kania, 'All Play and No Work: An Ontology of Jazz', *Journal of Aesthetics and Art Criticism*, Vol. 69, 2011: p. 391.
9. Ian Brodie, *A Vulgar Art: A New Approach to Stand-Up Comedy* (Jackson: University Press of Mississippi, 2014); Ian Brodie, 'Is Stand-Up Comedy Art?', *Journal of Aesthetics and Art Criticism*, Vol. 78, No. 4, 2020: pp. 401–418.
10. Frank Boardman, 'What Is a Stand Up Special?', *Aesthetic Investigations*, Vol. 5, No. 1, 2021: p. 55.
11. Baldesar Castiglione, *The Book of the Courtier*, trans. Charles S. Singleton (New York: Anchor Books, 1959), p. 43.
12. *Liam Withnail – MANCHESTER I'm back hosting …* [online video], www.instagram.com/reel/CYl3KzRsToX.
13. *natfromleicester – Drunk guy vs. Jimmy Carr* [online video], www.tiktok.com/@natfromleicester/video/7089548284829732102.
14. *John Grubb – Michael Richards Goes Crazy* [online video], www.youtube.com/watch?v=amjUNF_R_PY.

Further Reading

Brodie, Ian, 'Is Stand-Up Comedy Art?', *Journal of Aesthetics and Art Criticism*, Vol. 78, No. 4, 2020: pp. 401–418.

Brodie, Ian, *A Vulgar Art: A New Approach to Stand-Up Comedy* (Jackson: University Press of Mississippi, 2014).

DeCamp, Elise, 'Humoring the Audience: Performance Strategies and Persuasion in Midwestern American Stand-Up Comedy', *Humor*, Vol. 28, No. 3, 2015: pp. 449–467.

Deen, Phillip, 'Is Bill Cosby Still Funny? Separating the Art from the Artist in Stand-Up Comedy', *Studies in American Humor*, Vol. 5, No. 2, 2019: pp. 288–308.

Lockyer, Sharon and Lynn Myers, '"It's about Expecting the Unexpected": Live Stand-Up Comedy from the Audiences' Perspective', *Participations: Journal of Audience & Reception Studies*, Vol. 8, No. 2, 2011: pp. 165–188.

Quirk, Sophie, 'Containing the Audience: The "Room" in Stand-Up Comedy', *Participations*, Vol. 8, No. 2, 2011: pp. 219–238.

Rosenberg, Neil V., 'Big Fish, Small Pond: Country Musicians and Their Markets', in Peter Narváez and Martin Laba (eds), *Media Sense: The Folklore Popular Culture Continuum* (Bowling Green: Bowling Green State University Popular Press, 1986), pp. 149–166.

Rutter, Jason, 'Rhetoric in Stand-Up Comedy: Exploring Performer–Audience Interaction', *Stylistyka*, Vol. 10, 2021: pp. 307–325.

Straw, Will, 'Cultural Scenes', *Loisir et Société/Society and Leisure*, Vol. 27, No. 2, 2004: pp. 411–422.

Tomsett, Ellie, '"Less Dick Jokes": Women-Only Comedy Line-ups, Audience Expectations and Negotiating Stereotypes', in Oliver Double and Sharon Lockyer (eds), *Alternative Comedy Now and Then: Critical Perspectives* (Basingstoke: Palgrave, 2022), pp. 239–265.

COMEDIANS' INSIGHTS
Who Are You Onstage?

Edward Aczel (UK)

An anti-comedian, bad.

Stephen Bailey (UK)

I am a more confident version of me. On stage I say everything I am too scared to say without a spotlight.

Maria Bamford (USA)

Myself, but with more swearing and unnecessary exaggeration.

Angela Barnes (UK)

Onstage it is always my turn to speak, the rules of social engagement are clear and I'm in control. Onstage I don't have the anxiety of worrying that I am being annoying, or talking too much, or not enough. So I think my stage persona oozes a confidence that in real life I can only dream of. I don't apologise for myself onstage, because I am expected to take up the space and have the voice.

Jo Brand (UK)

I am a couldn't-give-a-shit, dismissive purveyor of self-deprecating, unfeminine, feminist, bad housewifery, husband abuse, one-liners and generally pessimistic bad tempered view of the world.

Nathan Caton (UK)

I would say I'm me, but turned up, times ten. Onstage I'm more of an extrovert and people-person. Offstage I'm more content if I'm chilling by myself as people annoy me more.

Jo Caulfield (UK)

The 'me' that I want to be twenty-four hours a day – but society frowns upon that.

Tanyalee Davis (Canada/USA/UK)

Me at my best.

Tiernan Douieb (UK)

I'm definitely very me onstage, with perhaps a heightened element of grumbling when performing to adults and of idiocy and overenthusiasm when performing to children.

Alexis Dubus (UK), Who Performs as Marcel Lucont (France)

These days I'm mostly a sardonic Frenchman called Marcel Lucont. I think people who meet me for the first time after seeing the act are often surprised, as I'm an optimistic and amenable person in real life, quite far-removed from the haughty stage persona. Someone suggested to me that perhaps Marcel was my outlet to channel negativity and remain a decent person myself, which kind of suggests I was a bit of a prick before inventing him.

Mary Gallagher (USA)

A gritty and optimistic single mom.

Richard Herring (UK)

I am a heightened version of myself – much more outgoing than in real life. Lou Sanders says I come alive onstage (which I think is a polite way of saying I am boring offstage). I try to be me and honest about myself, but I am not a hugely sociable person offstage and quite shy and that wouldn't really work as an act. I love performing, so maybe Lou is right and the bloke onstage is the real me.

Bec Hill (Australia/UK)

Just a more energetic version of who I am offstage: a massive dork with a short attention span.

Charmian Hughes (UK)

I am me, but crystallised into my essential worst and best characteristics – judgy, grudgy, and petty but also a 'mad aunt on acid'.

Robin Ince (UK)

I think I am the closest thing to the person in my head. I have often had people say, 'Have you been diagnosed with ADHD?' – it has taken me fifty-two years of being alive but only very recently I have really started to face up to what I can be and what I cannot be – I have spent too long panel beating myself into who I think you are meant to be.

Milton Jones (UK)

An idiot savant. A moron who thinks he wins. And given that the audience are paying to see him, maybe he does.

Myq Kaplan (USA)

Good question! I'm just a boy, standing in front of an audience, asking them to love me. Also doing my best to love myself and them and everyone. With jokes!

Athena Kugblenu (UK)

100 per cent myself – but if I wasn't an introvert.

Beth Lapides (USA)

Me. But funnier. More focused. More sparkly. A combo pack of a cheerleader, a ring master, a mad scientist, and a yogi.

Stewart Lee (UK)

A worse version of me.

Laura Lexx (UK)

A lot of different people and all of them slight variations on myself or who I want to be. Kind but cutting, clever but silly, and mostly thoughtful.

Trevor Lock (UK)

A cross, funny orchestra conductor and a supply teacher.

Pope Lonergan (UK)

I chose a stage name because I wanted to create a bit of a separation between me (onstage) and me (in life). And then I've isolated and enhanced certain aspects of my personality that are an identifiable type, so the audience have useful coordinates. For instance: cheeky, mouthy Essex boi. I'll lean into that. Drug addict – but a thoughtful, conscientious drug addict (which is pretty much me). And a thoughtful, conscientious drug addict – that READS! I'm just realising this onstage self cleaves so close to my *actual* self that they're practically the same person. So there's very little separation TBH.

Elf Lyons (UK)

A nightmare.

Andrew McClelland (Australia)

The heightened Andrew McClelland. Like most of us. Me, but with more energy and desperate to please. I consider myself an 'entertainer' and love to do exactly that.

Aditi Mittal (India)

The daughter my mother wishes she had.

Martin Mor (Northern Ireland/UK)

I am closer to being myself onstage than at any other point in my life.

Al Murray (UK), Who Performs as the Pub Landlord (UK)

The Pub Landlord is a know-all know-nothing. He's a giant, shining idiot with the charisma of idiocy. The charisma of certain foolishness. The thing is I absolutely do love doing it, so it's still me very much onstage. I don't perform him with a heavy heart or any of that sort of thing. And I find it, using the comic forcefield it creates, I find being behind that forcefield incredibly liberating.

Sander Õigus (Estonia)

The goal is to be as natural and true to myself as possible. I don't want to just make people laugh at whatever cost, I want to do it my way.

Anuvab Pal (India)

I'd like to think I'm a more middle-class, settled version of myself.

Lucy Porter (UK)

I think I'm more myself than I've ever been now, because I'm kind of a cheerful, careworn mum. Previously, I was just cheerful and careworn and people didn't really know what to do with that. When I was starting out, the comedy archetypes for women were either dollybird or battle-axe, and I was neither a wide-eyed ingénue or a cynical hag, but a bit of both. Now I've earned the right to a bit of scepticism. It's not necessarily having children, I think it's more an age thing. I think I needed to be of an age where my demeanour perfectly fitted. Women, as they age, I think you become more chatty. A bit less self-conscious. And a bit more tired. So I think I've occupied the niche that I was always searching for.

Rod Quantock (Australia)

Me.

John Scott (UK)

I'm an affable agitator.

John Simmit (UK)

Am definitely me, not a character. It's a tour around my thoughts which sometimes goes well.

Joe Wells (UK)

This sounds pretentious but I think I'm a truer version of myself onstage. As a neurodivergent person I am always pretending to be someone else. Stand-up is very freeing.

Nigel Williams (UK/Belgium)

Onstage I try to be who I am and how I feel in life. My shows used to be full of outrage, now it's more mellow as I give up on politics and find 'us' (me included) just unfathomable.

Bilal Zafar (UK)

I've been described as low-key, wry, and naturalistic which are all things I like.

CHAPTER 13

Persona

Oliver Double

In the summer of 2015, the non-binary British-based Canadian comedian Mae Martin is performing a short set at the Just for Laughs festival in Montreal. Martin immediately establishes themself as a cool, quirky presence – elfin face, stylishly tousled short blond hair, T-shirt sleeves half rolled-up, tasteful tattoos on each forearm. There's an interesting mismatch between the excitable way the audience applaud and cheer them onto the stage and Martin's relaxed delivery. They talk as if this is a genuine conversation, with perhaps one or two other people rather than a theatre crammed full of lively punters.

The routine is about the fact that Martin has dated both men and women, and hinges on breaking up with a boyfriend they had when they were thirteen, called Ian Peach. When they first mention him, there's a gag that precisely plays on the illusion of stand-up as genuine conversation. 'D'you guys know Ian Peach?' Martin says, shading their eyes as if looking for anybody in the audience who might.[1] This gets a laugh because it reveals the artifice of talking to an audience as if talking to small group of friends. The people in the auditorium are just there to see a comedy show, so the chances of one of them knowing Ian Peach is ridiculously small. They recognise the question as a jokey bluff.

However, on this particular occasion, a woman sitting at the front calls Martin's bluff, indicating that she does indeed know Ian Peach. Martin turns to her: 'Wait, seriously? [quiet laughter] Wait, you do?' The woman replies, 'Yeah, from Toronto?' Martin giggles nervously before exclaiming, '*Oh my God!*' There's a delighted response – laughter, clapping, even some screams. Martin asks the woman, '*Are you serious?*' and lets loose a yell that's full of apprehension: 'ShhaaAAUUUUGHH!! [laughter, clapping, and screams]'.

This short but remarkable exchange is revealing, because it sheds light on the essential slipperiness of stand-up comedy. Stand-up is a formal performance masquerading as an everyday conversation. There's a lack of clarity about how the person onstage relates to the self they are in everyday life, whether the things they say are true or invented. When the punter reveals she actually knows Ian Peach, the conversation becomes a real, two-way exchange of information, and the anecdote is authenticated, removing the ambiguity about truth and fiction. Now that we know it's true, the stakes are raised. Martin addresses some of their following comments directly to the woman, as if to placate her: 'You can tell him I'm over it. Like, I never even – talk about it publicly. [laughter]' As they later confessed on a podcast, 'I'd been doing that joke for a year and then of course the one time it's televised this woman in the audience … really did know him … And so after the show I was like, "Just please don't … tell him. How pathetic that I'm still talking about him!".'[2]

Ever since the turn of the twentieth century, when the monologists of American vaudeville and the comedians of British music hall started to evolve into what we now call stand-up comedy, the identity of the performer has been at its very core. As an article from *The Times* put it in 1923, music hall existed 'for the exhibition of personality, pure and simple'.[3] However, the comedians of that era – with their cartoonish costumes and greasepainted faces – couldn't easily be mistaken for somebody the audience might encounter in everyday life. Since then, there has been a gradual but radical shift away from exaggeration and theatrical artifice and towards authenticity and self-revelation.

As David Marc puts it, 'the stand-up comedian addresses an audience as a naked self, eschewing the luxury of a clear-cut distinction between art and life'.[4] For Joanne R. Gilbert, stand-up involves 'the autobiographical self – a multifaceted, protean entity that encompasses both onstage and offstage personae'.[5] Similarly, Sophie Quirk argues that '[n]o comic persona can accurately and fully represent the person who exists offstage, nor can any character act divorce completely from the real-life performer'.[6] What all of this suggests is that while persona draws on the performer's offstage personality, there is also a level of artifice involved. This is something that comedians themselves are aware of, to the extent that some have even joked about it onstage. For example, Shelley Berman confesses to the audience that he uses, 'Little tricks … to win your love, so if you don't like the act, at least you'll like me' and as a result the act is 'strewn with several tiny little *lies*. So that I have gotten to a point where *so help me God* – I don't know whether I'm talking sincerely to you or whether I'm conning the *hell* out of you. [laughter and scattered applause]'[7]

Still, while there are stand-ups who use exaggerated personas or even outright characters today, for most comedians the gap between who they are onstage and off has drastically narrowed. Thus, the boundary between private life and stage material has become ever more porous and permeable – as Martin's encounter with the woman who knew Ian Peach vividly demonstrates. This chapter examines the creative opportunities and challenges that this presents, as well as exploring the craft skills and artistic choices behind a performance genre that makes itself look so spontaneous and authentic.

An Update on How My Life Is Going

Sarah Millican hails from South Shields in northern England. She is known for her high-pitched, Geordie-accented voice, gleefully rude material, and warm, collusive rapport with the audience. She explains, 'I guess what you're doing when you come to see me is you're getting an update on *how my life is going at the moment*'. Her act is built from her lived experiences, which effectively makes them a renewable resource for her creative output. She has to take time off between tours because, 'I write about *me* [so] I have to live a bit. 'Cos otherwise I'm just writing about staying in hotels and driving on motorways.'[8]

The title of her 2016 show *Outsider* gives an idea of her appeal. She represents the person on the outside, the kid who was unpopular at school, and she flies in the face of the oppressive beauty standards expected of women. In one of her *Outsider* routines, she talks about a vet who advises her to let her dog put on weight as 'padding against illness'. Her response is typical: 'I said, "How come no doctor's ever suggested this to me?" [laughter] I reckon I could have six weeks of sickness and diarrhoea – [laughter] and still not be able to get into anything in Topshop. [laughter into applause]'[9] Lawrence E. Mintz argued that the comedian 'represents conduct to be ridiculed and rejected, and our laughter reflects our superiority, our relief that [her] weaknesses are greater than our own'.[10] In Mintz's terms, then, the audience laugh because they feel superior to Millican for her failure to conform to the body shape assumed by a high-street clothes shop. However, Mintz also conceded that the comedian can 'can become our *comic spokesman*',[11] which seems nearer the mark in this case. The joke seems to embrace the concept of 'padding against illness' as a *relief* against the pressure to be thin. The real target is not Millican but Topshop, which fails to provide clothes for larger women – and the audience's applause suggests support for her defiant stance.

Later in the show, Millican brings something from her private life onto the stage in a much more controlled way than Martin's chance encounter with Ian Peach's friend. She tells the audience that she's going to read them an email sent to her via her website from somebody called Lynn, who she knew at school. The email is smug and self-aggrandising, like the kind of round robin letters sent with Christmas cards. Almost a minute into it, Lynn starts to list the various places she's lived: 'We next moved to Denmark, where I gave birth to Giles – and then moved on to Rome where I gave birth to Harvey. Family complete, we moved to the Middle East. We moved from there to Monaco.' At this, Millican pauses to breathe out heavily, showing us how bored and fed up she is with what she's reading. This gesture of contempt gets seven seconds of laughter. Finally, the email ends. In the pause that follows, there's a murmur of laughter – audible anticipation – as Millican puts down the printed email. Then she announces, 'She was one of my bullies.' There's a loud response, in which the laughter is outweighed by a sound of sympathy: 'Ahhh.' Millican goes on to give an example of the psychological bullying that Lynn put her through at school. Then, after acknowledging that 'I might've misremembered things' or been 'overly sensitive at the time', she explains how she responded to the email: 'So this is all I sent, just the one line: "Hello, Lynn. To be honest, I probably won't reply any more fully than this, as I don't remember you very favourably."' This gets a huge, fifteen-second response, the laughter quickly overwhelmed by cheering and applause.

This routine tells us a lot about the relationship between affection and power in stand-up. The audience's affection for Millican is tangible, manifested in the 'Ahhh' of sympathy and the joyful cheering and applause. As a successful comedian, Millican is far more powerful than she was when she knew Lynn at school. Lynn acknowledges this in the email: 'My boys aged 11 and 10 are very impressed that mum went to school with someone famous.' Clearly Lynn was hoping to re-establish contact in order to enhance her own status. Instead, Millican is able to wield the obvious affection of her audience to enact a symbolic revenge. *She* has the power now and she comes back for more jabs later in the show, imagining Lynn's response to her reply ('I like to think she gathered them around and she said, "Mummy's friend from school, the one off the television, she's replied. Let's read the email all together, as a family." [laughter]'), and suggests she'll 'send her the fuckin' DVD'. This line gets another huge response, with laughter dissolving into twenty seconds' worth of cheering, whistling, and applause. The audience clearly enjoy seeing her right a wrong, sharing vicarious pleasure by witnessing the outsider triumphing against her former oppressor. This also extended to the larger audience watching the recording of the show. Within months of posting a clip of the routine on YouTube in 2021, it had logged almost three million views.

Process the Shame

Other examples are almost the polar opposite of this – an aspect of the comedian's private life can creep onto the stage with them whether they want it to or not, and they can be cast as the abuser rather than the abused. This was the situation faced by two American comedians identified by the #MeToo movement, Louis CK and Aziz Ansari. It must be acknowledged that – despite their apparent similarity – these cases are significantly different. Louis CK engaged in a repeated pattern of abusive behaviour involving masturbating in front of a series of female colleagues from the comedy industry. CK denied the rumours for years, before finally confessing in November 2017. The statement he issued acknowledged that he had abused his power as a comedian: 'I … took advantage of the fact that I was widely admired in my and their community, which disabled them from sharing their story and brought hardship to them when they tried because people who look up to me didn't want to hear it.'[12] By contrast, the single allegation against Aziz Ansari was made in an article on *Babe.net*, which described a sexual encounter in which the issue of consent was unclear and contested. The controversy and ambiguity of the case inspired a *Saturday Night Live* sketch in which restaurant diners are terrified to express a view on it. Even feminist journalists were hotly divided, some defending Ansari on the grounds of poor journalistic standards in the *Babe.net* article. As Caroline Framke put it: 'There are also some aspects of how they put the story together in the first place that are, to be frank, alarming.'[13] There was also a contrast in the fortunes of the two comedians after the accusations against them became public. CK's forthcoming Netflix special was cancelled, and HBO removed his work from their streaming services. Ansari's Netflix special went ahead.

Disturbing ethical issues aside, both men faced a similar situation – how to address an audience who would undoubtedly be all too aware of the controversy surrounding them. They dealt with this in very different ways, with very different outcomes, and with differing effects on their stage personas. Louis CK had been celebrated as a comedian who could play with taboos, exploring outrageous trains of thought which often ended up travelling to progressive conclusions. He was also known for his self-lacerating honesty. His 2008 special *Chewed Up* starts with him apologising because 'I ate too much and masturbated too recently', getting laughs by recalling running into a woman he knows before he could 'process the shame', and acknowledging that weighing himself is 'not guiding my behaviour', before concluding: 'Why am I bothering – [laughter] to find out exactly how much of a piece of shit I am? [laughter]'[14] When he finally confessed to his abusive behaviour, he revealed just how partial and selective this kind of onstage honesty was. Suddenly, the reference to masturbation became more troubling than funny.

However, the audience captured on his 2020 special *Sincerely Louis CK* – released via his own website – showed no sign of being troubled. Before he enters, they chant his name, and some rise to their feet as he's cheered onto the stage. He addresses the controversy almost immediately: 'How are you? How, how was *your* last couple o' years? [laughter] How was two thousand and eighteen and nineteen for you guys? [laughter]'[15] It's striking just how little he has to say for the audience to know what he's talking about. CK's public shaming is clearly at the top of their minds. He goes on to joke about not his actions – or his victims – but the experience of being on the receiving end of public shame: 'I learned a lot. I learned how to eat alone in a restaurant, with – [laughter] people giving me the finger from across the room. [laughter]' Towards the end of the show, he returns to the subject. The audience cheer and applaud for four seconds when he says, 'Right, you wanna talk about it, shall we talk about it?' He then gets a laugh by offering them 'some advice that really only *I* can give': 'If you ever ask somebody – may I – jerk off in front of you – and they say yes – just say, "Are you sure?" [laughter]' On the face of it, he's advising the audience to take more care with consent, but it's a double-edged gag that also implies his victims hadn't been clear enough about *not* giving him consent. Either way, his handling of the subject erases the impact of his actions on these women. The laughter he seeks does not allow any empathy with them, and indeed he soon returns to the subject of his own struggles with being shamed.

Despite the live audience's positive reaction, some critics were less convinced. The *New York Times*'s Jason Zinoman pointed out the problem for CK's persona in this post-#MeToo show: 'We know too much about his transgressions to see jokes that transgress in the same way.'[16] Similarly, the *Guardian*'s Brian Logan argued that 'this set is hard to watch through any lens other than that of CK's behaviour', concluding, '[p]erhaps, now the veil has slipped, CK can no longer be bothered pretending to the loftier ideals that used to offset his more cynical material'.[17]

Aziz Ansari's persona is very different from CK's. Although he tackles serious subjects such as racism in his stand-up, he tends to present himself as superficial, childish, and privileged, particularly in contrast with his first-generation immigrant parents. Like CK, Ansari addresses his public shaming twice in his show – a Netflix special called *Right Now* – once near the beginning and again at the end. Like CK, he enters to an audience welcoming him onto the stage by rising to their feet. Like CK, he starts by referencing his shaming in a joke. In this case, he recalls a fan approaching him in the street and praising him for a show that was actually by a different Indian American comedian, Hasan Minhaj. Realising his faux pas, the man starts listing things Ansari is known for to show that he does know who he is, ending with, 'And, er, you had that whole thing last year, sexual misconduct.' Ansari immediately cuts to his own reaction: 'NO NO NO NO NO NO NO NO NO NO NO NO NO NO!! [laughter] *That* – was Hasan. [laughter and applause]'

Having raised the subject with a joke, he immediately changes tone. His face and voice become more serious, more sincere. He talks in a way that suggests he's no longer chasing laughs, but rather wanting to share something deeper and more personal. For nearly a minute, he reflects on how he feels about the situation, and includes at least some acknowledgement of the other person's feelings: 'And ultimately – I just felt terrible – that this person felt this way. And – after a year or so – I just hoped – there was a step forward. And it moved things forward for me – made me think about a lot – I hope I become a better person.' Shortly afterwards, he brings the reflection to an end, by drawing attention to the unusualness of this type of serious reflection in this performance context: 'And – I know – this isn't the most hilarious way to begin a comedy show. [laughter] But it's important to me! That you know – how I feel about that whole thing – before we share – this night – together. [extended applause and some cheering] Well – that was pretty intense! [laughter]'[18]

Ansari's performance strategy is very different from CK's. Where CK meets opprobrium with jokes, Ansari chooses to push joking to one side and instead talk seriously. He explicitly frames this confessional moment as his attempt to clear the air before joking can begin again. At the end of the show, he returns to the subject with the same serious tone, and seems to acknowledge the effect the incident has had on his persona: 'That old Aziz who said, "Oh, treat yourself, whatever!" – he's dead. [quiet laughter]'

Not only did this strategy work for the audience in the theatre, it also received praise from some of the same reviewers who criticised CK's show. Jason Zinoman described *Right Now* as Ansari's 'finest work yet', arguing that, '[b]y framing the new special around his personal story … his act now coheres, taking on a new force and clarity, one that represents his finest, boldest and probably most polarizing work'.[19] Zinoman goes on to acknowledge that he previously found Ansari 'gifted if often glib … covering up mediocre material with high-energy performance', suggesting that the 'lower key' approach here works better, allowing for tighter writing and more nuance. Similarly, Doreen St Félix in the *New Yorker* called this 'Ansari's first authentic comedy special', arguing that 'the #MeToo story had liberated Ansari, forcing him to kill his old persona and give his new one teeth'.[20] The contrast with CK is very clear. Where the opprobrium and the way CK tackled it were seen as undermining his existing persona, Ansari's approach was seen as improving his persona, by forcing him to shed some of his superficiality and strive for greater authenticity.

Dead Dad Shows

Sometime in early 1980s, Tony Allen is performing in a show staged by Alternative Cabaret at the Elgin pub in Ladbroke Grove, London. After some material poking fun at the concept of immaculate conception, he goes into a ten-minute routine about what he's been doing in the last week, starting with being arrested after saying the word 'fucking' while speaking at Speakers' Corner. He finds himself in court, facing two magistrates who are middle-aged women. The clerk of the court tells him he can adjourn the case rather than face them. He considers it. To him, they look as stern and forbidding as Margaret Thatcher or the censorship campaigner Mary Whitehouse – not to mention his own mother.

He segues into a story about visiting his mother in Skegness and trying to get past their usual conflicts. He builds the atmosphere as they go for a walk: 'So we go on the beach. And it's beautiful. It's a summer morn, it's March, and – it's great. And the sun's glistening on the beach.' As they walk, his mother starts knocking a ball along with a golf club, and it lands on the golf course, leading to an altercation with its caretaker. When this '*jobsworth*, this bureaucrat' tells them they can't come onto the golf course, his mother responds by contemptuously blowing a raspberry at him. This leads Allen into some self-examination: 'And I thought, "I wonder where she gets that from?" [laughter] And then I sussed out – that that's where *I* get it from! [laughter] And I looked at her and I accepted her, and I – I *cried!* There, I fucking cried.' It's a delicate, tender moment in which the anarchist Allen suddenly realises he's inherited his rebelliousness from his mother, apparently resolving the long conflict between them. Crucially, when he realises how like his mother he is, he cries.

Now he cuts from this deeply personal moment back to the courtroom. The segue is so sudden and unexpected that it gets a laugh. He realises he may have misjudged the middle-aged magistrates just as he'd misjudged her mother: 'And so the – clerk of the court said to me – [laughter] "You, what do you want, d'you want the case adjourned?" An' I said – "No, they're cool." [laughter]' They dismiss the charges, and he concludes: 'And it was a good week! [laughter into applause]'[21]

This routine was performed at a moment of transition in British stand-up, when alternative comedy revolutionised the form both politically and stylistically. One of its many innovations was to change the nature of stage persona. Immediately before this, the main arena for stand-up in the UK was working men's clubs, and although many of the comedians who performed in them were ostensibly just performing *as themselves*, their material was almost exclusively made up of old gags. There was no expectation that stand-ups should generate their own material, nor was there any notion that material should be original. The same gags would turn up in the acts of many stand-ups. There was a small alternative to this in the form of comedians such as Billy Connolly and Jasper Carrott, who started out in folk music clubs and included more personal, anecdotal material. However, folk comedians were few and far between. Alternative comedy radically expanded the creative possibilities for British stand-ups, including allowing them to base their entire act on their own experiences and opinions.

The inspiration for this sea change came from across the Atlantic. The more personal approach had emerged much earlier in America, pioneered in the 1950s by comedians such as Mort Sahl and Lenny Bruce. Since then, a number of American comedians have created routines about intense personal experience, tackling subjects that might seem too distressing for audiences to laugh at. In May 1959, Jonathan Winters was hospitalised after a very public mental breakdown in San Francisco. A few months later, he was performing a routine about it, featuring this on his LP *The Wonderful World of Jonathan Winters*, released that December. In the 1960s, Lenny Bruce often talked onstage about the legal problems that would destroy his career and contribute to his early death, towards the end even reading court transcripts to the audience. From the 1970s through to the 1990s, Richard Pryor created hilarious routines from the many traumas he'd experienced, including a heart attack, major burns, and multiple sclerosis. In 2012, Tig Notaro decided to tell her audience at the Largo in LA about her recent diagnosis for cancer – among other traumas – and a recording of the performance became a bestselling album.

However, before alternative comedy there was no tradition of such material in British stand-up. For older comedians, intense personal experience was simply unsuitable for comedy. In 1994, towards the end of a career that started in variety theatres, Bob Monkhouse met with a TV producer to discuss his forthcoming special, *An Audience with Bob Monkhouse*. The previous year he had published his autobiography – the aptly titled *Crying with Laughter* – which included some of his more traumatic experiences. The producer picked some of these out as possible subjects for him to cover in the show. He shunned the idea:

> While the events she had listed were all true incidents in my life and had seemed quite suitable for the book, as comedy material they lacked the strength needed to sustain an hour of laughter … an in-depth interview … might require some truthful account of my life and times, [but] this was more the sort of show designed to be a vehicle for what I do best, which is stand-up comedy … While I could deliver a truthful lecture on these topics, it wouldn't be all that comical.[22]

This shows how remarkable it was for Tony Allen to be sharing such an intimate moment as early as 1980. There was no tradition of this kind of confessional material in British stand-up at this point. However, what Allen's routine foreshadowed – with its interwoven personal narratives, its tones and textures, its sad moment just before the end – was the so-called dead dad show, which would become a significant trend in the twenty-first-century UK comedy scene.

Dead dad shows are a product of the Edinburgh Fringe, and in spite of the name, they don't just refer to shows about losing a father. They are long-form, autobiographical shows based on traumatic experiences such as bereavement, physical illness, or mental health issues. Early examples include André Vincent's *André Vincent is Unwell* (2002), about suffering from kidney cancer; and Smug Roberts' *Me Dead's Dead* (2006) and Jason Cook's *Joy* (2008), both about losing a father. Since then, dead dad shows have become increasingly important. Since 2010, four of the eleven winners of the Edinburgh Comedy Award have won with this type of show: Russell Kane's *Smokescreens and Castles* in 2010, Richard Gadd's *Monkey See Monkey Do* in 2016, and Hannah Gadsby's *Nanette* jointly with John Robins' *The Darkness of Robins* in 2017. Indeed, these shows became so prevalent that in 2018, a *Guardian* critic wrote:

> The classic Edinburgh comedy show lasts an hour, with a strong narrative component and an inevitable 'sad bit'. But this rigid template is stifling creativity … So common is the sad bit now that not only is it a cliche in comedy circles, it's also become a cliche for standups to knowingly point it out with, 'OK, here's the sad bit of the show now.'[23]

Figure 13.1 Russell Kane performs in his production *Smokescreens and Castles* at the Pleasance as part of the Edinburgh Festival Fringe
Photo: Robbie Jack / Contributor / Corbis Entertainment / Getty Images.

Russell Kane's *Smokescreens and Castles* is arguably the best-known dead dad show to actually concern the loss of a father, but in fact bereavement is only touched on briefly (Figure 13.1). For most of the show, Kane uses the present tense to suggest his father is still around. The show paints a hilarious picture of Kane's upbringing in a working-class family in Essex, particularly focusing on his troubled relationship with his hypermasculine Thatcherite father, Dave. Kane brings Dave vividly to life through description and impersonation, and many of the routines focus on experiences that are too personal or upsetting to be an obvious fit for a stand-up show. One of the lighter themes is Kane's disapproval of his father's racism, and he confesses that he initially took a left-wing antiracist stance 'purely to spite him'. He imitates his father saying, 'Yeah. I hate all these people', before adopting an effete, middle-class voice to imitate his younger self's reaction to this: 'I love them then, Papa! [laughter]'[24]

Other routines cut deeper, uncovering a lack of warmth between father and son. Kane recalls Dave declaring, 'I love you son. I'd throw myself in front of a car for you. I love you. But I won't fucking speak to you between the ages of twelve and eighteen. [loud laughter] 'Cos I'm emotionally retarded by my own dad. And in turn, I'm attempting to retard *you*. [laughter]' Shortly afterwards, he delves deeper into his father's self-justification: 'D'you wanna know what he actually said? "Why d'you make out – I'm not a loving father? [whisper of laughter] I never fucking hit ya!" [laughter into applause] That was it! That's the total sum up – of love! That's all it takes, ladies and gentlemen! As long as you don't close your fist and beat the little shit. [laughter]' Then he digs deeper still:

> 'D'you know *why* I never hit ya?' And I'm still holding on. Pathetic! Still the eight-year-old boy on the inside. 'D'you know *why* I never hit ya?' 'Why, dad? Why?' And this is what he said. 'Cos if I'd started – I wouldn't've fucking stopped. [loud laughter into applause]' Murder! *Murder!* That's murder! Take a child – and punch it without stopping. [laughter] D'you know what'll happen? You'll kill it! It'll die! [whisper of laughter] And what's weird – is the look of pride that's on these men's face, when they say it! [laughter]

One thing that makes this show so radically different from the stand-up comedy of Bob Monkhouse's era is the level of emotional detail that's included. Often this is unnecessary for any upcoming punchline but instead adds texture and builds atmosphere. Towards the end of the show, there's a long routine about an incident in Dave's favourite curry house, the Akash. A fight kicks off on another table, and Dave moves his arm to protect his son:

> And just me and dad left in the corner of the bench, I'll never forget the warmth – of his bicep against my chest. Like, it sounds a bit of a – sentimental memory, but it's an amazing one for me, just the – there it is, across me, first time *ever*, some sort of affection, some sort of primal – connection – between father and son.

By telling the audience that this 'sentimental memory' is an 'amazing one for me', Kane emphasises the fact that he's sharing very personal experiences with them, deepening the emotional involvement and heightening the feeling of authenticity. This is not the only time he underlines the fact that he's making private memories public. Going into the routine, he recalls that Dave cried when the Akash closed down, 'more than he cried over anything *I've* ever done, how hurtful!' Then he makes the act of sharing quite explicit: 'D'you know the next sentence that came out of his mouth, I've never shared *this* before and now it'll go down on a DVD forever. It's not even funny, it's just bizarre – he would say it to an astounded eleven-year-old. "The Akash is closed, boy." "Why dad?" "Well. Abdul didn't do his VAT returns." [laughter into applause]'

It's only in the last two minutes of the show that Kane reveals the truth about his father. Picking up on his occasionally inconsistent use of tense when talking about him – 'I kept going from *was* to *is*' – he points to the box at the side of the stage where, as he has previously explained, his mother is sitting:

> He should be sat up there, course he should, right, but he's not there. And why is he not there? Well, it doesn't take Columbo to try and work out what I'm telling you, yeah? The sad truth of this fucking story, right? Is that he'll never see this show. He'll never know a DVD was made. And that's it, I'm drifting into my dad's voice now, what a sick, fucked-up way to close the show. Right? [laughter]

He continues in his father's voice, ventriloquising him from beyond the grave to tell the story of his own death and its aftermath. There's only one punchline in the whole sequence, and the show ends not with a big laugh but with a kind of wistful calm.

The Constant Sifting of Experience

In her broadly positive review of Aziz Ansari's *Right Now*, Doreen St Félix describes the quiet, confessional moment at the beginning of the show as 'crafted contrition'. The word *crafted* seems to suggest that there is something disingenuous about Ansari's words, as if something that is carefully constructed and calculated to have a certain impact cannot be sincere. The truth is, of course, that everything that appears in a stand-up show is carefully crafted. For all the emotional depth of *Smokescreens and Castles* – in spite of the way it presents personal, often painful memories – it's still a stand-up comedy show, with a rigorous construction process behind it. Kane put it together as he would any of his other shows. He describes how this works:

> It's a Darwinian process ... and Darwinian processes take a lot of time. So for example, even someone like me, who's pretty much just doing their personality onstage, if I want to take ten funny stories that have happened to me, I will preview a minimum of thirty times before I sell you a tour ticket. So that means a fifty-seater, everyone's paid four quid to get in, notes scattered on the floor – and in a Darwinian way, I'm advancing.[25]

In describing how he develops material in preview shows, he uses a striking phrase about his onstage identity: 'pretty much doing [my] personality onstage'. The suggestion is that he is simply *playing himself*, so that his personality is indivisible from his persona. However, he actually acknowledges that the stage persona is created by selecting and amplifying particular aspects of the personality: 'You also, in a longer way, over the first two, three, four, five years, advance in a Darwinian way which parts of the personality you show. "Oh, people find it really funny when I'm more Essex-y. People find it funny when I'm theatrically angry. I'll use more of that."'[26] This echoes Tony Allen's account of how comedians develop stage persona through 'a sort of strategic identity crisis' in which 'various sides of our personality come to our assistance. However idiosyncratic or inappropriate these minority personalities appear to be, they should all be given an audition.'[27]

As for finding the elements of his personal life to share in his act, this is a question of being constantly alert to anything with the kind of absurdity that gives it comic potential: 'You can learn spotting the incongruity. I mean, all you've got to do is, if you want to learn incongruity – did everyone just howl when I was out at what just happened? That goes in your [note]book.'[28] For this show, he had a particular process for finding material: 'I would go round each room of the house and think of a funny memory ... "Let's go into the lounge. What's going on there? Let's go into the bedroom, let's go into the garden, into the gym." So it's like a mental tour.'[29]

The final reveal of his father's death came very late in the process. After completing almost all the previews, Kane had the idea of finishing the show on a dramatic note. Trying it out in the last preview, right at the beginning of the Fringe, produced startling results: '[S]omeone started crying in the front row. I thought ... "Are they grieving, is something happening at home?" It took me a while to realise that people were crying at what I was saying.'[30]

The shift towards sharing ever more personal material in stand-up, constantly thinning the membrane that separates life and art, eliding the gap between persona and personality, could be seen as somewhat corrosive to the comedian. In 1992, the pioneering alternative comedian Alexei Sayle argued that the 'constant sifting of experience to see whether they can get a laugh out of it' can lead to 'the former most popular person in class becom[ing] a social amputee'. He recalled meeting a fellow comedian in the street, who told him his father has just died. When Sayle commiserated, the comedian replied: 'I'm really upset. I was hoping to get a five-minute routine out of it, but so far I've come up with nothing.'[31]

There are certainly ethical issues that arise for comedians who mine their personal lives for material, because this is likely to involve talking about not just themselves but also the friends and family with whom they share their lives. A positive review of Kane's show acknowledges some discomfort around this: 'There are moments when you feel old scores are being settled, and worry at the ethics of it all.'[32] In fact, Kane invited his mother to the preview shows to check she was happy with what he was saying: 'The only bit my mum hadn't seen was the moving ending. She'd come to see a preview and said, "Yeah." It's all true at the end of the day. It's true. I've not added anything. There's no slating there.'[33]

In a sense, Kane shares Sayle's cynicism, reflecting on his own work in a disarmingly matter-of-fact way. 'I have just monetised my personality', he explains, adding that comedians present 'pseudo truths' and the audience are attracted by the 'false persona game'.[34] He doesn't remember the creation of *Smokescreens and Castles* being driven by any kind of artistic idealism:

> I don't know what made it occur to me ... I think it doesn't go any deeper than, 'Oo, I'm at a poncy art festival. Wouldn't it be fun if there was a moving bit at the end?' That's as far as my thinking went. It wasn't, 'I sensed the structure would be amazing' or 'I'm a superior creative individual', I just, as a working-class person, wanted to show off to posh arts people, and think of an ending that would move people.[35]

He decided to reveal his father's death at the end of the show 'from the practical point of view [that] I couldn't work out how to tell an audience he was deceased at the top of the show and not sour the atmosphere ... I did stand-up for seven years pretending my dad was alive after he was dead – just purely out of sheer, people-pleasing cowardice.'[36] The phrase 'people-pleasing cowardice' is revealing, because it implies that it would have been braver and more admirable to be more honest, more willing to share this fact with an audience. The implication is that far from being corrosive, the comedian's willingness to share intimate details of their lives could be seen as a superior artistic approach.

Maybe That's an Arty Show

Throughout its existence as a recognisable form, stand-up has always put the identity of the performer at its centre. This chapter has explored how this identity has changed so that for many comedians, stage persona and off-stage personality have come ever closer, art and artist ever more indivisible. The rise of the dead dad show is just the latest manifestation of a tendency for any life experience, no matter how intense, personal, and seemingly lacking in comic potential to become the raw material for a stand-up show. Of course, there are considerable craft skills involved in transforming life experience into viable comedy material, and in constructing a persona from the careful selection and exaggeration of character traits. This process could be seen cynically as a commodification of self, with increasing demands to put even the most traumatic experiences into the act.

On the other hand, it could be seen more positively as a remarkable act of public sharing. When comedians talk about difficult experiences they have had, this can open up a wider range of audience responses than laughter alone. These might include anything from elation at the thrill of seeing a former bully brought down to size, to tears of empathy for a dead parent. Such shows might even affect the audience's worldview. The pragmatic Russell Kane argues against the idea of stand-up as an art form, except when the comedian's routine sticks in the memories of the people who laughed at it. The examples he gives are by other performers, but when pressed he acknowledges that he might have had such an effect with *Smokescreens and Castles*: 'Have I temporarily altered the way you see working-class masculinity? I'd like to think so. So maybe that's an arty show.'[37]

Notes

1. *Mae Martin – Why Are You Gay?* [online video], www.youtube.com/watch?v=YoUP6eIpU_U.
2. RHLSTP [podcast], www.youtube.com/watch?v=l9mJzFyUInc.
3. 'Personality – On Playing One's Self', *The Times*, 4 April 1923, p. 8.
4. David Marc, *Comic Visions* (Boston: Unwin Hyman, 1989), p. 13.
5. Joanne R. Gilbert, *Performing Marginality* (Detroit: Wayne State University Press, 2004), p. 51.
6. Sophie Quirk, *Why Stand-Up Matters* (London: Bloomsbury, 2015), p. 132.
7. Shelley Berman, 'A Sappy Thank You', on *The Edge of Shelley Berman* [LP] (USA: Verve Records, 1960).
8. 'This is a really, really arrogant diary ... ' – hmv.com talks to Sarah Millican about her new DVD *Outsider* [online video], www.hmv.com/video/sarah-millican-interview-home-bird-hmv.
9. Sarah Millican, *Outsider* [DVD] (UK: Universal, 2016).
10. Lawrence E. Mintz, 'Standup Comedy at Social and Cultural Mediation', *American Quarterly*, Vol. 37, Spring 1985: p. 74.
11. Lawrence E. Mintz, 'Standup Comedy at Social and Cultural Mediation', p. 74.
12. 'Louis C.K. Responds: "These Stories Are True"', *New York Times*, 11 November 2017, p. A13.

13. Caroline Framke, 'The Controversy around Babe.net's Aziz Ansari Story, Explained', *Vox*, 18 January 2018, www.vox.com/culture/2018/1/17/16897440/aziz-ansari-allegations-babe-me-too.
14. Louis CK, *Chewed Up* [DVD] (USA: Anchor Bay Entertainment, 2008).
15. Louis CK, *Sincerely Louis CK* [video download] (USA: Positive Image Video, 2020).
16. Jason Zinoman, 'Louis C.K. Doubles Down on the Value of Saying the Wrong Thing', *New York Times*, 4 November 2019, www.nytimes.com/2019/11/04/arts/television/louis-ck-tour-review.html.
17. Brian Logan, 'Sincerely Louis CK Review – Standup Returns with Not-Quite Apology', *The Guardian*, 7 April 2020, www.theguardian.com/stage/2020/apr/07/sincerely-louis-ck-review-standup-comedy-me-too.
18. Aziz Ansari, *Right Now* [online video] (USA: Netflix, 2019).
19. Jason Zinoman, 'Aziz Ansari Addresses Sexual Misconduct Accusation in "Right Now"', *New York Times*, 9 July 2019, www.nytimes.com/2019/07/09/arts/television/aziz-ansari-netflix.html.
20. Doreen St Félix, 'The Productive Ambivalence of Aziz Ansari in His Comeback Netflix Special', *New Yorker*, 13 July 2019, www.newyorker.com/culture/cultural-comment/the-productive-ambivalence-of-aziz-ansari-in-his-comeback-netflix-special.
21. Unpublished recording from the British Stand-Up Comedy Archive, University of Kent.
22. Bob Monkhouse, *Over the Limit* (London: Century, 1998), p. 66.
23. Paul Fleckney, 'Joke's Over: Why Standups Should Refresh the Tired "Edinburgh Show"', *The Guardian*, 28 August 2018, www.theguardian.com/stage/2018/aug/28/standups-edinburgh-show-sean-hughes-comedy-award-festival-fringe.
24. Russell Kane, *Smokescreens & Castles* [DVD] (UK: Universal, 2011).
25. Russell Kane interview, by Zoom, 11 August 2021.
26. Russell Kane interview.
27. Tony Allen, *Attitude: Wanna Make Something of It?* (Glastonbury: Gothic Image, 2002), p. 35.
28. Russell Kane interview.
29. Russell Kane interview.
30. Russell Kane interview.
31. Alexei Sayle, 'Deadly Serious Funny Men', *Independent on Sunday*, 26 April 1992, p. 22.
32. Dominic Cavendish, 'Finding the Funny in Family Trauma', *Daily Telegraph*, 23 August 2010, p. 23.
33. Russell Kane interview.
34. *Archive on 4* ('Stewart Lee: Unreliable Narrator') [radio], BBC Radio 4, 12 June 2021.
35. Russell Kane interview.
36. Russell Kane interview.
37. Russell Kane interview.

Further Reading

Allen, Tony, *Attitude: Wanna Make Something of It?* (Glastonbury: Gothic Image, 2002).

Double, Oliver, *Getting the Joke: The Inner Workings of Stand-Up Comedy*, 2nd ed. (London: Methuen, 2014).

Gilbert, Joanne R., *Performing Marginality: Humor, Gender and Cultural Critique* (Detroit: Wayne State University Press, 2004).

Marc, David, *Comic Visions* (Boston: Unwin Hyman, 1989).

Mintz, Lawrence E., 'Standup Comedy as Social and Cultural Mediation', *American Quarterly*, Vol. 37, No. 1, 1985: pp. 71–80.

Quirk, Sophie, *Why Stand-Up Matters: How Comedians Manipulate and Influence* (London: Bloomsbury, 2015).

CHAPTER 14

Stand-Up Comedy and Trauma
Hannah Gadsby's Nanette

Mary Luckhurst

Stand-Up and the Trauma Narrative

The narrative of trauma is an integral part of Hannah Gadsby's superstar comedy status, which they attained through *Nanette*, their Netflix comedy special, in 2018. Trauma can refer to physical as well as mental wounds and in a post-Freudian age its meanings have come to be understood as serious, disabling injury to a person's psyche, sense of identity, and experience of the world caused by an external agent. Many scholars understand trauma as a defining factor of a modernity marked by violence, war, and genocide. Cathy Caruth has quantified trauma as 'a central characteristic of the survivor experience of our time' and Mark Seltzer has argued that 'the modern subject has become inseparable from the categories of shock and trauma'.[1] The trauma narrative pervades *Nanette* just as it overwhelmed Gadsby's earlier life. In their bestselling memoir, *Ten Steps to Nanette: A Memoir Situation* (2022), Gadsby refers to trauma as fundamental to their understanding of stand-up and as critical to their health and their development of resilience: 'I owe stand-up my life', they state, 'it gave me the platform and the purpose to playfully interrogate my own story and unravel the immature and sometimes toxic versions of events that my younger, traumatised brain had settled on'.[2]

Born in 1978, Gadsby had enjoyed success as a writer, stand-up, and actor in Australia since 2006 but their Netflix launch on 19 June 2018 propelled them into new worlds of Hollywood celebrity that they are still trying to negotiate today.[3] *Nanette* debuted as a work in progress with a disastrous but instructive failure in Perth but it was later, in its evolutionary journey at the Melbourne International Comedy Festival in 2017, that it began to generate a critical ruckus (Figure 14.1).[4] Gadsby renounced their familiar, much-loved persona, delivered a coruscating deconstruction of what they perceived to be the abusive conventions of stand-up, and announced that they were quitting comedy in order to protect their mental health. Their familiar

Figure 14.1 Hannah Gadsby performs *Nanette* during the Assembly Gala Launch for the Edinburgh Festival Fringe at Assembly Hall, Edinburgh, 2 August 2017
Photo: Roberto Ricciuti / Contributor / Getty Images Entertainment / Getty Images.

Australian audiences were stunned and *Nanette* gained notoriety on the circuit both for the exposure of a new public identity defined by shocking traumatic events from the past and for outing stand-up as an ethically compromised medium. Gadsby had, it seemed, revealed ugly truths about stand-up as well as its performers and audiences. In the months of the live tour before *Nanette* reached the screen, it was unclear how long Gadsby could continue to do stand-up while making claims about the mental injury they were simultaneously sustaining. By the time of the Netflix special, filmed at the Sydney Opera House, Gadsby had refined the show into a highly crafted, metatheatrical act of high-wire, confessional storytelling moving fluidly between performance monologue, stand-up routine, and lecture. Gadsby won a Primetime Emmy Award for Outstanding Writing for a Variety Special and a Peabody award that recognised their powerful, enlightening, and invigorating story. These were in addition to awards and honours they had already accumulated in Australia and the UK.

Gadsby has been clear that the staging of her intention to quit was a dramatic conceit, a narrative hook, stumbled on accidentally and then deployed to lay bare their professional and personal conundrums as a comic and trauma survivor.[5] The conceit of announcing their departure from stand-up while performing a show is perhaps the most notorious and brilliantly executed comic device of recent times. It gave Gadsby 'the permission to say what I wanted to say' because they removed the stakes that they had hitherto attached to they career and persona and renegotiated them.[6] Critics and practitioners were fascinated by Gadsby's explosion of form and the reinvention of their performance persona.[7] Some American comedians even demanded Gadsby's cancellation because they thought of their work as hostile to comedy and detrimental to the stand-up industry. Gadsby's staging of their trauma has caused just as much controversy as their innovative experiments with comic form, and – depending how you view their work – these two things may or may not be linked. For Gadsby the one cannot be separated from the other. As they have explained, by October 2017 they had already removed themself from social media platforms 'because *Nanette* had inspired a bit of hate and a lot of sharing of trauma'.[8] The capacity of a trauma narrative to trigger trauma in others, its transmissibility between the narrator/victim and their listeners or viewers, is well documented and something of a preoccupation for Gadsby because of their own experience of trigger reactions.[9] But the phenomenon that became *Nanette* overtook all Gadsby's expectations, developed its own momentum and threatened to turn into a runaway monster, the power of which, in its many iterations, even frightened its author. Indeed, in their memoir Gadsby uses a containment strategy and personifies *Nanette* as an entity separate from themself, referring to the show with pronouns she/her:

> I understood that I was not just in control of a moment, but in control of people, real people, and I did not care for that feeling at all. That kind of power feels too big to comprehend, too dangerous for anyone to wield, but especially someone who was running the gauntlet of their own triggers and trauma. I had wanted to create a show that served as my tool, not my weapon.[10]

Since the 1960s, stand-up has been identified as a form ideal for exposing human rights abuses and social inequities and for bringing minority identity politics to the fore.[11] In *Nanette*, Gadsby's trauma narrative is inextricably linked to their sexual identity as a gender-non-conforming lesbian and to the violence they have been subjected to because of their sex, body shape, and gender expression. During the course of the show, Gadsby reveals that they were a victim of childhood sexual abuse and male assault as a teenager, and were raped by two men. They also describe how they were psychically brutalised by the discourses of criminality, Christian damnation, and homophobic shame surrounding gay identity that they absorbed in Tasmania as a child and young woman (where some of the harshest penalties for homosexual activity in the Western world were imposed until 1997).

Gadsby's focus on trauma within stand-up can be contextualised through Western society's contemporary fetishisation of real stories and the rise of the confessional culture, personified through figures such as Oprah Winfrey. Their interest in trauma makes Gadsby a performer of their time, though, as she pointed out in *Nanette*: 'Artists don't invent the zeitgeist; they respond to it.'[12] It is not new for a stand-up to incorporate personal experiences of trauma into their set. However, it is against the grain to investigate so forensically how the dramaturgical construction of conventional jokes can intensify silences, censor storylines, feed stigma, trigger depression, and worsen trauma responses. More to the point, it mattered to Gadsby's following that they had not felt able to share these stories with them before. Audiences had felt confident that Gadsby was knowable as well as a trustworthy political performer. Their relationship with her audiences, built up over her preceding eight shows, was premised on an openness about themself and their fans' knowledge of their struggles with their sexuality. Gadsby's audiences identified with their persona and felt they knew Gadsby, whereas, in fact, Gadsby had censored the most significant details of life out of crippling shame. It was also against the grain to suggest to their audiences that their pleasure in Gadsby's manipulation of their responses might be an unethical and abusive power dynamic that they should take the trouble to examine. Gadsby's revelations about their traumatic past simultaneously played out as a confession to audiences that they had been behaving inauthentically, deceiving others by concealing their pain and reinforcing their trauma in the interests of serving up effective jokes. In pleasuring audiences and giving in to their dramaturgical expectations, they had been trapped inside a house of horrors, inflicting intolerable injury to themself while complicit with a comedy ecosystem that seemed to depend on a denial of straight white male cisgender violence and a suppression of female trauma.

Trauma and the Dramaturgy of the Punchline

Before *Nanette*, Gadsby's comedy project had been to pre-empt negative judgements projected on to them by staging self-attack. 'They say that comedy is trauma plus time', they have observed, 'But I have never needed time. I have always written my stories for laughs at the same time as the humiliation is tearing my self-esteem to shreds.' The 'open hostility' that Gadsby has fielded centres on their sexuality, their looks, and their body, and in their memoir Gadsby lists examples of the abhorrent, pathological body-shaming they have been subjected to for 'most of my life'.[13] With *Nanette*, Gadsby disavowed their lifelong career strategy of self-deprecation and acknowledged – as have other notable female stand-ups – that self-destructiveness and self-hate are incompatible with self-care and advancing gender equality.[14] Self-deprecation reinforces trauma, argues Gadsby in *Nanette*: it is an act of self-harm and self-erasure.

> I have built a career out of self-deprecating humour and I don't want to do that anymore. [applause] Do you understand what self-deprecation means for someone who already exists on the margins? It's not humility. It's humiliation. I put myself down in order to speak, in order to seek permission to speak and I simply will not do that to myself anymore or to anyone who identifies with me. [applause, whoops, whistles]

The problem with the dramaturgy of the joke and the convention of stand-up, Gadsby asserts, is its two-part structure of set-up and punchline. Even American stand-up Tig Notaro, who famously broke convention by announcing her traumatic diagnosis in the opening sentences of *Live* (2012): 'Hello. Good evening. Hello. I have cancer, how are you?', insists on tightly defined limits of decorum. The job of the comedian,

Notaro enjoins, is to persistently 'deliver a lighter joke' and keep audiences laughing in order to spare them from what she has termed 'the dark hole'.[15] Gadsby, by contrast, was intensely focused on the dark hole in *Nanette* and of the view that a precipitous drop into it is exactly what their comedy needed. Gadsby remodels form and function to operate in opposing directions so that they can accommodate the detail that trauma narrative requires. Without warning, Gadsby plunges their audiences into some of the dark places of her past and requests that audiences acknowledge suffering appropriately – in stretches of intense silence bracketed with laughter, which is engineered with genius.

There is a recognition from Gadsby that their refusal to be driven by the laughline bemused and alienated as much as it fascinated and attracted an international fan base. *Nanette*'s dramaturgy is culturally at odds with the American model of stand-up which serves the consumer the kind of entertainment they expect – 'the lighter joke', the end that must be laughter. This is true even of comedians whom Krefting might classify as engaging in 'charged humour' protesting against social and political hegemonies, because of the market economy of laughter in America which is increasingly driven by mass consumer tastes and large-scale commercial platforms.[16] Many American stand-ups, Ellen DeGeneres included, did not know how to classify *Nanette* and argued that it was 'not stand-up'. For Gadsby that non-recognition is the very point of their interrogation of comedy and at the core of the intervention they were endeavouring to make: the measurement of comedy solely by laughter is not a straightforward marker of the efficacy of a show. Gadsby's take that 'laughter is rarely benign, but it is often malicious',[17] echoes uncomfortably in the entertainment industry; and their suggestion that many comedians might be on the wrong side of the line in terms of their ethical practices makes many nervous. A comedian *can* precipitate psychological damage and might do so more than they imagine, argues Gadsby in *Ten Steps to Nanette*. Similarly, a reactive stand-up 'might defend bigotry in the name of laughter' and delude themselves that their jokes are harmless while audiences laugh at them 'for their own harmful reasons'.[18] With *Nanette*, Gadsby is thinking through how she might develop a more ethically responsible approach to narrating trauma and how they can lessen anger and encourage empathy in the auditorium.

Gadsby's cultural difference as an Australian was also not legible to many American stand-ups, though the American public had little difficulty reading the humour. Gadsby has stressed that the Australian comedy scene is a world apart from the American model: 'my work is not simply a reflection of who I am as an individual but also very richly informed by the culture and circumstance of where I learnt my craft'.[19] This is an oblique commentary on the cult of the individual in American showbiz and on American stand-ups' strong self-referentiality to their own comedy gods, whom Gadsby has pointed out are not her own. Tellingly, she cites Andy Kaufman as one reference point, a self-styled anti-comedian who has deliberately defined himself against American traditions of live comedy. In a move designed to underscore their project to redefine the limits of comedy, Gadsby describes themself as a 'stand-up performance artist'.[20] Day-to-day Australian humour, inflected by past genocides, a convict history, and traumatic immigration, can often push at the boundaries of risk by cutting as close to the bone as possible and there is greater acceptance of the shock value of humour.[21] Gadsby's craft is rooted in her upbringing in Tasmania, an island with a history of its own (often interconnected) traumas with a present still marked by them – indigenous massacres, a convict past, a high record of violence against women, a functional illiteracy rate of 50 per cent, and the highest rate of poverty in Australia. Gadsby locates a particular trigger for their own self-hatred in the debates on the decriminalisation of homosexuality in Tasmania when they were a teenager in the 1990s, which permanently and deeply scarred them.[22] *Nanette* was fashioned in the context of the 2017 same-sex marriage equality debate in Australia, a toxic national conversation that demonstrated the brutal prejudice and discrimination to which LBGTIQ communities were routinely subjected. Although Australians voted in favour of same-sex marriage equality, the fallout from the plebiscite was bitter and a survey shortly afterwards found that the mental health impacts on LBGTIQ people had been devastating, fracturing relationships with family, work colleagues, and other communities.[23] Gadsby had already suffered their own traumas living in Tasmania at a time when homosexuality was criminalised. The plebiscite reopened those wounds as is made clear in their memoir. It was because of this political backdrop and the widespread retraumatisation of gay communities that Gadsby's determination to expose the dangers of stand-up conventions gained a new intensity.

The forward momentum of the punchline, Gadsby contends, requires the real story to be truncated and the pain and trauma to be erased. The now famous example that Gadsby gives in *Nanette* is of their teenage encounter with a man at a bus stop who berates them for flirting with his girlfriend and calls them 'a fucking faggot', realises he has mistaken her for a man, and apologises, saying that he never hits women. Gadsby had also narrated this event in previous shows and ended with the same heroic decision to walk away: 'I do understand that I have a responsibility to lead people out of ignorance at every opportunity but I left him there people. [applause] Safety first! [laughter]' Towards the end of *Nanette* they return to this narrative (executing what is effectively a reinvention of the callback) and reveals that the event actually ended quite differently but that the real-life situation did not lend itself to conventional comic architectonics. In fact, what happened is that the man returned having realised that Gadsby was 'a lady faggot' and, from his perspective, fair game: 'He came back to the bus stop to beat the shit out of me. *And nobody stopped him.*' Gadsby reflects on the fact that they neither reported the crime nor took themself to accident and emergency for treatment, despite their injuries:

> You know why I didn't? Because I thought it was all I was worth. And this is what happens when you soak a child in shame and give permission to another to hate. And that was not homophobia pure and simple. It was gendered. If I'd been feminine that would not have happened. I am incorrectly female. Incorrect. And that is a punishable offence [...] It is dangerous to be different.[24]

Analysing the effect of punchline dramaturgy or the laughter principle, Gadsby concludes that the trauma narrative is sacrificed to an insistence that the laugh must be the end-point and that the simplicity of the joke structure cannot 'undo the damage done to me in reality'.[25] This explicit imperative to find a means of articulating trauma and 'undo the damage', to treat their wounds and explore comedy as a salve that returns them to health, makes Gadsby quite different from the majority of professional stand-ups. In their TED talk, Gadsby speaks of their obsession to 'tell my truth – not to share the laughs but the literal visceral pain of my trauma'.[26] If the joke stifles the articulation of trauma, Gadsby proclaims in *Nanette* that 'laughter is not our medicine, stories hold the cure' and by that they mean the long-form story with its elaborate twists and turns and its sophisticated multiplicity of layers. 'I'd always been told that the way out of trauma was through a cohesive narrative' Gadsby declares in their TED talk: 'I realised I'd been telling my stories for laughs. I'd been trimming away the darkness, holding away the pain and holding on to my trauma for the comfort of my audiences. I was connecting other people through laughs and yet I remained profoundly disconnected.'[27] Gadsby's professional objective is highly ambitious. With *Nanette* the project of comedy *becomes* a search for the articulation of trauma. Gadsby is intent on springing the locks on a set of imposed conventions which limit their freedom of expression. They believe that stories, unlike jokes, can heal. By adhering to the punchline, Gadsby argues: 'I froze an incredibly formative experience at its trauma point and I sealed it off into jokes.'[28] By this analogy, joke structure is like setting an insect in amber or sealing a coffin: it emulates the traumatic response by arresting the moment and paralysing the speaker. The three-part structure of the story, on the other hand, with beginning, middle, and, crucially, an ending, allows for different kinds of narrative shapes and more detailed content. By breaking the conventions of the punchline and re-examining what the constituent parts of a stand-up routine might be, Gadsby could sculpt their material into a different shape, reforming it so that 'it could better hold everything I needed it to share'.[29] The comic George Carlin once famously said that it is the duty of the comedian to find out where the line is drawn and cross it immediately.[30] Gadsby has directly acknowledged that challenge and *Nanette* is their answer to it. 'The line I found is the definition of comedy itself, and given the considerable nerve I struck, I would say that makes me an excellent comedian.'[31]

Trauma, Audiences, and Ethics

A particular feature of the trauma narrative is its transmissibility and its capacity to precipitate traumatic reactions in others. The lack of a trigger warning in *Nanette* gave Gadsby an ethical conflict but the show relied on delivering a shock to audiences.[32] Vicarious traumatisation is a recognised phenomenon in therapeutic communities. Theorists have noted the collapse of psychological borders and emotional disturbances caused by processes of transference or suggestion between victims and their listeners or viewers, who can find themselves overwhelmed. The dangers of the trauma narrative's capacity to disrupt the distinction between self and other has been highlighted in Dominic LaCapra's work and he has emphasised the importance of empathy which establishes distance and preserves selfhood.[33] For Gadsby, the aim of *Nanette* is 'to repurpose comedy into something that could allow me to express the heat of my anger and the pain of my trauma, but without transferring it'.[34] From the outset, then, *Nanette* was underpinned by a strong sense of ethics in relation to audience. Individual reactions are not something that Gadsby could control but they were interested in creating a shared empathy and in providing a holding environment for that empathy. By the time the Netflix special was filmed, the #MeToo campaign, a social movement against sexual abuse and rape culture, had gained mainstream momentum, and audiences were especially responsive to survivors' narratives. To be clear, *Nanette* had become a phenomenon before #MeToo really lifted off but its screen reception was caught up in a mass public platform expressing outrage against sex offenders such as Harvey Weinstein and outpourings of compassion for victims of sexual assault and harassment.

In *Nanette*, Gadsby laments that '[p]unchlines need trauma because punchlines need tension and tension feeds trauma'. Punchlines preclude narrative complexity, realistic endings, and, as Gadsby sees it, stifle learning and arrest adult development. In *Ten Steps to Nanette*, Gadsby discusses their technical understanding of the show as '"stand-up catharsis", an experiment in the transmutation of trauma'. They state that their goal was 'to simulate a feeling in the room that was akin *to* trauma, because I wanted to see if I could create an experience of communal empathy in a roomful of strangers'.[35] So Gadsby was not interested in provoking trauma but in generating an experience which might, microcosmically, simulate an experience of traumatic pain which is ultimately met with compassion. In psychotherapy, catharsis is broadly defined as the release of strong, repressed emotions in order to overcome the problems associated with them. Gadsby's intent is to mould their trauma narrative into another form, to externalise it in the shape of a complex story in order for it to be apprehended, experienced, and valued. Stand-up staging lends itself well to this since it is without a fourth wall and the dynamic of tension (the withholding of an expression of emotion) and its release (laughter) is the dynamic of comedy. The metaphor of tension and release is Gadsby's metaphor for the suppression and expression of trauma. The comedian has to generate tension in order to diffuse it, and the audience buy tickets to experience that gratification, a power dynamic that Gadsby suggests is exploitative and unhealthy. If the art of comedy is tension-diffusion *Nanette* is an exploration of how far the comedian's refusal to release tension can be stretched. Gadsby's understanding of 'tension' equates to an interest in generating stress reaction. Stress is an emotional, physical, and psychological reaction to external stressors that require the subject's attention and, often, action. Stress can cause catastrophic clinical harm in a sufferer, especially if the exposure is prolonged. *Nanette* was an experiment that Gadsby knew would not have worked as 'a theatre-show gate-crashing a comedy stage' – it needed the dialogic form – but it did require an act of disassembly and reverse engineering: 'I took everything I knew about comedy, then I pulled it apart and built a monster out of its corpse.'[36]

In order to build the momentum towards the ending of *Nanette*, Gadsby's dramaturgy does incorporate a form of assault on their audience, a gradual crescendo of pressure, which they explain in their TED talk:

> I wrote a comedy show that did not respect the punchline, that line where comedians are expected to pull their punches and turn them into tickles. I punched through that line into the metaphorical guts of my audience. [...] I

wanted to take their breath away, to shock them so they could listen to my story and hold my pain as individuals not as a mindless laughing mob.[37]

The first half set-up is packed with punchlines and imitations of straight white cisgender men attacking gender difference and normalising sexual violence against women. This is Gadsby's evocation of the standard stand-up diet and its model consumer. The second half concerns the revelation of their trauma narrative and their refusal to indulge the conventional consumerist appetite for violence that they see as rooted in this dominant pathology. Gadsby's project in *Nanette* is to subvert those supposedly 'gender normal' misogynist pathologies and suggest that many 'supposed gender normals' (straight white cisgender men) in fact, do not qualify for the top of the human hierarchy, as is generally supposed, but perhaps barely scrape 'a subcategory of human'.[38] Gadsby then treats these 'gender normals' to some of the sexually charged verbal abuse that is customarily used against 'gender not normals', a routine that they have ventriloquised and parodied earlier but now invert. Gadsby divides their audience, inviting the women to cast judgement on the victims of the inversion, but, at times, Gadsby also turns on the whole room: 'Why do you stay with me? I just made you laugh with a joke about domestic violence. Comedy is nasty work.'[39] The 'punch in the metaphorical guts' is the building up of trust and familiarity in the first half which Gadsby then suddenly removes. The strategy is to allow the audience to relax and feel safe precisely so that Gadsby can 'take that safety away and not give it back': this, they argue, is 'the shape of trauma' and they have sculpted *Nanette* into that same shape.[40] To feel perpetually unsafe, constantly at risk, and trapped in a state of terror is the psychic condition of the trauma victim and recovery is dependent on the capacity to find a place of safety, retrain cognitive pathways, and calm the central nervous system. A specialist in trauma psychiatry, Judith Herman argues that the predominant features of psychological trauma are disempowerment and disconnection from others, and she conceptualises a recovery process of establishing safety, retelling the story of the traumatic event, and reconnecting with others.[41] This is the mirror of the journey Gadsby describes in their memoir and is a mapping of their lived experience of performing *Nanette*. The journey Gadsby structures for their audience is not the long traumatic path that Gadsby was forced down, but there is destabilisation, inversion, and disruption. Gadsby does not release them into laughter but suggests there is work to do: 'This tension, it's yours and I am not helping you anymore.'[42] Instead, *Nanette*'s ending is a gentle plea for mutual respect and empathy. In *Ten*

Steps to Nanette, the author explains the ending as an attempt to create a narrative catharsis, not just for themselves but 'for all the people who have gone to comedy shows and been triggered by all the rape celebrations, violence, misogyny, homophobia and transphobia'.[43] It is also a statement about why Gadsby has privileged their own needs first in performing *Nanette*:

> I am not a victim. I tell you this because I need you to know that I know that to be rendered powerless does not destroy your humanity. Your resilience is your humanity. The only people who lost their humanity are those who believe they have the right to render another human being powerless. [...] I will not allow my story to be destroyed.
>
> I needed my story to be heard, my story to be felt and understood by individuals with minds of their own. Because like it or not, my story is your story and your story is my story. [...] *Please* help me take care of my story. [...] The focus of the story we need. Connection. Thank you.[44]

Connection is healing and recovery from trauma and, for Gadsby, trauma is released through a deliverance *to* and sharing *with* others. Recovery involves the subject's recognition of the value of their life.[45] Gadsby has been quite explicit about the therapeutic benefits of *Nanette*, which they state worked to 'strip me of the worst effects of my residual trauma'.[46] Connection is what Gadsby finds through stand-up comedy, and the repeated encounters and negotiations they enact through *Nanette* constitute a process of healing and a restoration of self. It is highly unusual for a mainstream comic to so publicly discuss their professional work as a form of therapy even though it is widely acknowledged that much contemporary stand-up draws on lived experience.[47] Though many might be motivated for similar reasons, it is has been unfashionable to admit it, probably because of the stigma of mental health issues and a fear of appearing vulnerable. Gadsby's model of relating to audiences in *Nanette* proposes a way through the negativity and the toxic anger which they feel comedians have all too often spewed out and spread like a contagion. At the end of *Nanette* they make it clear that although their anger about the abuses they have suffered is justified, their right to infect others is not. If anger is the defensive response to a perceived threat to the self, Gadsby is trying to overcome her ingrained trauma responses and reach across their isolation. 'The damage done to me is real and debilitating. I will never flourish', Gadsby tells their audience matter-of-factly towards the end of the show. But in performing *Nanette* Gadsby can find visibility and self-recognition and their story does, as their success demonstrates, resonate with extraordinary power and has met with widespread acceptance. That a vehicle such as *Nanette*, which caused Gadsby such terror and pain in its making and moulding, could also be the same vehicle used to diminish terror and pain is one of the paradoxes of treating trauma. As the trauma scholar Roger Luckhurst has argued, 'the passage through trauma often works not to undermine but rather to *guarantee* subjectivity'; sequences of catastrophe, survival, and supersession, he suggests, can be read 'as trajectories that recompense the felt depredations to identity'.[48] For Gadsby, stand-up comedy is that passage and they are serious in their claim that it saved their life.

Selfhood, Safe Practices, and Healing

One of the extraordinary features of Gadsby's memoir are the insights they share about ensuring that they can perform *Nanette* with minimal harm to themself. These insights underline their concern with self-care and safe practices. Revealing and sharing a trauma narrative in such a public fashion was a significant risk and Gadsby reflects that, in hindsight, they would never advise anyone 'to write a show out of your own trauma and perform it two hundred times all over the world'.[49] However, paradoxically, Gadsby also knew that the stage was the only place they could tell their trauma with the complexity and the live dialogic dynamics they felt it needed to make the most resonant intervention. Only after the first live trial of their material did Gadsby realise just how dangerous her endeavour was and they describe a journey overwrought with physical and mental pain that they had to work at indefatigably to find ways of mitigating. 'Safety is being able to trust that those around you *want* to protect you from harm', Gadsby argues, but they also knew that they had to earn that protective response from audiences. Gadsby was affected by every single performance and terrified of experiencing meltdowns, shutdowns, and emotional outbursts; for the first few months of the tour the experience was a form of torture and they were flooded with stimulus that they had to learn to defend themself against.[50] Immediately after each performance she had to retreat to 'a quiet, dark and safe place and decompress'.[51] But Gadsby also understood that they were engaging in a form of exposure therapy for themself and that if they could push through the worst of the terror they might free themself from its shackles: 'I managed to take the worst of the sting out of my own trauma through performing *Nanette* over and over again.'[52] Aside from drawing on the safeguarding protectiveness of their family and the production team, Gadsby invents their own creative risk mitigations, their own 'life raft'. They write safety mechanisms into the show, soothing themself write with strategies such as summoning their mother's love by impersonating her and finding empowering mantras such as 'I am in my prime'.[53] In doing so Gadsby experiences 'profound catharsis' and discovers 'a new layer of protection'.[54]

Gadsby elucidates that the boundaries between themself and the show material were in constant flux and it was a titanic battle to control them. In their memoir, they refer to *Nanette* as both subject and object, themself and not themself, dynamic and lifeless, 'a monster', 'a corpse': '*Nanette* did not feel like a comedy show … she felt more like someone, me'.[55] But Gadsby's gradual mastery of the material and the show over time emulates Sigmund Freud's description of how an individual might overcome trauma – by 'mastering the amounts of stimulus which have broken in and are binding them, in the psychical sense, so that they can be disposed of'.[56] Effectively, *Nanette* serves as what psychoanalyst Donald Winnicott has termed 'a holding environment', and in shaping it Gadsby creates their own healing space, an environment in which they minimise their trauma narrative's threat levels to themself and others. 'Hold' and 'holding' are words that Gadsby invokes both in *Nanette* and in their memoir; they suggest a space where the comic can meet their audience as their traumatised self (the self which they have heretofore hidden) and find acceptance. Winnicott describes the holding environment as a space where the individual can experience the anxiety associated with a disintegration of self but remain intact, a space where negotiation and reintegration are possible.[57]

Nanette, then, is both a trauma narrative and story of healing. In the telling, Gadsby experienced an extraordinary power. 'There is nothing stronger than a broken woman who has rebuilt herself', Gadsby declares in *Nanette*, to thunderous applause.[58] And to the surprise of many, at the beginning of their subsequent show, *Douglas*, Gadsby declares themself 'fresh out of trauma'.[59] But their trauma narrative is in circulation, and as they have said, *Nanette* may be their creation but their trauma story has been internalised in a whole universe of other minds: 'I understood I had to let her go. *Nanette* belongs to the world now.'[60]

Notes

1. Cathy Caruth, 'Introduction to Psychoanalysis: Trauma and Culture II', *American Imago*, Vol. 48, No. 4: 1991: p. 417; Mark Seltzer, '"Wound Culture": Trauma in the Pathological Public Sphere', *October 80*, 1997: p. 18.
2. Hannah Gadsby, *Ten Steps to Nanette: A Memoir Situation* (Sydney: Allen & Unwin, 2022), p. 24.
3. Monica Lewinsky, 'Dealing with Trauma', interview with Hannah Gadsby, *Vanity Fair*, New Establishment Summit, New York, 2018.
4. Gadsby, *Ten Steps*, pp. 343–344.

5. Hannah Gadsby, 'Three Ideas. Three Contradictions. Or not.' TED talk, 2019, www.ted.com/talks/Hannah_gadsby_three_ideas_three_contradictions_or_not?language=en.
6. Kerrie O'Brien, interview with Hannah Gadsby, *The Age, Spectrum*, 1 July 2017, p. 9.
7. Mary Luckhurst, 'Hannah Gadsby: Celebrity Stand-Up, Trauma, and the Meta-theatrics of Persona Construction', *Persona Studies*, Vol. 5, No. 2, 2019: pp. 53–66; Rebecca Krefting, 'Hannah Gadsby: On the Limits of Satire', *Studies in American Humor*, Vol. 5, No. 1, 2019: pp. 93–102.
8. Gadsby, *Ten Steps*, pp. 19 and 359.
9. E. Ann Kaplan, *Trauma Culture: The Politics of Terror ad Loss in Media and Literature* (New Brunswick: Rutgers, 2005).
10. Gadsby, *Ten Steps*, p. 349.
11. For example, see the work of American stand-up activists such as Dick Gregory in the 1960s whose work addressed racism and bigotry in America; and Maxine Feldman in the 1970s, a campaigner against racism and for gay rights who needed police protection from the Ku Klux Klan for shows in 1977.
12. Hannah Gadsby, *Nanette* (Netflix, 2018). All references to *Nanette* in this essay refer to this Netflix special.
13. Gadsby, *Ten Steps*, pp. 220–225.
14. See Luckhurst, 'Hannah Gadsby'.
15. Tig Notaro, *I'm Just a Person: My Year of Death, Cancer and Epiphany* (London: Pan Macmillan, 2016), pp. 139–140.
16. Rebecca Krefting, *All Joking Asides: American Humor and Its Discontents* (Baltimore: Johns Hopkins, 2014).
17. Gadsby, *Ten Steps*, pp. 19–21.
18. Gadsby, *Ten Steps*, p. 21.
19. Gadsby, *Ten Steps*, p. 18.
20. Gadsby, *Ten Steps*, p. 19.
21. For further information see the following celebrated accounts: Frank Welsh, *Great Southern Land: A New History of Australia* (London: Penguin, 2004); Robert Hughes, *The Fatal Shore* (London: Vintage, 2003); Tom Keneally, *The Commonwealth of Thieves: The Story of the Founding of Australia* (London: Vintage, 2007); Geoffrey Blainey, *The Story of Australia's People: The Rise and Fall of Ancient Australia* (Melbourne: Viking, 2015); Noel Pearson, *Up from the Mission* (Melbourne: Black Inc., 2011).
22. Gadsby, *Ten Steps*, pp. 299–300.
23. Saan Ecker, Ellen D. B. Riggle, Sharon R. Rotowsky, and Joanna M. Byrnes, 'Impact of the Australian Marriage Equality Postal Survey and Debate on Psychological Distress among Lesbian, Gay, Bisexual, Transgender, Intersex and Queer/Questioning People and Allies', *Australian Journal of Psychology*, Vol. 71, No. 3, 2019: pp. 285–295.
24. Gadsby, *Nanette*.
25. Gadsby, *Nanette*.
26. Gadsby, TED talk, 2019.
27. Gadsby, TED talk, 2019.

28. Gadsby, *Nanette*.
29. Gadsby, TED talk, 2019.
30. Lewis Black, *The Best of George Carlin* (New York: Hachette, 2021).
31. Gadsby, *Ten Steps*, p. 19.
32. Gadsby, *Ten Steps*, p. 340.
33. Dominic Lacapra, *Writing History, Writing Trauma* (Baltimore: Johns Hopkins, 2001), p. 21.
34. Gadsby, *Ten Steps*, p. 331.
35. Gadsby, *Ten Steps*, p. 22.
36. Gadsby, *Ten Steps*, p. 22.
37. Gadsby, TED talk, 2019.
38. Gadsby, *Nanette*.
39. Gadsby, *Nanette*.
40. Gadsby, *Ten Steps*, p. 22.
41. Judith Herman, 'Recovery from Psychological Trauma', *Psychiatry and Clinical Neuroscience*, Vol. 52, No. 51, 2002: pp. 598–103.
42. Gadsby, *Nanette*.
43. Gadsby, *Ten Steps*, p. 22.
44. Gadsby, *Nanette*.
45. Herman, 'Recovery from Psychological Trauma'.
46. Gadsby, *Ten Steps*, p. 357.
47. Oliver Double, 'Tragedy plus Time: Transforming Life Experience into Stand-Up Comedy', *New Theatre Quarterly*, Vol. 33, No. 2, 2017: pp. 143–155.
48. Roger Luckhurst, *The Trauma Question* (Abingdon: Routledge, 2008), p. 119.
49. Gadsby, *Ten Steps*, p. 337.
50. Gadsby, *Ten Steps*, pp. 336, 340, 371.
51. Gadsby, *Ten Steps*, p. 351.
52. Gadsby, *Ten Steps*, p. 340.
53. Gadsby, *Ten Steps*, pp. 338–340.
54. Gadsby, *Ten Steps*, p. 338.
55. Gadsby, *Ten Steps*, p. 334.
56. Sigmund Freud, 'Beyond the Pleasure Principle', in *Penguin Freud Library*, Volume 11 (Harmondsworth: Penguin, 1984), p. 301.
57. D. W. Winnicott, 'The Theory of the Parent–Infant Relationship', *International Journal of Psychoanalysis*, Vol. 41, 1960: pp. 4–6.
58. Gadsby, *Ten Steps*, p. 271. In 2023 Hannah Gadsby declared her preference for using the pronouns they/them.
59. Hannah Gadsby, *Douglas* (Netflix, 2020).
60. Gadsby, *Ten Steps*, p. 25.

Further Reading

Balkin, Sarah, 'The Killjoy Comedian: Hannah Gadsby's Nanette', *Theatre Research International*, Vol. 45, No. 1, 2020: pp. 72–85.

Levy, Shawn, *In on the Joke: The Original Queens of Stand-Up* (New York: Knopf, 2022).

Martin, Rod, *The Psychology of Humour: An Integrative Approach* (Amsterdam: Elsevier, 2004).

Oppliger, Patrice A. and Eric Shouse (eds), *The Dark Side of Stand-Up Comedy* (New York and London: Palgrave, 2020).

Scepanski, Philip, *Tragedy Plus Time: National Trauma and Television Comedy* (Austin: University of Texas, 2021).

COMEDIANS' INSIGHTS

Why Do You Do Stand-Up?

Edward Aczel (UK)

Because it's a pleasure.

Stephen Bailey (UK)

Growing up on a council estate I was told far too often that things like 'that don't happen to people like us' and things like 'know your place'. I decided to change the narrative to prove that where you start doesn't define you, but it can make you.

Tom Ballard (Australia)

I'm able to be closer to 'me' when improvising onstage or interacting with an audience member. Having a genuinely funny, genuinely spontaneous moment onstage is still probably the greatest thrill of doing stand-up for me: it's a feeling of being 100 per cent present, real, and connected to the people around me.

Maria Bamford (USA)

It feels good, the hours are WONDERFUL, I am the CEO (for good and for bad) and – if you get a following – you can get paid well above a living wage.

Daman Bamrah (UK)

Stand-up is a unique opportunity to tell a story in the most palatable way. As a British Sikh, our experience is rarely shared on a wider scale. Performing stand-up has helped me bring that experience to a mainstream audience, allowing me to build connections and bridges between my life, my culture, and the wider population as I present life through my lens in a way that is entertaining but easy to digest. Because laughter as a knee-jerk reaction can bypass preconceptions and prejudices.

Angela Barnes (UK)

With stand-up comedy, every day is different, I have a lot of autonomy, and I get to work with different people in different places. For someone with ADHD who is always seeking that next dopamine hit, comedy is the only job that has been able to deliver.

Jo Brand (UK)

'Cause I like it, it feels great to make people laugh, and I wanted to see more women comics so had to put my money where my mouth was and it gave me a forum to insult back all the fuckwits who have verbally abused me over the years in the form of attacking them as an everyman type.

Jo Caulfield (UK)

I have no choice. Stand-up comedy chooses you, you do not choose stand-up comedy.

Tanyalee Davis (Canada/USA/UK)

It's what I was meant to do. It's now lead me to doing more motivational and inspiring stories. #UnstoppableMe

Tiernan Douieb (UK)

I don't think I have a choice. If a week goes by without a show in a it, I get itchy feet and become irritable. I think I have to do comedy now. During the pandemic I started to wonder if I should give it up, and within one gig back I was reminded that I am driven by a need to do comedy to live audiences and the thrill and gratification I get from it is like nothing else.

Alexis Dubus (UK), Who Performs as Marcel Lucont (France)

I still get a real buzz out of connecting with an audience, there's something really fulfilling about making people happy (even via the medium of Gallic pessimism).

Andy Erikson (USA)

It's exhilarating and addicting. I love getting to explore ideas while also exploring who I am as a person. It's scary in a fun way.

Mary Gallagher (USA)

I do it to learn how to speak up for myself. This has changed my life and I believe it also is what gave me the courage to leave a bad marriage and to never abandon myself again.

Justin Herman (USA)

Stand-up to me is a sociological experiment to see if I can convince a room full of strangers to laugh at what I think is funny; whether I succeed or fail it's my favourite way to engage the world.

Richard Herring (UK)

I always loved comedy and people who could make me laugh. I have had a nice life and not any of the tragedy or stress that sometimes drives people to perform. I wanted to be able to emulate the comedians I loved and make people laugh. It's the best feeling to have an audience in the palm of your hand so I am sure there is some sort of ego in it too. But I think it's mostly a love of comedy and wanting to get as good at it as I can.

Bec Hill (Australia/UK)

I think the same reason anyone does anything creative – because of the *urge*. It took me a long time to learn the difference between *urge* and *want*. Sometimes I don't *want* to do stand-up – maybe due to fear, or doubt – which is when I know that I definitely NEED to do it. Other times, I don't have the *urge* – usually because my creative energy is focused elsewhere – and it's those times I have to take a break. Stand-up is hard and just as unforgiving as it is rewarding, but the *urge* is a bulletproof vest which protects you from the negatives. If you don't have the *urge*, it's like walking onto a firing range in your underpants. You might survive, but it could take you a long time to recover.

Harry Hill (UK)

It's an artistic journey for me. A huge challenge to get a laugh in a way that no one else has – that's the aim.

Matt Hoss (UK)

To add positivity to people's life, including my own.

Tom Houghton (UK)

I can't imagine anything else making me as happy.

Charmian Hughes (UK)

I found something that I am good at that gives me instant gratification. Stand-up performances exist only in the now, when it is over it evaporates like life itself leaving hardly an echo.

Robin Ince (UK)

I have to for my sanity and my insanity. It may sound stupid or highfaluting but it really is the time when everything is alive in me.

Milton Jones (UK)

I like to make people laugh. The process is creative and challenging. If you work hard, you can earn a living. You can also get to meet unusual people and go to amazing places.

Myq Kaplan (USA)

I love it.

I love having conversations with audiences where I get to share meaningful parts of who I am.

It's a sort of communion, really.

With a two-communion-wine minimum.

Jackie Kashian (USA)

Fell into it and it felt like, I assume, what falling into a vat of heroin would be like. In other words – I don't know quite why I *started* – but I cannot seem to stop. It gave me self-esteem and friends and a purpose. And then I realised what it did not give me and that was offstage life outside the stage. Which I realised 15–20 years into my career I *also* wanted. So I put more attention to that and now I'm pretty happy.

Athena Kugblenu (UK)

It's the best medium for the things I am trying to say and do with my life. And I enjoy it.

Beth Lapides (USA)

I love to laugh. It helps me pay attention. Plus, connection – to the big thing, the audience, myself, my story, the now.

Stewart Lee (UK)

Fear of everything else.

Laura Lexx (UK)

Um, I do it because I love it. I find it a very immediate form of art: I like the close contact with the audience, and the lack of gatekeepers on my ideas. The speed between having an idea and taking it to the audience is amazing. It's fun and short – that suits my attention span and it opens my world up to lots of other areas of art and entertainment.

Elf Lyons (UK)

Because otherwise I wouldn't know how to breathe.

Tom Mayhew (UK)

Because it can change people's lives, like it changed mine. It made me feel less alone as a teenager, and I want to do that for others like me.

Jimmy McGhie (UK)

Because it feels like someone has given you the cheat codes to life.

Andrew McClelland (Australia)

The joy of it. A need to be on stage. Narcissism possibly or the need to be loved by strangers. Again, the usual I think. Also a little bit of advocacy for leftist progressivism.

Aditi Mittal (India)

I don't know how to do anything else. Even stand-up I'm barely managing.

Alfie Moore (UK)

I'm a risk-taker by nature and stand-up is one of the 'safer' (less damaging) outlets.

Al Murray (UK), Who Performs as the Pub Landlord (UK)

I became a stand-up because I wanted to perform but I needed to set my own terms. It was very much about that, about wanting to perform on my own terms – and not through the filters and gatekeepers that stand between an actor and getting onstage. Whereas stand-up, the audience is the filter, the gatekeeper. And sometimes a promoter and someone running a club. But basically, the direct link between you and it working is the shortest possible. The line is the shortest.

Sander Õigus (Estonia)

Because the first time I got on stage I felt like I'm home.

Anuvab Pal (India)

Essentially to tell stories you don't often hear on stand-up stages. As in veering away from domestic woes to more historical, societal, international cross-cultural things.

Rayen Panday (Netherlands)

It is the only form where my honesty is appreciated.

Lucy Porter (UK)

It's probably daddy issues, that I was trying to kind of get my dad's attention. He always wanted to be a doctor, and he really liked comedy. And my sister's become a doctor and I've become a comedian. So I think there's your answer right there, it was the only avenue left to me to impress my dad. And also the big reason is because I could never hold down a proper job and it kind of saved my life really. I – like so many people – have recently had an ADHD diagnosis. And it all makes sense, and you go, 'Yeah, the kind of people who end up doing comedy are the kind of people for whom other avenues are closed down.' I always felt like an outsider, and the Manchester stand-up circuit in the nineties was full of interesting misfits.

Rod Quantock (Australia)

Because I can, because it's fun, and because I can get weight of this crazy world off my shoulders.

John-Luke Roberts (UK)

You sound just like my mother.

John Simmit (UK)

Because I can't box, run fast, or sing.

Joe Wells (UK)

I find it a therapeutic artistic outlet and I couldn't hold down a real job with my mental health intact.

Nigel Williams (UK/Belgium)

Stand-up is me having therapy and getting paid to do it instead of paying for it.

Bilal Zafar (UK)

With stand-up, I can think of something and perform it that evening. I also love that you can be from any background, any age etc. to get into it.

Select Bibliography

Aarons, Debra and Marc Mierowsky, 'Obscenity, Dirtiness and Licence in Jewish comedy', *Comedy Studies*, Vol. 5, No. 2, 2014: pp. 165–177.
Ajaye, Franklin, *Comic Insights: The Art of Stand-Up Comedy* (Los Angeles: Silman-James Press, 2002).
Allen, Tony, *Attitude: Wanna Make Something of It?* (Glastonbury: Gothic Image, 2002).
Auslander, Philip, *Liveness: Performance in a Mediatized Culture*, 2nd ed. (Abingdon and New York: Routledge, 2008).
Balkin, Sarah, 'The Killjoy Comedian: Hannah Gadsby's *Nanette*', *Theatre Research International*, Vol. 45, No. 1, 2020: pp. 72–85.
Banks, Morwenna and Amanda Swift, *The Joke's on Us: Women in Comedy from Music Hall to the Present* (London: Pandora, 1987).
Barreca, Regina, *They Used to Call Me Snow White… But I Drifted: Women's Strategic Use of Humor* (Hanover: University Press of New England, 1992).
Baum, Devorah, *The Jewish Joke* (New York and London: Pegasus, 2018).
Beale, Sam, *The Comedy and Legacy of Music Hall Women 1880–1920: Brazen Impudence and Boisterous Vulgarity* (Cham: Palgrave Macmillan, 2020).
Bell, Nancy, 'Reactions to Humor, Non-Laughter', in Salvatore Attardo (ed.), *The Encyclopedia of Humor Studies*. Volume 2 (Los Angeles, London, New Delhi, Singapore & Washington, DC: Sage, 2014), pp. 628–629.
Bennett, Joe, 'The Critical Problem of Cynical Irony: Meaning What You Say and Ideologies of Class and Gender', *Social Semiotics*, Vol. 26, No. 3, 2016: pp. 250–264.
Berger, Phil, *The Last Laugh: The World of Stand-Up Comics* (New York: Cooper Square Press, 2000).
Bhargava, Rashi and Richa Chilana (eds.), *Punching Up: Stand-Up Comedy Speaking Truth to Power* (Abingdon, UK and New York: Routledge, 2023).
Bingham, Shawn Chandler and Sara E. Green, *Seriously Funny: Disability & the Paradoxical Power of Humor* (Boulder: Lynne Rienner Publishers, 2016).
Borns, Betsy, *Comic Lives: Inside the World of American Stand-Up Comedy* (New York: Simon & Schuster, 1987).
Borum Chattoo, Caty and Lauren Feldman, *A Comedian and an Activist Walk into a Bar: The Serious Role of Comedy in Social Justice* (Oakland: University of California Press, 2020).

Brodie, Ian, *A Vulgar Art: A New Approach to Stand-Up Comedy* (Jackson: University Press of Mississippi, 2014).
Brodie, Ian, 'Is Stand-Up Comedy Art?', *Journal of Aesthetics and Art Criticism*, Vol. 78, No. 4, 2020: pp. 401–418.
Bruce, Kitty (ed.), *The Unpublished Lenny Bruce* (Philadelphia: Running Press, 1984).
Bruce, Lenny, *How to Talk Dirty and Influence People* (St Albans: Panther, 1977).
Butler, Nick and Dimitrinka Stoyanova Russell, 'No Funny Business: Precarious Work and Emotional Labour in Stand-up Comedy', *Human Relations*, Vol. 71, No. 12, 2018: pp. 1666–1686.
Carter, Judy, *The Comedy Bible: From Stand-up to Sitcom – The Comedy Writer's Ultimate How To Guide* (New York: Simon & Schuster, 2001).
Cohen, John (ed.), *The Essential Lenny Bruce* (New York: Ballantine Books, 1970).
Cohen, Yael, *We Killed: The Rise of Women in American Comedy* (London: Picador, 2013).
Cook, William, *Ha Bloody Ha: Comedians Talking* (London: Fourth Estate, 1994).
Cook, William, *The Comedy Store: The Club That Changed British Comedy* (London: Little, Brown, 2001).
Curtis, James, *Mort Sahl and the Birth of Modern Comedy* (Jackson: University Press of Mississippi, 2017).
Dates, Jeannette and Mia Moody Ramirez, *From Blackface to Black Twitter: Reflections on Black Humor, Race, Politics, and Gender* (New York: Peter Lang US, 2018).
Dauber, Jeremy, *Jewish Comedy: A Serious History* (New York: W. W. Norton, 2017).
DeCamp, Elise, 'Humoring the Audience: Performance Strategies and Persuasion in Midwestern American Stand-up Comedy', *Humor*, Vol. 28, No. 3, 2015: pp. 449–467.
Deen, Phillip, 'Is Bill Cosby Still Funny? Separating the Art from the Artist in Stand-up Comedy', *Studies in American Humor*, Vol. 5, No. 2, 2019: pp. 288–308.
Dessau, Bruce, *Beyond a Joke: Inside the Dark Minds of Stand-Up Comedians* (London: Arrow Books, 2012).
Double, Oliver, *Stand-Up! On Being a Comedian* (London: Methuen, 1997).
Double, Oliver, *Britain Had Talent: A History of Variety Theatre* (Basingstoke: Palgrave Macmillan, 2012).
Double, Oliver, *Getting the Joke: The Inner Workings of Stand-up Comedy*, 2nd ed. (London: Methuen Drama, 2014).
Double, Oliver, *Alternative Comedy: 1979 and the Reinvention of British Stand-Up* (London: Methuen Drama, 2020).
Double, Oliver and Sharon Sharon Lockyer (eds.), *Alternative Comedy Now and Then: Critical Perspectives* (Basingstoke: Palgrave Macmillan, 2022).
Douglas, Mary, 'Jokes', in Mary Douglas (ed.), *Implicit Meanings: Selected Essays in Anthropology*, 2nd ed. (London: Routledge, 1999), pp. 146–164.
Edgerton, Gary R., *The Columbia History of American Television* (New York: Columbia University Press, 2007).

Epstein, Lawrence J., *The Haunted Smile: The Story of Jewish Comedians in America* (New York: PublicAffairs, 2001).

Frances-White, Deborah and Marsha Shandur, *The World's Best Stand-Up Comedians Get Serious about Comedy* (London and New York: Bloomsbury Academic, 2015).

Frances-White, Deborah, *The Guilty Feminist* (London: Virago, 2018).

Freud, Sigmund, *Jokes and Their Relation to the Unconscious* (Harmondsworth: Penguin, 1976).

Friedman, Budd, *The Improv: An Oral History of the Comedy Club That Revolutionized Stand-Up* (Dallas: BenBella Books, 2017).

Friedman, Sam, *Comedy and Distinction: The Cultural Currency of a 'Good' Sense of Humour* (London and New York: Routledge, 2014).

Gadsby, Hannah, *Ten Steps to Nanette: A Memoir Situation* (Sydney: Allen & Unwin, 2022).

Gilbert, Joanne R., *Performing Marginality: Humor, Gender and Cultural Critique* (Detroit: Wayne State University Press, 2004).

Gilbert, Joanne R., 'Lesbian Stand-Up Comics and the Politics of Laughter', in Peter Dickinson, Anne Higgins, Paul Matthew St. Pierre, Diana Solomon and Sean Zwagerman (eds.), *Women and Comedy: History, Theory, Practice* (Lanham: Farleigh Dickinson Press, co-published with Rowman & Littlefield, 2013), pp. 185–197.

Gilbert, Joanne R., 'Laughs Last: Gender, Power, and Comic Identity', in Louise Peacock (ed.), *A Cultural History of Comedy in the Modern Age* (London: Bloomsbury Academic, 2020), pp. 87–111.

Goldman, Albert and Lawrence Schiller, *Ladies and Gentlemen – Lenny Bruce!!* (New York: Penguin Books, 1991).

Gray, Frances, *Women and Laughter* (Charlottesville: University of Virginia Press, 1994).

Haller, Beth and Sue Ralph, 'John Callahan's Pelswick Cartoon and a New Phase of Disability Humor', *Disability Studies Quarterly*, Vol. 23, No. 3/4, 2003.

Harris, Richard, *Punch Lines: Twenty Years of Australian Comedy* (Sydney: ABC Books, 1994).

Hartblay, Cassandra, 'Welcome to Sergeichburg: Disability, Crip Performance, and the Comedy of Recognition in Russia', *The Journal of Social Policy Studies*, Vol. 12, No. 1, 2014: pp. 111–124.

Hunt, Leon. 'Near the Knuckle? It Nearly Took My Arm Off! British Comedy and the "new offensiveness"', *Comedy Studies*, Vol. 1, No. 2, 2010: pp. 181–190.

Ince, Robin, *I'm a Joke and So Are You: A Comedian's Take on What Makes Us Human* (London: Atlantic Books, 2018).

Kanfer, Stefan, *A Summer World: The Astonishing History of the Jews in the Catskills* (New York: Farrar Straus Giroux, 1990).

Keane, Webb, 'On Semiotic Ideology', *Signs and Society*, Vol. 6, No. 1, 2018: pp. 64–87.

Keisalo, Marianna, 'The Invention of Gender in Stand-up Comedy: Transgression and Digression', *Social Anthropology*, Vol. 26, No. 4, 2018: pp. 550–563.

Keisalo, Marianna, 'Perspectives of (And On) a Comedic Self: A Semiotics of Subjectivity in Stand-up Comedy', *Social Analysis*, Vol. 62, No. 1, 2018: pp. 116–135.

Kercher, Stephen, *Revel without a Cause: Liberal Satire in Postwar America* (Chicago: University of Chicago Press, 2006).

Kibler, Alison, *Censoring Racial Ridicule: Irish, Jewish, and African American Struggles over Race and Representation, 1890–1930* (Chapel Hill: University of North Carolina Press, 2015).

Kift, Dagmar, *The Victorian Music Hall: Culture, Class and Conflict* (Cambridge: Cambridge University Press, 1996).

Krefting, Rebecca, *All Joking Aside: American Humor and Its Discontents* (Baltimore: John Hopkins University Press, 2014).

Krefting, Rebecca, 'Hannah Gadsby: On the Limits of Satire', *Studies in American Humour*, Vol. 5, No. 1, 2019: pp. 93–102.

Krefting, Rebecca, 'Hannah Gadsby Stands Down: Feminist Comedy Studies', *JCMS: Journal of Cinema & Media Studies*, Vol. 58, No. 3, 2019: pp. 165–170.

Laineste, Liisi, 'Stand-up in Estonia: From Soviet Estrada to Comedy Estonia', in L. Laineste, D. Brzozowska, and W. Chłopicki (eds.), *Creativity and Tradition in Cultural Communication* Volume 1: Jokes and Their Relations (Tartu: ELM Scholarly Press, 2012), pp. 73–90.

Lee, Stewart, *How I Escaped My Certain Fate: The Life and Deaths of a Stand-Up Comedian* (London: Faber & Faber, 2010).

Levy, Shawn, *In on the Joke: The Original Queens of Stand-Up* (New York: Knopf, 2022).

Lhamon, W. T. Jr., *Raising Cain: Blackface Performance from Jim Crow to Hip Hop* (Cambridge: Harvard University Press, 1998).

Limon, John, *Stand-Up Comedy in Theory, or, Abjection in America* (Durham: Duke University Press, 2000).

Lockyer, Sharon and Michael Pickering (eds.), *Beyond a Joke: The Limits of Humour* (Basingstoke: Palgrave Macmillan, 2005).

Lockyer, Sharon and Michael Pickering, 'You Must Be Joking: The Sociological Critique of Humour and Comic Media', *Sociology Compass*, Vol. 2, No. 3, 2008: pp. 808–820.

Lockyer, Sharon, 'Dynamics of Social Class Contempt in Contemporary British Television Comedy', *Social Semiotics*, Vol. 20, No. 2, 2010: pp. 121–138.

Lockyer, Sharon and Lynn Myers, '"It's about Expecting the Unexpected": Live Stand-up Comedy from the Audiences' Perspective', *Participations: Journal of Audience & Reception Studies*, Vol. 8, No. 2, 2011: pp. 165–188.

Lockyer, Sharon, 'From Comedy Targets to Comedy-makers: Disability and Comedy in Live Performance', *Disability & Society*, Vol. 30, No. 9, 2015: pp. 1397–1412.

Lockyer, Sharon, '"It's Really Scared of Disability": Disabled Comedians' Perspectives of the British Television Comedy Industry', *The Journal of Popular Television*, Vol. 3, No. 2, 2015: pp. 179–193.

Lockyer, Sharon, 'Performance, Expectation, Interaction, and Intimacy: On the Opportunities and Limitations of Arena Stand-up Comedy for Comedians and Audiences', *The Journal of Popular Culture*, Vol. 48, No. 3, 2015: pp. 586–603.

Marc, David, *Comic Visions* (Boston: Unwin Hyman, 1989).

Martin, Nicola, 'A Preliminary Study of Some Broad Disability Related Themes within the Edinburgh Festival Fringe', *Disability & Society*, Vol. 25, No. 5, 2010: pp. 539–549.

Martin, Rod, *The Psychology of Humour: An Integrative Approach* (Amsterdam: Elsevier, 2004).

Martin, Steve, *Born Standing Up* (London: Simon & Schuster, 2007).

Maus, Derek C. and James J. Donahue (eds.), *Post-Soul Satire: Black Identity after Civil Rights* (Jackson: University Press of Mississippi, 2014).

Meier, Matthew R. and Casey R. Schmitt (eds.), *Standing Up, Speaking Out: Stand-Up Comedy and the Rhetoric of Social Change* (New York and London: Routledge, 2017).

Mesropova, Olga, 'Stand-up Comedy', in Tatiana Smorodinskaya, Karen Evans-Romaine and Helena Goscilo (eds.), *Encyclopedia of Contemporary Russian Culture* (London: Routledge, 2014), p. 293.

Miles, Tim, '"It's not the jokes, it's what lies behind 'em": Towards a Phenomenological, Performance-based Methodology for Analysing Live Stand-up Comedy' (Doctoral dissertation, University of Surrey, 2018).

Mills, Brett, 'A Special Freedom: Regulating Comedy Offence', in Chiara Bucaria and Luca Barra (eds.), *Taboo Comedy: Television and Controversial Humour* (London: Palgrave Macmillan, 2016), pp. 209–226.

Mintz, Lawrence E., 'Standup Comedy as Social and Cultural Mediation', *American Quarterly*, Vol. 37, No. 1, Spring 1985: pp. 71–80.

Mizejewski, Linda and Victoria Sturtevant (eds.), *Hysterical: Women in American Comedy* (Austin: Texas University Press, 2017).

Molineux, Christopher, 'Life Memory Archive Translation Performance Memory Archive Life: Textual Self-documentation in Stand-up Comedy', *Comedy Studies*, Vol. 7, No. 1, 2016: pp. 2–12.

Morgan, Danielle Fuentes, *Laughing to Keep from Dying: African American Satire in the Twenty-First Century* (Champaign: University of Illinois Press, 2020).

Nachman, Gerald, *Seriously Funny: The Rebel Comedians of the 50s and 60s* (New York: Pantheon Books, 2003).

Nesteroff, Kliph, *The Comedians: Drunks, Thieves, Scoundrels and the History of American Comedy* (New York: Grove Press, 2015).

Oppliger, Patrice A. and Eric Shouse (eds.), *The Dark Side of Stand-up Comedy* (New York & London: Palgrave Macmillan, 2020).

Oring, Elliott, *The Jokes of Sigmund Freud: A Study in Humor and Jewish Identity*, 3rd ed. (US, UK and Canada: Rowman & Littlefield, 2007).

Paterson, Richard, 'Drama and Entertainment', in Anthony Smith (ed.), *Television: An International History*, 2nd ed. (Oxford: Oxford University Press, 1998), pp. 57–68.

Pérez, Raúl, *The Souls of White Jokes: How Racist Humor Fuels White Supremacy* (Stanford: Stanford University Press, 2022).
Peters, Lloyd and Sue Becker, 'Racism in Comedy Reappraised: Back to Little England?', *Comedy Studies*, Vol. 1, No. 2, 2010: pp. 191–200.
Quirk, Sophie, 'Containing the Audience: The "Room" in Stand-up Comedy', *Participations*, Vol. 8, No. 2, 2011: pp. 219–238.
Quirk, Sophie, *Why Stand-Up Matters: How Comedians Manipulate and Influence* (London: Bloomsbury Academic, 2015).
Quirk, Sophie, *The Politics of British Stand-Up Comedy: The New Alternative* (London: Palgrave Macmillan, 2018).
Quirk, Sophie, 'Comedy Clubs That Platform Marginalised Identities: Prefigurative Politics in Sophie Duker's Wacky Racists', *European Journal of Cultural Studies*, Vol. 25, No. 2, April 2022, pp. 373–388.
Reid, D. Kim, Edy Hammond Stoughton and Robin M. Smith, 'The Humorous Construction of Disability: "stand-up" Comedians in the United States', *Disability & Society*, Vol. 21, No. 6, 2006: pp. 629–643.
Richler, Mordecai, 'The Catskills: Land of Milk and Money', Holiday Magazine, July 1965.
Rosenberg, Neil V., 'Big Fish, Small Pond: Country Musicians and Their Markets', in Peter Narváez and Martin Laba (eds.), *Media Sense: The Folklore Popular Culture Continuum* (Bowling Green: Bowling Green State University Popular Press, 1986), pp. 149–166.
Rutter, Jason, 'Rhetoric in Stand-up Comedy: Exploring Performer-Audience Interaction', *Stylistyka*, Vol. 10, 2021: pp. 307–325.
Sahl, Mort, *Heartland* (New York and London: Harcourt Brace Jovanovich).
Scepanski, Philip, *Tragedy Plus Time: National Trauma and Television Comedy* (Austin: University of Texas, 2021).
Straw, Will, 'Cultural Scenes', *Loisir et Société / Society and Leisure*, Vol. 27, No. 2, 2004: pp. 411–422.
Tafoya, Eddie, *The Legacy of the Wisecrack: Stand-up Comedy as the Great American Literary Form* (Boca Raton: Brown Walker Press, 2009).
Time Magazine, 'Nightclubs: The Sicknicks', July 13, 1959.
Tomsett, Ellie, '"Less Dick Jokes": Women-only Comedy Line-ups, Audience Expectations and Negotiating Stereotypes', in Oliver Double and Sharon Lockyer (eds.), *Alternative Comedy Now and Then: Critical Perspectives* (Basingstoke: Palgrave Macmillan, 2022).
Tomsett, Ellie, *Stand-Up Comedy and Contemporary Feminisms* (London: Bloomsbury Academic, 2023).
Washbourne, Neil, 'Social and National Difference in the High-Speed, Popular Surrealism of Tommy Handley and Ronald Frankau's Double Acts, 1929–1936', in Helen Davies and Sarah Ilot (eds.), *Comedy and the Politics of Representation: Mocking the Weak* (London: Palgrave Macmillan, 2018), pp. 117–136.
Watkins, Mel, *On the Real Side: A History of African American Comedy from Slavery to Chris Rock* (Chicago: Lawrence Hill Books, 1999).
Weaver, Simon, *The Rhetoric of Brexit Humour: Comedy, Populism and the EU Referendum* (London and New York: Routledge, 2016).

Weaver, Simon, *The Rhetoric of Racist Humour: US, UK and Global Race Joking* (London and New York: Routledge, 2016).
Weaver, Simon and Karen Morgan, 'What's the Point of Offensive Humour', *The Conversation*, 2017. Available at https://theconversation.com/what-is-the-point-of-offensive-humour-76889
Wenzel, John, *Mock Stars: Indie Comedy and the Dangerously Funny* (Golden, CO: Speck Press, 2008).
Willett, Cynthia and Julie Willett, *Uproarious: How Feminist and other Subversive Comics Speak the Truth* (Minneapolis: Minnesota University Press, 2019).
Williams, Elsie, *The Humor of Jackie Moms Mabley: An African American Comedic Tradition* (New York: Garland Pub., 1995).
Wilmut, Roger and Peter Rosengard, *Didn't You Kill My Mother-in-Law? The Story of Alternative Comedy in Britain from The Comedy Store to Saturday Live* (London: Methuen, 1989).
Wisse, Ruth R., *The Schlemiel as Modern Hero* (Chicago: University of Chicago Press, 1971).
Wisse, Ruth R., *No Joke: Making Jewish Humor* (Princeton: Princeton University Press, 2013).
Wood, Katelyn Hale, *Cracking Up: Black Feminist Comedy in the Twentieth and Twenty-First Century United States* (Iowa City: University of Iowa Press, 2021).
Womack, Ytasha L., *Afrofuturism: The World of Black Sci-fi and Fantasy Culture* (Chicago: Chicago Review Press, 2013).
Zoglin, Richard, *Comedy at the Edge: How Stand-Up in the 1970s Changed America* (New York: Bloomsbury Academic, 2008).

Index

Aczel, Edward, 13, 61, 97, 222, 290
Afrofuturism, 147–148, 152–153
Allen, Keith, 33
Allen, Tony, 1, 33–35, 262–264
alternative comedy, 32–39, 55–56, 73, 116–117, 263
Alternative Comedy Experience, The, 39
Anderson, Drew, 125
André, Eric, 150–153
  illustration, 151
Ansari, Aziz, 259–262, 267
Apollo Theatre, 49–50, 143
Ayers, Kyle, 77

Bailey, Stephen, 13, 290
Ballard, Tom, 97, 222, 290
Bamford, Maria, 2, 13, 57, 61, 97, 222, 290
Bamrah, Daman, 13, 290–291
Baram, Daphna, 97
Barnes, Angela, 13–14, 61, 97, 222, 291
Bea, Aisling, 212
Belgium, 6–7
Berman, Shelley, 1, 166, 256
blackface, 26, 43–47, 49–50, 141–142
Bob the Drag Queen, 129, 132
Bobolink Bob, 43
Borscht Belt, 51–52, 70, 159–162, 164, 167
Boyle, Frankie, 192–193
Brand, Jo, 14, 61, 98, 116–117, 223, 291
  illustration, 118
Brown, Roy Chubby, 113–114
Bruce, Lenny, 2, 34, 165, 170, 192, 195, 263
  illustration, 167
Buress, Hannibal, 146
Burnham, Bo, 94
Byer, Nicole, 148–150, 152, 155

CK, Louis, 67, 74, 259–262
Caine, Marti, 30, 110
cancel culture, 201
Carlin, George, 281
Carr, Jimmy, 193, 243–244
Carrott, Jasper, 263

Case, Charley, 48
Caton, Nathan, 62, 223
Caulfield, Jo, 14, 62, 98, 223, 291
Chappelle, Dave, 77, 146, 193
Chitlin' Circuit, 48–52, 70, 142–143
Christie, Bridget, 119
Civeris, George, 126, 128
Clark, Laurence, 177, 179–182
Comedians, The, 30, 113
Comedy Cellar, 67, 74
  illustration, 75
Comedy Central, 39, 146, 148
Comedy Store (London), 6, 32–35, 117, 234
Comedy Store (Los Angeles), 53, 71–72
Comedy Store (Mumbai), 6, 9–10
Comic Strip, 32–33, 116
Connolly, Billy, 263
Conran, Lou, 98, 223
Cook, Dane, 79
Cosby, Bill, 144, 236
Covid-19 pandemic, 68, 78–79, 209, 211
crowdwork, 99, 102, 241–243

Dangerfield, Rodney, 79
David, Larry, 172
Davis, Tanyalee, 14, 62, 98, 223, 291
dead dad shows, 10, 264, 269
Def Comedy Jam, 35, 145
DeGeneres, Ellen, 278
Diller, Phyllis, 171
Douglas, Mary, 190, 201, 215–216
Douieb, Tiernan, 14, 98, 291
Dubus, Alexis, 62, 98, 224, 291
Dunn, Finlay, 2

Early, John, 134
Edmondson, Ade, 32
Erikson, Andy, 62, 99, 224, 292
Estonia, 6–7, 9, 65

Farrow, Alex, 14, 62, 224
Fay, Frank, 48

Feimster, Fortune, 125, 132–133
Fields, W. C., 69, 113
Foley, Erin, 129
Frances-White, Deborah, 206–218
  illustration, 207
French & Saunders (Dawn French and Jennifer Saunders), 116
Freud, Sigmund, 163, 166, 286
Friedman, Budd, 71–72

Gadsby, Hannah, 132, 134, 273
  illustration, 274
  Nanette, 10, 57, 130–132, 264, 273, 277–286
Gallagher, Mary, 14, 99, 292
Georgio, Solomon, 135
Gilligan, Mo, 35–37
  illustration, 36
Gregory, Dick, 144
Griffin, Eddie, 145
Guilty Feminist, The, 206–219
  illustration, 207

Hagen, Sofie, 206, 218
heckling, 33, 99, 101, 117, 161, 243–245
Herford, Beatrice, 48, 52
Herman, Justin, 15, 99, 224, 292
Herring, Richard, 62, 210, 224, 292
Hill, Bec, 15, 63, 99, 225, 292
Hill, Harry, 15, 99, 225, 292
Hindi, 9
Hinglish, 8–9
Hoss, Matt, 15, 99, 293
Houghton, Tom, 15, 99, 293
Hughes, Charmian, 15, 100, 225, 293
hungry i, 70, 165

Iapalucci, Adrienne, 67, 77
Improvisation, the, 71
Ince, Robin, 15, 63, 100, 225, 293
Isac, Radu, 5–6, 16, 100

Jalees, Sabrina, 124–125, 127, 135
Jay, Sam, 127–128, 132–133
Jones, Leslie, 153–155
Jones, Milton, 16, 63, 100, 225, 293
Jones, Rosie, 179, 182–183
  illustration, 178

Kane, Russell, 265–270
  illustration, 265
Kaplan, Myq, 225–226, 293
Kashian, Jackie, 16, 63, 226, 293
Kay, Peter, 120
Keith, B. F., 47, 69
Kiley, Brian, 16, 101

Kim Booster, Joel, 135
Knutt, Bobby, 30
Kugblenu, Athena, 16, 63, 226, 294

Lapides, Beth, 16, 55, 63, 100, 226, 294
Lecoat, Jenny, 116
Lee, Stewart, 16, 23–24, 39, 64, 101, 211, 226, 294
Leno, Dan, 25–26
Lexx, Laura, 100, 294
Live at the Apollo, 62, 185
liveness, 83–86, 89, 91, 93–94
Lloyd, Marie, 114–115
Lock, Trevor, 101
Lonergan, Pope, 17, 101
Long, Josie, 38–39
Lyons, Elf, 17, 64, 101, 226, 294

Mabley, Jackie 'Moms', 50, 143
Manning, Bernard, 29–30, 113–114
Markham, Dewey 'Pigmeat', 50
Maron, Marc, 172
Martin, Mae, 255–256
Martin, Steve, 54
Mayall, Rik, 16, 32
Mayhew, Tom, 101, 227, 294
McClelland, Andrew, 4, 17, 64, 227, 294
McGhie, Jimmy, 17, 101, 294
McIntyre, Michael, 9, 37
McLeod, Janet A., 5, 9
Melbourne, 4–5
Melbourne International Comedy Festival, 4, 273
Melville, Pauline, 34
Men Behaving Better, 214–215
Miller, Max, 28–29
Millican, Sarah, 120, 257–259
Mittal, Aditi, 17, 64, 102, 227, 295
Mooney, Paul, 144
Moore, Alfie, 17, 227, 295
Mor, Martin, 17, 227
Mumbai, 6, 10
Murphy, Eddie, 54, 144
Murray, Al, 18, 64, 102, 227, 295
music hall, 2, 24–27, 39, 110, 115

Netflix, 5, 93, 148
Noble, Ross, 86, 212

Õigus, Sander, 7, 18, 65, 102, 228, 295
Omielan, Luisa, 109
Ormiston Chant, Laura, 115
Oswalt, Patton, 73

Pal, Anuvab, 6, 8–9, 18, 65, 102, 228, 295
Panday, Rayen, 6, 18, 228, 295
Pascoe, Sara, 209–210, 212

Perkins, DeWayne, 134
Playboy Club (Chicago), 144
Porter, Lucy, 18, 65, 102, 295–296
Pryor, Richard, 54, 144, 192, 263

Quantock, Rod, 3–4, 19, 65, 103, 228, 296

radio, 69, 86, 88–89
Reed, Nori, 125, 129
Regan, Jarlath, 212, 214
Rice, T. D. (Thomas D. Rice), 49, 141
Richards, Michael, 245
Rickles, Don, 70
Rivers, Joan, 171
Roberts, John-Luke, 103, 228, 296
Rock, Chris, 145–146
Roper, George, 29
Ryan, Katherine, 109

Sahl, Mort, 1, 70, 165–168, 172
Saturday Night Live, 54, 91, 259
Sayle, Alexei, 32–33, 268
Scott, John, 103
Seinfeld, Jerry, 172
Sharp, Josh, 126, 128
Shore, Mitzi, 53, 72
sicknicks, 164–165
Silverman, Sarah, 171
Simmit, John, 35–37, 103, 229, 296
Simmonds, Mark, 19, 229
Simmons, Russell, 145
Sykes, Wanda, 136, 146

Tarri, Suzette, 27–28
Taylor, Fin, 214–215
television, 51, 53–54, 85–87, 89–90, 196
Theatre Owners Booking Association (TOBA), 49–50, 142
Thomas, Mark, 19
Tich, Little, 39
Tom, Jes, 126, 128
Twain, Mark, 2
Tyler, Robin, 54

UnCabaret, 55

variety theatre, 2, 24, 26–29
vaudeville, 2, 46–49, 68–69, 161
Vee, Sindhu, 209

Washington, Sydnee, 125
Wells, Joe, 65, 229, 296
Williams, Nigel, 6, 19, 65, 103, 296
Winters, Jonathan, 263
Withnail, Liam, 242–243
working men's clubs, 3, 29–31, 35, 110, 113, 263

Yiddish, 161–162, 164, 167, 169
Youngman, Henny, 162–164
Young-White, Jaboukie, 132, 135–136

Zafar, Bilal, 20, 66, 296
Zezeran, Louis, 6–7, 9

For EU product safety concerns, contact us at Calle de José Abascal, 56–1°, 28003 Madrid, Spain or eugpsr@cambridge.org.

www.ingramcontent.com/pod-product-compliance
Ingram Content Group UK Ltd.
Pitfield, Milton Keynes, MK11 3LW, UK
UKHW022103150326
469019UK00019B/1433